SIGNLESS SIGNIFICATION IN ANCIENT INDIA AND BEYOND

Cultural, Historical and Textual Studies of South Asian Religions

The volumes featured in the **Anthem Cultural, Historical and Textual Studies of South Asian Religions** series are the expression of an international community of scholars committed to the reshaping of the field of textual and historical studies of religions. Titles in this series examine practice, ritual, and other textual religious products, crossing different area studies and time frames. Featuring a vast range of interpretive perspectives, this innovative series aims to enhance the way we look at religious traditions.

Series Editor

Federico Squarcini, University of Florence, Italy

Editorial Board

Piero Capelli, University of Venice, Italy
Vincent Eltschinger, ICIHA, University of Vienna, Austria
Christoph Emmrich, University of Toronto, Canada
James Fitzgerald, Brown University, USA
Jonardon Ganeri, University of Sussex, UK
Barbara A. Holdrege, University of California, Santa Barbara, USA
Sheldon Pollock, Columbia University, USA
Karin Preisendanz, University of Vienna, Austria
Alessandro Saggioro, Sapienza University of Rome, Italy
Cristina Scherrer-Schaub, University of Lausanne and EPHE, France
Romila Thapar, Jawaharlal Nehru University, India
Ananya Vajpeyi, University of Massachusetts Boston, USA
Marco Ventura, University of Siena, Italy
Vincenzo Vergiani, University of Cambridge, UK

SIGNLESS SIGNIFICATION IN ANCIENT INDIA AND BEYOND

Edited by Tiziana Pontillo and Maria Piera Candotti

With a Preface by Giuliano Boccali

ANTHEM PRESS
LONDON · NEW YORK · DELHI

Anthem Press
An imprint of Wimbledon Publishing Company
www.anthempress.com

This edition first published in UK and USA 2014
by ANTHEM PRESS
75–76 Blackfriars Road, London SE1 8HA, UK
or PO Box 9779, London SW19 7ZG, UK
and
244 Madison Ave. #116, New York, NY 10016, USA

First published in hardback by Anthem Press in 2013

British Library Cataloguing in Publication Data
A catalogue record for this book is available from the British Library.

Library of Congress Cataloging in Publication Data
A catalog record for this book has been requested.

ISBN-13: 978 1 78308 332 9 (Pbk)
ISBN-10: 1 78308 332 8 (Pbk)

This title is also available as an ebook.

Contents

Preface by Giuliano Boccali 9

Part I
Technical and Speculative Reflections on Signless Signification

Alberto Pelissero
Much Ado about Nothing: Unsystematic Notes on śūnya 17

Elisa Freschi, Tiziana Pontillo
When One Thing Applies More than Once: tantra *and* prasaṅga *in Śrautasūtra, Mīmāṃsā and Grammar* 33

Maria Piera Candotti, Tiziana Pontillo
The Earlier Pāṇinian Tradition on the Imperceptible Sign 99

Paolo Corda
The Infinite Possibilities of Life: Interpretations of the śūnyatā *in the Thinking of Daisaku Ikeda* 155

Part II
Reflections on Signless Signification in Literature and Arts

Cinzia Pieruccini
Presences and Absences in Indian Visual Arts: Ideologies and Events 177

MIMMA CONGEDO, PAOLA M. ROSSI
Rethinking the Question of Images (Aniconism vs. Iconism) in the Indian History of Art 195

PATRIZIA MUREDDU
Denotation in absentia *in Literary Language: The Case of Aristophanic Comedy* 223

RUBEN FAIS
The Birth of the Buddha in the Early Buddhist Art Schools 239

PREMA BHAT, PAOLO BRAVI, IGNAZIO MACCHIARELLA
Untranslatable Denotations: Notes on Music Meaning Through Cultures 261

Summary of Papers 283

Università degli Studi di Cagliari

Publication of the Dipartimento di Filologia Classica,
Glottologia e Scienze Storiche dell'Antichità e del Medioevo,
financially supported by the University of Cagliari,
"Fondo per il sostegno della ricerca di base
e per lo start-up dei giovani ricercatori".

Giuliano Boccali

Preface

The present volume of Proceedings of the Workshop "Il segno e il vuoto" (April 8-9, 2011) hosted by the Dipartimento di Filologia Classica, Glottologia e Scienze Storiche dell'Antichità e del Medioevo" of the University of Cagliari, follows a common thread, which is robust and identifiable, even though it is not explicitly stated. It is a survey, albeit by far incomplete, of the debates, difficulties and provisional answers raised in classical Indian culture with some excursions outside by the awareness of the existence of some asymmetries or dissonances within the otherwise well established casual pattern found in phenomenal, linguistic or aesthetic reality. Its boldest expression coincides with the well known *mādhyamika* Buddhist refusal of the *svabhāva* of any phenomenon, i.e. with the metaphysic cancellation of the intrinsic nature of each appearance, which as a consequence relies on its absolute 'depending upon other nature' (*parabhāva*) or on the 'dependent origination' (*pratītyasamutpāda*). Precisely by means of a reflection on the conceptual dependence between the three linguistically considered factors e.g. of movement, i.e. action, agent and object of going, Nāgarjuna shows that cause and effect cannot be endowed with an intrinsic nature (*svabhāva*). Otherwise the movement itself should be suppressed. The relevant background is of course the idea of the world which results as "becoming" instead of as "being".

In linguistic terms, such speculation focused on the non-homogeneous relationship occurring between the phono-morphological level of the communication (a sign, in Saussurian terms) and the conveyed meanings (or the signified), and has long been developed and discussed, through the advancement of solutions quite distant from each other. From this point of view and also from the ritual one the starting point gives the impression of being diametrically opposite to the already mentioned *mādhyamika* premise: *śabda*/ word and *artha*/ meaning are connected to each other by means of a strong ontological relation and this strict correspondence is extended to the sub-units of *pada*s/ inflected words themselves. Yet there are numerous linguistic examples where this relation is, so to say, blurred, cases where a word seems to convey more than one meaning (like in homonyms) or where a meaning is understood in the absence of an otherwise expected sign, as it happens in cases managed by Pāṇini through zero-replacement of a morph or even of an entire inflected word. This last kind of substitution is only taught by one Pāṇini rule (*Aṣṭādhyāyī* 5.3.82), but widened to a great extent by Kātyāyana and by Patañjali, for instance in order to explain the compulsory integrations required by the analysis of *bahuvrīhi*-compounds. Substitution with zero contribute in shaping an interpretation of language as a positional sequence of information bits, where position itself is significant also in absence of any other specific information, something akin to the positional value of zero (and other signs) in mathematics. On a late commentary on Patañjali's *Yogasūtra* we read:

> *Yogasūtrabhāṣya* 3.13: *yathaikā rekhā śatasthāne śataṃ daśasthāne daśaikaṃ caikasthāne yathā caikatve 'pi strī mātā cocyate duhitā ca svasā ceti*, "Just as one (same) stroke is one hundred in the place of the hundreds, in the place of the tens is ten and one in the place of units, in the same way a women, despite being one is called a mother, and a daughter and a sister."

This grammatical device perfectly matches with an analogous ritual pattern, which probably constituted its technical antecedent, applied every time that an *artha* can be obtained also *in absentia* of its recognizable (*pratyakṣa*) cause. In the description of the ritual praxis, the supporting structures of the linguistic mechanism are better distinguishable: the effect of a cause, i.e. the signification conveyed by a sign can be extended from an X place which is eccentric with respect to the Y context, where that specific effect occurs or where that specific signification is required. There are two available distinct schemas. The first (*tantra*) provides for a radial extension, which expands around only one element, perceptible in the middle of a series of several different contexts where it is absent, albeit unquestionably required, as has been proven on the basis of an implicit comparison with analogous cases. The second pattern (*prasaṅga*) works via contiguity, from a place which is extraneous to the context where that signification is required, to this context itself, which shares at least one detail with the extraneous one. The linguistic mechanism of anaphora relies on the former, while the latter one grants that the whole system of denotation *in absentia* can be properly governed and limited, so that the feared undue over-extensions of whatever element (*sarvaprasaṅga*) which is simply not present, can be avoided. Otherwise the risk should really be the incommunicableness between sender and receiver of the message. Not just any element can be postulated where a zero occurs, by assuming that zero can be a substitute of whatever. It is 'the place' left void that helps in identifying the specific value to which each zero-realisation is linked. Only on the basis of a plain analogy, observed in everyday language, every zero must be proven to be a veritable substitute of some specific expected element, i.e. of something which is automatically implied by a specific context, which nevertheless does not include it perceptibly. We could even say that zero, at least in linguistic, is an inherently relational term, being always zero 'of' something. Again the similarity with mathematics is striking.

This substitution pattern, both in its ritual and grammatical dimension, might have constituted an important starting point for the reflections elaborated by the *alaṃkāraśāstra*-writers on *upamā, rūpaka, śleṣa* and on the broad constellation of poetic significations which variously "replace with zero" some 'signs' which by contrast, have to be included within the denotation, provided that the context has the power to entail them, for instance by mentioning some other objects which can be superimposed on the absent ones and at least partially overlap each other. Patañjali, for instance, emphasizes that the integration of the stem *priyadarśanā* 'pleasant to the sight' is compulsory in a classical attribute referred to a woman's face such as *candramukhī* 'pleasant to the sight like the moon', even though the moon's qualities are many, such as its round shape, its brightness, its whiteness. It is extremely clear that more than one *guṇa*/ attribute can be considered as a good candidate for the role of substituend, but not whatever, and as a consequence not just any nominal stem can be integrated in order to analyse the meaning of the compound. Everyday linguistic usage assures this limit as an underlying layer of communication by which the sender is allowed to reach the receiver with his message, as far as it is creative. The meaning has to be actually shared by the two actors of the communicative event. The semantic potentialities of such devices are well known and used in all cultures for poetic effects but also, as shown in the case of Aristophanes, to create the comic effect precisely on the basis of the shared knowledge and the collaboration of the audience.

The substitution of the object directly denoted by a word with another object, which is only partially comparable, seems to be exactly the remote foundation of the majority of definitions of figures as recorded in the *alaṃkāraśāstras*. See for instance the definitions of *upamā, śliṣṭa* and *rūpaka* in Bhāmaha's *Kāvyālaṃkāra*:

> 2.30 *viruddhenopamānena deśakālakriyādibhiḥ / upameyasya yat sāmyaṃ guṇaleśena sopamā*, "*Upamā* is that which pertains to the first term of comparison and which is equivalent – as far as a small portion of quality is concerned – to the second term of comparison, which on the contrary is opposite as far as its place, time and action are concerned."

> 3.14-15 *upamānena yat tattvam upameyasya sādhyate / guṇakriyābhyāṃ nāmnā ca śliṣṭāṃ tad abhidhīyate // lakṣaṇaṃ rūpake 'pīdaṃ lakṣyate kāmamatra tu / iṣṭaḥ prayogo yugapad upamānopameyayoḥ*, "The real essence of the subject of comparison, when it is realized by the standard by means of quality, action and name is denoted as *śliṣṭa*. But this is the essential feature which also characterizes a *rūpaka* – only if we want. The simultaneous usage of subject and object of comparison is preferred."

From the distant, perhaps original Ṛgvedic intuition of an Emptiness contained in the cosmic Egg, an Emptiness which is more fecund than the embryo and which precisely consists in the cause (i.e. the place) of the potentiality of the caused effect, the Indian way of reflection on the possible dissymmetric relationships between cause and effect results as being a very long and fascinating story, with regard to both the technical and speculative point of view and the practical aesthetic experiments. With regard to the origin, I am hinting at the famous, discussed and also traditionally rearranged image, which was inaugurated in *Ṛgveda* X.129.3 (cf. the recent contribution Daniele Maggi, *Sul "vuoto" in Ṛgvedasaṃhitā* X.129.3c, in "Studi Linguistici in onore di Roberto Gusmani", vol. 2, pp. 1011-22, and bibliography quoted there): *tama āsīt tamasā gūḷham agre 'praketaṃ salilaṃ sarvam ā idam / tucchyenābhv apihitam yad āsīt tapasas tanmahinājāyataikam*, "Darkness was hidden by darkness in the beginning; with no distinguishing sign, all this was water. The life force that was covered with emptiness, that one arose through the power of heat" (transl. by Wendy Doniger O'Flaherty, *The RigVeda. An Anthology*, London 1981, p. 25).

Of course the opposite belief is also attested in the *Ṛgveda* (X.90.1-3, the *puruṣasūkta*, transl. by W. Doniger O'Flaherty) where the whole and overflowing Being is put at the origin of everything: "The Man has a thousand heads, a thousand eyes, a thousand feet. He pervaded the earth on all sides and extended beyond it as far as ten fingers. It is the Man who is all this, whatever has been and whatever is to be. He is the ruler of immortality, when he grows beyond everything through food. Such is his greatness, and the Man is yet more than this. All creatures are a quarter of him; three quarters are what is immortal in heaven." Perhaps by forcing these images just a little, albeit in a legitimate way, since we are dealing with some primeval Myths, the future dialectics between a position which considers the Emptiness as the cause of (or at least as a condition for) the appearance of everything in the universe, and a different view which asserts the inexpressible and incomprehensible oneness of Being, might be recognized in these two quoted Vedic passages.

Both Poetry and the Figurative Arts seem to have repeatedly pursued the non-overt vocation of Silence to become Word, i.e. the vertigo of Absence which aims at becoming a presence made of Signs, or vice versa the presence which strives to enter into the Silence from which it originated, playing at propelling the absent unit elsewhere as far as time or place are concerned, albeit with measurable fancy and precise awareness, beyond every disapproved vague ambiguity. In fact it is not "an objective measure of ambiguity" of Sanskrit which rendered this language "inherently more *śleṣa* friendly than another", as Yigal Bronner maintains in his important work on the history of *śleṣa* published in 2010. The Sanskrit language rather "is unprecedented in its accurate description and its complex and elegant metalinguistic conceptualization of vast linguistic phenomena" and poetry itself resulted as being empowered by this granted shared intimate knowledge of the language. For instance Sanskrit came to possess a near-perfect description of the euphonic glides and assimilations, which *śleṣa*s can often rely on, precisely since they were studied and memorized by every educated person (Yigal Bronner, *Extreme Poetry: The South Asian Movement of Simultaneous Narration*. New York 2010, pp. 14-5). It is higly probable that the historical reflections on the signless signification also played a role in the historical advancement of this "flexible" language to exploit its potentialities. Therefore the foreseen steps of the present inquiry are also desirable and are undertaken here with a large wealth and appropriateness of suggestions, both in order to enlighten the formerly merely hypothesized relationship between ritual, grammatical and poetical science with regard to the subjects of "absence", "integration" and "simultaneous or multiple signification", and in order to investigate the historical context, which from the most ancient Upaniṣads onwards might have at the very least determined such an emphasis on the topic of substitution.

Part I

Technical and Speculative Reflections on Signless Signification

Alberto Pelissero

Much Ado about Nothing: Unsystematic Notes on śūnya*

Please don't ask us the slogan that could open worlds to You,
only some syllables, dry and bent like a branch.
Today only this we can tell You:
what we are not, what we do not want.

Eugenio Montale, *Cuttle-fish Bones*

Śūnya means 'void', 'bereft', and in mathematical scientific literature, 'zero'. It derives from *śūna,* being the past passive participle of root *śvi,* 'to grow', 'to swell', according to Pāṇini (7.2.14). So *śūna* means swelled, swollen, increased, grown. According to *Ṛgvedaprātiśākhya* (14.2) it indicates a fault in Vedic recital, consisting in an utterance with a swollen mouth.[1] The term *śūnya* occurs within Upanisadic literature in the *Maitryupaniṣad* (2.4; 6.31; 7.4), together with other epithets referred to brahman, epithets that mean 'pure', 'clear', pacified' (*śuddha, pūta, śānta*). Etymologically *śūnya* should therefore mean a void space, a hole determined by a borderless opening, by an unlimited disclosing. According to lexicographers (*Amarakośa* 3.1.56), its synonyms are 'sapless', 'meaningless', 'void', 'vane', 'hollow' (*asāra, phalgu, vaśika, tuccha, riktaka*). This kind of voidness is conceived first of all as a sort of deprivation, as we can see from a well-known literary 'good saying' (*subhāṣita*) centred around the term *śūnya:*

* Antonio Rigopoulos kindly accepted to check my English version of this paper, originally written in Italian: all mistakes and misunderstandings are obviously mine, not his.

[1] Abhyankar 1986, p. 393.

'Void is the house for he who is sonless, void is the time for he who is friendless, void are the four cardinal points for he who is silly, void is the whole world for he who is poor' (Śūdraka, *Mṛcchakaṭikā* 1.8).[2] The reference to the cardinal points (*diś*) is not at all a trivial one, because it explains why the term *śūnya* could be made synonym with 'ethereal space', 'atmospheric space', 'heaven' (*ākāśa, kha, vyoman*).

The abstract derivate *śūnyatā* is recorded in Buddhist literature, mainly of the *mahāyāna* type, first of all in Nāgārjuna, as meaning 'voidness', 'the fact of being void', and even (though this kind of translation is *sub iudice*) as 'vacuity', 'emptiness'. The mathematical zero cannot be compared to any other number, being their very precondition, and in consideration of such a meaning it is tendentially compared with the concept of infinite (*ananta*). Which of the three main shades of meaning of *śūnya* first suggested the other two? Did the mathematical, the grammatical, or the Buddhist philosophical meaning come first? There is a great deal of debate on this question. First of all it may be noted that, even if the concept of zero grade is important and well-known within Indian grammatical tradition (*vyākaraṇa*), the term *śūnya* is actually never employed in this context. Phonic zero, intended as absence of any sound whatsoever, to be found in alternation with sound, especially within vocalic gradation (apophony), is widely known, and used as the apophonic grade. But we must note that the grades known in Western use as normal or full grade and extended or lengthened grade, both correspond to a Sanskrit technical term, respectively *guṇa* (a, e, o) and *vṛddhi* (ā, ai, au), which among other things can be taught as a replacement of a, i, u respectively (A 1.1.3). By contrast the grade that we call weak or reduced or zero grade does not correspond to a univocal Sanskrit technical word, because it is treated exactly as the other zero-replacements of phonemes, and, what is most important, it never takes the name of *śūnya.* It is not a mere chance that what we call zero grade is not described by Indian grammarians in positive words, but only as an exception, subject to specific rules of application, to *guṇa* and *vṛddhi* grades (e.g. A 1.1.5 suffixes with K and Ṅ markers): it is impossible to describe an absence, a deprivation, a limitation in positive terms. The technical term used in such cases is *lopa* (e.g. 1.1.4; 1.1.62), a name given to the meaning of *adarśanam* 'non-perception' by means of metarule 1.1.60.

[2] This passage is echoed by *Cāṇakyaśataka* 47, quoted in Vatsyayan et al. 1992, p. 400. Translations from Sanskrit are by the author, unless otherwise indicated.

Therefore, even if we cannot rule out the possibility that the apophonic zero could be the base of the mathematical zero, it is only the latter that takes the name of *śūnya*. The doubt whether or not the philosophical use could precede the mathematical one, still remains. Even in the field of architecture, the value of the void asserts itself: it is sufficient to think of what we define as the *sanctum* (Indians call it *garbhagṛha*, 'house of the embryo') in the sanctuary of Śiva Naṭarāja in Chidambaram, enclosing the signum 'made of space' (*ākāśaliṅga*), technically a void space, that represents the icon being worshipped by the devotees.

Within the mathematical field, zero is the base of the system of numerical positional notation on the decimal scale: it is the void space that permits the passage from units to tens and so on. The *Yajurveda* (*Vājasaneyisaṃhitā* 17.2) enumerates the names of the powers of ten starting from 100 *eka* up to 1012 *parārdha*. The synonyms of zero to be found in mathematical, astronomical and astrological texts (*jyotiḥśāstra*), are all specifications of a semantic field that generally covers the concept of 'space'. But it is a large sphere that combines different notions, and is variously declined as ethereal space, surrounding space, void space, atmospheric space (*ākāśa, ambara, kha, gagana*). Other kinds of synonyms are more interesting, because they range from an apparent antonym meaning 'full' (*pūrṇa*), to the term for 'point' (*bindu*), up to the little circle used in writing as a sign for zero (*chidra, randhra*, both words meaning 'hole'). It is possibly not a mere chance that the first quotation of zero as a mathematical symbol is to be found within a metrical text (Piṅgala, *Chandaḥsūtra* 8.28-31).[3] Obviously, quotations from mathematical literature are numerous (*Āryabhaṭīya* 1.2; *Pañcasiddhāntikā* 1.17; *Bṛhatkṣetrasamāsa* 1.69-71; *Tattvārthādhigamasūtra* 3.11).

At least in the Vedic period, within priestly circles the value of fullness (*pūrṇatā*) and full (*pūrṇa*) prevails, e.g. in passages such as 'full that, full this, from the full this full is born, having taken the full from the full, full only remains' (*Bṛhadāraṇyaka-upaniṣad* 5.1.1). This primacy of fullness does not entail any sort of undervaluation of voidness, because without the void the full itself could not hold ('in the beginning indeed this was not being, from this the being is based [...] who could live, who could breathe, if within space [*ākāśa*] there was not bliss?' (*Taittirīyopaniṣad* 2.7). This fact entails a twofold consequence. First of all, being and not being (*sat, asat*), full and void, are complementary entities, each one is indispensable to the other. In some way, each one is the matrix of the other (*Ṛgvedasaṃhitā* 10.129.1-4). Thanks to the

[3] Thus Sarma 1992, p. 400-11, but cf. Bronkhorst 1994.

doctrine of the different levels of truth, each one can be derived from the other. Secondly, bliss is associated to the void. Buddhism will highly value both concepts.

In the Buddhist field, *śūnya* and its abstract *śūnyatā* cannot be considered as signs of a nihilistic doctrine. Vedantic doxographical tradition will put a conscious distortion into practice that rejects the 'emic' denomination of Nāgārjuna's school, 'followers of the middle path' (*mādhyamika*), preferring an ambiguous term (doomed to a certain degree of success), i.e. nihilists (*śūnyavādin*): in fact *śūnya* cannot be considered as a *vāda*, a valid doctrine, from Nāgārjuna's point of view, but only a convenient dialectical device. Void and voidness only signify the mere negation of every possible sort of positive assessment within the field of experiential reality. It is not proper to ascribe the status of doctrine (*vāda*) to *śūnya* and *śūnyatā*.

The concept of vacuity or emptiness, *śūnyatā*, so relevant in Nāgārjuna, is already entirely theorized in the literary genre of the 'transcendent gnosis', *prajñāpāramitā*, where we can find different lists, ranging from four to twenty elements. The list including eighteen terms, the most widely accepted one, considers the following varieties: 1) vacuity relative to the interior realm (*adhyātmaśunyatā*), where the six awarenesses (*vijñāna*, five related to the senses and the sixth a mental one) are revealed as empty; 2) vacuity relative to the exterior realm (*bahirdhāśūnyatā*), where both sensory and mental objects are revealed as empty ones; 3) vacuity relative to interior and exterior (*adhyātmabahirdhāśunyatā*), where the very same distinction between interior and exterior is revealed as empty; 4) vacuity of vacuity (*śūnyatāśūnyatā*), where the very same notion of vacuity is revealed as empty; 5) great vacuity (*mahāśūnyatā*), where space is revealed as empty; 6) vacuity of absolute reality (*paramārthaśūnyatā*), where transcendent reality is revealed as empty; 7) vacuity of all composite entities (*saṃskṛtaśūnyatā*), where every compounded entity is revealed as empty, because it depends on causes and conditions; 8) vacuity of non-composite entities (*asaṃskṛtaśūnyatā*), where every non compounded entity is revealed as empty, beginning with *nirvāṇa*; 9) final vacuity (etymologically 'vacuity beyond the limit', *atyantaśūnyatā*), where the very same border dividing permanence and destruction is revealed as empty; 10) beginningless and endless vacuity (*anavarāgraśūnyatā*), where the whole cycle of transmigration (*saṃsāra*) is revealed as empty; 11) vacuity of what is not subject to scattering (*anavakāraśūnyatā*), where *nirvāṇa* is revealed as empty; 12) vacuity of the object-principle (*prakṛtiśūnyatā*); 13) vacuity of all phenomena whatsoever (*sarvadharmaśūnyatā*); 14) vacuity of what is self-defining (*svalakṣaṇaśūnyatā*), where what is self-defining (*svalakṣaṇa*), i.e. the point-instant (*kṣaṇa*), is revealed as empty; 15) vacuity of what is not known (*anupalambhaśūnyatā*), where all events, considered as cut off from any reference with the time in which they take place (past in the future, future in the past, present in the future and in the past), are revealed as empty; 16) vacuity of the absence of one's own mode of being, or of not existence (*asvabhāvaśūnyatā*, or sometimes *abhāvaśūnyatā*), where the very same absence of one's own mode of being (*svabhāva*) of the dharmas is revealed as empty; 17) vacuity of one's own mode of being (*svabhāvaśūnyatā*); and finally 18) vacuity of non existence and of one's own mode of being (*abhāvasvabhāvaśūnyatā*), where the very same distinction between real and unreal is revealed as empty. As we can see, the path towards theologizing and hypostatizing the concept of vacuity has already been outlined. It will be one of the main concerns of Nāgārjuna, as a champion of the anti-intellectual trend of the followers of the middle path, to deconstruct the huge doctrinal building of the followers of the transcendent gnosis.

Nāgārjuna's thought is particularly reluctant to be pigeonholed within discursive categories. It is characterized by a background of anti-intellectualism, and it makes use of eristical techniques which are most useful in debate. It will be sufficient to mention here the doctrine of the double truth, absolute and wordly (*paramārthasatya, saṃvṛtisatya*); the use of the logical tetralemma (*catuṣkoṭi*) in order to defeat any metaphysical assessment whatsoever; the concept of vacuity or emptiness (*śūnyatā*) as a category in effect identical with the process of conditioned coproduction (*pratītyasamutpāda*); the dialectical use of the *reductio ad absurdum* (*prasaṅga*); the concept of insubstantiality (*niḥsvabhāvatā*).

As we have seen, the Vedantic interpretation (first of all in such works as the *Sarvadarśanasaṃgraha*) of *mādhyamika* (or *madhyamaka*) doctrine as *śūnyavāda*, 'doctrine of the void', a term generally rendered with 'nihilism', is based on a great equivocation, and causes a gnoseological misunderstanding. Following Mādhava's statement of *śūnyavāda*, we will be confronted with a position according to which the gnoseological triad, formed by the knowing subject, the known object and knowledge, effectively amounts to fully interdependent elements. In such a case, the reality of each and every element of the triad depends on the reality of the other two elements. So it will be sufficient to prove the falseness of one single element in order to deduce the falseness of the other two. When we erroneously perceive the snake instead of the rope, the snake is no doubt false; so, even the subject perceiving a false object, and the very same knowledge deriving from such a perception, are equally false. Thus reality withdraws more and more, until it wholly disappears, and universal falseness can be translated as void, *śūnya*, or as an abstract principle such as vacuity, emptiness, insubstantiality, *śūnyatā*. First of all, we should note that this is a conscious doxographical distortion of *mādhyamika* thought. In fact, the *mādhyamika* school refers to the 'middle path' evoked by the Buddha, the path standing as intermediate between two opposite conceptions, eternalism and annihilationism (or, less properly, nihilism) (*śāśvatavāda*, *ucchedavāda*). If nihilism is one of the two risks that must be avoided, it is not possible to attack the school with the charge of nihilism. Secondly, *mādhyamika* thought does not deny reality at all (for this would amount to accepting a metaphysical position); rather, it criticizes from its very root the concept of substantiality of the phenomenal world, of what is apparent within the domain of the senses and of the mind. Beyond the phenomenal world there is no substance whatsoever, mental or extramental, there is only the void, *śūnya*. And the void, in turn, cannot be made into a substance. The term 'void', *śūnya*, covers two entirely different shades of meaning: it may indicate the phenomenal world as it is 'void of one's own nature' (*svabhāvaśūnya*), or it may indicate the absolute reality as it is 'void of the manifoldness of manifestation' (*prapañcaśūnya*). So the term may be rendered both as 'void' and as 'devoid, deprived'. This last meaning restates the character of (inter)relation that is typical of *śūnya*: it always means a deprivation of something else, it is not a self-contained term, it cannot be reified within positive self-sufficient terms.[4]

Candrakīrti will declare that vacuity, *śūnyatā*, acts for intellectual activity as a purge acts for the body, purifying it and being expelled together with the pathogenic factors carried away by its action. That being the case, vacuity cannot cling to the intellect as a conceptual construction, but it must be carried away in its turn when it has carried out its goal. Otherwise, it will be a cause of further problems, in the same way as if a purge could not be carried away, flowing out of the body. In these conditions, the description of reality can be made only in negative terms, it can only negate substantiality, and this negation does not equate at all with the same conceptual predicament as if it could positively assess unsubstantiality. The real nature of objects and of the world cannot be ascertained, it can only be described in negative terms such as through the category of void, an intrinsically empty predicament. In fact, what is real must be wholly independent from any other element, in order that it may be described in conceptual terms. But universal interdependence, deriving from *pratītyasamutpāda*, negates every sort of independence of

[4] Following the proposal of Sharma 1960, pp. 86 f.

anything whatsoever. So the very same reality of the world is negated. But this does not mean that the world can be described as unreal, because what is unreal (the aerial city of the heavenly musicians on the clouds, *gandharvanagara*) never comes into being. On the contrary, the world does come into being, it is manifest, and everyone can testify to this fact. Neither can we say that the world is real and unreal at the same time, nor that it is neither real nor unreal. This eristic or dialectical practice applies a fourfold negation to a thesis A in four steps (not A, not non-A, not either-A-and-non-A, not neither-A-nor-non-A). It is mainly applied to the category of being, *sat*, as not being, not non-being, not either-being-and-non-being, not neither-being-nor-non-being, so as to thwart any ontological claim. It will take the name of tetralemma (*catuṣkoṭi*), and it will become the main device of negative dialectic (eristic) of the *mādhyamika* school, being able to deconstruct any possible conceptual construction whatsoever, with rigid and pitiless grace. An adequate description of reality being impossible, its best approximation is the term vacuity (*śūnyatā*), that has in itself its own antibodies, being able to prevent any possible reification of itself in terms of a substance. The 'things' of the world appear, are manifest to us, but when we try to analyse them, they escape any possible definition in terms of reality, non-reality, either-reality-and-non-reality, neither-reality-nor-non-reality. In the *Madhyamakakārikā* the method of the tetralemma is successfully applied to vanify concepts such as motion, causation, and so on. This deconstruction definitely proves the inadequacy of common sense and of trivial thought, which cannot efficiently and authentically describe the complexity of phenomena. Interdependence affirms itself as the preferential entry to reality, even if it is an apophatic and limited approach. Interdependence and vacuity are the same thing, they are synonyms: *pratītyasamutpāda*, interdependent coproduction, and *śūnyatā*, vacuity or emptiness, are two different ways to describe the same situation. There is no feature (*dharma*) that might be considered independent, so every feature is intrinsically devoid of one's own nature. One's own way of being, the essential nature (*svabhāva*) of a thing (*dharma*), its being non factitious (*akṛtrima*), not dependent on anything whatsoever for its own being, is not ascertainable in any way at all. So universal interdependence, say emptiness, is just as well rendered as absence of one's own nature (*niḥsvabhāvatā*). Indeed, the concept of emptiness, vacuity (*śūnyatā*), in its extreme shade of meaning, refers properly to the absence of one's own way of being (*svabhāva*). It can therefore be indicated as *niḥsvabhāvatā*, absence of one's own nature or of one's way of being. This does not only concern the empirical reality, but the whole of the *dharmas*. Each and every *dharma* is conceived as devoid of one's own nature, we could even say that each and every *dharma* is unsubstantial (but this could be interpreted as a tendentially metaphysical assessment). Following Candrakīrti *ad* Nāgārjuna, the term 'one's own way of being' can be understood in three ways: 1) essential property, e.g. heat in the case of fire; 2) essential feature of a single *dharma*, absolute specificity, *svalakṣaṇa*; and finally 3) existence which is not dependent upon other factors. In this last meaning, *svabhāva* indicates an absolute non-subjugation to change in the past, present or future, independence from causes and conditions, unborn and unproduced nature. Nāgārjuna's criticism hits precisely this last shade of meaning, disclosing every object whatsoever as being void, unsubstantial. Nāgārjuna is fully aware of the risk, i.e. of transforming the doctrine of vacuity, originally a mere dialectical device, into a new sort of substantialism: he strongly reaffirms the emptiness, the ineliminable self-contradictory nature of any thesis (*pratijñā*) whatsoever, positive or negative.

Nevertheless, an underlying reality is beyond the range of phenomena, a reality which is no less authentic, even if our power of understanding and our expressive capacity fail to grasp it firmly. It is the reality of extinction (*nirvāṇa*), proclaimed by the Buddha: the extinction of pain, of the grief bound to human worldly experience. If this extinction were unreal, there would be no use in undertaking the way doomed to lead to it; the Four Noble Truths would be overcome, together with the Noble Eightfold Path. The unknowability of the real through ordinary gnoseological tools does not clash with this underlying reality. Contradiction is avoided through the medium of a doctrine of double truth. There is indeed a trivial, empirical, temporary, conditioned truth, the truth of worldly affairs, *saṃvṛtisatya* (etymologically 'covering truth'), and in addiction to it, an underlying, eternal, unconditioned truth, the absolute truth, *paramārthasatya*. The distinction between *saṃvṛtisatya* and *paramārthasatya* probably arises from a dichotomy present in the *sarvāstivāda*, where there is the opposition between what is existent *qua* substance, *dravyasat*, and what is existent *qua* convention, *prajñaptisat*, even if the two sets of criteria do not completely overlap. According to *mādhyamika* thought, the very same reality that from the ordinary point of view appears as interdependence, transmigration, *saṃsāra*, if it is observed from the point of view of the higher truth, is manifested as extinction, *nirvāṇa*. So *saṃsāra* and *nirvāṇa* are the two faces of the same coin. The description of *nirvāṇa* can be attempted only in apophatic terms; the same is true for the description of the 'so gone' or 'he who comes and goes in the same way', *tathāgata*, the being who has fully realized in himself this kind of truth. The silence of the Buddha with reference to metaphysical questions can thus be explained as a programmatic silence, full of meaning, the silence of he who declares that some questions are undecidable: they cannot be worked out in conceptual and verbal terms, but only with apophatic tools. Mādhyamika apophatism has often been compared with Upanisadic and Vedantic apothatism (mainly with reference to Gauḍapāda and Śaṅkara), giving life to a sort of game in the looking glass, involving mutual charges of cryptovedantism and cryptobuddhism (with reference to Nāgārjuna and Śaṅkara). In particular the incipit of *Madhyamakakārikā* can be read as an attempt to reinterpret Nāgārjuna's terminology in Vedantic terms. But the direction of the loan is not clear at all: who lends, who borrows, within this hermeneutical circle? The *incipit* of the *Madhyamakakārikā* contains, with reference to *pratītyasamutpāda*, a series of epithets clearly of vedantic appearance. First of all, we have the eight negations relative to cessation, birth, annihilation, eternity, unity, multiplicity, going and coming (*anirodha, anutpāda, anuccheda, aśāśvata, anekārtha, anānārtha, anāgama, anigama*), and subsequently more specific epithets, such as 'appeasement of the display of discursive thought' and 'kindly disposed' (*prapañcopaśama, śiva*), which are present in the *Māṇḍūkyopaniṣad.* So the Upanisadic references present in the text, which show a sort of similarity in the concept of void with terms such as 'pure', 'appeased', 'full' and 'bliss' (*śuddha, śānta, pūrṇa, ānanda*), acquire a new meaning: they are appropriated from a Buddhist point of view.

The process of conditioned coproduction (or interdependent co-origination), *pratītyasamutpāda,* is a good hermeneutical tool, but it cannot be reified in its turn. This reification would involve the violation of unsubstantiality: it is not possible to consider any concept whatsoever a substance. Even the concept of the self is critically deconstructed: there is no substance which is independent from its qualities; there is no self which is independent from the states of consciousness; an agent exists only with reference to action, and action with reference to an agent, but in absolute terms neither of the two exists as a substance. The very same knowledge is a logical impossibility, it cannot exist, because it depends entirely on difference. For instance, a cow is not defined in positive terms, but only negatively, as not non-cow, i.e. as different e.g. from a horse or a sheep (foreshadowing the *apoha* theory): the cow exists in so far as it is not existent as a horse or a sheep, as it is not existent as something different from it. Any knowledge whatsoever is relative, *rectius,* it is relational. Thought cannot grasp the world, even less could it grasp itself. Truth can be compared with silence, the semantically pregnant silence of the Buddha with reference to vain questions. True knowledge consists in the awareness of the impossibility of knowing anything with discursive and argumentative tools, because the world does not fit logical criteria. Indeed, not even the Buddha, the Tathāgata, exists: from the absolute point of view there is no distinction whatsoever between truth and error, *saṃsāra* is the same as *nirvāṇa*, there are neither death nor birth, neither unity nor multiplicity.

So we can now examine the last term that can help us in our attempt to understand the subject-matter of the paper. The term has already been incidentally introduced. Its use and diffusion are due to the great master of the so-called logico-epistemological school of Buddhism, Dignāga (or Diṅnāga). The term is *apoha*, 'exclusion'.

Dignāga reduces the field of application of perception to the particular (*svalakṣaṇa*, 'one's own feature') and the field of application of inference to the universal (*sāmānyalakṣaṇa*, 'common feature'), and in so doing he negates a pillar of the *nyāya* (logical) school, maintaining the suitability of different means of knowledge to the very same object (*pramāṇasamplava*). The *svalakṣaṇa* is endowed with causal efficiency (*arthakriyā*, the power to produce its object), different from any other object, inexpressible in words, unknowable with the help of signs different from itself, being able to determine a difference in the form manifested into cognition; a real fire is a fire being able to illuminate and to heat; a fire that cannot illuminate nor heat is an unreal one. *Svalakṣaṇa* is a key term, not entirely defined by Dignāga, being glossed and interpreted by Dharmakīrti and Mokṣākaragupta. Real, unique, determined by the time, space and form that are peculiar to it, *svalakṣaṇa* is also an undivided instant (*kṣaṇa*). Perception is free from conceptual constructions (*kalpanāpoḍha*, where *kalpanā* means a cognition being associated with a linguistic expression), and is error-proof (*abhrānta*). It comprehends sensorial perception, but in addition to it, even mental awareness of perceptions and emotions, and the supernatural perception typical of the *yogin* (*yogipratyakṣa*). Existence is equated with efficiency, and efficiency is change; what is changeless is not efficient, therefore it is unreal, because reality is change, instantaneous, perpetual kinesis, according to the theory of universal flux. All the same, causality is not a sort of functional production, but merely and exclusively interdependence. The cause cannot produce the effect because it does not have not the necessary time to do so: it is instantaneous like any other thing. All we can say is that the cause precedes the effect, and the effect follows the cause. Existence is efficiency, and efficiency itself is the cause. As *mādhyamika* thought had already demonstrated, things cannot arise from themselves, from 'non themselves', from both or from neither. Effects are not at all produced, they only functionally depend upon their causes. Therefore all *dharmas* are inactive, forceless (*nirvyāpāra, akiñcitkāra*), there is no efficiency beyond existence, existence itself equates with causal efficiency (*sattvaiva vyāpṛti*), and causality is only invariable precedence (*ānantaryaniyama*), the fact that the cause invariably precedes the effect. In other words, the effect is distinguishable from the cause only because it invariably follows the cause, it cannot come before it. Causality is the determination of the successive states through the preceding states. The universal, being the object of inference, is conceived in strictly apophatic terms, in order to avoid its reification current within Brahmanical schools, and is thus defined as 'exclusion of other' (*anyāpoha*).

The linguistic theory of exclusion (*apoha*) can now be entirely spelled out. A word expresses its objects only through a negative way, denying other meanings, different from it. The semantical sphere of each and every word is obtained by cutting out every other possible extraneous meaning, i.e. it is not possible to delineate any meaning in positive terms. So e.g. the horse will be described as a living being (excluding non living beings), four-footed (excluding two-footed beings, snakes and so on), not endowed with horns (excluding cows and so on), a cloven-footed quadruped (excluding cloven-footed animals such as pigs and so on), cutting out the semantic sphere of the term by progressively excluding further specifications, through a series of successive negations. Language is the sole tool of communication for discursive thought, it does not express universals which are present in particular objects in an undivided way. This last position is maintained by the followers of epistemological realism (first of all, the *nyāya* school). Language for Dignāga expresses only a 'difference', *bheda*, through the exclusion of what is different from itself, of everything that, in its extreme variety, can be combined into a whole only by the fact that it is different from something else, that it has different effects from something else. The own way of being of a thing, its intrinsic nature, is something inexpressible, it is a mere difference. The only common feature is the exclusion of what is different from itself: this feature in fact replaces the notion of universal, because it takes on such attributes as unity, permanence, invariable presence with reference to its particulars. The denotation of the meaning of a word is inseparable from the exclusion of other meanings. Difference and exclusion are not separable, either from a gnoseological or from a conceptual point of view. Difference indeed cannot be considered as a real existing thing, a *vastu*, and the same is true for exclusion. It is only a relative, interdependent term, it has no reality in and of itself. Only the form, *rūpa*, should be considered as existent in itself (but the interest of the school lies in epistemology, not in ontology): but the word is not concerned with form, *rūpa,* rather only with difference, *bheda.* The three main positions of the school with regard to *apoha* can be summarized as follows. The word expresses: 1) only negation (Dignāga, Dharmakīrti); 2) firstly a positive entity, secondly, only by implication, the exclusion of all other entities (Śāntarakṣita, Kalamaśīla); 3) a positive entity, being qualified by the exclusion of all other entities (Jñānaśrīmitra, Ratnakīrti). A word denotes only the 'portion' of the thing corresponding to the exclusion of all the other. So the 'thing' perpetually escapes the word, it is continually elusive. A word may only aspire to remove the causes of misunderstanding of the thing, but it can never grasp its essence, its intimate core.

Śāntarakṣita and Kalamaśīla subsequently elaborate more and more upon the notion of exclusion, *apoha,* noting the existence of two types of negation: relative negation or exclusion properly, *paryudāsa,* and absolute negation or denial, *niṣedha.* Relative negation is itself divided into two types: due to a conceptual difference (*buddhyātma*), and due to an objective difference (*arthātma*). Things are in and of themselves reciprocally different one with respect to the other, but due to a limited power (*niyataśakti*) some of them develop some sort of conception of similarity. On the basis of such a conception, a kind of reflection (*pratibimbaka*) arises. This reflection is erroneously conceived as an 'object'. *Apoha* is only the conception of such a reflection. The denotative function of the word is only the production of such a reflection, the exclusion of other objects from its own semantic sphere. Relative negation is known directly, whereas absolute negation is known through implication. In order to better understand the distinction between the two types of negation, we may remember that it dates back to grammatical thought, where we find the distinction of two different shades of application of the negative particle *na.* This happens through the dichotomy between *paryudāsa* and (*prasajya*)*pratiṣedha* (this last term being replaced with *niṣedha* within Buddhist epistemology). The process can be summarized as follows: the composition of *na* with a noun (*abrāhmaṇa,* one who is not a priest) in order to indicate a negation; and composition of *na* with a verbal form, in order to indicate a prohibition. Negation being limited to a nominal form, it can generate a certain amount of semantical choice. See e.g. the phrase 'this is polite': when verbally negated it becomes 'this is not polite', when nominally negated it becomes 'this is impolite'. But when we apply the double negation we can generate such a phrase as 'this is not impolite'. This phrase is not entirely semantically equivalent with 'this is polite', because nominal negation (*paryudāsa*) does entail the possibility of a choice. The way is paved for the possible existence of a kind of behaviour which is intermediate between polite and impolite. The object cow and the object no-cow are both well delimited, their respective boundaries are clear. But the word cow is unreal, because it depends on the will of those who use it in speech. Words do not know external objects, only their reflections. Due to ignorance, we take these internal reflections as if effectively representing external objects. But no word can ever directly 'touch' its own object: a word is always a mere verbal abstraction. The word 'cow', definable as 'not no-cow', is entirely different from the object 'no-cow', it never enters in contact with it. A word is imprisoned within the net of its own conceptual definitions, it never succeeds in tearing this net, in order to directly enter in contact with reality. Reality is not negated by this school, it is merely revealed as not accessible to our understanding, it is understandable only through the severe rigid mediation of language. From the epistemological point of view, the *apoha* theory corresponds to the same extension of the mere absence of observation (*adarśanamātra*) of that which is not denoted by the semantical sphere, and in so doing it is eventually elevated to the rank of inference. Inference is that special type of exclusion which excludes from itself the object not denoted by it (*vyavacchedānumāna*). From the point of view of the different levels of reality, we may conclude that Dignāga equates the level of perception with the dependent level, *paratantra,* the level of inference with the imaginary level, *parikalpita,* and the level or pure consciousness with the absolute level, *pariniṣpanna.*

As a conclusion, we may note that Indian mystics tried to follow three different paths in order to express what is ineffable.[5] The first path is the path of poetic language through the use of metaphor, the main way, the other two being subordinate to it. The limits of expressibility are transcended by poetic language, and mystics use this tool of communication in order to reach what is ineffable. The second path is paradox, the use of contradictory predicates in order to characterize the specific experience we want to communicate. Within Jainism, this path is present in the type of the systematic simultaneous application of predicates that are authentical but at the same time mutually contradictory, with reference to a metaphysical assessment. Thus, from a certain point of view it is possible to assert a proposition, and from another point of view it is possible to negate the same proposition. E.g. the phrase 'John does not drink' may be intended as valid with reference to the fact that John does

[5] Following Matilal 1990, pp. 151 ff.

not drink spirits, but it is invalid with reference to the fact that John does effectively drink water (it is not possible to conceive the hypothesis that John does not drink any liquid substance whatsoever). The third path is apophatism, negative dialectics, according to the Upanisadic dictum 'not so, not so' (*neti neti*), further elaborated by *mādhyamika* eristic into an antisubstantialist device. To assign any possible predicate to a mystical object is but a vain venture, every sort of predication being successively negated. But if we are able to reiterate this process more and more, progressively negating every variety of possible descriptions, we will be able to convey the desired meaning in a negative way. Within this last perspective, it might not have been entirely useless to make much ado about nothing.

References

Abhyankar, Kashinath Vasudev (1896). *A Dictionary of Sanskrit Grammar.* Baroda: Oriental Institute, p. 393, s.v. *śūna.*

Bronkhorst, Johannes (1994). "A Note on Zero and the Numerical Place-value System in Ancient India." In: *Asiatische Studien* 48, No. 4, pp. 1039-42.

Matilal, Bimal Krishna (1990). *The Word and the World, India's Contribution to the Study of Language.* Oxford: Oxford University Press.

Sarma, S.R. (1992) "*Śūnya*: Mathemathical Aspect." In: *Kalātattvakośa. A Lexicon of Fundamental Concepts of the Indian Arts.* Ed. by Kapila Vatsyayan. New Delhi: Indira Gandhi National Centre for the Arts and Motilal Banarsidass, vol. 2 *Concepts of Space and Time.* Ed. by Bettina Bäumer, pp. 400-11.

Sharma, Chandradhar (1964). *A Critical Survey of Indian Philosophy.* Delhi: Motilal Banarsidass [Rider, London 1960].

Vatsyayan, Kapila, S.R. Sarma and G.C. Pande (1992). "*Śūnya/śūnyatā.*" In: *Kalātattvakośa. A Lexicon of Fundamental Concepts of the Indian Arts.* Ed. by Kapila Vatsyayan. New Delhi: Indira Gandhi National Centre for the Arts and Motilal Banarsidass, vol. 2 *Concepts of Space and Time.* Ed. by Bettina Bäumer pp. 399-428.

Bibliography for Further Research

Arnold, Dan (2006). "On Semantics and *saṃketa*: Thoughts on a Neglected Problem with Buddhist *apoha* Doctrine." In: *Journal of Indian Philosophy* 34, No. 5, pp. 415-78.

Bhattacharyya (Chakrabarti), Bhaswati (1979). "The Concept of Existence and Nāgārjuna's Doctrine of *śūnyatā*." In: *Journal of Indian Philosophy* 7, No. 4, pp. 335-44.

Bugault, Guy (2000). "The Immunity of *śūnyatā*: is it possible to understand *Madhyamakakārikās* 4, 8-9?". In: *Journal of Indian Philosophy* 28, No. 4, pp. 385-97.

Dargyay, Lobsang (1990). "What Is Non-existent and What Is Remanent in *śūnyatā*." In: *Journal of Indian Philosophy* 18, No. 1, pp. 81-91.

De Jong, Jan Willem (1972-1974). "Emptiness." In: *Journal of Indian Philosophy* 2, No. 1, pp. 7-15.

Duckworth, Douglas D. (2010). "De/limiting Emptiness and the Boundaries of the Ineffable." In: *Journal of Indian Philosophy* 38, No. 1, pp. 97-105.

King, Richard (1989). "*Śūnyatā* and *ajāti*: Absolutism and the Philosophies of Nāgārjuna and Gauḍapāda." In: *Journal of Indian Philosophy* 17, No. 4, pp. 385-405.

Lopez, Donald S. Jr. (1988). "Do *śrāvakas* Understand Emptiness?". In: *Journal of Indian Philosophy* 16, No. 1, pp. 65-105.

Siderits, Mark (2004). "Causation and Emptiness in Early Madhya-maka." In: *Journal of Indian Philosophy* 32, No. 4, pp. 393-419.

Frederick J. Streng (1970-1972), "The Buddhist Doctrine of the Two Truths as Religious Philosophy." In: *Journal of Indian Philosophy* 1, No. 3, pp. 262-71.

Tola, Fernando and Carmen Dragonetti (1981). "Nāgārjuna's Conception of 'Voidness' (*śūnyatā*)." In: *Journal of Indian Philosophy* 9, No. 3, pp. 273-82.

Elisa Freschi and Tiziana Pontillo

When One Thing Applies More than Once: tantra *and* prasaṅga *in Śrautasūtra, Mīmāṃsā and Grammar*[*]

1 General Introduction

The present article is part of a wider project focusing on the function of absent elements and trying to answer this basic question: How can an absent element perform a function notwithstanding its absence? How come that an effect can be grasped in absence of its cause? Eventually, the question boils down to the status of absence. Is it a distinct category, as maintained by Bhāṭṭa Mīmāṃsā authors (see Freschi 2010) or nothing more than the negation of presence, as maintained by Buddhist Epistemologists?

Grammarians and linguists are familiar with the idea of a function of the "absence" of morphemes which is currently called "zero". Western linguists beginning with de Saussure's work of 1879 (Saussure 1879 [1878], see Pontillo 2002, pp. 559 ff.) have often postulated the existence of the so-called zero-morpheme where the actual perceptible linguistic form does not match its relevant semantic and syntactic content. They resorted to this de-

[*] All translations are the authors', unless explicitly stated. Other authors' translations have been reproduced for the sake of comparison, only in case of significant divergence. This paper is the result of a joint work entirely discussed and shared by both authors. However, Elisa Freschi is responsible for sections 1.1-1.3, 2.1-2.3, 2.4.3, 2.5, 3-3.3 (except 3.2.1), 3.5, 4 (except 4.1.1) and 5; Tiziana Pontillo for sections 1 (except 1.1-1.3), 2.4 (except 2.4.3), 3.2.1, 3.4, 4.1.1. We are grateful to Saroja Bhate for her comments (in 2008) on a preliminary version of the study on the technical terms *prasaṅga* and *tantra*, on which the present article is based. The Śrautasūtra-occurrences here analysed have been detected through the consultation of the *prasaṅga*-call slips in the Scriptorium of the Dictionary Project at the Deccan College of Poona. We are hence grateful to the Director Vinayaka P. Bhatta who allowed T. Pontillo to access the slips at the end of November 2007.

vice on the basis of a significant opposition pointed out between comparable morphological structures. By contrast, as elaborated by Al-George, the Indian linguistic zero is not a mere device adopted for a descriptive purpose (see also Pontillo 1999; Pontillo 2000 [2003], pp. 159 ff., Candotti and Pontillo 2012, § 2.2).[1]

More in general, the answer to the problem will be the elaboration of a complex net which allows an element to be applied to a specific case, even though it is not explicitly there. This net may work through various devices, i.e., analogical extension (*atideśa*), centralised simultaneous application (*tantra*), associative extension of what is automatically involved (*prasaṅga*), substitution (*ādeśa, vikāra, pratinidhi*), zero-replacement (*lopa*). The present article aims at showing how this topic was well present with a high degree of technicalities in Indian thought, within and outside Linguistics.

1.1 Conceptual tools for dealing with substitution and absence in the Śrautasūtras: Comparisons with Grammar

In order to illustrate the way in which the basic framework of the 'general methodological division in Śāstra between the general (*samānya*) and the special (*viśeṣa*)' works (Kahrs 1998, pp. 183-5), Kahrs explains (pp. 184-5):

> Thus, the methodology employed revolves around such concepts as *prakṛti* 'prototype' and *vikṛti* 'modification'. This is also referred to in terms of an image from the art of weaving as *tantra* 'warp' and *āvāpa* 'woof' denoting respectively the basic model which is the constant part of a ritual and the special features which differ from one ritual to another.

This opposition between general and specific rules, which has been commonly resorted to by every kind of scientific explanation, and which has been probably inaugurated by the Kalpasūtra-tradition in the Indian culture, is often considered as a good antecedent of the grammatical substitution-pattern. Nevertheless, the Pāṇinian Vyākaraṇa tradition has attained a higher degree of structural complexity and terminogical precision.

We shall have several occasions below (§ 3.5) to deal with the possible comparison between the ritual descriptive schemas and the linguistic pattern of substitution. In spite of the differences, what seems to be noteworthy is that the dichotomy between a general/ archetypal instruction and specific/ ectypical single

[1] As it happens to be presented, e.g., in Pandit 1990. By contrast for an interpretation of Pāṇini's *lopa* as a notion 'linked to a structuralistic approach in grammar', see Wicher 2008, pp. 46 ff.

rules[2] is already well established in the former tradition. Furthermore, the archetypal instruction is that which is taught explicitly, whereas the ectypal ones are analogically inferred and do not need to be stated, as long as there is no difference with the archetype. Accordingly, the archetypal instruction is said to be *vyākhyāta* ('explained') and, more frequently, *upadiṣṭa* ('directly taught'), in passages such as the following ones:[3]

> We shall explain the midday pressing [of Soma]; its ritual disposition has been explained by means of the morning pressing; we shall [now] list the modifications.[4]

> *iṣṭis*, animal- and Soma-sacrifices have been enunciated by means of the Full moon sacrifice.[5]

This usage of *upadiṣṭa* sounds very close to the grammatical concept of *upadeśa*, i.e., the first enunciation of a linguistic unit.

In sum, both Grammar and Ritualistic share the common idea described by Kahrs as follows:

> If we have a map – and I think it is justified to call the ritual and linguistic descriptions of the ancient Indians a map – [...] [r]eminding ourselves that the map is not the territory, we may [...] ask what features of the territory are represented on the map. If the territory is absolutely uniform, nothing would be represented on the map except the borders of the territory. Otherwise, what will be represented on a map is really differences of various kinds – differences in height, vegetation, surface, population structures, etc. (Kahrs 1998, p. 184)

Kahrs' metaphor has the further advantage of pointing at the dimensional perspective of these texts. Although the temporal dimension of their recitation is inherent in all texts, Grammatical and Ritualistic texts seem to also presuppose a space where the sacrifice/ language takes place, so that substitutions may be described as happening "in place of", i.e., at the place which might be occupied by... Similarly, elements which are not prescribed by the rule we are currently examining can be introduced, as if they were available somewhere else, in a different portion of the sacrificial/ linguistic "space". We shall see (§ 4.1) how this spatial metaphor

[2] "Archetype" and "prototype" have both been used to translate *prakṛti*, the former is more common in translations of Mīmāṃsā and ŚrSū literature and has therefore been used also in the current study.

[3] On an hypothetical chronology of the ŚrSū, see below, § 2.1.

[4] *madhyaṃdinaṃ savanaṃ vyākhyāsyāmaḥ. tasya prātaḥsavanena kalpo vyākhyātaḥ. vikārān anukramiṣyāmaḥ* (BhŚrSū 14.1.3).

[5] *paurṇamāseneṣṭipaśusomā upadiṣṭāḥ* (ĀśvŚrSū 2.1.1).

works in the case of *tantra* and *prasaṅga*, but it might be worth remembering that an absence in space is never an absolute absence.

1.2 tantra *as opposed to* prasaṅga

tantra is one of the terms with several distinct technical meanings, departing from its complex Vedic usage: 'In Vedic ritual literature, *tantra* indicates the standard form of a ritual, including both what is common to all rituals of the same class, and what constitutes the model for several rituals' (Gonda 1977, pp. 492, n. 22; 510; see also Gonda 1980, pp. 180, 421). Within Mīmāṃsā, it became a technical term indicating the device by means of which an auxiliary element is performed only once and applied wherever needed, on certain conditions: 'There are certain Subsidiaries which, if performed once, effectually help, by that single performance, more than one Act; this help accorded by a single performance of the Subsidiary to several Primaries has been called "*tantra*" (Centralisation, Collectivation)' (Jha and Mishra 1964, p. 307, p. 348 of the 1942 edition).

prasaṅga shares a partly similar meaning insofar as it indicates the possibility of something to be applied to its own case and also to a further one.[6]

Both terms *tantra* and *prasaṅga* are used in the Pāṇinian tradition, though to the best of our knowledge, except in Bhartṛhari, they are never explicitly contrasted in the same passage (Pontillo 2008, 94). Some crucial occurrences of *prasaṅga* in Patañjali precisely deal with the phenomenon occurring when the sense of a speech unit is intended, in spite of the absence of the speech unit itself.

1.3 *Questions*

tantra and *prasaṅga* are first juxtaposed and contrasted in Bhartṛhari's commentary on the M and in Śabara's (5th c. CE?) one on the *Mīmāṃsāsūtra*. Does it mean that they oppose each other? Do Bhartṛhari and Śabara faithfully represent the M and MS (2nd c. BC?) stances on them? And can one detect the stages of the development of *tantra* from its Vedic usage, through the ŚrSū one, to the Mīmāṃsā one and further? And what about *prasaṅga*? Is it a linear development, or are there mutual contaminations between the ŚrSū and the Mīmāṃsā and Vyākaraṇa usages?

[6] Cf. Pandurangi 2006, p. xxvii: 'Tantra is the technique of single performance with reference to many, while *prasaṅga* is the technique of one item serving the purpose of another also. These two are intended to avoid repetition and economize the effort.'

Furthermore, what exactly is *tantra*? The application of a subsidiary (as when one says that something is applied more than once *tantreṇa* or the subsidiary itself (as when one says that X is *tantra*)? Which of the two usages is metaphorical?

2 tantra

2.1 tantra *in the Śrautasūtras*

The relative chronology of the ŚrSū is still a controversial topic and its settlement lies outside the scope of the present article. The following table is merely tentative and is based on previous studies (mainly Gonda 1977 and Brucker 1980, which have been elaborated independently of each other). Moreover, Gonda 1977, p. 483 himself is cautious about attempting a chronology of the ŚrSū and Bodewitz 1984 convincingly argues that Brucker's results are far from being conclusive. The only reason for attempting a chronological table, which merely concerns the works which are actually quoted in the present paper, is to make readers aware of the fact that the presence of one or the other shade of meaning of *tantra* and *prasaṅga* in the ŚrSū might also have historical reasons.

group	name of the ŚrSū
most ancient ŚrSū	BaudhŚrSū, LāṭyŚrSū
middle ancient	ĀsvŚrSū, ŚŚrSū, BhŚrSū, ĀpŚrSū
most recent	KātyŚrSū

2.1.1 tantra *as basic procedure*

The term *tantra* is found in the ŚrSū primarily in its meaning of '(basic) procedure'.

A standard occurrence of *tantra* as 'basic procedure' is the locative form *saumike tantre* 'in the procedure of a Soma-sacrifice' in BaudhŚrSū 21.18.[7] The meaning of 'procedure', in the precise sense of an "ordered series of actions conducted in a certain manner" has to be assumed in BaudhŚrSū 23.8: *antas tantram eva yūpe virūḍhe prāyaścittaṃ kuryād iti śālīkiḥ*, 'One should perform the prescribed expiation only if the post sprouts within the time of the procedure, according to Śālīki.'

[7] As it has also been recently confirmed by Parpola (Parpola 2011, p. 342) the BaudŚrSū is generally considered as the earliest ŚrSū.

Another of the most ancient ŚrSū, LāṭyŚrSū, includes a definition of *tantra*, after two *sūtras* mentioning it as a device:

daśarātrāt ṣāḍahikāny aṣṭamanavamayoś caitāny ahīnatantrāṇi. 6.9.10 [...] *kalpasaprāyāṇy ṛksāmāni yatra samavayanti tad āśīstantraṃ yathābhicaraṇīyeṣu.* 6.9.12 *bhūyiṣṭhaṃ tantralakṣaṇam.* 6.9.13

These basic procedures of the Ahīna [sacrifices] referring to the six-day [sacrifice] and the eight- and nine- [day ones] [are derived] from the ten-day sacrifice.[...] [The procedure] where stanzas and songs having a similar ritual arrangement are combined, is the *āśīs-tantra* "the Blessing procedure", as in the case of exorcisms. The definition of *tantra* is that which is most present.

Similar instances can be found throughout the ŚrSū as well as in the GṛSū.

2.1.2 *"Just once" vs. repeatedly*

tantra is employed as a concise technical formula denoting a 'common/ combined procedure' opposed to the modality of single procedures repeated (*abhivṛt-*) for each ritual act in the most ancient Ritual Sūtras, both in BaudhŚrSū 25.31 (12 times) and 25.34 (2 times) and in BhŚrSū 8.25.11 and 14.25.6. The shift from the first meaning of *tantra* to this second one may be better understood through cases such as BaudhŚrSū 13.1.1, which is a good example of the meaning of *tantra* as a 'basic procedure':

Now we shall explain the *iṣṭis* in detail. Their basic procedure, following that of the Full and New moon Sacrifices, is pointed out once and for all.[8]

It is noteworthy here that the basic procedure needs to be explained only once (*sakṛt*) and then applies for all cases. Similarly, the later, Mīmāṃsā meaning of *tantra* will point to a subsidiary which is performed only once and with its function lasting throughout the whole sacrifice.

A technical opposition similar to the one generally conveyed by the terminological pair *tantra/ abhivṛt-* 'to repeat' also occurs 9 times in the ĀpŚrSū. Consider, for instance, ĀpŚrSū 21.3.4:

According to one [opinion], the enumeration of the *ṛṣi*-ancestors of those who belong to one and the same *gotra* should be repeated after the intervention of a different *gotra*; according to another [opinion] even if there is the intervention [of the enumeration

[8] *athāta iṣṭīr vyākhyāsyāmaḥ. tāsāṃ sakṛt pradiṣṭam eva dārśapaurṇamāsikaṃ tantram* [...].

> of the ancestors of one belonging to a different *gotra*], [the *ṛṣi*-ancestors of all those who belong to one and the same family should be enumerated] only once.[9]

ĀpŚrSū 24.4.16-17 seems to imply even the further step of *tantra* as a 'simultaneous application':

> Since the cooking pot, the spit and the two-pronged fork are capable [of being used for all victims] there should be [their] common application. By contrast, when there is a difference in the sort [of victim], the [cooking tool] should be distinguished, because the cooking is different.[10]

The connection of *tantra* and *sakṛt* 'once' is also present in the GṛSū.

2.1.3 tantra *as part of the basic procedure*

Also in a passage of ŚŚrSū (14.39.5), *tantra* seems to shift from the meaning of 'basic procedure' to a different one. Consider Caland's translation and note thereon:

> *tantraṃ dīkṣopasadaḥ.*
>
> The ceremonies of consecration and the *upasads* (of both the sacrifices) are the regular paradigma.
>
> This must mean they are performed ones for the two sacrifices, cf. JB *tayoḥ saha dịkṣā saha krayaḥ sahopasadaḥ.* (Caland 1953)

One could even suggest here a Mīmāṃsā-like translation (see infra, § 2.3): '*dīkṣā* and *upasad* are simultaneously applied.'

And:

> *prāsmā agnim bharatovadhyagoham iti tantram uttamaḥ prayājaḥ parivapyau*[11] *ca.*
>
> [The words of the *adhrigu*-formula]: 'Bear ye the fire forwards for it' (up to): 'Dig in the earth a hole for the undigested food' are the regular paradigm (they are neither repeated nor altered al-

[9] *nānāgotravyavāyād eva samānagotrāṇām ārṣeyavaraṇam abhyāvartetety ekam. vyavete 'pi tantram evety aparam* (Thite 2004).

[10] *kumbhīśūlavapāśrapaṇīprabhūtvāt tantraṃ syāt. jātibhede tu bhidyeta paktivaiṣamyāt.* The other 7 occurrences are ĀpŚrSū 14.5.16; 14.7.5; 14.7.7; 21.3.8; 21.5.6; 24.3.22; 24.12.5. By contrast, 21 occurrences display *tantra* in the probably more ancient sense of 'procedure'.

[11] 'Read *parivapyau* instead of *-vāpyau* (Āp 7.20.9 and 21.2). For all the *vāpas* they are repeated once' (Caland 1953, *ad loc.*).

> though more victims than one are immolated), the same prevails for the last fore-offerings and the two libations before and after the offering of the omentum. (Caland 1953, *sū.* 15.1.26)

It is noteworthy that this *sūtra* follows ŚŚrSū 15.1.23 almost immediately, where *tantra* seems to mean just 'basic procedure', once again showing the semantic connection of these two meanings, since it is unlikely that two different, yet technical, uses of a term would be found within four *sūtras*.

Similarly, ĀpŚrSū 14.5.3 makes a further step towards what will be discussed later (§ 2.3), i.e., *tantra* as denoting each element of the basic procedure:

> *tantram aṅgāni vibhavanti.*
>
> The subsidiaries which are *tantra* are sufficient [and need not be repeated].

2.1.4 tantra *and* āvāpa

At the beginning of the Karmānta-section, precisely in BaudhŚrSū 24.3 *tantra* is formally opposed to *āvāpa*, in order to distinguish the standard form of *iṣṭis* from some of their special features. The *āvāpas* are rites inserted within the basic procedure (*tantra*). From these original meanings, the oppositional couple developed within Mīmāṃsā into 'common application' vs. 'repetition' of a certain rite. In fact, rites which belong to the basic procedure are performed once and for all, whereas *ad* hoc insertions are to be repeated whenever needed. Within the opposition between basic procedure and insertions to be repeated, a peculiar case is the one of elements which *tantrasthānaṃ bhajante*, literally 'take part to/ get a place within/ the basic procedure'. These seem to be elements which are inserted in a preexisting basic procedure, but which are, then, incorporated in it.

A further evidence of the status of *tantra* as something which can be reached is ĀśvŚrSū 11.1.15:

> *pūrṇaḥ pūrṇaś ca ṣaḷahas tantratām eva gacchati.*
>
> The six-day ritual so completed in each case gains the status of a basic procedure.

2.1.5 Conclusions on the meaning of tantra *in the Śrautasūtras*

But what does the fact of taking part in the *tantra* entail? Consider the following instance: *tataḥ saṃsthājapa iti paśuḥ tantram* (ĀśvŚrSū 3.6.28). The animal to be sacrificed is *tantra*, since it becomes part of the structure of the sacrifice and remains valid in regard to all the rites of the sacrifice. In this way, an element can continue to be valid although it is absent in a particular instance *tantreṇa*, i.e., since it has become part of the basic procedure of the ritual, which is present at each moment of its performance.

From a more general perspective, *tantra* seems to act in a centralised way upon elements which are ultimately related insofar as they are part of the same basic structure. Therefore, it only functions within the same ritual. On the full development of these two conditions, see infra, § 2.3 and § 2.3.1.

2.2 The semantic web of tantra *in the Śrautasūtras*

2.2.1 tantra *and* prakṛti

The meaning of *tantra* as 'basic procedure' makes it quite akin to *prakṛti*, in the sense of 'archetypical procedure', that is, the basic form of a ritual – the one out of which details are analogically transferred to the derivative forms (*vikṛti*). In fact, both these terms and – with a more limited semantic overlapping – *kalpa* occur in some quite similar contexts, such as in the following passages:[12]

ĀśvŚrSū 1.1.3: *darśapūrṇamāsau tu pūrvaṃ vyākhyāsyāmas tantrasya tatrāmnātatvāt.*

But we shall explain the New and Full moon sacrifices at first, because the basic procedure has been handed down in that context.

BhŚrSū 5.17.1-3: *punarādheyam vyākhyāsyāmah. tasyāgnyādheyena kalpo vyākhyātaḥ. vikārān anukramiṣyāmaḥ.*

We shall explain the re-establishment of the fire; its (ritual) arrangement (*kalpa*) has been explained through [the explanation concerning] the establishment of the fire; we shall [now] list the modifications.[13]

BhŚrSū 6.15.4-5: *āmāvasyam tantraṃ bhavati. tatraiṣo 'tyantapradeśaḥ. sarveṣv iṣṭipaśubandheṣu dārśapaurṇamāsikā dharmā anuyanti.*

The New moon sacrifice is the basic procedure; in this context there is the indication reaching all [performances]: in all *iṣṭi*s and animal sacrifices, the usual properties of the New and Full moon sacrifices go on.

[12] The order of the quotations follows the relative chronology as proposed by Brucker 1980. See also Pontillo 2003 [2004].

[13] An analogous opposition between *kalpa* and *vikāra* occurs in BhŚrSū 14.1.3.

ŚŚrSū 1.16.1: *vyākhyātau darśapurnamāsau prakṛtir iṣṭipaśubandhānām.*

The New and Full moon sacrifices which have been explained are the archetype for the *iṣṭis* and for the animal sacrifices.

The term *kalpa* is rarely found, apart from its chief role in identifying the class of Kalpasūtras. Its intersections with *tantra* and *prakṛti* are not yet clear, although its etymology may point more to the sense of a ritual "arrangement", which builds order within rituals.

In this context it is not surprising that *prakṛti* and *tantra* at a certain point assume almost synonymous meanings, although it might be suggested that *prakṛti* refers more to the originative model (the archetype one) in its static aspect, whereas *tantra* stresses this model's application to all needed instances. Furthermore, the latter evolves as an operational noun, indicating the way an action is implemented.

2.2.2 Playing with the base tan-: tantra *and* tati

In the Karmānta-section of the BaudhŚrSū another terminological pair, namely *pūrva-* and *uttara-tati*, seems to convey an analogous opposition between archetypical and non-archetypical rites, focusing on the time and the place occupied by them and as a consequence on their sequence. A similar focus on the sequence of mention can also be observed in ĀpŚrSū 24.4.15.[14]

pūrva-tati and *uttara-tati* are defined as 'the antecedent and the subsequent series of ceremonies. The standard (ritual) is *pūrvā tatiḥ*, and what one arranges (modifies) is *uttarā tatiḥ*; (for instance,) the establishment of the ritual fires is *pūrvā tatiḥ*, the re-establishment *uttarā tatiḥ*; of the vegetarian sacrifices (*iṣṭi*) the Full and New moon sacrifices are the *pūrvā tatiḥ*, all the optional rites (*kāmyā iṣṭayaḥ*) the *uttarā tatiḥ*' (Gonda 1977, p. 510). The initial question about *pūrva-* and *uttara-tati* in BaudhŚrSū 24.5 thoroughly sounds as a replica of the question about *tantra* and *āvāpa* from BaudhŚrSū 24.3: *katham u khalv etaj jānīyād idam tantram ayam āvāpa iti.*

katham khalv etaj jānīyād iyaṃ pūrvā tatir iyam uttareti. yā prakṛtiḥ sā pūrvā tatiḥ. atha yad vidadhāti sottarā tatiḥ. agnyādheyaṃ pūrvā tatiḥ, punarādheyam uttarā tatiḥ. darśapūrṇamāsāv iṣṭīnāṃ pūrvā tatiḥ, sarvāḥ kāmyā iṣṭaya uttarā tatiḥ. aindrāgno nirūḍhapaśubandhānāṃ pūrvā tatiḥ sarve kamyāḥ paśava uttarā tatiḥ. jyotiṣṭomaḥ somānāṃ pūrvā tatiḥ sarve somā uttarā tatiḥ. śyenacid agnīnāṃ pūrvā tatiḥ,

[14] *prakṛteḥ pūrvoktatvād apūrvam ante syāt*, 'As the basic procedure is mentioned first, that which is not the first one should be at the end.'

sarve kāmyā agnaya uttarā tatiḥ. dvirātro 'hīnānāṃ pūrvā tatiḥ, sarve 'hīnā uttarā tatiḥ. dvādaśāho 'harganāṇāṃ pūrvā tatiḥ, sarve 'harganā uttarā tatiḥ. gavāmayanaṃ sāṃvatsarikāṇāṃ sattrāṇāṃ pūrvā tatiḥ, sarvāṇi sāṃvatsarikāni sattrāṇy uttarā tatiḥ.

How should one know 'This is the antecedent ritual act, this is the subsequent?' The antecedent ritual act is the archetype, the one that one arranges [presupposing this ritual act] is the subsequent. The establishment of the ritual fires is the antecedent ritual act, the re-establishment is the subsequent. The Full and New moon sacrifices are the antecedent ritual act among the *iṣṭis*. All optional animal [offerings] are the subsequent (insofar as their descriptions presuppose elements already described in regard to the Full and New moon sacrifices). The [offering] to Indra and Agni is the antecedent ritual act among the compulsory animal sacrifices, all optional ones are the subsequent ritual act. The Jyotiṣṭoma is the antecedent ritual act among the Soma-[offerings], all Soma-[offerings] are the subsequent ritual act. The one piled up in the [form of a] hawk is the antecedent of all fire-[altars]. All optional fire-[altars] are the subsequent. The two-day festival is the antecedent among the [sacrifices] lasting several days. All [sacrifices] lasting several days are the subsequent. The twelve-day one is the antecedent among the series of sacrificial days. All series of sacrificial days are the subsequent. The Gavāmayana is the antecedent among the yearly Sattras. All yearly *sattras* are the subsequent.

In the first sentences, *pūrvā tati* refers to the first instance of a ritual act, along the lines of which a second one is performed. But later in the text it also seems to refer to whatever is presupposed by a later re-elaboration. Hence, the *pūrvā tati* seems the "premiss", following which the *uttarā tati*, i.e., the "elaboration" is arranged. It seems to entail a link with the way one arranges things and is not confined to an act, and even less to a series of acts.

Göhler (2011, pp. 105-6) also directly links *pūrvā tati* and *uttarā tati* with *prakṛti* and *vikṛti*. Oddly, he then translates without further explanation, *tati* with *Sequenz* and renders the answer to the initial question in BaudhŚrSū rather freely. Similarly, the meaning of 'series of sacrificial acts' proposed by Gonda (1977, p. 510]), who translates *pūrva-* and *uttara-tati* as 'the antecedent and the subsequent series of ceremonies' (cf. Kashikar 2003b, p. 1539: 'the first of the series... the next') does not seem to rely on grammatical analysis. The *kṛt tati* is in fact derived from the verbal base *tan-* 'to extend, to weave' as a *nomen actionis* according to A 3.3.94; the form of the base *ta-* instead of *tan-* is determined by A 6.4.39. The transitive sense of the deverbal *nomen actionis tati* 'the action of tending the sacrificial act' might have been opposed to the intransitive sense of the matching deverbal noun *tantu* 'thread' 'succession of the sacrificial acts', and both to the deverbal noun *tantra* as the 'web, the woven work'. All three nouns might have insisted on the sense of spatiotemporal continuity already attributed to the Ṛgvedic verb *tan-* by Silburn 1955, 14; 44; 59; 68.[15]

2.3 tantra *in Mīmāṃsā*

How can an actually absent subsidiary have any effect on a part of the ritual occurring well after its execution? Possibly because it is recognised as belonging to an underlying basic form of the ritual (again: *tantrasthānaṃ bhaj-*, about which see § 2.1.4), which is simultaneously present in all its parts. The whole picture is, however, far more complex. In fact, *tantra* is a common term in Mīmāṃsā, but it has no less than three technical meanings:

1. the basic structure of the ritual (as in the ŚrSū)
2. a device through which an element is performed just once, but automatically applying to all the sacrifice's parts (as in Jha and Mishra 1964, see § 1.2)
3. an element of the sacrifice which is performed just once, but automatically applies to all the sacrifice's parts

A possible pathway to the latter two from the Vedic meaning, which is also more common in the earlier ŚrSū, could be the following:

tantra as basic procedure

↓

the basic procedure is explained only once (*sakṛt*)

↓

tantra is, hence, opposed to *āvāpa*, inserted rites,
which are inserted more than once, whenever need arises

↓

whatever element remains valid for the whole rite and
needs not to be repeated
is said to have a place within the *tantra* (*tantrasthānaṃ bhaj-*)

↓

hence, the device through which an element remains valid
for the whole ritual is itself called *tantra*

The shift from the Meaning 1 to 2 could be explained as a case of metonymy (*pars pro toto*), whereas the one from 2 to 3 could be a case of metaphor (the function instead of the element to which it applies). Furthermore, this passage could have

15 For the transitive sense of the deverbal nouns in *-ti* opposed to the intransitive sense of the deverbal nouns in *-tu*, see Lazzeroni 1997.

been influenced by the parallel of *prasaṅga* (explicitly contrasted to *tantra* already before Śabara, see infra, § 4.1.2), which denotes the function and not the element to which it applies.

All the distinct items listed above are well documented, whereas the shifts of meaning merely constitute our reconstructive hypothesis.

Interestingly, all three meanings remain in use throughout the history of Mīmāṃsā. However, No. 1 (the Vedic meaning) is just implicitly accepted, as if it were not a technical term requiring an additional explanation. No. 2 and 3 are, by contrast, object of a particular focus, although the authors seem not to distinguish sharply between them and their definitions of the technical usage of *tantra* may focus on 2 (so Śabara) or 3 (so MNS), with no apparent reason.

It might also be useful to remember that *tantra* in Meaning 1 is not opposed to *prasaṅga*.

2.3.1 tantra *in Jaimini*

According to Śabara, MS 11 is dedicated to *tantra* and MS 12 to *prasaṅga*. The first term is, in fact, very frequent throughout MS 11 (*pāda*s 2, 3 and 4) and it can also be found at the beginning of MS 12 (and once outside these two books). It is often contrasted to *bheda*. It often retains the Vedic meaning of *Grundform* (so Mylius), i.e., the basic structure of the ritual (Meaning 1),[16] to which an operative meaning is added (Meaning 3).[17] The 'basic procedure' is the one which encompasses the whole ritual and enables an element to be present in the whole sacrifice, without being repeated again and again. Each of its elements might also be said *tantra* (Meaning 2).[18]

In MS 11.2, Jaimini discusses with a PP on the conditions for the application of *tantra* using the case of complex sacrifices:

1. coming together (*samavāya*) of various ritual elements[19]
2. unity of place and time[20]
3. unity of the injunction prescribing the sacrifice

[16] E.g., *na vā svāhākāreṇa saṃyogād vāṣaṭkārasya ca nirdeśāt tantre tena vipratiṣedhāt* (MS 8.4.11). All quotations from Abhyankar and Jośī 1970.

[17] E.g., *daśapeye krayapratikarṣāt pratikarṣas tataḥ prācāṃ tatsamānaṃ tantraṃ syāt* (MS 11.2.58).

[18] MS 11.2.11 and 11.4.19.

[19] See MS 11.4.1.

[20] On the unity of time, see also MS 11.3.22: *subrahmaṇyā tu tantraṃ dīkṣāvad anyakālatvāt.*

4. unity of the sacrificial act
5. unity of the performers
6. unity of the Deity to whom the offering is meant[21]
7. unity of function[22]

It might be suggested that the first conditions overrule the latter ones, although in all cases of conflict Jaimini rather seems to aim at persuading the opponent that there is no conflict at all. The following *sūtra* is the only exception we could detect, although it is difficult to say whether it must be attributed to a PP or to the S (as claims Śabara):

> But, in the case of different injunctions, there can be a simultaneous performance of [rites] which have come together, because of their connection with a [single] time.[23]

In other words, it might be the case that there are separate originative injunctions (*utpattividhi*) referring to distinct elements of the same ritual. Yet, the unity of time and their contiguity (*samavāya*) in the performance might be enough to justify a simultaneous application.

2.3.1.1 Semantic web of tantra *in Jaimini*

A little bit later in MS 11.3, Jaimini seems to indirectly define *tantra* as that which is *sarvārtha* 'having all [elements] as its purpose',[24] as *sādhāraṇa* 'common' (see MS 11.3.9) and as an antonym to *āvṛtti* 'repetition' (see MS 11.3.5).

Within MS 11.3, *tantra* might also have Meaning 1, thus showing the contiguity of all meanings in the awareness of the Mīmāṃsā listeners.[25]

The opposition between *tantra* and *bheda* reminds one of that between *vākya* and *bheda*. Both *tantra* and *vākya* are principles implemented to build a unity within the textual passages regarding a

[21] On this principle: 'There must be a split [in the simultaneous application] in the case of a different Deity, since [otherwise] there would be doubt' (*bhedas tu sandehād devatāntare syāt*, MS 11.4.30).

[22] On this principle: 'In the case of the [rites composing] the animal sacrifice, there is the condition of being *tantra* (i.e., being performed once and for all) of the pot, the iron stake and the two-pronged fork, since they include [all functions to be performed through them]' (MS 11.4.29).

[23] *codanāpṛthaktve tu aikatantryaṃ samavetānāṃ kālasaṃyogāt* (MS 11.4.21).

[24] *dravyasya karmakālaniṣpatteḥ prayogaḥ sarvārthaḥ syāt svakālatvāt* (MS 11.3.2).

[25] E.g., *svarus tantrāpavargaḥ syād asvakālatvāt* || 11.3.8 || *paśau ca puroḍāśe samānatantraṃ bhavet* || 11.3.17 || *vākyasaṃyogād votkarṣaḥ samānatantratvād arthalopād ananvayaḥ* || 11.3.55 ||

sacrifice. If their conditions do not apply, however, there must be a split (*bheda*) in the sentence or in the simultaneous application.[26]

2.3.2 What are the differences between the Mīmāṃsā and the Śrautasūtras' usage of tantra*?*

The more common usage of *tantra* in the ŚrSū is that meaning 'basic procedure'. However, each element of the basic procedure can also be said to be *tantra*. And this usage easily leads to the consequence that what belongs to the basic procedure does not need to be repeated.

What does the Mīmāṃsā usage add besides this?

1. systematicity: *tantra* consistently functions as a principle within Mīmāṃsā,
2. structure: Jaimini seems to have a clear framework of rules for *tantra*,
3. flexibility: (this latter point probably applies only after Jaimini) once it has become a principle, *tantra* might be used even without the precinct of ritual; *tantra* is, for instance, often used in order to explain the role of a verb within a sentence (it is not repeated, although it applies to all *kārakas*).

2.4 tantra *in Grammar*

2.4.1 tantra *in Pāṇini*

The technical term *tantra* is not employed by Pāṇini, apart from the interesting sequence:[27]

svatantraḥ kartā || 1.4.54 ||
tatprayojako hetuś ca || 1.4.55 ||

The independent one is called kartṛ.
Its promoter, the hetu, also [is called *kartṛ*].

The expression *svatantra* did not fail to raise some recent and less recent discussions. A 1.4.54 supplies the semantic basic definition for the last *kāraka* by describing *kartṛ* as that *kāraka* which does not depend on others involved in an action. Given the assumed identification of a prototypical ritual agent in the com-

[26] See *vartamānāpadeśād vacanāt tu tantrabhedaḥ syāt* (MS 11.4.12).

[27] Moreover in A 5.2.70 *tantra* occurs as a common noun (meaning 'loom') to which a *taddhita* rule is applied. All quotations of the A are from Sharma 1987-2003.

pound *svatantraḥ* (specially in its masculine gender),[28] it seems reasonable to wonder whether the lexical choice itself, i.e., the use of *tantra* is somehow ultimately related to the ritual terminology. In fact, Patañjali commenting on this rule appears to be uncertain at least about the etymological sense of the term:

> – Is a *svatantra* a person who has his own warp (*sva-tantra*)? And what follows from that? It would result that [*svatantra* means] 'weaver'.
> – This is not a shortcoming. Certainly the word *tantra* is employed in the sense of 'extended [cloth]', e.g., *āstīrṇaṃ tantram* 'the warp has been stretched', *protaṃ tantram* 'the warp has been strung'. [In such cases] 'extended [cloth]' is meant but [the word *tantra*] might also be employed in the sense of what is principal: e.g., when one says 'this *brāhmaṇa* is *svatantra*', it is meant that he is self-dependent (i.e., that the principal [thing] for him is himself, that he is his own master).[29]

Although the hypothesis of a ritual background behind Pāṇini's *svatantra* is intriguing, there is no explicit hint at whatever ritual background exists for Pāṇini's use of the term nor for the three M occurrences of *tantra* (apart from *tantraśabda*) included in this passage.

2.4.2 tantra *in Patañjali*

In the M there are 18 other occurrences of the inflected noun *tantra*, 4 of which involve the noun *tantra* as a linguistic example. The remaining 14 occurrences are intended as the positive principle corresponding to a-*tantra* (which is found 11 times: vt. 1X; M 10X), which is the expression employed by the grammatical tradition from Kātyāyana onward in order to detach some features of the precise wording from Pāṇini's rules.

2.4.3 Are gender and number of a word in the Aṣṭādhyāyī tantra*?*

Nāgeśa's PBh 73, *sūtre liṅgavacanam atantram,* translated in Abhyankar 2001 as 'The (particular) gender and number in which a word is put down in a rule, are not (intended) to teach anything', seems to resume Patañjali's conclusions to the questions tackled by his commentaries on A 1.2.39 (*tantram* 1X; *atantram* 1X); 3.3.18

[28] Deshpande 1991, p. 471.

[29] *kiṃ yasya svaṃ tantraṃ sa svatantraḥ. kiṃ cātaḥ. tantuvāye prāpnoti. naiṣa doṣaḥ. ayaṃ tantraśabdo 'sty eva vitāne vartate. tad yathā. āstīrṇaṃ tantram. protaṃ tantram. vitāna iti gamyate. asti prādhānye vartate. tad yathā. svatantro 'sau brāhmaṇa ity ucyate svapradhāna iti gamyate* (M 1.338 ll. 17-20 *ad* A 1.4.54). For the translation of *vitāna* as 'warp' see Joshi and Roodbergen 1975, pp. 266-8.

(*tantram* 2X; *atantram* 1X); 3.4.21 (*tantram* 2X; *atantram* 1X); 4.1.92 (*tantram* 2X; *atantram* 1X); and 5.2.47 (*tantram* 1X).

An illuminating instance is A 3.3.18 *bhāve*, which teaches the application of the affix *kṛt GHaÑ* to denote a condition of being, i.e., to derive an action noun. Since the condition of denotation is expressed by a noun which is masculine singular (*bhāvaḥ*), vt. 1 (M 2.144 l. 8 *ad* A 3.3.18: *bhāve sarvaliṅgo nirdeśaḥ*) propounds the addition of a specific mention of all genders, to avoid that derivatives are exclusively masculine singular. M rejects the vt. through two different solutions, the first of which involves our terminology. It consists in denying that the specific mention of masculine expression is *tantra*. We propose that this sentence might have meant that the questioned specific mention was not a case of *tantra* (Meaning 2, see above § 2.3), in the sense of having no jointly multiple value, no extension out of the mere wording of that rule. And this is because it was not an essential part of the basic structure of the rule, the one which is ideally present in each instance of the rule's application (just like the basic structure of the ritual is present in each of its details).

> –[S:] Here the specific mention is not a *tantra*. –[PP:] How could it be that exactly the [word] through which the mention [of *bhāva*] is made is not a *tantra*? –[S:] Sir, you are disputing something you [alone] created! Here the mention is made by means of masculine gender and singular number, because they are intrinsically present [in the same word *bhāve*].[30] The mention has to be made by means of some ending and some gender. For example, when one looks for cereals, one gets the whole bundle of rice with husks and stalks since they are intrinsic parts [of rice]. After taking away what has to be taken away, he casts away husks and stalks. In the same way, when one looks for meat, one gets fish with fish-scales and bones since they are intrinsic parts [of fish]. After taking away what is supposed to be taken away, he casts away fish-scales and bones. In such a manner, also in our case, the specific mention is made by means of masculine gender and singular number since [gender and number] are intrinsic parts [of each word].[31] Here the specific mention is not a *tantra*. The mention has to be made by means of some ending and some gender.[32]

[30] He probably alludes to the definition of "word" (*pada*) as an exclusively "inflected word" (A 1.4.14 *suptiṅantam padam*, '*pada* is an item terminating in nominal or verbal endings'), i.e. furnished with its number mark according to the standard list of triplets which distinguishes singular, dual and plural of every nominal case-ending (A 4.1.2).

[31] For the translation of the four occurrences (here included) of the expression *nāntarīyakatvād*, cf. Filliozat 1980, p. 112 and Scharfe 1961, p. 12.

[32] *nātra nirdeśas tantram. kathaṃ punas tenaiva ca nāma nirdeśaḥ kriyate tac cātantraṃ syāt. tatkārī ca bhavāṃs taddveṣī ca. nāntarīyakatvād atra puṃlliṅgena nirdeśaḥ kriyata ekavacanena ca. avaśyam kayācid vibhaktyā kenacic ca liṅgena*

The second solution advanced by M, which is however clearly a less preferred one, does not ultimately end up as being so distant from the former with regard to the kind of arguments used. In fact, Patañjali argues that *bhāva* as an abstract noun might indicate what is common to all the actions (*kriyāsāmānyavācin*), which each verb denotes, although it also denotes a particular action (*kriyāviśeṣavācin*). To explain this assumption, Patañjali mentions the parallel of a man who is a teacher as well as a maternal uncle: when a student asks his teacher's nephew to greet his teacher, the latter is referred to as a teacher, although he will be greeted by his nephew in virtue of the fact that he is the maternal uncle of this nephew, i.e., of the person who will effectively meet and greet him.[33] Once again the opposition between an overarching feature of rules and some other specific ones is at stake.[34]

2.4.4 Is the comparative suffix in the Aṣṭādhyāyī tantra*?*

Vyāḍi's PBh 60 *atantraṃ taranirdeśaḥ*, translated in Wujastyk 1993 as 'The specification of *-tara* is not the main point', seems to summarise the conclusions reached by all the remaining M occurrences of *tantra/ atantra*, except one. These occurrences (M 1.210 ll. 5; 8; 12; 14; 15 *ad* A 1.2.33: *tantram* 2X; *tantre* 1X; *atantram* 2X; M 1.435 l. 18-436 l. 14 *ad* A 2.2.34: *tantram* 2X, *atantram* 3X, atantre 2X) deal with the implications of the comparative suffix *-tara*. In fact, the affix *-tara*, employed in A 1.2.35, 1.2.40 and 2.2.34, should have been used there, according to the meanings prescribed by A 5.3.57 (*dvivacanavibhajyopade tarabīyasunau*), that is, on condition that '[the *taddhita*s derived by means of this affixation denote "superiority, excellence"], provided that they co-occur with a *pada* which is an expression of two things or with a *pada* which distinguishes one from another'.

Rule A 2.2.34, e.g., teaches that in a *dvandva*-compound, the *pada* which contains fewer vowels must precede. The doubt is whether the taught sequence of *pada*s is restricted to *dvandva*s

nirdeśaḥ kartavyaḥ. tad yathā. kaścid annārthī śālikalāpaṃ satuṣam sapalālaṃ āharati nāntarīyakatvāt. sa yāvad ādeyaṃ tāvad ādāya tuṣapalālāny utsṛjati. tathā kaścin māṃsārthī matsyān saśakalān sakaṇṭakān āharati nāntarīyakatvāt. sa yāvad ādeyaṃ tāvad ādāya śakalakaṇṭakāny utsṛjati. evam ihāpi nāntarīyakatvād puṃlliṅgena nirdeśaḥ kriyate ekavacanāntena ca. na hy atra nirdeśas tantram. kayācid vibhaktyā kenacic ca liṅgena nirdeśaḥ kartavyaḥ (M 2.144 ll. 12-6).

[33] See also Scharfe 1961, pp. 12-3; Wezler 1986, p. 95; Cardona 1999, pp. 232-3, p. 308 fns 126-7.

[34] With regard to the other three occurrences and the possible source of the recurring double image of rice and fish, see Pontillo 2008 and Freschi and Pontillo forthcoming.

with two members or has to be extended to each *dvandva*, regardless of the number of members.

> – Is this specific mention of *-tara* a *tantra* or an *atantra*? – [PP:] And what follows from that? –[S:] If it is a *tantra*, there is a restriction in case of two [*padas*] and no restriction in case of many [*padas*]. – [PP:] In this case, what is the shortcoming? – [S:] [The *dvandva*-compound] *śaṅkha-dundubhi-vīṇānām* 'of a conch, a drum and a *vīṇā*' cannot be formed. The first place of the word *dundubhi* [would] be obtained.[35] Alternatively, it is not a *tantra*. [In this way,] 'the drum, the conch and the flute (*mṛdaṅga-śaṅkha-tūṇavāḥ*) are played separately in the assembly' and 'in the palace of Dhanapati, Rāma and Keśava (*dhanapatirāmakeśava*)' cannot be formed. – [PP:] Let it be as you like. – [S:] [No whimsical solution might be accepted. Let us examine the issue again]. To begin with, let us assume that it is a *tantra*. – [PP:] But has it not been said that there is a restriction in the case of two [*padas*] and no restriction in the case of many [*padas*]? If this is so, [the *dvandva*-compound] *śaṅkha-dundubhi-vīṇānām* cannot be formed. The first place of the word *dundubhi* [would] be obtained. – [S:] There is not this shortcoming. I'll say that *alpāctaram* 'containing fewer vowels' is actually *alpāc* 'containing few vowels'. Alternatively, let us assume again that it is not a *tantra*. – [PP:] But [in this way] it has been said that [the expressions] 'the drum, the conch and the flute (*mṛdaṅgaśaṅkhatūṇavāḥ*) are played separately in the assembly' and 'in the palace of Dhanapati, Rāma and Keśava (*dhanapatirāmakeśava*)', cannot be formed.[36]

The final view on this conundrum is expressed immediately thereafter, it coincides with the second alternative and is stated by a vt. (M 1.436 l. 6 *ad* A 2.2.34 vt. 1), which precisely involves the term *atantra* and which furthermore shows that the use of this terminology is not an innovative choice by Patañjali: *atantre taranirdeśe śaṅkhatūṇavayor mṛdaṅgena samāsaḥ*, 'If the specific mention of the suffix *-tara* is an *atantra*, the compound [is made] of *śaṅkha-tūṇavau* with *mṛdaṅgaḥ*.'

In fact, if we adopt the *atantra* view, we manage both to justify *mṛdaṅga-śaṅkha-tūṇavāḥ* by resorting to a two-word compound-

35 In other words no rule would teach the correct sequence of *padas* in case of plurimember *dvandvas*.

36 *kim ayaṃ tantraṃ taranirdeśa ahosvid atantram. kiṃ cātaḥ. yadi tantraṃ dvayor niyamo bahuṣv aniyamaḥ. tatra ko doṣaḥ. śaṅkhadundubhivīṇānām iti na sidhyati. dundubhiśabdasyāpi pūrvanipātaḥ prāpnoti. athātantraṃ. mṛdaṅgaśaṅkhatūṇavāḥ pṛthaṅ nadanti saṃsadi. prāsāde dhanapatirāmakeśavānām ity etan na sidhyati. yathecchasi tathāstu. astu tāvat tantram. nanu coktaṃ dvayor niyamo bahuṣv aniyama iti tatra śaṅkhadundubhivīṇānām iti na sidhyati dundubhiśabdasyāpi pūrvanipātaḥ prāpnotīti. naiṣa doṣaḥ. yad etad alpāctaram iti tad alpāj iti vakṣyāmi. athavā punar astv atantram. nanu coktaṃ mṛdaṅgaśaṅkhatūṇavāḥ pṛthaṅ nadanti saṃsadi prāsāde dhanapatirāmakeśavānām ity etan na sidhyatīti* (M 1.435 l. 18-436 l. 5 *ad* A 2.2.34).

formation, and to block ***dundubhi-śaṅkha-vīṇānām*, by resorting to a three-word compound-formation.[37] By contrast, we would not be able to block this latter formation, if we had adopted the *tantra* view. In fact, M leads us to conclude – as Radicchi 1985-1988, p. 112 demonstrates – that this rule is valid for the bi-member compounds, while the pluri-member ones are not governed by any grammatical rules but rather by usage.[38]

In a M passage following the one mentioned above (M I.436 l. 11 *ad* vt. 1 *ad* A 2.2.34) Patañjali speaks of *pūrvanipātaprasaṅga* ('a chance to get the first place for many [*padas*]' within a compound). We deem that Patañjali's use of the term *prasaṅga* is thoroughly significant, since it precisely denotes a chance to extend the application of a rule, once stated that it is not a case of *tantra* (see § 3.4.3).

2.4.5 tantra *vs.* nipātana

There is only one occurrence of the term *tantra* which escapes from the two late Paribhāṣās quoted above. This refers to A 6.4.24, '*lopa*-replacement of the penultimate phoneme *n* of a verbal stem ending in a consonant and not including I as marker before an affix with marker *K* or *Ṅ*' (e.g., *srans-* 'fall' + *Kta* = *srasta-* 'fallen'). vt. 4 *ghinuṇi nipātanāt siddham*, defines the *lopa*-replacement of *n* in *aṅga rañj-* before the affix *GHinUṆ* as "already established" out of a *nipātana*, i.e., by means of the incidental mention of an irregular, so to say ready-made linguistic form given without explaining its derivation as if it accidentally had dropped (*ni-pat-* 'to drop') into some rule. In this case *rajA* without the phoneme n quoted in A 3.2.142 instead of the verbal base *rañjA* is proposed for being considered as a *nipātana*.

M 3.194 l. 24-195 l. 1 *ad* vt. 4 *ad* A 6.4.24 rejects the vt. 4, insofar as it refuses to consider a *nipātana* as a *tantra*:

> *aśakyam dhāturnideśe nipātanaṃ tantra āśrayitum.*
>
> If there is the mention of a verbal base (such as in A 3.2.142 where *rajA* is quoted as a left context, i.e., as a verbal base according to A 3.1.91), it is not possible to resort to a *nipātana* (which furthermore generally is a pada or at least a derived stem) as to a *tantra*.

A *nipātana* which is a special rule superseding a general rule[39] cannot intrinsically be a *tantra*, i.e., something which is extended

[37] Cf. Joshi and Roodbergen 1974, p. LXVIII.
[38] For "three-word" vs. "two-word" compounding see Joshi 1968, pp. 22-5.
[39] Cf. Kielhorn 1887, p. 125 (reprinted in Staal 1972, pp. 123-34).

out of the rule where it is mentioned, such as a *dhātu* should be considered.

2.4.6 Conclusions on tantra *in Grammar*

In conclusion, the extensive use of the terms *tantra* and *atantra* in the M, including one case of *atantra* in the vt., and one of *tantra* distinct from *prasaṅga* in the M, suggests that this grammatical classification of parts of single rules might be ultimately related to some culturally evident Sanskrit categorization, arguably to the context of the ritual arrangement of rules.

2.4.7 What are the differences between the Grammar's and the Mīmāṃsā-Śrautasūtras' usage of tantra*?*

The surveyed ŚrSū occurrences of the term *tantra* as part of the sacrifice which overpasses the boundaries of a rite to encompass all the rites of the sacrifice, acting in a centralised way (cf. § 2.1), sound undeniably close to M usages analysed here above. Alongside the last but one step reconstructed in § 2.3 for the history of MS usage of the term *tantra* as 'whatever element remains valid for the whole rite and needs not to be repeated is said to have a place within the *tantra*' could be even supposed as an etymon for the attributive use of *tantra/ atantra* in M.

Nonetheless, in the early Grammar, *tantra* is used in regard to rules, in order to discern whether one of their elements has to apply to all possible cases or not. No similar instances of the usage of *tantra* have been found in Mīmāṃsā.

2.5 Semantic analysis of tantra

As already seen, *tantra* might assume a descriptive or an operative meaning. In the following table one can find in the line above the contexts in which *tantra* is more likely to be discussed, and in the line below, its meanings.

prakṛti | *sakṛd eva*

↘ ↙

tantra

↗ ↖

basic structure | single performance applying to all elements

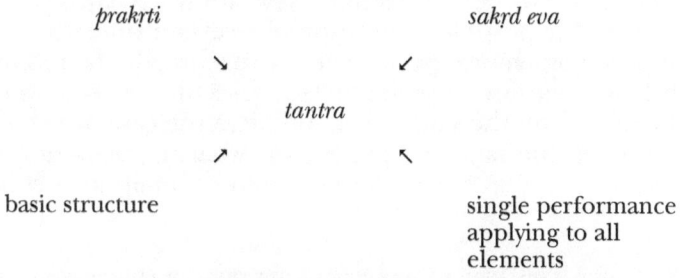

3. prasaṅga

prasaṅga is attested in several meanings. Are they connected? What is the object of *prasaṅga* as a technical device? An element or its function? What are the conditions for *prasaṅga*? Does *prasaṅga* as a device have any Vyākaraṇa counterpart?

3.1 How to translate prasaṅga

We have long been struggling to find a single suitable translation for *prasaṅga* in its technical usage. At the end of our enquiry into ŚrSū, Grammar and Mīmāṃsā, we are sure of its general sense of "what happens automatically, unless one blocks it". The *prasaṅga* is what would happen, if one were not to block it. It is used often in regard to rules, referring to the rules which would be applied, if there were not a contrary, more specific, rule blocking them.

In the context of *lopa,* Benson 1990, pp. 124-40 often translates *prasaṅga* as "possible appearance" (and *prasakta* as "something which would appear", p. 131), which works smoothly whenever a certain suffix "could appear" if it were not blocked by the *lopa* rules. However, we decided not to use "possible appearance" because it is too interpretative (i.e., it is an interpretation, not a translation) and it seems to overemphasize the mere effect of *prasaṅga* over its action.

Benson 1990, p. 129 translates *sarvaprasaṅga* as "possible application to all". This translation is, we believe, correct, but also tends to emphasize an aspect (the application of the rule) which is not exactly the point at stake.

In some contexts, Benson's translation of *prasakta* as what would be "otherwise expected" sounds good and is quite close to the technical sense we are going to analyze below, but we have to admit that this translation presupposes that there is someone expecting that something will occur. And this is an undue assumption.

Hence, we considered translating *prasaṅga* in a more neutral way, one which – ideally – should not have privileged a particular aspect of it. We tried "possible association". A *prasaṅga* would have been the possible association of a certain rule, which might be blocked by a more specific rule. We eventually abandoned this translation because "association" suggests that the two associated elements are on the same level, unlike in the case of *prasaṅga.*

Stressing the fact that *prasaṅga* is what happens unless one blocks it[40] and that it is what one would normally expect to hap-

[40] Cf. the translation of *prasaṅga* as "provisional occurrence" proposed in

pen, Benson translates *prasakta* as "otherwise expected". Following the same kind of reasoning (although independently of Benson's writing), we considered using "entailment" or "involvement" for *prasaṅga* and *prasakta*. We then decided to abandon the first one because we feared it would have conveyed the sense of a logical implication (which is, hence, unavoidable), whereas *prasaṅga* regards much more material implications, which are expected, but not unavoidable.

Last, we decided to use "involvement" as much as possible, although the verb (to be involved) seems to work better than the corresponding noun.

3.2 prasaṅga *in the Śrautasūtras*

prasaṅga is not frequent in the ŚrSū and we failed to find a definition of it. Hence, one has to reconstruct its meaning indirectly, through its usage in the ŚrSū, through its usage in Grammar and Mīmāṃsā, and possibly also through its etymological meaning. Every translation is therefore intrinsically tentative.

In its sole occurrence in the *Aśvalāyana Śrautasūtra* (AśvŚrSū 1.1.22, about which see also infra, § 3.2.2) it is opposed to *apavāda* (certainly meaning 'exception'):

prasaṅgād apavādo balīyaḥ.

Mylius (Mylius 1994, p. 29a) translates:

Eine Ausnahme (-Regel) ist gewichtiger als eine allgemeine Regel ('An exceptional [rule] is more forceful than a general rule').

But the meaning seems, more precisely, to be 'default occurrence'. The *prasaṅga* is what one expects to happen; what follows by default from the previous discussion. Only secondarily, does it define the "general rule". Hence, our proposed translation:

An exception is stronger than what is automatically involved.

3.2.1 prasaṅga *in KātyŚrSū*

The rather late KātyŚrSū, which might have been authored by the same Kātyāyana who wrote the *vārttikas* on the A, or be coeval with him,[41] testifies to four cases of *prasaṅga*. One of these displays

Cardona 1967 in the context of the current opposition between an operation prescribed by a general rule, which is 'allowed to occur provisionally' and its negation (*pratiṣedha*).

[41] For the hypothesis according to which the author of the *vārttikas* on

the shift from the above meaning to Śabara's one (see infra, § 4.1):

> *pratikarmoddharaṇam aprasaṅge.* (Ranade 1978, *sū.* 1.3.27, Thite 2006, *sū.* 1.3.26)

That is,

> The taking away of a brand from the Gārhapatya-fire to supply other fires [is done] for every rite, if no [different rule] is automatically involved.

The context of this rule seems to rely on the distinction between the repetition of a rite for each sacrificial action on the one hand, and the technical chance of resorting to a procedure resembling the *atideśa* (i.e., the analogical extension of a rule) on the other.[42] Accordingly, *prasaṅga* in 1.3.26-27 means first of all the application of a default situation, which could have already enjoined something about the *uddharaṇa* (Meaning 1). If no such rule is automatically involved from the above (*a-prasaṅga*), there is the simultaneous application of the same act (of *uddharaṇa*) to more than one rite. Consequently, *prasaṅga* might be seen as denoting the simultaneous application itself (Meaning 2).

Again in KātyŚrSū:

> *vrate prasaṅgo na niyamaśabdāt.* (Thite 2006, *sū.* 1.4.8)

The commentary (in Weber 1859) specifies that the *prasaṅga* regards *pratinidhi* and the context is, in fact, about substitution. Accordingly, one could translate as follows (note the two alternatives):

> In the case of a vow [of feeding on milk only], due to a restrictive statement, there is no automatic involvement [of anything else]/ [of any substitute at hand].

In other words, whenever there is a specific prescription enjoining a specific item, one cannot automatically substitute it.

3.2.2 Meaning of prasaṅga *in the Śrautasūtras and difference from* tantra

As an event, *prasaṅga* assumes the form of a possible extended use of a ritual function already introduced for a preceding per-

the A might have been the same as that of the KātyŚrSū, see Paranjpe 1922 (summarised in Göhler 2011, p. 31, n. 46). For further arguments and for the identification of this author with the one of the *Vājasaneyīpratiśākhya* (white Yajurveda) see Parpola 1994, pp. 298 ff.

[42] See the *sūtras* immediately following.

formance. It implies an incidental association between one act, which is subsidiary to a rite, and another, which is subsidiary to another rite. It might further require that the function of what has been employed for one rite is needed for the other also.

This mechanism is prevented from working if the subsidiary at stake is explicitly linked to a specific purpose of the previous rite alone.[43] More in general, the ritual texts point out the exceptions and the restrictions (see above, Kahrs' quote about map and territory, § 1.1). ĀśvŚrSū 1.1.22 (see § 3.2), for instance, shows that an *apavāda* is needed precisely in order to block the automatic *prasaṅga*. Whenever nothing like this occurs and there is a specific need, *prasaṅga* occurs automatically.

According to the same principle of noting the exceptions rather than the default behaviour, *prasaṅga* is often used in the negative. If this intepretation is correct, *aprasaṅge* or *aprasaṅgāt* indicate the interruption in the default involvement of what precedes in what follows.

To sum up, on the basis of these occurrences of *prasaṅga* in the ŚrSū, the etymological meaning and the occurrence in Mīmāṃsā (Meaning 3) and in the M (Meanings 1 and 2), one might attempt a sketch of the semantic history of this technical term:

1. the temporary and incidental coming into contact of two functions or rites
2. the chance, i.e., occasion, for an extended application caused by this temporary association

This latter meaning is akin to the one common in M and might produce the later, Mīmāṃsaka one, which seems foreshadowed in some ŚrSū usages:

3. the fact that something happens automatically, through a transport from one rite to another, unless there is an opposite prescription, in similar cases and if need arises

It is worth stressing that, unlike in *tantra*, what is transported is not an element, but rather the function it performs. *prasaṅga* does not regard an altar in itself (as a *dravya*), but its function of holding things during the ritual.

Furthermore, the transport does not depend on a centralised instance (as occurs in the case of *tantra*). Rather, it depends on a mar-

[43] See KātyŚrSū 1.3.27 in Thite 2006 = Ranade 1978, *sū.* 1.3.28.

ginal contact, resulting in a temporary association which is based on a specific need. *tantra* occurs within a ritual, *prasaṅga* outside it.

A *tantra*-like journey would be that of a whole school sharing the same ship or train, booked especially. The ship has been booked once and for all, since everyone belongs to the same set. A *prasaṅga*-like journey would be the relation between a hitchhiker and the car-driver who gives him a lift. Their association is temporary and based on the former need for an element already in use by the latter.

3.3 prasaṅga *in Mīmāṃsā*

According to Śabara and all subsequent Mīmāṃsakas, *prasaṅga* is the topic of MS 12. Its standard definition in mature Mīmāṃsā runs more or less as follows:

> *so 'yam anyārthānuṣṭhitāṅgair anyasyo 'pakārarūpaḥ prasaṅgo dvādaśa ucyate.* (MNS 12.1.1)

> This is *prasaṅga*, which has the form of assistance for one thing by means of subsidiaries performed for the sake of another, and which is spoken of in the Twelfth Book. (Benson 2010, p. 766)

In other words, *prasaṅga* refers to a *function* (and not a substance), which applies to *more than one item*, insofar as it has been *made for the purpose of one item, but then ends up helping another, too.*

This definition, however, does not make explicit some of the features of *prasaṅga*. For instance, a further requirement which is explicit in Śabara (see infra, § 4.1) and only implicit in the above definition, is an explicit prescription prescribing assistance for a certain rite – this assistance happens to have been already performed for a previous one and is still available. In fact, *prasaṅga* is the procedure through which a function is extended from the case for which it was originally meant to a further case. What is extended is not structurally part of the sacrifice, on the contrary, it is usually extended from a different context (typically, a preceding sacrifice or rite). Since there is no structural need for the extension, this is only ruled by an *ad* hoc prescription enjoining it. In other words, one only extends to a later rite the function of, e.g., staying awake, if in the context of the latter rite the fact of staying awake is prescribed.

To sum up, all elements prescribed in the context of the Full and New moon sacrifice apply through *tantra* to all the six rites composing it, independently of whether they are actually needed there, just because the six rites share the same basic procedure (Meaning 1 of *tantra*). By contrast, the assistance offered through *prasaṅga* applies to a sacrifice different from the one it had been initially performed for. Therefore, it only applies to this later sacrifice if it is explicitly needed there, i.e., if in the later sacrifice there is a prescription enjoining the same assistance.

Examples

The late Mīmāṃsaka Mahādeva Vedāntin explains that in the case of the Soma sacrifice, the altar already built for the Soma offering applies through *prasaṅga* to the subsequent *iṣṭi* as well (Benson 2010, *ad* 12.1.3). Similarly, in the Kauṇḍapāyināmayana sacrifice, the same fire Gārhapatya is used, where the Agnihotra is offered every day (Benson 2010, *ad* 12.1.6). In both cases, since the needed function is already performed by something at hand, one does not build a new altar or kindle a new fire for this purpose. This happens whenever:

1. There is no explicit indication to the contrary
2. The function to be extended is needed there
3. The place is the same
4. The time is the same
5. The sacrifice for which the element (whose function is extended through a *prasaṅga* procedure) was prepared is not affected by the element's extension

To summarize:

tantra	*prasaṅga*
structural	non-structural
centralised	lateral
applies anyway	applies only if prescribed
same sacrifice	different sacrifice or rite

In the following paragraphs, we shall investigate the history of how *prasaṅga* acquired these meanings and its inner-Mīmāṃsā and inner-Grammar history.

3.3.1 prasaṅga *in Jaimini*

According to Śabara and to all subsequent Mīmāṃsakas, the whole MS 11 is dedicated to *tantra* (Meanings 2 or 3) and the whole MS 12 is dedicated to *prasaṅga*. The paucity of occurrences of the latter term in the two books and the fact that they never appear together as a contrastive couple makes Śabara's interpretation far from smooth. In MS, the opposition *tantra/ prasaṅga* seems less central than the one between *tantra* and *āvāpa*, pointing at what belongs to the structure of the ritual as opposed to what must be inserted each time, separately.

The paucity of occurrences of *prasaṅga* in both MS and the ŚrSū has led us to anticipate the common Mīmāṃsā understanding of *prasaṅga* and then to adjust it to Jaimini's case, rather than the opposite. Readers are however given many instruments to judge by themselves, since many occurrences in MS and in the ŚrSū have been reproduced.

prasaṅga occurs three times in MS, all very close to each other, in MS 12.1.10-11 and 15. The context is that of the *prakṛti-vikṛti* relationship and of the way elements are analogically translated from the former to the latter.

The first of these three *sūtras* is traditionally read as a PP, possibly depending on the *vā* found in the subsequent one:

> *pātreṣu ca prasaṅgaḥ syād dhomārthatvāt.* (10)
> *nyāyyāni vā prayuktatvād aprayukte prasaṅgaḥ syāt.* (11)

A provisional translation could sound like this:

> [PP:] And, as regards the vessels, [their function] might be automatically involved (in a subsequent rite), since they are for the sake of the oblation.
> [S:] Better: since [they] are [already] in use, they are regularly [to be employed]. The involvement applies [only] in regard to something which is not already in use.

If the attribution to a PP is right, the objector argues that, in regard to the vessels, one might "apply" (i.e., analogically translate) them from the *prakṛti*, since both *vikṛti* and *prakṛti* have a common purpose, i.e., the oblation. The PP is here implementing the instrument of knowledge (for deciding what has to be analogically extended) called *artha*, that is, inferring the proper element to be translated from its purpose (rather than out of a specific mention in the text, etc., see MNP 199, 201 in Edgerton 1929). The *siddhāntin* replies that the vessels are to be employed regularly, since they are in use. This does not seem to confute the preceding *sūtra*. It accepts the employment of the vessels, not out of their translation from the *prakṛti*, rather out of their being already in use. Further conditions (in the present case, *prasaṅga*) only apply if there is not something which is already in use. On the meaning of *prayukta*, see MS 12.1.12, also stressing the fact that if something is already in use (for a different rite), then it takes precedence.

In other words, the principle of involvement only applies if something is not already in use (and hence does not need any involvement). We are understanding *prasaṅga* in *sūtra* 11 as a principle and not a concrete act of involvement because one would have no reason to repeat that the concrete involvement does not occur, given that this is already established in the first half of the *sūtra*.

Next come MS 12.1.14-5:

havirdhāne nirvapaṇārthaṃ sādhayetāṃ prayuktatvāt. (14)
asiddhir vānyadeśatvāt pradhānavaiguṇyād avaiguṇye prasaṅgaḥ syāt. (15)

whose provisional translation is:

[PP:] The two oblation carts should accomplish the intended pouring, because they are already in use.[44]
[S:] Rather, no [automatic application of an element (in more than one rite)] is realized, since the principal [rite] would be affected [by it] because the place is different (and hence, the ritual cart would be removed from it and the function of carrying could not be accomplished by it anymore). An automatic involvement of an element can occur [only] in case the [principal rite] is not affected.

That is, the PP proposes that since the two carts are already in use for a previous rite, the prescribed offering may well occur in one of these and there is no need to bring in a further one. However, argues the S, employing one of the carts which are already in use would mean displacing it. Consequently, the principal rite would no longer have it at its disposal. Hence, it is required that the *prasaṅga* only regards functions fulfilled by elements found in the same place (and, one could imagine, at the same time). In fact, if the place were not the same, one would have to move the element away and it would be lacking in the main rite.

As in *sūtra* 11, the final clause of *sūtra* 15 apparently expresses a general condition for the *prasaṅga*-principle to apply.

3.3.2 Meaning of prasaṅga *in Jaimini and difference from* tantra

In sum, *prasaṅga* occurs only if:

1. something is not already in use (cf. MS 12.1.11)
2. there is no damage to the principal rite (cf. MS 12.1.15)
3. there is a specific purpose (cf. 12.1.10)

Hence, *prasaṅga* has a role only *faute de mieux*, that is, it fills up empty spaces.

[44] So Clooney 1990, p. 117. Basu understands *havirdhāne* as a locative (Basu 1923-1925).

But why does Jaimini not use the term *tantra* in all the above cases? The difference seems to consist in the following: Through *tantra*, what is performed once counts twice (or thrice, etc., see MS 11.1.54-67 and Clooney 1990, p. 123, n. 48), because it becomes part of the basic procedure of the ritual, the one presupposed by each additional rite. *prasaṅga*, on the other hand, seems to refer to the possibility of applying the same ritual function to more than one rite, without implying that the element whose function is applied through *prasaṅga* becomes part of the general procedure of the ritual. In sum, an element is implied *tantreṇa* if it is postulated that it belongs to the basic core of the ritual and that it is hence supposed to be present in each of the ritual's elements, as if the rites to which it applies were on the circumference of the ritual's structure and each ray would connect the rite with it. This pictorial description could also suit the metaphorical one by Śabara (see infra, Fig. 2 in § 4.1), referring to a lamp at the centre of a group of Brahmans.

By contrast, *prasaṅga* does not presuppose anything like this. It is only the application, by default, of an element's function in more than one rite, unless contrary evidence arises. The metaphor used to represent this by Śabara (see infra, Fig. 1 in § 4.1), in fact, refers to a lamp within a house also illuminating the contiguous street, which has, however, nothing to do with the house. Hence, unlike in the case of *tantra*, *prasaṅga* does not presuppose the fact of being part of a same substrate (the same sacrifice or a single house).

Furthermore, it is also possible that in Jaimini (like in Śabara and probably also in the ŚrSū) *prasaṅga* regards an item's function rather than the item itself. Since we lack a specific statement on this, this latter point is however purely speculative.

3.3.3 prāsaṅgika *in Jaimini*

This term is found twice in MS (5.1.28 and 9.4.28) and has been translated as "incidental" or "accidental" by Basu 1923-1925 and by Jhā 1933-34-36. Can any resemblance to *prasaṅga* (as described above) be found?

MS 5.1.28 discusses the order of rites within an ectype. A prescription says that the post-sacrifices (*anuyāja*) should be postponed and the PP suggests that this also includes the Piṣṭalepahoma and the Phalīkaraṇahoma. The S answers that this is not the case, because the two groups are not related:

prāsaṅgikaṃ ca notkarṣed asaṃyogāt

The point seems to be that the postponement does not apply automatically, by default, to more than one element. Hence,

> The [elements whose function has been] automatically involved should not be postponed, since there is no connection [with the post-sacrifices, about which a prescription says that they must be postponed].

This *sūtra* indirectly confirms the non-structural nature of *prasaṅga*. Since what is automatically involved in the after-sacrifices is not an intrinsic part of them, whatever happens to them does not regard the *prāsaṅgika* component.

A further instance: If one has taken fire out of the Gārhapatya fire for the Agnihotra sacrifice but the new fire is extinguished before the Agnihotra, one needs to perform an expiatory rite (*prāyaścitta*). MS 9.4.28 discusses whether this expiatory rite should be performed even in the case that the fire which has been taken out was never meant for the Agnihotra. The PP proposes that an expiatory rite has to be performed in any case, whereas the S utters the *sūtra*, concluding that no *prāyaścitta* is necessary:

> *prāsaṅgike prāyaścittaṃ na vidyate* [...]

Which we understand as follows:

> In the case of something which has been automatically involved [from a previous rule, in this case the one about the need for an expiation if the Agnihotra fire is extinguished before the Agnihotra is performed], no expiatory rite takes place [...].

These two cases also display a strong link between *prasaṅga* and *vidhi* and *artha*, which will also be highlighted afterwards, in regard to Śabara.

3.3.4 Summary on the semantics of prasaṅga

To sum up, *prasaṅga* applies in Mīmāṃsā:

- (most likely) in regard to an element's function
- when there is a specific need of the function which is said to be automatically involved
- by default, filling up an empty and contiguous space
- without referring to an underlying structure, as it is the case with *tantra*
- without referring to an overruling hierarchy of rules, as is the case with *utsarga* and *apavāda*[45]
- if there is no contrary prescription

[45] An *apavāda* prevails over a *prasaṅga*, but just because the former is more specific.

We shall see in the next section in further detail how this meaning of *prasaṅga* can be connected to the one current in Grammar. Grossly speaking, *prasaṅga* in Grammar denotes the procedure which one expects to happen. The comparison with the ŚrSū and most of all Mīmāṃsā shows that this does not mean that *prasaṅga* is a general rule. Rather, it is that which happens automatically, if one does not explicitly want to do otherwise. Thinking of the Mīmāṃsā examples of *prasaṅga*, if one needs a support, one will just use the *mahāvedi* available, unless something different has been prescribed.

Can this "automatic involvement" also be interpreted etymologically? Can it, in other words, be considered as a case of 'attachment' (from the verbal base *prasañj-*)? Yes, we think so, insofar as the element involved through *prasaṅga* is attached to the following rite although it comes from the previous one. It applies by default (it just "attaches" itself to what follows), but is interrupted by specific restrictions, such as the fact of being already in use and the fact of affecting the ritual.

In this way, we might recognise three distinct, yet related, spheres of meaning:

1. *prasaṅga* as attachment,
2. *prasaṅga* as the principle through which a function meant for X also applies to whatever comes after it,
3. *prasaṅga* as the procedure that one expects to happen.

The connection of *vidhi* and prescription, as in Mīmāṃsā (see infra, § 4.1, is also noteworthy.

3.3.4.1 prasaṅga *and* vidhi

As we shall see below (§ 4.1), for Śabara the presence of a prescription enjoining it, is a necessary condition for *prasaṅga*. In Jaimini and in the ŚrSū, *prasaṅga* fills a need, unlike *tantra* which applies independently of any particular requirement for the element to apply more than once. We could not see any explicit indication of the requirement of a prescription in Jaimini and one might think that the only requirement is the need for the element to apply more than once. However, indirect evidence of the need of a prescription might be derived from a ŚrSū:

> The main [acts] if they are enjoined in one and the same context, share the same prescriptions. The context has a suspending effect on the prescriptive rules.[46]

[46] *ekaprakaraṇe codyamānāni pradhānāni samānavidhānāni. prakaraṇena vidhayo badhyante* (ĀpŚrSū 24.2.26-7).

These *sūtras* seem to connect the fact of sharing the same ritual context (i.e., belonging to the same ritual) and the presence of a specific prescription, insofar as a single prescription continues to have value only within one ritual context. The fact that *prasaṅga* usually regards different rituals, is a further element which makes the presence of an *ad hoc* prescription enjoining it necessary.

3.3.5 prasaṅga *in Mīmāṃsā: Similarities with Grammar?*

These basic points (sharing the same context, vs. not sharing the same context and requiring an *ad hoc* prescription) remind one of the opposition between the *utsarga/ apavāda* model (where the same context is shared) and the *ādeśa* one (which functions independently of a context). Does the Mīmāṃsā couple *tantra/ prasaṅga* correspond to them?

3.4 prasaṅga *in Grammar*

Whereas no wording of Pāṇini's rules involves the term *prasaṅga*, there are more than 450 occurrences of this term as a simple noun or as a member of a compound (very frequent is *atiprasaṅga*) in the M and in the vt. (source: Gretil text of the M). Our survey takes into account 16 vt. occurrences and 62 M occurrences, singled out on the basis of the Index by Pathak and Chitrao 1935, i.e., all the passages which involve at least once the simple noun *prasaṅga* (for details, see Freschi and Pontillo forthcoming). The term *prasaṅga* had already been singled out by Paranjpe in his study on the common terminology of Kātyāyana's *vārttikas* and Jaimini's *Mīmāṃsāsūtra* (Paranjpe 1922, pp. 33; 79), where it is translated as 'conséquence nécessaire, conséquence indésirée, possibilité vicieuse' (p. 60) and the following clarification is added: (p. 67) 'Dans les J.S. *prasaṅga-* signifie une nécessité, tandis que dans le Vārt. on a gardé le sens dans plusieurs passages et on l'a modifié dans d'autres. Le sens modifié est de "conséquence nécessaire qui est indésirée".'

3.4.1 prasaṅga *in Kātyāyana's* vārttikas

From the syntactic point of view, in the 16 *vārttikas* analysed, *prasaṅga* as an *uttarapada* of a compound, prevails with 11 occurrences over the 5 occurrences as a simple noun. A single occurrence uses the term as a *pūrvapada* in a compound inflected in the ablative ending.

3.4.1.1 prasaṅga *as an automatic involvement to be tested*

The absolutely first vt. occurrence of the term is a denial of *prasaṅga*, in vt. 11 *ad* A 1.1.1 (M 1.41 l. 7). Neither definition nor explanation of the term is supplied, as if it were immediately understandable, perhaps part of a shared knowledge. Paranjpe's interpretation as "necessity" can be temporarily adopted for translating it as "necessity of applying":

> *anyatra sahavacanāt samudāye saṃjñāprasaṅgaḥ* (=*aprasaṅgaḥ*)
>
> Because of the mention of *saha* elsewhere, there is no necessity of applying these names (*vṛddhi* and *guṇa*) to the whole group.

It supposedly makes known that, e.g., the use of the denomination *vṛddhi* does not refer to the whole group of the phonemes included in the *pratyāhāra āDaiC*, rather it only refers to the suitable one out of the three phonemes.[47] If Pāṇini had meant to refer to all of them taken together, he would have included the indeclinable *saha* in the rule.

However, to better understand vt. 11, we need to take a step back into its immediate context: the two vts. preceding this aim, so to say, at the core of Pāṇini's work. They end up stating the veritable target of a grammar like the A.

vt. 9[48] solves the flaw consisting in the possible mutual dependence between the name *vṛddhi* and the named units matching it, i.e., the phonemes *ā*, *ai*, *au* by resorting to the permanent nature (*nityatva*) of these phonemes and consequently to the priority of their existence compared with the assignment of the name. In other words, grammar does not create linguistic elements, nor do *saṃjñās* create the elements to which they refer (their *saṃjñin*). Thus, when Pāṇini uses the name *vṛddhi* to enjoin the replacement of a linguistic unit, he is actually accounting for something which is already there. Therefore, vt. 10[49] claims that the grammatical *śāstra* is useful, although it does not produce any linguistic form, insofar as it excludes the incorrect linguistic forms (*nivartakatva*). Consequently, one is led to ponder what linguistic forms are to be excluded.

The example proposed by Patañjali is the teaching of *vṛddhi* for the verbal base *mṛj-* 'to wipe' according to A 7.2.114 *mṛjer vṛddhiḥ*. vt. 11 notices that the *saṃjñā* "*vṛddhi*" could automatically involve the whole list of augmented vowels which could substitute the vowel *ṛ* of *mṛj-* and then excludes it (*a-prasaṅga*). It

[47] Pāṇini does not include *ār* and *āl* in the series of *vṛddhi*-substitutes mentioned in A 1.1.1. See below A 1.1.51 for the rule which enjoins adding *r* or *l* to the substitute *ā* when the substituend is *ṛ* o *ḷ*.

[48] M I.40 l. 26 vt. 9 *ad* A 1.1.1: *siddhaṃ tu nityaśabdatvāt.*

[49] M 1.41 l. 1 vt. 10 *ad* A 1.1.1 *kimarthaṃ śāstram iti cen nivartakatvāt siddham.*

follows that the specific task of grammar here is not to create a linguistic substituted form, but rather to lead to the selection of the only correct linguistic form, among the results of the multiple rules potentially involved.

3.4.1.2 prasaṅga *as the involvement of something which is not there*

An analogous kind of selection among possible options, leading from potential operations to actual linguistic forms, seems to also be the target of the occurrence involved in vt. 3 *ad* A 1.1.51. Here the term *prasaṅga* is employed to select the object of a substitution-rule, which has not been univocally identified elsewhere. In fact, rule A 7.3.84, which logically precedes A 1.1.51, merely teaches a *guṇa*-replacement of the final vowel of a pre-suffixal stem before the verbal terminations, without specifying whether *a*, *e* or *o* has to be used.[50]

vt. 1 (M 1.125 l. 1) assumes that the precise purpose of rule A 1.1.51 (*ur aṇ raparaḥ*, '*a*, *i*, or *u* replacing *ṛ* is followed by *r* or by *l*') is not to enjoin the replacement of *ṛ* with the vowels *a*, *i*, *u*, but rather to enjoin adding the phoneme *r* after the vowel, when *ṛ* is replaced by the vowels *a*, *i*, *u*. Therefore, according to this rule, *ṛ* could be indifferently replaced by vowels *a*, *i*, *u* or by all other vowels. As a consequence, another issue is tackled by vt. 2 (M 1.126 l. 1): when a *guṇa*- or a *vṛddhi*-replacement is enjoined without any other piece of information about the replacement (right- and left-contexts apart) – such as by A 7.3.84 – there is no rule which establishes whether, e.g., *ṛ* has to be replaced by *a* or by some other *guṇa* unit in order to derive *kar-tṛ* which is the classical example mentioned in this connection. Indeed, the name *guṇa* automatically evokes the whole set listed by A 1.1.2, i.e., the vowel a and the diphthongs *e* and *o*.[51] vt. 3 aims to solve this difficulty (M 1.126 l. 14), by focusing on a specific restriction determined by the association between the *sthānin* *ṛ* and the only *ādeśa* which is allowed when its right-hand side is the consonant *r*:

> *siddhaṃ tu prasaṅge raparatvāt.*
>
> That [*a* substitutes *ṛ*] is nevertheless established because r follows when there is this automatic involvement (of *aṆ* and *ṛ*, i.e., when *ṛ* is replaced by *aṆ*).

[50] A 7.3.84: *sārvadhātukārdhadhātukayoḥ*, 'A substitute *guṇa* vowel (*a*, *e*, *o*) replaces the *aṅga* final of verbal stems ending in *i*, *u*, *ṛ*, *ḷ* before *sārvadhātuka* and *ārdhadhātuka*.'

[51] Differently from current modern phonetics, A 1.1.2 does not include *ar* and *al* in the series of *vṛddhi*-substitutes.

Thus, the involvement of the *ādeśa* a by its *sthānin ṛ* determines the presence of the following *r*. Therefore, the term *prasaṅga* introduces here the possible involvement of something, like the *ṛ*, which although it is actually not there, as it has been replaced by *a*, influences its substitute.

Furthermore, the parallelism between the locative *sthāne* of vt. 2 (*uḥ sthāne*, 'in place of ṛ') and the locative *prasaṅge* (paraphrased by M 1.126 l. 15 as *uḥ sthāne 'ṇ prasajyamāna*, '*aṆ* which is involved in place of *ṛ*') of vt. 3 is noteworthy. And M 1.126 ll. 16-7 does not fail to emphasize this:

> – Has this [word *sthāne*] to be added? – No, indeed. – How shall that which is not said be understood? – There is *anuvṛtti* of 'sthāne'. And the word *sthāna* is an expression of *prasaṅga*.[52]

3.4.1.3 prasaṅga *as the involvement of a rule or of a segment of rule*

From a slightly different point of view, *prasaṅga* is also the process of involving another rule or a segment of another rule. The rule (or its segment) at stake is thus transferred from one context of application to another, provided that this is comparable (e.g., the morpho-phonic left-context and/ or the condition of meaning must be the same). This process is put into action for instance by means of the *anuvṛtti* in M 1.201 l. 6 vt. 1 *ad* A 1.2.22:

> There is optionally the potential involvement [of the prohibition of the property of functioning like an affix with *anubandha K*] for the affixes *Ktvā* and *niṣṭhā* [which receive the augment *iṭ*] after *pū-* because of the context of *seṬ*.[53]

As there is the *anuvṛtti* of na, which is taught for *seṬ*, i.e., the affix which receives the augment *iṭ* in A 1.2.18, such a property can potentially be denied.[54]

More directly, *prasaṅga* seems to be evoked as a well known principle by means of the expression *prasaṅgasāmarthya* involved in a vt. *ad* A 1.1.44 (*na veti vibhāṣā*, '*vibhāṣā* means "rather not"').[55] The *vārttikas* thereon explain how each prohibition is based on a rule which is automatically involved by the context at stake and recall that nevertheless in such cases one is faced with a conflict.

[52] *iṃ vaktavyam etat. na hi. katham anucyamānaṃ gaṃsyate. sthāna iti vartate sthānaśabdaś ca prasaṅgavācī.* A 1.1.51 is read through the *anuvṛtti* of *sthāne* as if it were *uḥ sthāne aṇprasaṅge raparaḥ*. Hence, the meaning of *sthāne*, i.e., *prasaṅge*, is taken twice.

[53] *pūṅaḥ ktvāniṣṭhayor iṭi vā prasaṅgaḥ seṭprakaraṇāt.*

[54] See also M 2.325 l. 1 vt. 3 *ad* A 4.3.155 and M 2.327 l. 17 vt. 2 *ad* A 4.3.163.

[55] On *vibhāṣā* as the preferred option, see Kiparsky 1979.

Then, M 1.103 l. 13 vt. 9 *ad* A 1.1.44 underlines that *na vā* establishes both the application of the potentially involved rule and its prohibition in the two distinct domains which are demarcated by the formula *na vā*: *na vā prasaṅgasāmarthyād anyatra pratiṣedhaviṣayāt*, '"Rather not", by force of its being automatically involved [by the rule to be applied], (the rule at stake is realised) elsewhere than under the dominion of the prohibition.'

3.4.1.4 Conflict between prasaṅga*s*

The term *prasaṅga* in the occurrences reviewed above can be considered as a *vox media*, the use of which does not include the negative sense of "undesired" potential involvement of some rule, although some occurrences deal with a refuted possibility. In other cases, *prasaṅga* defines each of two rules potentially involved, one of which has to be refuted in order to solve the conflict. In M 1.368 l. 9 vt. 14 *ad* A 2.1.1 the compound *dvisamāsaprasaṅga* introduces two alternative ways of forming the same attested compound (*rāja-gavī-kṣīra* 'milk of Bos Grunniens').

The two *prasaṅgas* consist in combining two inflected nouns in a compound with a third *pada* (1) or vice versa one *pada* with a compound derived from the combination of the second and third *pada* (2). As a matter of fact, only the former possibility is correct, since *rājagavī* is a lexicalised compound meaning 'Bos Grunniens'.

An analogous, more technical, vt. occurrence is included in the definition of 'conflict' proposed in M 1.304 l. 13 vt. 1 *ad* A 1.4.2:

> *dvau prasaṅgāv anyārthav ekasmin sa vipratiṣedhaḥ.*
>
> When there are two rules potentially involved with a different aim (for each rule) in a single place (i.e., in the same phono-morphological context or under the same conditions of meaning), this is a conflict (between two rules).

3.4.1.5 Is prasaṅga *an undesired consequence?*

A real sense of "undesired" can be deduced from the four occurrences of the expression *sarvaprasaṅga* 'the potential involvement of any unit', i.e., the risk of overextension of a rule to all the units taught by whatever potentially involved rule – a circumstance which has of course to be avoided (M 1.120 ll. 15-6 vt. 1 *ad* A 1.1.50; 1.158 l. 9 vt. 2 *ad* A 1.1.60; 1.291 l. 1 vt. 2 *ad* A 1.3.67; 3.152 l. 8 vt. 5 *ad* A 6.3.34). For instance, vt. 1 *ad* A 1.1.50 discusses the choice of the correct substitute among the many substitutes which can be simultaneously involved by their single substituend:

Since there is a potential involvement of any unit, because both a single substituend and conversely many substitutes are expressly mentioned, it is said *sthāne 'ntaratamaḥ*.[56]

The status of vox media of the term *prasaṅga*, which nevertheless often results in conveying the sense of an undesired automatic involvement of some rule, is indirectly confirmed by the *tatpuruṣa aniṣṭaprasaṅga* in M 1.130 l. 15 vt. 2 *ad* A 1.1.52:

itarathā hy aniṣṭaprasaṅgaḥ.

In fact, otherwise there is a potential involvement of something (a rule or part of a rule) which is undesired.

This vt. explains the risk to which a rule is exposed, if some specific restriction does not intervene. This need to avoid a potential involvement of something undesired is elaborated in M 1.130 l. 13 vt. 1 *ad* A 1.1.52 *alo 'ntyasyeti sthāne vijñātasyānusaṃharaḥ*. This describes rule A 1.1.52 (*alo 'ntyasya*, 'a substitute replaces the final phoneme [of the substituend]') as an abrogation (*anusaṃhāra*) of what is already known (*vijñāta*) in case of *sthāne* 'in place of', i.e., as an important restriction of the general rule A 1.1.49 *ṣaṣṭhī sthāneyogā*, 'The genitive ending is used to denote the relation "in place of".' The possible involvement tout court of A 1.1.49 is overcome by A 1.1.52.[57]

3.4.2 Conclusions on prasaṅga *in the* vārttika*s*

To sum up, the term *prasaṅga* in the vt. occurrences conveys the sense of a potential involvement of a rule which is automatically evoked, so that a prohibition, a restriction or some other kind of specific demarcation of rule-domain becomes necessary, in order to regulate the otherwise uncontrolled process of rule-extension. The potential involvement which is focused on, depends both on substitution mechanisms (the *saṃjñā*-one included) and on the *anuvṛtti*-system.

Often Kātyāyana seems to question the extension of a rule (e.g., a *saṃjñā*-rule) which results as being more general than the operational rule (i.e., the rule which teaches a *kārya*) associated to it. At least once (vt. 3 *ad* A 1.1.51, see § 3.4.1.2) it is the *prasaṅga*,

[56] *sthānina ekatvanirdeśād anekādeśanirdeśāc ca sarvaprasaṅgas tasmāt sthāne 'ntaratamavacanam* (M 1.120 ll. 15-6 *ad* A 1.1.50).

[57] Cf. M 1.130 l. 14 *ad* vt. 1 *ad* A 1.1.52: *alo 'ntyasyety ucyate sthāne vijñatasyānusaṃhāraḥ kriyate sthāne prasaktasya*, '*alo 'ntyasya* is said. An abrogation of that which is already known is realised in case of *sthāne* "in place of" i.e. "in place of that which is potentially associated".'

meant as a potential involvement of a substituend, which realises the requested restriction by itself. In four cases the concurring rules of a conflict are classified as *prasaṅgas* themselves.

The relation between the discussed rules never seems to amount to a fixed kind of hierarchy. It rather depends on the specific point of view which is assumed every time with the target of justifying some linguistic form actually occurring in the language.

The used translation of the term as "risk" seems to be too interpretative, insofar as it relies on the consequences of all contexts, taken as a whole rather than on the actual sense of the passages analysed. The three occurrences involving the sense of "conflict" also suggest discarding the choice of "necessity" as a translation of *prasaṅga.*

3.4.3 prasaṅga *in the Mahābhāṣya*

The total number of M occurrences of *prasaṅga* is 62. Our survey has also been extended to the 22 occurrences of the term *prasakta,* since its use appears to often be strictly connected to the term *prasaṅga.*[58]

We encounter two kinds of occurrences of *prasakta,* namely, as an adjective agreeing with a substantive (12X), aiming to present a potential involvement which is essentially undesired, and as a substantive defining a rule which has a chance of being applied (10X).

Out of the 62 M occurrences of *prasaṅga,* 34 are thoroughly independent from vt. ones, i.e., they refer to A rules whose *vārttikas* do not include this term. Nevertheless, sometimes the problem at stake is the same as that dealt with by a different vt. involving this term. For instance, M 1.47 ll. 22-4 *ad* vt. 7 *ad* A 1.1.3 takes into consideration the same pair of rules, which vt. 11 *ad* A 1.1.1 discusses by involving the expression *a-prasaṅga.*

3.4.3.1 Multiplicity of potential involvements

The exigency of some further specification for the domain of a certain rule lies at the heart of a number of M occurences of *prasaṅga,* which at least three times particularly stress the cognitive process involved in the dichotomy between the multiplicity of potential associations of a linguistic fact with different rules and the single operational rule to be actually applied. For instance,

[58] Nevertheless, in order to remain within the limits of this contribution we are forced to refer to Freschi and Pontillo forthcoming for a detailed explanation of the different collected typologies of occurrences. Consequently, the following account on the M is almost wanting in citations and argumentations.

vt. 11 *ad* A 1.1.1 (quoted above, end of last §) reflects on the potential involvement – within the *saṃjñā* "*vṛddhi*" which is evoked by the operational rule A 7.2.114 – of the whole list of of *vṛddhi*-substitutes of A 1.1.1, i.e., *ā, ai, au*. Consequently, Patañjali's introduction to this vt. (M 1.41 ll. 2-6 *ad* vt. 10 *ad* A 1.1.1) pays special attention to the process, which consists in moving the speaker from the notion conveyed by a *guṇa*- or *vṛddhi*-substitution rule and not further specified, to a specific prohibition concerning the *guṇa* or *vṛddhi* substitutes which have to be rejected:

> –[S:] The *śāstra*'s function is to exclude [incorrect linguistic forms]. –[PP:] How? –[S:] *mṛj*- is taught to someone without specifications. His notion of *mṛj*- automatically involves any [form of the verb *mṛj*-]. In its regards, the exclusion [of incorrect linguistic forms] is realised by means of this [Vyākaraṇa *śāstra*]. When *mṛj*- is automatically involved [since it is the basic form of the root], *mārj*- instead of *mṛj*- is right, except before affixes with *anubandhas* *K* or *Ṅ*. –[S:] We have to say that the names *vṛddhi* and *guṇa* are [to be applied] one by one (to the phonemes named as *āDaiC* and *aDeṄ*). –[PP:] What is the purpose [of your statement]? –[S:] This should not be, that [these names] are applied to the whole group [of them].[59]

3.4.4 Comparison between prasaṅga- *and* ādeśa-*system in the Mahābhāṣya*

The assumption of a substantial overlap between the rule-extension based on the substitution and the reference system on which the *prasaṅga*-occurrences seem to rely, is tempting. Yet, it should be premised that it does not result in a bi-univocal relation.

On this topic, a long discussion on A 3.1.33 could be very instructive, since here the system of the opposition between general and special rules (*utsarga/ apavāda*) is compared with their arrangement in *sthānin/ ādeśa* in order to decide which is the best model for describing how *lakāra*s are related to each other.

After several unsuccessful proposals, the final although not absolute solution is to consider *ŚaP* (the affix -*a*- of the verbs of the first class) as a *sthānin* for the *vikaraṇa*s (conjugational affixes) of all the present verbal classes, by classifying *ŚyaN* etc. taught from A 3.1.69 onward as *ādeśa*s of *ŚaP*, and to govern the tense- and mode-conjugational affixes (such as *sya* taught in A 3.1.33) as *apavāda*s, which are often taught before their *utsarga*.

[59] *nivartakaṃ śāstram. katham. mrjir asmā aviśeṣeṇopadiṣṭaḥ. tasya sarvatra mṛjibuddhiḥ prasaktā. tatrānena nivṛttiḥ kriyate. mṛjer akṅitsu pratyayeṣu mṛjiprasaṅge mārjiḥ sādhur bhavatīti. pratyekaṃ vṛddhiguṇasaṃjñe bhavata iti vaktavyam. kiṃ prayojanam. samudāye mā bhūtām iti.* Cf. also M 1.60, ll. 24-6 *ad* vt. 1 *ad* A 1.1.8.

But before this final solution, one encounters an interesting definition of *apavāda*:

> (M 2.42 l. 19 *ad* A 3.1.33): *apavādo nāma bhavati yatrānekalakṣaṇaprasaṅgaḥ.*
>
> An *apavāda* occurs where more than one rule is potentially associated.

It seems noteworthy that even in a passage discussing the comparison between the *utsarga/ apavāda* system and the benefits of a *sthānin/ ādeśa* arrangement of rules, the term *prasaṅga* is just involved in the context of the former, definitely confirming that the relationship between the *prasaṅga*- and the substitution-horizons cannot be considered as a bi-univocal matter.

The coincidence of the meaning of the units taught by the concurring rules is a condition for evoking a *prasaṅga*-mechanism. In other words, it is compulsory that a "well established place" exists, where two or more rules are potentially applied. This place consists in the specific meaning or function conveyed by all the morphemes which are taught by the concurring rules (on the spatial metaphor inherent in this, see also above, § 1.1). This is also emphasized in two other passages which involve both the term *prasaṅga* and the opposition between *utsarga* and *apavāda*, i.e., M 2.81 ll. 3-6 *ad* vt. 10 *ad* A 3.1.94 and M 2.140 l. 25-141 l. 2 *ad* A 3.3.10.

Nevertheless, when Patañjali reflects on the substitution, it is apparent that the *prasaṅga* terminology is crucial. Generally speaking, substitution results as being a more restrictive case of the *utsarga/ apavāda* system of rule-extension. In the commentary on the main rule of substitution, i.e., on A 1.1.56 (*sthānivad ādeśo 'nalvidhau*, 'A substitute has the status of its substituend (*sthānivat* "[behaves, is treated] in the same manner as a substituend") except in respect of an operation that depends on an original sound (*analvidhau*)', Cardona 1997, p. 58), the term *prasaṅga* (together with the strictly related term *prasakta*) is focused on once again, precisely in the cognitive interpretation of the substitution already seen above (§ 3.4.3).

The remote target is to overcome the problem of the fixedness (*nityatva*) of language, which has been established since the first vt. *ad* A. Such fixedness seems to prevent the possibility itself of the *ādeśa* having the status of its *sthānin* (M 1.137 l. 3 vt. 12 *ad* A 1.1.56: *anupapannaṃ sthānyādeśatvaṃ nityatvāt*). vt. 14 (M 1.137 l. 12 vt. 14 *ad* A 1.1.56: *kāryavipāriṇāmād vā siddham*) advances the hypothesis that this status of the *ādeśa* can be accepted by relying on a change of the effect which occurs purely on the cognitive level, namely, as a difference in the knowledge conveyed by the linguistic unit.

Before the linguistic application of this interpretation of substitution, M 1.137 ll. 19-23 *ad* vt. 14 *ad* A 1.1.56 proposes an example drawn from common life:

> For instance, someone says to someone else: 'East of the village there are mango trees'. His notion of mango trees automatically involves any [tree being East of the village, since he does not know anything about mango trees]. Thereafter, [the first one] says: 'The [trees also found East of the village and] which are sappy, with aerial roots and broad-leaves are banyans.' [The listener] thus gains the notion of banyan trees [which he also perceives to the East of the village] by means of the notion of mango trees [the only ones whose place had been established by a precise instruction]. Then he perceives that mango trees are removed and banyan trees are acquired by his notion (i.e., the mango trees have been replaced by the banyans in his intellect). Mango trees are permanent in their domain and banyan trees too, but his notion has changed.[60]

Next, the *upadeśa* of a linguistic unit (in the present case, the verbal base *as-* 'to be'), for which no domain is specified, is confronted with a specific substitution rule (its replacement with *bhū-* according to the conditions of A 2.4.52, i.e., before *ārdhadhātuka* affixes). Because both units are permanent in the language (and both taught in the Dhātupāṭha, respectively in the *adādi-* and in the *bhvādi-*class), the replacement is based on the analogous change of the speaker's notion which precisely moves from the *sthānin as-* to its *ādeśa bhū-*.[61]

This is only one out of two devised explanations respectively based on the conception of *sthānin* as a *bhūtapūrva* or as an *abhūtapūrva*. According to the latter view, i.e., the one just quoted, *sthānin* as a *bhūtapūrva* is 'something which was really there before'. Namely it occupies the place where the substitute will be afterwards. This place is clearly the speaker's *buddhi* as the real place where the substituted notion is formed in place of the substituend's one. In fact, no change would be acceptable for permanent entities, unless this change were limited to the cog-

[60] *tad yathā. kaścit kasmaicid upadiśati prācinaṃ grāmād amrā iti. tasya sarvatrāmrābuddhiḥ prasaktā. tataḥ paścād āha ye ksīriṇo 'varohavantaḥ pṛthuparṇās te nyagrodha iti. sa tatrāmrābuddhyā nyagrodhabuddhiṃ pratipadyate. sa tataḥ paśyati buddhyāmrāṃs cāpakrṣyamāṇān nyagrodhāmś cādhīyamānān. nityā eva ca svasmin viṣaya āmrā nityāś ca nyagrodha buddhis tv asya vipariṇāmyate.*

[61] M I.137 ll. 23-6 *ad* vt. 14 *ad* A 1.1.56.

nitive level: a permanent linguistic unit can only be replaced by another in the speaker's mind, although both units continue to be permanent in the language.

The latter to some extent opposite assumption is expounded just before the passage quoted above: *sthānin* is considered as an *abhūtapūrva*, i.e., as something which has never been in the place where the substitute occurs. Here another example is drawn from common life, followed by a Vedic example (M 1.137 ll. 8-11 *ad* vt. 13 *ad* A 1.1.56):

> *siddham etat. katham. yathā laukikeṣu vaidikeṣu ca kṛtāntesv abhūtapūrve 'pi sthānaśabdo vartate. loke tāvad upādhyāyasya sthāne śisya ity ucyate na ca tatropādhyāyo bhūtapūrvo bhavati. vede 'pi somasya sthāne pūtīkatṛnāny abhiṣuṇuyād ity ucyate na ca tatra somo bhūtapurvo bhavati.*
>
> – This (status of the *ādeśa*, namely that fact that it has the status of the *sthānin*) is established. – How? – As happens for instance in the precepts relative both to common life and to Vedas: the word *sthāna* occurs exactly in the sense of "something which has never been there before". In common life it is said: 'the pupil in place of the teacher', but the teacher had never been there. In the Vedas it is also said: '*pūtīka*-herbs have to be pressed in place of Soma', but Soma had never been there.

A certain similarity between this latter (*vaidika*) example and some Kalpasūtra-passages (e.g. BaudhŚrSū 24.1) enjoining some *pratinidhi*s cannot go unnoticed. Furthermore, rules like this which explain the recommended conduct to be adopted towards the potential substitutes of the teacher, are frequent in Dharmasūtras (for further details, see Freschi and Pontillo forthcoming).

3.4.4.1 Rule-extension as a common practice

This mechanism of rule-extension is explained by M 1.133 ll. 22-4 *ad* A 1.1.56 in the following way:

> We have to behave in the presence of the preceptor's son as if we were in the presence of the preceptor, i.e., that which has to be done (*kārya*) in the presence of the preceptor is extended in the presence of the preceptor's son. Analogously that which has to be done (the application of the rule/-s) when there is the *sthānin*, is extended when there is its *ādeśa*.[62]

[62] *guruvad asmin guruputre vartitavyam iti gurau yat kāryaṃ tad guruputre 'tidiśyate. evam ihāpi sthānikāryam ādeśe 'tidiśyate.*

Nevertheless, Patañjali objects to the necessity of teaching the *sthānivadbhāva* for *ādeśas* because this kind of extension of rules is actually a common practice, and there is no need for its specific enunciation. The chosen example is not so far from the one based on the guru's son's rights, since it deals with the rights and honours deserved by a pupil when he is called to replace his teacher in some ritual performance. Although – to the best of our knowledge – it does not match any Dharmaśāstric rule, the example seems fit enough as evidence of the assumed non-artificialness of this practice. *prasaṅga* is again a key-word:

> This is also established from the point of view of common life. As in common life when one obtains the privileges which are due to the one, one has been associated with. For instance, a pupil gets the seat of honour etc. when he reaches the clan for which he is going to perform a sacrifice.[63]

It is noteworthy that the pupil's chance to perform the sacrifice does not derive from his birth, i.e., it does not constitute a sort of right due to a fixed status of this pupil, which can be acquired once and for all. It rather depends on a possible association with his teacher. When his teacher is designated as the performer of a sacrifice, his pupil can be called to take his place, more precisely to play the same role of performer. It is almost as if the call of the teacher (who is the placeholder) worked as a potential device for entailing his pupil to cover the same role, i.e., to perform the same function. By contrast, the role itself is strictly connected to the first call, without which the replacement could never take place, since the substitute would lack above all the investiture for the function to be performed. Analogously, the *upadeśa* is a sort of warrant for the *ādeśa*. Without the *upadeśa*, which teaches the function, the meaning and often the morphological context which are required for a given linguistic unit, no *ādeśa* could be applied. This transference of information from the *sthānin* to the *ādeśa* takes the form of an effect *in absentia*. In other words, function, denotation, right- and left-context and all the other details taught elsewhere for a unit which is replaced, also really work for the substitute. This functioning not in *praesentia* and not as an effect of a diachronic sequence is emphasized by Patañjali – as seen above – with regard to the couple of examples pertaining to the Soma's and the preceptor's substitutes: both the Soma and the preceptor, respectively replaced by the *pūtīka*-herbs and the pupil, "have never been there".

[63] *lokata etat siddham. tad yathā. loke yo yasya prasaṅge bhavati labhate 'sau tatkaryāṇi. tad yathā. upādhyāyasya śiṣyo yājyakulani gatvāgrāsanādīni labhate* (M 1.133 ll. 24-134 l. 2 *ad* A 1.1.56).

3.4.4.2 What does sthānivat *mean?*

In his commentary *ad* A 1.1.56, Patañjali seems to aim at singling out the specific feature of the substitution and it is interesting to note that he chooses to compare it with the *utsarga/ apavāda* model. In fact, vt. 15 (M 1.138 l. 1 *ad* A 1.1.56) already proposes to clarify the *ādeśa* method by suggesting an overlap between the two paradigms:

> *apavādaprasaṅgas tu sthānivattvāt.*
>
> There is indeed a potential involvement [of the corresponding *utsarga*] within the *apavāda*, because of this condition *sthānivat* 'like a *sthānin*'.

The statement which is crucial for our subject is M 1.138 l. 6 vt. 17 *ad* A 1.1.56:[64]

> *siddhaṃ tu ṣāṣṭhinirdiṣṭhasya sthānivadvacanāt.*
>
> By contrast, [the right derivation] is established by force of the mention of *sthānivat* referred to [the unit] which is expressly mentioned with the sixth ending.

In other words, the *sthānivadbhāva*, i.e., the rule-extension from the *sthānin* to the *ādeśa*, is unequivocally limited to a unit mentioned in the genitive case. As Patañjali points out in M 1.138 ll. 7-9 *ad* vt. 17 *ad* A 1.1.56, there is also no need for further restrictions, since the standard pattern of the substitution is taught by means of the explicit usage of the sixth *vibhakti* in A 1.1.49:

> Such being the case, then should an additional mention of *ṣaṣṭhīnirdiṣṭasya* 'of a unit expressly indicated in the genitive case' be made? It does not need to be made. The subject under discussion continues. Where has this been introduced? In rule A 1.1.49.[65]

3.4.4.3 Conclusions on the comparison between substitution and prasaṅga

Patañjali's necessity of further limiting the system of the extension of rules by resorting to a more precise model than the *utsarga/ apavāda* one is here and elsewhere recursively attested

[64] For some further details about this passage see Candotti and Pontillo 2012, § 1.4.

[65] *tat tarhi ṣaṣṭhīnirdiṣṭagrahaṇaṃ kartavyam. na kartavyam. prakṛtam anuvatate. kva prakṛtam. ṣaṣṭhī sthāneyogā iti.*

in his commentary. The process itself according to which the substitute has the status of its substituend is considered obvious and any explicit statement about it is deemed to be superfluous. It is consistent with some well known and shared worldly and Vedic attitudes (see the examples quoted above, p. 37). As a consequence, the expression *sthānivat* itself, without the following *analvidhau* restriction, is provisionally proposed to be eliminated as a superfluous part of the rule-wording, by resorting to two implicit senses (*jñāpaka* 'indirect revealer') explained in M 1.134 ll. 2-9 *ad* vt. 1 *ad* A 1.1.56. By contrast, it is the negation (*analvidhau*) which is considered as the veritable target of rule A 1.1.56. The scheme of rule A 1.1.56, including a prohibitive part, once again matches the same Dharmaśāstric kind of rules quoted above (M 1.136 l. 1 *ad* vt. 8 *ad* A 1.1.56, see p. 37):

> We have to behave in the presence of the preceptor's son as if we were in the presence of the preceptor, except with regard to the act of eating his leftovers and of reverentially clasping his feet.[66]

It is noteworthy that the M restriction concerning leftovers and clasped feet, which is only supplied in this quotation is reserved to those acts which are closer to the material (corporal, i.e., perceptible) features of the preceptor, exactly as the restriction *analvidhau* concerns the more physical (phonic) features of the *sthānin*.

To sum up, the *sthānin/ ādeśa* relationship, inscribed in the general frame of the *utsarga/ apavāda* opposition, is peculiarly identified both from the metalinguistic point of view according to A 1.1.49 by limiting the pattern of the substitution to the explicit usage of the genitive case for the substituend, which technically figures as the *prasakta*, and by stating a specific condition, i.e., the *niyama analvidhau*, which excludes what is strictly connected to the material feature of the language from being transferred.

An analogous restriction is proposed and refuted because of secondary reasons in M *ad* vt. 4 *ad* A 1.1.60, see Candotti and Pontillo 2012, § 1.4.

3.4.5 Conclusions on prasaṅga *in the M*

To sum up, the term *prasaṅga* in the M results as being used to describe the involvement of some rule which is evoked by a linguistic unit and made possible by a specific place (a specific morpho-

[66] *guruvad asmin guruputre vartitavyam anyatrocchiṣṭhabhojanāt padopasaṃgrahaṇāc ceti.*

phonic context) or through a specific sense or function as a space shared by two or more rules. It is this precise place which allows the transference of some detail from a peculiar kind of *utsarga*, i.e., from the *sthānin* or 'place-holder', to its technically taught *apavāda*, i.e., to the *ādeśa.* Furthermore, it is noteworthy that both *prasaṅga* and *prasakta* are terms involved in some worldly and Vedic examples involved in Patañjali's commentary, in order to illustrate grammatical rules. It does not seem unreasonable that these kinds of examples involving the concept of *prasaṅga* constituted a sort of easier and perhaps currently well accepted pattern of governing the relationship among Kalpa-rules as well as some mundane behaviours. This detail could bear witness to the assumption of Patañjali's terminological dependence on the Kalpasūtra tradition.

If we read the almost all-inclusive Pāṇini's opposition between *utsarga* and *apavāda* in the terms of the so called Elsewhere Condition introduced into generative grammar by Kiparsky 1973[67] and reportedly descended from Pāṇini himself, we have to consider *vārttika* and M reflections on *prasaṅga* as deepening *ante litteram* the comprehension of its functioning.

According to the "Elsewhere Principle" a more specific form is preferred over a more general one where both are grammatically correct forms. In other words, the availability of more specific forms excludes the use of more general ones. The comparison of the two different applications of the *prasaṅga* concept, which is involved in the A respectively in the mere frame of the pattern of general vs. specific rules and in the more specific and circumstanced substitution-scheme, highlights a specific outcome of this principle which is systematically adopted for the descriptive method of (grammatical or ritual) rules. In fact, the more general rule, whose object is however superseded by the more specific rule, is suitable for supplying all the information which is not taught for the specific rule and becomes valid by means of a mere transference mechanism.

3.4.6 prasaṅga/ *attachment*

The etymological meaning of *prasañj-* as 'to adhere to', 'to attach to', 'to supply with' could have determined the use of the term *prasaṅga* as an 'automatic (even undesired) consequence of something' (i.e., that which automatically attaches to it).[68]

[67] More precisely this principle was at first only applied to the phonological rules by "'Elsewhere' in Phonology" and then extended to the morpheme structure conditions in the lexicon, e.g., in Clements 1982.

[68] The most ancient occurrences of forms derived from the verb *prasañj-* seem to be AV 7.52.3 (*īḍe agniṃ svāvasuṃ namobhir iha prasakto vi cayat kṛtaṃ naḥ,*

At Patañjali's time this etymological sense might have still been alive, as it almost seems to be synchronically confirmed by the use of *prasaṅga* ('association, adherence, attachment') as even 'intercourse' of a human couple in GDhSū 2.9.16 (= 18.16 Stenzler 1876): *pravrājete tu nivṛttiḥ prasaṅgāt*, 'But if [the husband] has renounced domestic life, [his wife must] refrain from intercourse [with other men].'[69] Cf. also MBh 6.40.34 (*Bhāgavadgītā* 18.34): *yayā tu dharmakāmārthān dhṛtyā dhārayate 'rjuna | prasaṅgena phalākāṅkṣī dhṛtiḥ sā pārtha rājasī*, 'O Arjuna, Pṛthī's son, the resolve by which one sustains with attachment duty, desire, and wealth, craving their fruits, is descended from passion' (Sukthankar, Belvalkar, and Vaidya 1933-1971).

3.4.7 Conclusions on prasaṅga *and* tantra *in Grammar*

The opposition between *tantra* (present as a function, besides the usage of the term), and *prasaṅga* in Vyākaraṇa may throw some light on their relationship. *tantra* as used in Mīmāṃsā and in Vyākaraṇa refers to the extension of something to elements participating in the same set. *prasaṅga* seems to be depicted, by contrast, as if it were a substitution-rule: it has to be explicitly indicated (as with Śabara, see infra) and one needs two elements (one occurring normally, the *prasakta*, and one to be introduced *ad hoc*). *Faute de mieux*, *prasaṅga* is applied.

3.5 Different approaches to substitution: ādeśa *and* vikāra

In the Kalpasūtras there is no trace of a distinction between the concept of "modification, transformation" referred to a model, called *vikāra*, and the Pāṇinian term for the 'substitute', i.e., *ādeśa*, which rather seems to be merely used to convey the sense of a 'specific instruction'. For instance, the two terms *ādeśa* and *vikāra* co-exist in the Śaunakīya Prātiśākhya, and at present it is difficult to tell whether they refer to distinct kinds of substitution.[70] To sum up, the meaning of 'ectype' and that of 'substitutes' might not have been conflated yet in the early ritual literature.[71]

'I praise Agni, who owns good things, with acts of homage; here, may he (Agni), to whom we are attached, distribute what we have won', Vishva Bandhu 1961), ŚB 1.7.3.21 (*rudriyeṇa paśūn prasajed*, 'He would impose Rudra's power on the cattle', Weber 1964), ŚB 1.7.4.12, 3.8.2.20, 4.2.5.13 and 5.3.2.2.

[69] Cf. the relative and absolute chronology proposed in Olivelle 2000, pp. 8-9.

[70] Deshpande advances the hypothesis that the Śaunakīya Prātiśākya 'implicitly had a doctrine of *sthānivadbhāva*' comparable to A 1.1.56 (Deshpande 1997, p. 210; cf. also pp. 176; 281).

[71] Beside this one, the problem of some Brāhmaṇa- and Upaniṣad-

However, since *vikāra* in the post-Pāṇini linguistic-grammatical tradition is treated as a quasi-synonym of *ādeśa*, or intentionally ignored in favour of it, one might be induced to extend the Grammatical usage to the Kalpasūtra one and consider *vikāras* as "substitutes" instead of "ectypes" also in the Kalpasūtras and in the late Vedic texts.

3.5.1 vikāra

vikāra is the specific term employed in the Prātiśākhyas, which introduce phonic substitutions by mentioning the substituted unit (called *vikārin*, 'possessing modification') in the nominative ending and the substitute (*vikāra*, 'modification') in the accusative ending, in order to express the sense of "X becomes Y" or "Y instead of X".[72]

3.5.2 ādeśa

The Kalpasūtras seem to neatly preserve the etymological meaning of *ādeśa* as a "specific instruction", unlike in the case of Vyākaraṇa. See, for instance, passages such as ŚŚrSū 15.11.15: *anādeśe prakṛtir dakṣiṇānām*, 'Unless there is a specific instruction, the archetype regarding the fees of the officiant priest [remains valid]' and AśvŚrSū 2.1.8: *adṛṣṭādeśe nitye*, 'When a specific instruction is absent, both [usual formulas][73] are compulsory.'[74] Such passages overtly suggest the archetype vs. ectype pattern as their background.

Then, Pāṇini's grammar fixed once and for all the technicalities of the so called substitution system with its terminological and syntactic equipment, but it is not impossible to maintain that Pāṇini's Grammar had, as its background for the development of the rules of substitution, the concept of *ādeśa* as a "specific instruction" as developed in the Kalpasūtras. Through the concept of *ādeśa*, Pāṇini manages to build a descriptive model

occurrences of *ādeśa* has also been tackled many times: see in particular Thieme 1968, p. 718; Wezler 1972, p. 7; Kahrs 1998, p. 181. There are many Upaniṣadic passages where *ādeśa* is translated by Olivelle as 'rule of substitution', see, e.g., BṛĀrUp 2.4.6. We could not access a further study, Ikari 1969, in Japanese.

72 For the terminology and the syntactic schema used for enjoining substitution-rules, see Liebich 1919-1920, pp. II, 41; Thieme 1968; Thieme 1971, p. 753; Kahrs 1998, p. 175.

73 The dual refers to *yājya* and *anuvākya*, mentioned before, AśvŚrSū 2.1.7.

74 Both passages have been drawn from two works dating back to the most ancient phase of ŚrSū according to Brucker 1980 (about which, see above, § 2.1). Comparable occurrences of the expression *anādeśe* are in AśvŚrSū 1.1.13; KātyŚrSū 1.8.37; 9.5.19.

of the phono-morphological phenomena of Sanskrit which can be compared with those based on the opposition between morphemes and allomorphs in the current grammatical systems in the West (see Pontillo 2000 [2003], p. 130, Pontillo 2002, pp. 542-48 and the bibliography quoted there). Patañjali's emphasis on the comparison between the *utsarga/ apavāda* and *sthānin/ ādeśa* reviewed here (see above, p. 36) seems to supply further evidence of a Kalpasūtra-style influencing the arrangement of rules in the M.

4 Śabara (and Bhartṛhari) and Thereafter

In Śabara, just like in Bhartṛhari among the Grammarians, *tantra* and *prasaṅga* figure as a structured couple of mutually distinct devices. Śabara and Bhartṛhari do not seem to improve much on the concept of *tantra*, whereas their treatment of *prasaṅga* as an alternative to *tantra* is noteworthy. *prasaṅga* is scarcely found in ŚrSū and MS and it is probably only through a conscious effort that the opposing couple has been elaborated. After Śabara and Bhartṛhari, the opposition between *tantra* and *prasaṅga* develops further, so that the balance found in these two authors (see § 4.1.2) is superseded by new ones (see Freschi and Pontillo forthcoming, § 4.1.2).

Consequently, this whole study derives its title and framework, namely an enquiry into *tantra* and *prasaṅga*, from Śabara's and Bhartṛhari's approach to the topic.

4.1 Śabara on tantra *and* prasaṅga

Jaimini and all commentators agree that MS 11 discusses *āvāpa* and *tantra*, which are thought of opposites of each other. Jaimini uses *prasaṅga* just three times in MS 12 (*ad* 1.10, 11, 15) and in a very few other instances (whereas *tantra* is largely employed). Hence, it is difficult to say whether Jaimini already wanted to structure a systematic distinction of *tantra* and *prasaṅga*, rather than implementing *prasaṅga* just for specific cases. What is quite sure, by contrast, is that Śabara systematises Jaimini's lore by classifying *tantra* and *prasaṅga* as distinct devices with specific functions and objects. In accordance with this agenda, Śabara mentions *prasaṅga* in his commentaries to all *sūtras* 12.1.1-15. That this was not just his own personal concern is proven by a verse he quotes at the beginning of his discussion on *tantra* and *prasaṅga* (MS 11.1.1), which also aims at distinguishing the two.

Probably, Śabara or the author of the verse before him, looked for the common elements in Jaimini's few instances of *prasaṅga*, and in the other instances they might have been aware of, in texts and in actual practice, and generalised them into a better structured *tantra-prasaṅga* opposition.

If we focus just on the beginning of his commentary on MS 11 and 12, we have two sets of evidences for Śabara's treatment of *tantra* and *prasaṅga*; on the one hand the verse he quotes and comments upon, at the beginning of MS 11.1.1, and on the other hand, the examples he mentions and his own, short definition:[75]

> *anyatra kṛtasyānyatrāpi prasaktiḥ prasaṅgaḥ.*
>
> *prasaṅga* is the further application to another occasion of something done on a certain occasion.

Through their comparison (about which more infra), one notices that Śabara differentiates *tantra* and *prasaṅga* through the following points:

1. presence of a prescription (*vidhi*): which is necessarily present in the case of *prasaṅga*
2. position in regard to the rite: whereas *tantra* is centralised, *prasaṅga* is lateral, that is, the element which applies more than once applies outside its main sphere and its direct purpose[76]
3. what is applied more than once: an auxiliary in the case of *tantra*, its function in the case of *prasaṅga*

These three characteristics can be easily summarised by the *prasaṅga*-example of Śabara and by its *tantra*-counterpart, in the preceding book. A lamp which is lit at the centre of a group of Brahmans and helps them all is *tantra* (ad MS 11.1.1). A lamp which is placed in a building and also throws light outside onto the street is *prasaṅga* (ad MS 12.1.1). In the first case, the lamp is in common; in the second, its enlightening function is in common.[77] Moreover, the extended application regards something which was not intended for it. Lastly, nothing is said in the example about a specific prescription enjoining the street's illumina-

[75] A detailed analysis of all occurrences of *tantra* and *prasaṅga/ prasakta* in the ŚBh goes beyond the scope of the present work. For further details, see Freschi and Pontillo forthcoming.

[76] The lateral position of *prasaṅga* also means that it does not presuppose a unity of purpose. Provided that it can serve the material exigency at stake, the auxiliary function does not need to originally have had the same purpose. This point is discussed in ŚBh *ad* MS 12.1.8-9 and 12.1.10-1.

[77] This last detail distinguishing the two examples and the presence of a prescription as the focus of Śabara's comparison between *tantra* and *prasaṅga* have already been pointed out in Pontillo 2008, p. 93, and n. 19.

tion, but the street is said to be a *rājamārga*, a 'principal road'. Hence, one may safely assume that there were public ordinances prescribing that such a road had to be illuminated (or at least that the street's illumination was needed, and need is one of the criteria of *prasaṅga* in the ŚrSū, see above, § 3.3.4).

light in the house
↓
street

Fig. 1. *prasaṅga*: the light meant for the house reaches the street

brāhmaṇa		brāhmaṇa		brāhmaṇa
	↖	↑	↗	
brāhmaṇa	←	light	→	brāhmaṇa
	↙	↓	↘	
brāhmaṇa		brāhmaṇa		brāhmaṇa

Fig. 2. *tantra*: a centralised light reaches all the people meant to be reached, independent of their needs

Only this requirement (presence of a prescription) is explicit in Śabara's treatment, that is, in the verse he quotes about *tantra* and *prasaṅga* at the beginning of the 11th *adhyāya* and in his subsequent discussion of it (see § 4.1.2), whereas, by contrast, the lamp-example stresses exactly the two aspects of *prasaṅga* which are not explicitly stressed in the verse (i.e., its being lateral and its referring to a function) while, vice versa, it does not emphasise the presence of a prescription about the street having to be enlightened.

To summarise, the example does not completely harmonise with the description of *prasaṅga* as found in Śabara's interpretation of the verse. One is inclined to think that the example Śabara repeats is a traditional one, and in fact it is also found in Bhartṛhari; also that the verse is a text he inherited, which had been however composed having in view a slightly different concept of *prasaṅga*. Presumably, neither constitutes Śabara's best description of the distinction between *tantra* and *prasaṅga*, which might however be reconstructed by means of noticing what he adds or what he stresses in what he inherited.

4.1.1 Bhartṛhari and the verse on tantra *and* prasaṅga

Bhartṛhari also quotes the same verse on *tantra* and *prasaṅga* in his commentary on the M. The object of the passage is the proposal (included in the M Paspaśā) of adding a prohibition of using some incorrect vowels not listed in the Śivasūtras, but which could nevertheless descend from them.[78] After a long list of defects in the pronunciation of phonemes (*varṇa*), lastly M 1.13 l. 27-14 l. 1 *ad* vt. 18 refutes the proposed addition, by assuming that the prohibition at stake can be plainly deduced from the *gaṇas* like Gargādi or Bidādi which are recited precisely without these defects. The starting point for the M reflection depends on this last statement. In fact, these *gaṇas* would have a double function as a consequence, i.e., they would serve two aims simultaneously, as they teach both the whole (each whole word derived from each member of the *gaṇa*) and the part (each sound involved in the stems listed in the *gaṇa*). The words involved in the two mentioned *gaṇas* would convey two different meanings at the same time.

> [If this is so], then both things are realized by this [recitation], namely the recitation itself is made specific and [the defects] beginning from the inarticulate drone are excluded. – How indeed could two things be obtained by means of one single effort? – He[79] said that they can be obtained. – How? – There are also causes (*hetu*) reaching two objects (*dvigata*), such as when mango trees are watered and the pitṛs are satisfied. Analogously there are sentences which have a double aim, such as *śveto dhāvati* (1) 'the white one runs'; (2) 'the dog (*śvā*) runs from here (*itaḥ*)', or *alambusānāṃ yātā,* (1) 'he will go (to the country) of the Alambusas'; (2) 'he is able to reach (*alam yatā*) the waters'.[80]

Bhartṛhari's comment elaborates further on the examples themselves, by putting them in a more specific and technical frame. To the best of our knowledge, this passage is among other things the first text where this terminological pair, i.e., *tantra* and *prasaṅga*, occurs side by side in the grammatical tradition.[81]

[78] M 1.13 l. 21 vt. 18.

[79] An unidentified grammarian according to Joshi and Roodbergen 1986, p. 208, n. 879.

[80] *evaṃ tarhy ubhayam anena kriyate pāṭhaś caiva viśeṣyate kalādayaś ca nivartyante. kathaṃ punar ekena yatnenobhayaṃ labhyam. labhyam ity āha. katham. dvigatā api hetavo bhavanti. tad yathā. āmrāś ca siktāḥ pitaraś ca prīṇitā iti. tathā vākyāny api dviṣṭhāni bhavanti. śveto dhāvati. alambusānāṃ yāteti* (M 1.14 ll. 10-4 *ad* vt. 18). This statement is somehow anticipated by M 1.14 ll. 1-2 *ad* vt. 18 (*asty anyad gargādibidādipāṭhe prayojanam. kim. samudāyānāṃ sādhutvaṃ yathā syād iti,* 'There is another purpose in the recitation of the "Garga etc." and "Bida etc." lists').

[81] Also in VP 2.77 we find both terms occurring in the same context:

Bhartṛhari's gloss can be divided into three parts. The first one is close to the commented text and formally accepts the thesis that a single cause is capable of bringing about two distinct effects. Nonetheless – as we shall see below – Bhartṛhari already seems to aim at underlining some details of the example which makes it more suitable for a *prasaṅga*-reading, although Bhartṛhari also seems to be eager to propose his own interpretation of how a simultaneous application can take place, insofar as he stresses the character of renunciation (*tyāgalakṣaṇa*), which is absent in both the accounts of *tantra* and *prasaṅga* examined so far. In fact, the second and the third parts of Bhartṛhari's commentary are respectively devoted to originally introduce a *prasaṅga*- and a *tantra*- interpretation of Patañjali's proposal.

D1.37 ll. 5-11: *dvāv arthau gatāḥ dvigatāḥ. hetavaḥ kāryanirvṛttau samarthāḥ. iha loke eka eva hetur dvayor arthayoḥ prasādhako dṛṣṭaḥ. ekam udakam. tadviṣayā kriyā tyāgalakṣaṇā āmramūle kṛtā pitṛtarpaṇe druseke ca sama eko hetuḥ. anyatra tad evodakaṃ na dvigataṃ bhavati yadā devadattayajñadattau tarpayitavyau bhavataḥ. āmrā api viprakṛṣṭadeśāt sektavyā bhavanti. tatra yathaivodakadānaṃ dṛṣṭam adṛṣṭārthaṃ sādhayituṃ samartham ity evaṃ buddhyā prakramya pravartamānam ubhayaṃ niṣpādayati evaṃ gargādibidādipāṭhaḥ samarthaḥ ubhayaṃ kartum avayavān samudāyaṃ ca kārye pravartamāna iti.*
dvigata are [things] reaching two objects. *hetu* are [things] capable of bringing about effects. In this world it happens that one single cause (*hetu*) is seen to accomplish two goals. The water is only one. The action having this object (the water) and characterized by renunciation, once performed on the root of a mango tree, it constitutes a single cause which is the same both for satisfying the *pitṛ*s and for watering the trees. In other cases this water is certainly not reaching two objects, [for instance] when Devadatta and Yajñadatta have to be satisfied (and each needs his own amount of water) and mango trees also have to be watered because of [a cause being in] a distant place.[82] In this case (that of mango trees and *pitṛ*s being simultaneously satisfied), in the way that the offering of water brings about both things which

prāsaṅgikam idam kāryam idaṃ tantreṇa labhyate. idam āvṛttibhedābhyām atra bādhasamuccayau, 'The operation which is *prāsaṅgika*, that which is obtained through *tantra*, that which [is obtained] through repetition and distinction: here, there is exclusion and combination.'

[82] The text is unclear. A possible suggestion is that the speaker refers here to the case of Devadatta and Yajñadatta and proposes to interpret the case of mango trees and *pitṛ*s in the same way, insofar as both mango trees and *pitṛ*s need their own water and mango trees cannot be satisfied through the water being in a "distant place", i.e., next to the *pitṛ*s. The *siddhāntin* replies that in this case mango trees and *pitṛ*s may be simultaneously satisfied. This is made easier because mango trees and *pitṛ*s pertain to two different cognitive levels of reality, namely the perceptible- and the non-perceptible one.

> take place – provided that one proceeds keeping in mind that the perceptible offering of water is capable of accomplishing a non perceptible goal – in the same way the recitation of the Gargādi and Bidādi *gaṇa*s is capable of realizing both parts and whole, when their operational effect takes place.

With regard to our hypothesis on the possible presence of some strategical anticipations of *prasaṅga*-details, it is noteworthy that the action (*kriyā*) of pouring water is the only recognized cause which attains the two mentioned goals, i.e., both satisfying the *pitṛ*s and watering the trees. By contrast, no role is played directly by the water element, and any personal interest of the performer is explicitly denied, thus making it clear that he is not the one for the sake of whom the action has been undertaken (*kriyā tyāgalakṣaṇā*). In this regard, the Devadatta and Yajñadatta's case is of course quite different.

The second part focuses on the *prasaṅga*-interpretation of the same M example of the mango trees, which are described as the only *prayojaka*s of the action. They prompt the action, but not in a centralised way, so that it could be simultaneously extended to the *pitṛ*s. The latter take advantage of a mere associative mechanism.

> Or the establishment of the goal is characterised by an automatic involvement (*prasaṅga*). If [something] attains a goal through something else, while not prompting the attainment of that goal, it is called *prasaṅga*. For example, one who desires [food] is a promoter for the [obtainment of] food but he is not a promoter for the putting [of the saucepan] on the fire, like one who eats leftovers [and hence does not prompt the usage of fire]. [...] In the same way, the mango trees prompt the watering separately (i.e., on their own); the *pitṛ*s do not prompt anything. In their case, they experience the offering of water, which is prompted [by the mango trees], by means of *prasaṅga*. (Similarly, the teaching regarding the vowels does not prompt the utterance of the *gaṇa*s, it is only entailed in it).[83]

Afterwards, D 1.37 l. 17-38 l. 1 introduces the *tantra*-principle while commenting on the second M passage quoted above (M 1.14 l. 14 *ad* vt. 18), the more linguistically oriented one, according to which 'there are sentences which are double-aimed'. The comparison with the *prasaṅga*-pattern is apparent.

Next, through the lamp-image, Bhartṛhari seems to go further in suggesting two different patterns of a simultaneous central-

[83] *atha vā prasaṅgalakṣaṇārthasiddhiḥ. yady arthāprayojako 'nyadvāreṇārthaṃ pratipadyate sa prasaṅga ity ucyate. yathā bhojanenārthī yaḥ prayojako 'dhiśrayaṇasya ca vighasāśivad aprayojakaḥ.* [...] *evam āmrāḥ pṛthak sekasya prayojakāḥ pitaro 'prayojakāḥ. tatra prayuktam udakadānaṃ prasaṅgenānubhavantīti* (ll. 11-6).

ised application (*tantra*) of signification. The illuminating function of a single lamp can be extended to more than one person or to more than one exigency of the same user. Similarly, the same linguistic unit (e.g., *śveto dhāvati*) pronounced by a single speaker can convey the same meaning to more than one listener and more than one meaning to a single listener. It is noteworthy that this multiple communication occurs independently of the speaker's intention. The word X, e.g., is used to convey the meaning Y. Suppose that X ends up conveying meanings which are connected with Y, but different from it. VP 2.298-299 compares it with a lamp (*dīpa*) which through proximity (*sānnidhya*) reveals in an object (e.g., a jar) elements other than that for the illumination of which it had been originally employed (*prayuj-*). The final effect of *tantra* on linguistic units is described as a sort of process of multiplying the single utterance of a speaker, which ends up producing more than one utterance.

Bhartṛhari concludes that the *gaṇas* make both wholes and parts known, exactly by relying on the *tantra*-device (D 1.38 l. 1 *ad* vt. 18: *tasmād ihāpi gargādibidādipāṭhas tantrābhyupāyaḥ samudāyāvayavayoḥ pratipādaka iti*, 'Therefore the recitation of the *gaṇas* Gargādi and Bidādi here assisted by the *tantra*-device causes [listeners] to understand both wholes and parts'). The extension of this reflection and the remarkable concurrence of VP passages closely comparable to this D text, seem to suggest that Bhartṛhhari cherished this topic indeed. The close comparison with the commented text of Patañjali unequivocally shows the distance between the two grammarians regarding the supposed descriptive and operative pair of *prasaṅga*- and *tantra*-patterns. In fact, Bhartṛhari

1. mentions both terms side by side
2. explicitly opposes them as two well-known different mechanisms of rule-extension
3. explains their relevant peculiar features by introducing both – broadly speaking – ritual examples and linguistic ones, with reference to both polysemous words and sentences which can be segmented in more than one way

It is not unlikely that these steps in the grammatical tradition derive from the Mīmāṃsā tradition, maybe from Bhavadāsa's work (Bronkhorst 1986, p. 79; Bronkhorst 1989, p. 112), which is lost but must have been known to Bhartṛhari, who on the contrary was not acquainted with the ŚBh. By contrast, if we evaluate the great effort and the recurring attention paid to the *prasaṅga*-mechanism and, in a completely independent way, to the *tantra*-concept by Patañjali, we are not able to exclude that such steps in the history of these two specific principles of rule-extension might have been an original achievement slowly accomplished by the grammatical tradition. Nevertheless, a thorough extraneousness of grammatical and ritual-mīmāṃsaka tradition is absolutely not plausible.

4.1.2 *Śabara and the verse on* tantra *and* prasaṅga

It is now time to return to the verse (mentioned above), which Śabara quotes from a former scholar. Śabara starts his investigation on *tantra* (at the beginning of his commentary on MS 11.1.1) as follows:

> That which is done once and helps many, is called *tantra*. For instance, a light done in the middle of many Brahmins. What helps through [its] repetition, is *āvāpa*, like the anointing with oil of those same Brahmins (which has to be done to each of them in order for each to benefit from it). [Scholars] mention (*udāhṛ-*) a verse as an illustration.[84]

Immediately thereafter:

> *sādhāraṇaṃ bhavet tantraṃ parārthe tv aprayojakaḥ |*
> *evam eva prasaṅgaḥ syād vidyamāne svake vidhau ||*[85]

As already hinted, this verse proves that Śabara had a further source. *sādhāraṇa* is used in regard to *tantra* also in the MS[86] and *parārtha* seems to be a technical term already in the MS.[87] Moreover, Śabara introduces the verse as 'exemplifying' (*udāhṛ-*), that is, he seems to imply that the verse summarises a lore about *tantra*. Hence, possibly a sort of common agreement about the essential characters of *tantra* and *prasaṅga* was already arising among Mīmāṃsakas and/ or *yājñikas* before Śabara. Nonetheless, Śabara's interpretation of the verse is far from plain and testifies

[84] *yat sakṛt kṛtaṃ bahūnām upakaroti tat tantram ity ucyate. yathā, bahūnāṃ brāhmaṇānām madhye kṛtaḥ pradīpaḥ. yas tv āvṛttyopakaroti sa āvāpaḥ. yathā, teṣām eva brahmaṇānām anulepanam. ślokam apy udāharanti.*

[85] Possibly: 'The *tantra* must be what is common [to more than one rite], by contrast the *prasaṅga*, though similar, does not promote [the assistance which then helps the rite], since it has a different purpose, [and] it occurs only when there is its own prescription', but the translation is controversial, see immediately below.

[86] Consider the sequence *svarus tantrāpavargaḥ syād asvakālatvāt* (11.3.8) and *sādhāraṇe vā 'nuniṣpattis tasya sādhāraṇatvāt* (11.3.9). The two *sūtras* discuss whether the *svaru* should be only one (*sādhāraṇa*) or not.

[87] See MS 11.1.4 (*śeṣasya hi parārthatvād vidhānāt pratipradhānabhāvaḥ syāt*) where *parārthatva* represents the feature of a subsidiary rite, which is subordinate to a main rite, insofar as it aims at the object of this main rite. See also MS 11.2.6 (*śrutiś caiṣāṃ pradhānavat karmaśruteḥ parārthatvāt*).

to the possible presence of disagreement about how the distinction between *tantra* and *prasaṅga* was to be understood.

Commenting on the verse, Śabara writes:

> ***tantra* must be what is common**, its meaning has already been stated [before the verse]. **By contrast, it does not promote, being for another purpose**: what arises for a certain purpose and while being performed for that very purpose, helps another [rite], this is not its promoter. For instance, the slaughter of the [sacrificed] animal, occurring for the sake of the sacrifice and being performed just for that purpose, also helps the acts of [getting rid of] blood and dung [which are not the promoters of the slaughter]. ***prasaṅga* must be just the same thing**. This is, by contrast, [their] difference: **when there is its own prescription**. Even if another prescription regarding it (auxiliary function to which *prasaṅga* applies) is available, the [auxiliary function] is not made [again] through [that] other prescription, since its purpose is [already] accomplished. For instance, the fore-sacrifices are acquired [as something to be done] both through the injunction of the [sacrificial] animal and [through that] of the animal rice-cake. However, once they are done only for the sake of the animal, they [also] help the animal rice-cake. Hence, they are not made again for the sake of the latter.[88]

In his commentary, Śabara takes *aprayojakaḥ* as a noun and accords it with *tantram*, although at first sight one might be inclined to think of it as an adjective referring to *prasaṅgaḥ*. Kumārila's commentary does not comment on this passage of the ŚBh, nor could we find any other Mīmāṃsā text dealing with it.[89]

However, Bronkhorst (1986) notes that the interpretation of *aprayojakaḥ* as a noun referring to *tantra* instead of an adjective referring to *prasaṅga* is far-fetched. He would prefer the following translation of the *pāda*s bc:

> *Prasaṅga*, on the other hand, is just like [*Tantra*] (*evam eva*), while not aiming at the other object.

[88] *sādhāraṇaṃ bhavet tantram ity uktārtham. parārthe tv aprayojaka iti. yaḥ parārtham utpannas tadartham eva cānuṣṭhīyamānaḥ parasyopakaroti, sa parastasyāprayojakaḥ. yathā, paśvālambho yāgārtham utpannas tadartham eva cānuṣṭhīyamāno lohitaśakṛtkarmaṇor apy upakarotīti. evam eva prasaṅgaḥ syāt. ayaṃ tu viśeṣaḥ. vidyamāne svake vidhāv iti. yady apy asyānyo vidhir vidyate, paravidhinā tu kṛtārthatvān na kriyate. yathā, prayājāḥ paśor api codakena prāptāḥ paśupuroḍāśasyāpi. paśvarthā eva tu kṛtāḥ paśupuroḍāśasyopakurvantīti na punas tadarthaṃ kriyante.*

[89] The MS uses *prayojakatva* and not *prayojaka* alone as a substantive, see MS 11.3.40 (*utpattir vā prayojakatvād āśiravat*, [11.3.39 in Jhā's translation]) where *prayojakatva* refers to the fact of being the cause, i.e., the promoter, the element prompting a rite.

He then adds:

> In this way, the lines agree perfectly with our understanding of *Prasaṅga*. The light in the house is just like the light amongst the Brahmins in that it lightens its different objects, viz. the inside of the house as well as the road outside. The essential difference is that the light in the house 'does not aim at the other object', i.e., it is not meant to lighten the road. (Bronkhorst 1986, p. 78)

Bronkhorst's interpretation is probably based on Bhartṛhari, who describes *prasaṅga* alone as *aprayojaka*:[90]

> *yady arthāprayojako 'nyadvāreṇārthaṃ pratipadyate sa prasaṅga ity ucyate.*
>
> If [something], while not aiming at an object, attains [that] object through something else, that is called *prasaṅga*. (D 14b 4-5, quoted and translated in Bronkhorst 1986, p. 79)

Note that *prayojaka* is here translated as 'aiming at', whereas Śabara seems to presuppose the meaning 'instigating' (used also by Bronkhorst, while translating a later passage by Bhartṛhari, Bronkhorst 1986, p. 80).

To sum up, we could either think that Śabara deliberately altered the meaning of the verse, possibly for fear that *tantra* might be interpreted as capable of promoting a ritual, and inserted it therefore in a context where *aprayojaka* referred to the promotion of further rituals, or that Bhartṛhari stressed an aspect of *prasaṅga* as central, although this might also be applied to *tantra*. An inquiry into the other instances of *a/ prayojaka* in MS and ŚBh (such as *prayojakatvād ekasmāt kriyerañ cheṣasya guṇabhūtatvāt*, MS 3.4.42) shows that they all seem to hint at the capability of a ritual element to promote something else. Furthermore, this uncertainty, does not alter our understanding of *tantra* and *prasaṅga*, which both do not promote the undertaking of a ritual.

4.1.2.1 aprayojaka

Such a ritual background of the verbal stem *prayuj-* also shows that *aprayojaka* has nothing to do with a subject's intention. It rather refers to the structural hierarchy of elements within a ritual (and, accordingly, to whatever can be described through a similar pattern).[91] The inadequacy of the concept of intentional-

[90] For our interpretation of this passage, see above, § 4.1.1.
[91] On intentionality as the main target of *tantra*, see Bronkhorst 1986, p. 78:

ity in regard to *tantra* is further clear, if one takes into account the context of the passages on *tantra* and *prasaṅga* in Patañjali and Bhartṛhari (about which see above and Pontillo 2008, pp. 91-3). For instance, Bhartṛhari adds that the lamp is not necessarily needed by all Brahmans (D I p. 37 ll. 21-4 *ad* vt. 18).

5 *Conclusions*

1. Śrautasūtra, Mīmāṃsā and Vyākaraṇa often share the same technical terms. It is however impossible to detect a single direction of borrowing/ influence. Hence, rather than uni-directional borrowings, a common prehistory should be postulated. Further studies are likely to show the inclusion of Dharmaśāstra in the same prehistory.
2. The texts examined so far do not speak of the "disappearance" of something. They rather explain the absence of something in such a spatial way, as the blank cell in a grid (representing the ritual space), whose blank value can be substituted through something else (see Kahrs 1998). An absence can be filled, i.e., a blank cell can be substituted by something else, in various ways, namely through *tantra*, *prasaṅga*, *atideśa*, *pratinidhi*, etc. All of them extend an element, which is already present in another place of the grid, to the blank cell.
3. *tantra* and *prasaṅga* refer to two different models of multiple application. *tantra* presupposes a common texture, of which all elements benefit. *prasaṅga*, on the other hand, represents an extended application, to be carried out if it makes things easier and if needed. It is available by default and without further requirements. Unlike in the case of analogical extension, it does not need a structural connection between two rites.

Abbreviations

A	*Aṣṭādhyāyī* – Sharma 1987-2003
ĀpDhSū	*Āpastambadharmasūtra* – Olivelle 2000
ĀpŚrSū	*Āpastambaśrautasūtra* – Thite 2004
ĀsvŚrSū	*Āśvalāyanaśrautasūtra* – Vidyāratna 1864-1874
AV	*Atharvaveda* – Vishva Bandhu 1960-1962

'In the case of *tantra* the multiple function is intentional' and Pandurangi 2006, p. 221: 'However, if the application of the auxiliaries to many is intentional, it is *tantra*'.

BaudhŚrSū	*Baudhāyanaśrautasūtra* – Kashikar 2003b
BhŚrSū	*Bhāradvājaśrautasūtra* – Kashikar 2003a
BṛĀrUp	*Bṛhadāraṇyakopaniṣad* – Olivelle 1998
D	*Dīpikā* (on the M) – Bronkhorst 1987
GDhSū	*Gautamadharmasūtra* – Olivelle 2000
GṛSū	Gṛhyasūtra
KātyŚrSū	*Kātyāyanaśrautasūtra* – Thite 2006
LāṭyŚrSū	*Lāṭyāyanaśrautasūtra* – Ranade 1978
M	*Mahābhāṣya* – Kielhorn 1880-1885
MB	*Mahābhārata* – Sukthankar, Belvalkar, Vaidya 1966
MDhŚā	*Mānavadharmaśāstra* – Jhā 1999
MNP	*Mīmāṃsānyāyaprakāśa* – Edgerton 1929
MNS	*Mīmāṃsānyāyasaṅgraha* – Benson 2010
MS	*Mīmāṃsāsūtra* – Abhyankar, Jośi 1970-1976
Nāgeśa's PBh	Nāgeśa's *Paribhāṣenduśekhara* – Abhyankar 1960-1962
PBh	*paribhāṣā*, metarule
PP	*pūrvapakṣin*, objector
S	*siddhāntin*, upholder of the final view
ŚB	*Śatapathabrāhmaṇa* – Weber 1855
ŚBh	*Śābarabhāṣya* – Abhyankar, Jośi 1970-1976
ŚŚrSū	*Śāṅkhāyanaśrautasūtra* – Caland 1953
ŚrSū	Śrautasūtra
sū.	*sūtra*
vt.	Kātyāyana's *vārttika* in M
Vyāḍi's PBh	– Wujastyk 1993

References

Abhyankar, Kashinath Vasudev, ed. (2001). *The Paribhāṣenduśekhara of Nāgojībhaṭṭa.* Edited and explained by Franz Kielhorn. Part II: Translation and Notes. 2nd (1st ed. 1960). Poona: Bhandarkar Oriental Research Institute.

Abhyankar, Kashinath Vasudev and Ganesasastri Ambadasa Jośī, eds. (1970). *Śrīmajjaiminipraṇite Mīmāṃsādarśane: Mīmāṃsākakaṇṭhīrava-Kumārilabhaṭṭapraṇita-Tantravārtikasahita-Śābarabhāsyopetaḥ.* Pune: Anandasrama.

Basu, Benjamin David, ed. (1923-1925). *Mīmāṃsāsūtra.* Sacred Books of the Hindus 27. Allahabad.

Benson, James (1990). *Patañjali's Remarks on* aṅga. South Asian Studies Series. Delhi: Oxford University Press.

Benson, James, ed. (2010). *Mīmāṃsānyāyasaṅgraha. A Compendium on the Principles of Mīmāṃsā,* edited and translated by James Benson. Wiesbaden: Harrassowitz.

Bodewitz, H.W. (1984). "Review of Egon Brucker's Die spätvedische Kulturepoche nach den Quellen der Śrauta-, Gṛhya-

und Dharmasūtras. Der Siedlungsraum". In: *Indo-Iranian Journal* 27, No. 3, pp. 207-210.
Bronkhorst, Johannes (1986). "*tantra* and *prasaṅga*". In: *Aligarh Journal of Oriental Studies* III.2, pp. 77-80.
Bronkhorst, Johannes, ed. (1987). *Mahābhāshya-Dīpikā of Bhartṛhari*, Fascicule IV, Āhnika I. Critically edited. Poona: Bhandarkar Oriental Research Institute.
Bronkhorst, Johannes (1989). "Bhartṛhari and Mīmāṃsā". In: *Studien zur Indologie und Iranistik* 15, pp. 101-17.
Brucker, Egon (1980). *Die spätvedische Kulturepoche nach den Quellen der Śrauta-, Gṛhya- und Dharmasātras: der Siedlungsraum.* Wiesbaden: Steiner.
Caland, Willem (1953). *Śāṅkhayana-śrautasutra, Being a Major yajñika Text of the Rgveda.* Translated into English for the first time by W. Caland. Edited with an introduction by Lokesh Chandra. Ed. by Lokesh Chandra. Nagpur: International Academy of Indian Culture.
Candotti, Maria Piera and Tiziana Pontillo (2012). "The Earlier Pāṇinian Tradition on the Imperceptible Sign". In: *Ancient India and Greece Reflections on Denotation in absentia.* Ed. by Maria Piera Candotti and Tiziana Pontillo. London: Anthem.
Cardona, George (1967). "Negations in Pāṇinian Rules". In: *Language* 43.1, pp. 34-56.
Cardona, George (1997). *Pāṇini. His Work and its Traditions. Volume One. Background and Introduction.* 2nd ed. Delhi: Motilal Banarsidass.
Cardona, George (1999). *Recent Research in Pāṇinian Studies.* Delhi: Motilal Banarsidass.
Clements, George Nick (1982). "A Remark on the Elsewhere Condition". In: *Linguistic Inquiry* 13, No. 4, pp. 682-5.
Clooney, Francis X. (1990). *Thinking Ritually. Rediscovering the Pūrva Mīmāṃsā of Jaimini.* Wien: De Nobili.
Deshpande, Madhav M. (1991). "Prototypes in Pāṇinian Syntax". In: *Journal of the American Oriental Society* 111, No. 3, pp. 465-480.
Deshpande, Madhav M., ed. (1997). *Saunakīya Caturādhyāyikā: a Prātiśākhya of the Saunakīya Atharveda with Commentaries Caturādhyāyībhāṣya, Bhārgava-Bhāskara-Vṛtti and Pañcasandhi.* Harvard Oriental Series 52. Cambridge Mass.
Edgerton, Franklin (1929). *Mīmāṃsānyāyaprakāśa of Āpadeva. Introduction, Sanskrit Text, English Translation and Notes.* New Haven: Yale University Press
Filliozat, Pierre-Sylvain, ed. (1980). *Le Mahābhāṣya de Patañjali avec le Pradīpa de Kaiyaṭa et l'Uddyota de Nāgeśa, traduction II (Adhyāya 1 Pada 2).* Pondichéry: Institut Français d'Indologie.

Freschi, Elisa (2010). "Facing the Boundaries of Epistemology: Kumārila on Error and Negative Cognition". In: *Journal of Indian Philosophy* 38, No. 1, pp. 39-48.

Freschi, Elisa and Tiziana Pontillo (forthcoming). *Rule-extension-strategies: Śrautasūtra, Mīmāṃsā and Grammar on tantra- and prasaṅga- principles.*

Göhler, Lars (2011). *Reflexion und Ritual in der Pūrvamīmāṃsā. Studie zur frühen Geschichte der Philosophie in Indien.* Beiträge zur Indologie 44. Wiesbaden: Harrassowitz.

Gonda, Jan (1977). *The Ritual Sūtras.* Vol. I. *A History of Indian Literature* edited by Jan Gonda 2. Wiesbaden: Otto Harrassowitz.

Gonda, Jan (1980). *Vedic Ritual: the Non-solemn Rites.* Handbuch der Orientalistik : Abt. 2, Indien: Bd 4, Religionen 1. Leiden [u.a.]: Brill. 54

Ikari, Yasuke (1969). "A Study on the Upaniṣadic Term *ādeśa*". In: *Indogaku Bukkyōgaku Kenkyū (Journal of Indian and Buddhist Studies)* 17, No. 2, pp. 684- 9.

Jhā, Gaṅgānātha, ed. (1933-34-36). *Shabara-bhasya, Translated into English, Index by Umesha Mishra.* Baroda: Oriental Institute.

Jhā, Gaṅgānātha, ed. (1999). *Manusmṛti. With the 'Manubhāṣya' of Medhatīti.* English Translation. 2nd ed. (1st Calcutta 1920-1939). Delhi: Motilal Banarsidass.

Jhā, Gaṅgānātha and Umesha Mishra (1964). *Purva-Mimamsa in its Sources.* Library of Indian philosophy and religion 1. Varanasi.

Joshi, Shivram Dattatray, ed. (1968). *Patañjali's Vyākaraṇa-Mahābhāṣya Samarthâhnika.* Poona: University of Poona.

Joshi, Shivram Dattatray and Jouthe Anthon Fokko Roodbergen, eds. (1974). *Patañjali's Vyākaraṇa-Mahābhāṣya. Bahuvrīhi-dvandvāhnika (P 2.2.23-2.2.38). Text, Translation and Notes.* Poona: Publications of the Centre of Advanced Study in Sanskrit.

Joshi, Shivram Dattatray and Jouthe Anthon Fokko Roodbergen, eds. (1975). *Patañjali's Vyākaraṇa-Mahābhāṣya. Kārakāhnika (P. 1.4.23-1.4.55), Introduction, Translation and Notes.* Class C 10. Poona: Publications of the Centre of Advanced Study in Sanskrit.

Joshi, Shivram Dattatray and Jouthe Anthon Fokko Roodbergen, eds. (1986). *Patañjali's Vyākaraṇa-Mahābhāṣya. Paspaśāhnika, Introduction, Text, Translation and Notes.* Publications of the Centre of Advanced Study in Sanskrit Class C 7. Poona.

Kahrs, Eivind (1998). *Indian Semantic Analysis : the Nirvacana Tradition.* Cambridge, U.K.; New York: Cambridge University Press.

Kashikar, Chintaman Ganesh, ed. (2003a). *Sūtras of Bhāradvāja. Critically Edited and Translated.* Vol. 2. Poona: Vaidika Samsodhana Mandala.

Kashikar, Chintaman Ganesh, ed. (2003b). *The Baudhayana Srautasutra.* New Delhi: Indira Gandhi National Centre for the Arts; Motilal Banarsidass Publishers.

Kielhorn, Franz, ed. (1880-1885). *The Vyākarana-Mahābhāshya of Patañjali*, 3 vols. Bombay.

Kielhorn, Franz (1887). "Some Devices of Indian Grammarians". In: *Indian Antiquary* 16, pp. 244-252.

Kiparsky, Paul. "'Elsewhere' in Phonology". In: *A Festschrift for Morris Halle.* Ed. by S.R. Anderson and Paul Kiparsky. New York: Holt, Rinehart and Winston, pp. 93-106.

Kiparsky, Paul (1979). *Pāṇini as a Variationist.* Ed. by S.D. Joshi. Cambridge, Mass. and Pune: MIT Press and Centre of Advanced Study in Sanskrit, University of Poona.

Lazzeroni, Romano (1997). "La transitività come categoria linguistica. I nomi d'azione indoeuropei". In: *Incontri Linguistici* 20, pp. 71-82.

Liebich, Bruno (1919-1920). *Zur Einführung in die indische einheimische Sprach-wissenschaft, I. Das Kātantra* [1919]; *II. Historische Einführung und Dhātupāṭha* [1919]; *III. Der Dhātupāṭha* [1920]; *IV. Analyse der Candra-Vṛtti* [1920]. Sitzungsberichte der Heidelberger Akademie der Wissenschaften, Philosophisch-historische Klasse 15. Heidelberg: Carl Winter's Universitäts- buchhandlung.

Mylius, Klaus, ed. (1994). *Āśvalāyana-Śrautasūtra. Erstmalig vollständig übersetzt, erläutert und mit Indices versehen.* Texte und Übersetzungen 3. Wichtrach: Inst. f. Indologie.

Olivelle, Patrick, ed. (1998). *The Early Upanisads. Annotated Text and Translation.* Oxford: Oxford University Press.

Olivelle, Patrick, ed. (2000). *Dharmasūtras. The Law Codes of Āpastamba, Gautama, Baudhāyana and Vasiṣṭha, Annotated Text and Translation.* Delhi.

Pandit, M.D. (1990). *Zero in Pāṇini.* 12. Poona: Publications of the Centre of Advanced Study in Sanskrit class B.

Pandurangi, Krishnacharya Tamanachary, ed. (2006). *Pūrvamīmāṃsā from an Interdisciplinary Point of View.* New Delhi: Centre for Studies in Civilizations.

Paranjpe, Vasudev Gopal (1922). *Le Vârtika de Kâtyâyana: une étude du style, du vocabulaire et des postulats philosophiques.* Heidelberg.

Parpola, Asko (1994). "On the Formation of the Mīmāṃsā and the Problems Concerning Jaimini with Particular Reference to the Teacher Quotations and the Vedic Schools (Part II)". In: *Wiener Zeitschrift für die Kunde Südasiens* XXXVIII, pp. 293-308.

Parpola, Asko (2011). "Codification of Vedic Domestic Ritual in Kerala: *Pārvaṇa-sthālīpāka* – the model of rites with fire-offerings – in *Jaiminīya-Gṛhya* 1,1-4 and in the Malayāḷam

Manual of the *Sāmaveda* Nampūtiri Brahmins of Kerala, the *Sāma-Smārta-Caṭṭaṅṅu*". In: *Le Veda-Vedāṅga et l'Avesta entre oralité et écriture. Veda, Vedāṅga and Avesta between orality and writing.* Ed. by Julieta Rotaru and Jan E.M. Houben. Vol. III. Bucarest: Biblioteca metropolitana Bucuresti, pp. 261-354.

Pathak, Shridharashastri and Siddheshvarshastri Chitrao (1935). *Word index to Pāṇini-Sūtra-pāṭha and Pariśiṣṭas.* 2nd (1st ed. 1927). Poona: Bhandarkar Oriental Research Institute.

Pontillo, Tiziana (1999). "Allomorfi e morfema "zeromorfi" in Pāṇini: sostituzione di morfemi con zero fonico". "Dottorato in Glottologia e Filologia" XII Ciclo 1996-1999. Italy: Faculty of Arts and Humanities of the University of Milan.

Pontillo, Tiziana (2000 [2003]). "Morfi "zeromorfi" in Pāṇini: un'introduzione alle regole specifiche di formazione con zero fonologico nella posizione di dati morfemi". In: *AIΩN. Sez. Linguistica* 22, pp. 129-84.

Pontillo, Tiziana (2002). "La prima ricezione del modello morfologico di Pāṇini nella linguistica occidentale: il caso dello zero". In: *Idee e parole. Universi concettuali e metalinguistici.* Ed. by V. Orioles. Vol. 3. "Lingue, linguaggi, metalinguaggio". Roma: Il Calamo, pp. 535-87.

Pontillo, Tiziana (2003 [2004]). "Il prototipo e le regole specifiche della letteratura rituale come modello della tecnica di sostituzione di Pāṇini: il verbo *lup-* e il sostantivo *lopa-* nei *Kalpa-Sūtra.*" In: *Annali della Facoltà di Lettere e Filosofia dell'Università degli Studi di Cagliari,* n.s. XXI, LVIII, pp. 5-42.

Pontillo, Tiziana (2008). "The Edible Part of the Rice in the *Mahābhāṣya* Imagery: what are the husks of rules? What is *a-tantram*?". In: *Pandanus.* Ed. by Jaroslav Vacek, pp. 79-96.

Radicchi, Anna (1985-1988). *La teoria pāṇiniana dei Samāsa secondo l'interpretazione delle scuole grammaticali indiane dal quinto all'ottavo secolo d.C.* Firenze: Elite.

Ranade, Hari Govind, ed. (1978). *Kātyāyana Śrauta Sūtra: Rules for the Vedic Sacrifices.* Translated into English. Pune.

Saussure, Ferdinand de (1879 [1878]). *Mémoire sur le système primitif des voyelles dans les langues indo-européennes.* 1st ed. (2nd in Recueil des publications scientifiques de F. de Saussure, Heidelberg 1922). Leipzig.

Scharfe, H. (1961). *Die Logik im Mahābhāṣya.* Berlin: Akademie Verlag.

Sharma, R.N., ed. (1987-2003). *The Aṣṭādhyāyī of Pāṇini.* Vols. 6. New Delhi: Motilal Banarsidass.

Silburn, Lilian (1955). *Instant et cause : le discontinu dans la pensée philosophique de l'Inde.* Paris: J. Vrin.

Staal, Frits, ed. (1972). *A Reader on the Sanskrit Grammarians*. MIT Press.

Stenzler, Adolf Friedrich, ed. (1876). *The Institutes of Gautama (Śrīgautamadharmaśāstram)*. London: Trübner.

Sukthankar, Vishnu Sitaram, Shripad Krishna Belvalkar, and Parashuram Lakshman Vaidya, eds. (1933-1971). *The Mahābhārata*. Vols. 19 Poona.

Thieme, Paul (1968). "*Ādeśa*". In: *Mélanges d'Indianisme à la mémoire de L. Rénou*. Vol. VIII. Publications de l'Institut de Civilisation Indienne 28. Paris: De Boccard, pp. 715-23.

Thieme, Paul (1971). "Buchbesprechung von: *L. Renou, Terminologie grammaticale du sanskrit, Paris 1957*". In: *Kleine Schriften*. Ed. by G. Buddruss. 2nd (1st ed. 1958 in *Göttingische Gelehrte Anzeigen* 212, pp. 19-49). Vol. II. Wiesbaden, pp. 727-57.

Thite, Ganesh Umakant, ed. (2004). *Āpastamba Śrauta Sūtra. Text with English Translation and Notes*. Delhi: New Bharatiya Book Corp.

Thite, Ganesh Umakant, ed. (2006). *Kātyāyana-śrautasūtra: Text with English Translation and Notes*. Delhi: New Bharatiya Book Co.

Vidyāratna, Rāmanārāyaṇa, ed. (1864-1874). *The Śrauta Sūtra of Āśvalāyana, with the comm. of Gārgya Nārāyaṇa*. Bibliotheca Indica 49. Calcutta.

Vishva Bandhu, ed. (1961). *Atharvaveda (Śaunaka) with the Padapāṭha and Sāyaṇācārya's Commentary*. Hoshiarpur: Vishveshvaranand Vedic Research Institute.

Weber, Albrecht, ed. (1859). *Çrauta-Sūtra of Kātyāyana: With Extracts from the Commentaries of Karka and Yājñikadeva. Vājasaneyi Saṃhitā*. Berlin: Ferd. Dümmler.

Weber, Albrecht, ed. (1964). *The Śatapatha-Brāhmana in the Mādhyandina-śākhā with Extracts from the Commentaries of Sāyaṇa, Harisvāmin and Dvivedagaṅga*. 2nd (1st ed. 1885). Chowkhamba.

Wezler, Albrecht (1972). "Marginalien zu Pāṇini's Aṣṭādhyāyī I *sthānin*". In: *Zeitschrift für Vergleichende Sprachforschung* 86, pp. 13-8.

Wezler, Albrecht (1986). "Zum Verständnis des Bhaṣya zu Pāṇini 3.3.18 (Studien zu Patañjali's Mahābhāṣya II)". In: *Wiener Zeitschrift für die Kunde Südasiens Archiv für Indische Philosophie* 30, pp. 91-108.

Wicher, Irene (2008). *'Zero' in the Aṣṭādhyāyī*. New Delhi: Aditya Prakashan. 57

Wujastyk, Dominik, ed. (1993). *Metarules of Pāṇinian Grammar. Vyāḍi's Paribhāṣāvṛtti. Critically Edited with Translation and Commentary*. Vol. V. Groningen Oriental Studies. Groningen.

Maria Piera Candotti and Tiziana Pontillo

*The Earlier Pāṇinian Tradition on the Imperceptible Sign**

Ø. Introduction

The reflection on whether and on what grounds the absence of a sign turns out to be as just significant as the sign itself inevitably leads, in the linguistic field, to concentrating one's attention on the heterogeneous set of linguistic phenomena which modern linguistics generally refers to with the term 'zero'. Examples are easily found in many languages, such as in Engl. *sheep* (sing.) vs. *sheep* (pl.); *cut* (present) vs. *cut* (past)[1] or, even more interesting, as it involves a transcategorisation, *cheat* (noun) vs. *cheat* (verb).[2] In all these and many other examples the 'absence of an otherwise necessary sign' to stay with Whitney's words may be recognised either through analogical reasoning (which allows one to postulate for example the necessity of an *s* to mark the morphological function of plural as in *brook* vs. *brooks* etc.) or through opposition which highlights the morphological role of some absences of sign like in Czech *žena* 'woman' (nom.sg.), *ženy* 'women' (nom. pl.) opposed to *žen* 'of women' (< asl. *ženu*).[3]

* All translations are by the authors, unless explicitly stated. This paper is the result of a joint work entirely discussed and shared by both authors. However, Maria Piera Candotti is responsible for §§ 0; 1.1.3; 1.4.2; 2; 3.2; 4.2; Tiziana Pontillo for §§ 1.1; 1.1.1-2; 1.2-4; 1.4.1; 3; 3.1; 3.3-4; 4.1; 4.3. Many thanks are due to Pandit Anjaneya Sarma of the EFEO in Pondicherry (École Française d'Extrême Orient), who in January 2010 led us in reading the more recent tradition of the rule *adarśanam lopaḥ*.

[1] Examples taken from Bloomfield 1933, § 13.7, pp. 215-8.

[2] Kastovsky 1969, p. 8.

[3] Example taken from CLG, p. 123 who comments: 'On voit donc qu'un

Similar phenomena have also been taken into account in the first Sanskrit grammar ever written, the *Aṣṭādhyāyī* of Pāṇini (4th c. BC) in 239 rules involving the technical device of *lopa* lit. 'suppression, erasing'.[4] 212 of these rules are operative ones, of which 95 can be considered as teaching the zero of sounds (either a single sound or sequences of sounds), 117 the zero of morphs (either inflectional or derivative affixes), 1 rule the zero of an inflected word (*pada*), and 1 rule the zero of its, i.e. of the so-called 'markers' used by Pāṇini to connect some rules to some specific units.[5]

A short typological schema of relevant rules with some examples should suffice to show the kind of linguistic facts that are accounted for in these rules.

(1) Zero of sounds

(1a) zero of a single sound

A 6.1.66 *lopo vyor vali*, '*lopa* in the place of a *v* or *y* before a consonant sound except *y*.'
knūy- 'to be humid' (Ø of *y*) + *p* + *-aya-* + *-ti* → *knū-p-aya-ti* > *knopaya-ti* 'to wet'

(1b) zero of a sequence of sounds

A 6.4.142 *ti viṃśater ḍiti*, '*lopa* of *ti* of the <pre-affixal base> *viṃśati* <when it is a base of the type *bha*[6]> before affixes with the marker *Ḍ*.'
viṃśati 'twenty' (Ø of *ti*) + *-aka-*[7] → *viṃśaka-* 'bought by twenty [coins]'

As it can be seen in example 1b, these rules are not bound to be purely phonic: zeroed sounds may be targeted as selected parts of morphemes. These parts are therefore singled out whithin a unit which is endowed with boundaries and is aimed at

signe matériel n'est pas nécessaire pour exprimer une idée; la langue peut se contenter de l'opposition de quelque chose avec rien'.

[4] From here on we will use, according to the tradition, *lopa* as a cover term subsuming all the procedures accounted for through the technical terms *lopa, ślu, luk* and *lup*. The detailed survey of *lopa*-rules in the A is the subject of Pontillo 1999.

[5] Of the remaining 24 rules, 6 are metarules governing the specific treatment of different kinds of *lopa*. The other 16 rules involve *lopa* as a condition for applying some different operative rules.

[6] A preaffixal stem is called *bha*, following the definition rule given in A 1.4.18, before affixes beginning with *y* or with a vowel with the exception of flectional *sarvanāmasthāna* affixes.

[7] Taught in the abstract form *ḌvuN* in A 5.1.24.

expressing some specific meaning,[8] all features which currently are object of morphology.[9] Nevertheless, zeroing of sounds is not treated by Pāṇini differently than other kinds of zero: differences arise, as we have shown elsewhere[10], when it comes to deciding which rules to apply, or not to apply, to the zeroed units.

(2) Zero of morphs

Zero of morphs, in Pāṇini, amounts to zero of affixes (*pratyaya*), be them inflectional or derivational affixes, without distinction. In fact there is an important distinction that shapes the grammatical treatment of zero of morphs yet it is an altogether different one. It is grounded on rule A 1.1.61 *pratyayasya lukślulupaḥ* that introduces, besides the generic technical term *lopa*, the three specific terms *luK*, *Ślu* and *luP* subsequently grouped under the cover term *lumat* 'having *lu*-'. The reason for keeping these two classes distinct is taught by the two subsequent rules A 1.1.62 and 63, stating that, while in case of the *lopa* of an affix the rules conditioned by that affix will, as expected, still apply (A 1.1.62 *pratyayalope pratyayalakṣaṇam*)[11] this will not happen in the case of zero of the *luK*-, *Ślu*- and *luP*-type: A 1.1.63 *na lumatāṅgasya*, 'The affix which is subject to zero when it is termed with a name which contains *lu*- does not condition operations in the place of [a part of] the *aṅga* "pre-affixal base".' As a consequence, the real discrimen which is taken into account by Pāṇini with regard to the zero of morphs is this opposition between *lopa*s of affixes taught by means of *lumat*-terms (78X) showing no effect on their bases, or by means of the term *lopa* itself (39X).[12]

(2a) A 6.4.51 *ṇer aniṭi*, '<*lopa*> of the [causative affix] *Ṇi* when an *ārdhadhātuka* affix without the initial augment *i*- follows.'
ex. *kṛ*- + Ø of *ṆiC* + *LyuṬ* (= *ana*) + *ṬāP* → *kāraṇā* 'instigation'.

Consider how the *vṛddhi*-replacement determined by the affix *ṆiC* (according to the general rule A 7.3.84) is perceived even

[8] To the best of our knowledge, rules of type 1b (by far the commoner) never show a purely phonic context. On the other hand the type 1a is almost rare.

[9] This group of rules includes e.g. 8 cases of *lopa* of the *abhyāsa* (reduplication syllable).

[10] Cf. Candotti and Pontillo 2004.

[11] We consider A 1.1.62 as purely functional to the following restriction taught by A 1.1.63. In fact, as we will show later, the fact that rules pertaining to an affix are still valid even in the case of the zero-variants of that affix is already granted by the general rules on the transfer from substituends to substitutes (A 1.1.56-59). Cf. Candotti and Pontillo forthcoming.

[12] This latter class is almost uniquely represented by cases of *lopa* of suffixes consisting in one single sound (14X) or of fictitious suffixes (25X).

though this last unit is not perceptible. This is by contrast prohibited for the *lumat* kinds of zero:

(2b) A 4.3.163 *phale luk*, '*luK* <of an affix[13] introduced after a nominal stem ending in the sixth ending in the meaning of "modification [of that]", "part [of that]"> when it means a fruit.'
ex. *jambū-* 'the black plum tree' + Ø of *-a-* (*aÑ*) → *jambu-* 'the black plum fruit'.[14]

The effect of the affix *aÑ*, which elsewhere would be to trigger the *vṛddhi*-replacement of the final vowel of the presuffixal base (*aṅga*) taught by A 7.2.115, is blocked by A 1.1.63.

(2c) A 5.3.98 *luP manuṣye*, '*luP* <of the affix *kaN* introduced in the meaning of "similar to"> <as an epithet> for a man.'
ex. *cañcā-* 'puppet' + Ø of *-ka-* → *cañcā* 'the Puppet', said of a man acting like a puppet.

Even more interesting is the example 2c where there is perfect homophony between the derived noun and the noun included in the relevant formation-rule (this latter matching with its – so to say – etymological base).[15] The meaning of the derived nouns can be considered as a sort of metonymic usage of the basic noun.

(3) Zero of inflected words

There is only one rule teaching the zero-replacement of an inflected word:[16]

A 5.3.82 *ajināntasyottarapadalopaś ca*, '<The affix *kaN* is introduced after a nominal stem consisting of a personal name> and when it is co-occurring with the term *ajina* there is also *lopa* of the final member.'
ex. *vyāghra-* 'tiger' + Ø of *ajina-* 'skin'+ *ka-* → *vyāghraka-* 'poor "Tiger skin"'.

Three other rules A 8.1.45; 8.1.62; 8.1.63, though not teaching the zero of a whole word, nevertheless mention it – respectively the zero of *kiṃ*, of *ca* and *aha* and of all the particles of the *gaṇa cādi* – as a condition for several different operations,

[13] The genitive here, contrary to the preceding example, is supplied by the definition itself of *luK*, *luP* and *Ślu* as being taught of affixes (cf. A 1.1.61).

[14] Thanks to A 1.2.49 the *luK* of this affix also involves the *luK* of the feminine secondary affix of the derivational base.

[15] Here we follow Scharfe's (1965) interpretation of this kind of rules. Cf. Pontillo 2010.

[16] However Kātyāyana's *vārttikas* already extend the domain of *lopa* of an inflected word in composition well beyond the strict limits established by A 5.3.82.

(4) Zero of markers

A 1.3.9 *tasya lopaḥ* governs the interpretation of forms with markers, by teaching an unconditioned *lopa* (i.e., not restricted by means of some specified left or right context) of all the elements previously defined as *it* 'markers' (A 1.3.2-8). Markers are somehow suspended between existence and non existence because of this unconditional zeroing: no trace of markers remains directly in the form of the unit to which they are attached but the grammatical operations they recall are nevertheless applied where needed.[17]

By its extension and complexity *lopa* is a foundational device of Pāṇini's grammar and certainly one of its great achievements. The history of its interpretation by later tradition is yet to be written and may prove useful not only to gain important linguistic insights but also to unveil some philosophical concepts, first of all on how to think of absence, even in a linguistic context. This paper will focus on this last perspective, concentrating on the earlier authors of the pāṇinian tradition, namely Patañjali (2th c. BC) and Bhartṛhari (5th c. AD), thus tracing the first steps of this much longer history.

1 Framework of lopa *in the* Aṣṭādhyāyī*: An Analysis of the Rule A 1.1.60*

1.1 Pāṇini's teaching of lopa *as 'non-perception'* (adarśaṇa)

Pāṇini gives an explicit instruction on what is to be understood by the term *lopa* in his grammar, the metarule

A 1.1.60 *adarśanaṃ lopaḥ*, 'Non-perception is called *lopa*.'

Taken literally, the terms *darśana/ adarśana* should specifically refer to visual perception, but even though the faculty of hearing occupies a sovereign place in the context of the *Śruti* and consistently of the *Vedāṅga* traditions, the faculty of sight is often used as a generic name for all the sense faculties. Commentaries are unanimous in stating that the term is equivalent here to *anupalabdhi* 'the fact of not grasping/not comprehending', a classical expression in philosophical terminology.

1.1.1 Non-perception does not entail non-existence

The *Kāśikā* gives a series of more or less strict synonyms of the term that even goes far beyond this equivalence: *adarśanam*

[17] See Candotti and Pontillo 2012.

aśravaṇam anuccāraṇam anupalabdhir abhāvo varṇavināśa ity anarthāntaram, '*adarśaṇa* is not hearing, not pronouncing, not perceiving, not existing, the annihilation of a sound: there is no difference in meaning.' The *Padamañjarī* (*ad* A 1.1.60) explains this series as a way of assuring that *lopa* does not only teach the non-hearing (*aśravaṇa*) of a linguistic unit but also its not being uttered (*anuccāraṇa*) which is its counterpart from the point of view of the speaker. It is thus a 'non-perception' that involves all the parts at stake in a given communication act and that amounts to the absence of the zeroed units in certain conditions and contexts. By rules teaching *lopa* of linguistic units 'their (i.e. of the zeroed linguistic units) absence (*abhāva*) in some given context (*asmin viṣaye*) is explained; [those rules] do not teach not to pronounce (*an-uccāranam*) [the units which] are found [there].'[18] In other words, the term *lopa* targets an absence that is independent [from grammatical explanation]: *svābhāvika abhāva.*

It is this discussion that Nageśa probably had in mind when, commenting on the same rule, he resorted to an unorthodox and indeed only provisional Patañjali's re-definition of *lopa* as meaning 'non-existence/ absence' (*abhāva*),[19] in order to affirm straightforwardly that *adarśana* should be interpreted as meaning *abhāva.* The key point of Nāgeśa's suggestion is thus not to crudely equate non-perception and non-existence but rather to qualify non-perception as, to stay with the author's words, being concomitant with non-existence/absence.[20] That is, as pointing at an absence which that can be experienced in everyday language. This does not amount to making any assumption about the absolute existence or non-existence of what is not being perceived.

In fact it would be quite difficult to accept without further ado that the fact of not perceiving something is equivalent to its non-existence and early commentators were perfectly aware of this. Existent things or properties may remain unperceived because of some external condition such as darkness,[21] because

[18] PM 1.191 *ad* A 1.1.60: *asmin viṣaye tayor abhāva eva vyākhyāpito bhavati na hi vidyamānayor anuccāraṇam upapadyati.*

[19] See M. 1.356 l. 15-357 l. 11 *ad* A 1.4.110 vt. 1-3. The proposal is stated by Patañjali in the context of an utterly hypothetical interpretation of the technical term *avasāna* as meaning *abhāva* 'non existence', instead of *virāma* 'cessation' (of something that was there before). The proposed definition has the advantage of being co-extensive with a hypothetical definition of *lopa* as *abhāva* and thus one single technical term could account for both phenomena.

[20] U 1.478 *ad* A 1.1.59[=60] vt. 1: *adarśanaśabdena tatsamāniyato varṇābhāva evātreti bodhyam.*

[21] See, for example, M 1.411 ll. 11-2 *ad* A 2.2.6.

of tininess[22] or swift movement or even due to the (temporary) inactivity of the manifesting cause. Bhartṛhari's interpretation of an example given by Patañjali in order to justify the uniqueness of sounds is interesting in this last respect: where we think we perceive different sounds, separated by time or by other sounds (such as the two *a* different *a*-sounds in *daṇḍaḥ*) there could in fact be one single sound moving swiftly from one place to another like birds in a row.[23] Bhartṛhari explains the reasoning behind such an imaginative argument: 'that which you conceptualise as an interruption by time or other sounds it is not a real interruption. What is it, then? These two are the apprehension and non-apprehension [of the thing] due to the application and suspension of the manifesting cause. The manifesting cause of the sound *a* not being active when the cause of manifestation of another sound is active, does not make the sound *a* known but when it is active it does.'[24]

1.1.2 Pāṇini exploits the semantic ambiguity of the term (a)darśaṇa

Thus, from a purely conceptual point of view, grammarians agree that a lack of perception of an object does not entail the absence of that same object. But even if we stay with the specific meaning of *adarśana*, avoiding taking sides as far as the ontological existence of the non-perceived object is at stake, there are

[22] See Kātyāyana and Patañjali's discussion on the meaning of sounds, developed while commenting on the fifth *akṣarasāmāmnāya* (M 1.30-1 *ad akṣarasāmāmnāya* 5 vt. 12). vt. 12 states that, since the wholes composed of sounds are meaningful, the single sounds are also meaningful. For example (M 1.31 ll. 1-2): *ekaś cakṣuṣmān darśane samarthas samudāyaś ca śatam api samartham / ekaś ca tilas tailadāne samarthas tatsamudāyaś ca khāryāpi samārthā*, 'A single sighted person is capable of seeing and a group of a hundred of people is also capable of this; and a single sesame seed is capable of giving oil as much as a measure of a *khārī*.' The point in the two examples is the perceptible or non perceptible presence of a given quality/ function in the parts, as Bhartṛhari points out, while commenting on this very passage (D 2.33 ll. 6-8 *ad akṣarasāmāmnāya* 5 vt. 12): *darśanam adarśanaṁ ca hetu / yathā tile 'sti kācit tailamātrā evaṁ varṇeṣv apy asti kācid arthasaṁbodhanamātrā / anekavarṇoccāraṇe tu paripakvā buddhir arthaṃ pratipadyata iti*, 'Perception and non-perception are the reason: just like in a sesame seed there is some quantity of oil in the same way there is some capacity of arousing meaning in phonemes. But when a certain number of sounds have been pronounced the mind (*buddhi*), when it is ripe, understands the meaning.' Similar examples are found in M 1.220 ll. 17-9 *ad* A 1.2.45 vt. 11.

[23] M 1.18 ll. 9-15 *ad akṣarasāmāmnāya* 1 vt. 12.

[24] D 2.8 l. 19 and ff.: *yo 'yaṁ vyavāyaḥ parikalpyate bhavatā kālaśabdabhyām nāyaṁ vastuno vyavāyaḥ / kiṁ tarhi? vyañjakasya nimittasya pravṛttinivṛttibhyām upalabdhyanupalabdhī ete / yad abhivyañjakanimittatvam akārasya tad varṇāntarābhivyañjake nimitte pravṛtte apravartamānam nopalambhayati akāram punaḥ pravartamānam upalambhayati.*

some deep ambiguities in the term chosen by Pāṇini that need to be addressed. The primary derivative suffix *-ana* is one of the most productive in Sanskrit, principally used to form agent nouns, as in *nandana* lit. 'rejoicer' but 'son' (A 3.4.67),[25] action nouns such as *hasana* 'laughter' (A 3.3.115) and nouns denoting the instrument (*śravana* 'ear') or the *locus* (*-dohanī* 'a pail where the cow is milked') as taught by A 3.3.117. Other meanings are then accounted for by A 3.3.113 *kṛtyalyuṭo bahulam.*

In fact the three main meanings of the term *darśana* as recorded in the current lexica are that

a) of *nomen agentis* (with a definite adjectival touch and often at the end of composites) indicating the seeing (one)
b) of *nomen actionis,* that is the act of seeing/perceiving and
c) that of a kind of *nomen rei actae:* the perceptive mental content as the result of the act of perceiving.

Meanings b) and c) are also currently found in usages of the negative compound *a-darśana,* which may thus mean b) the absence of sight/not seeing or c) the lack of vision, the absence of visual perception. The meaning d1) of 'not showing, non apparition' – typically said of the non-appearance of a divinity – may easily be derived from meaning c) and likewise, its interesting specialisation d2) as 'absence of mention, not being available in a text' as registered in EDSHP *sub voce.* Both the above-mentioned meanings b) and c) are found in technical and non-technical literature, which is contemporary or immediately subsequent to Pāṇini. Let us recall here, remaining within the domain of technical literature, Kāt.Śr.S. 26.2.3: *patnyadarśanam,* which enjoins that a given rite should be performed 'without the wife seeing it' (meaning b) or on the other hand, Kāt.Śr.S. 1.6.22: *nādarśanāt,* stating that a given Sattra rite supposed to last for one thousand years is not possible because [such a living being] is not seen (meaning c). In many occurrences, the difference between the two meanings might look like a tiny one. Yet it ultimately entails, at the very end, the difference between something that is simply not perceived in a given place (but might be there though unseen – like the rite which the wife does not attend) and what does not appear, does not show up in a given place.[26]

[25] This is the most common meaning according to Debrunner 1954 § 81 a, who adds that the terms thus formed in this way have a 'mehr oder weniger adjektivischem Character.'

[26] These Kalpasūtra-occurrences have already been pointed out in Pontillo 2003.

Now, what kind of non-perception is the meaning of the linguistic technical term *lopa* in the *Aṣṭādhyāyī*? The usage of the term *(a)darśana* is rare and semantically erratic in the text. There are only three occurrences besides the one in A 1.1.60, and one occurrence of the term *darśana*. Among these, there is at least one (A 1.4.28) clearly resorting to the action noun (namely to the act of seeing rather than the fact of being seen).[27] Another occurrence, despite appearances, is in fact an occurrence of the term *darśana* in the meaning a) 'the seeing (one)':

> A 5.4.76 *akṣṇo 'darśanāt*, '<The taddhita affix *aC* occurs after a compound nominal stem which contains> *akṣi* 'eye' as its final constituent, not in the sense of 'seeing/ the seeing (one)'. e.g. *lavaṇākṣa-* 'having beautiful eyes' used as an epithet but not in the case of *brāhmaṇākṣi-* 'seeing like a brahman/ having the (in) sight of a brahman.'

As it is quite evident, we are not confronted here with the lexicalised compound *adarśana* but rather with the technical usage of negation in the *Aṣṭādhyāyī* to block the application of a rule, under some given conditions. The same value a) of the term is to be found in the only occurrence of the term *darśana* alone.[28]

The occurrence of the term in A 1.2.55 is much trickier to handle. It is a rule not commented on by Patañjali and part of a section that is strongly suspected of being a later interpolation:

> A 1.2.55 *yogapramāṇe ca tadabhāve 'darśanaṃ syāt*, 'Even if one relies on the combination [of formatives], when this is absent, there should be non-perception [of the derived form].'

The rule (together with the preceding one) questions the possibility of forming secondary derivatives with zero of the affix. Rule A 1.2.54 assumes the final form as given and argues that the corresponding analytical form could not be explained, while A 1.2.55 goes the other way round and assume as given, for the sake of the argument, the analytical string/combination of formatives (*yoga*). Let us analyse the stock example of the toponym *pañcālāḥ* in the meaning 'country of the Pañcāla warriors' which is formed through A 4.2.81 *janapade lup* teaching the zeroing

[27] A 1.4.28 *antarddhau yenādarśanam icchati*, 'He by whom one wishes not to be seen (lit. the not seeing) <is termed *apadāna* (which matches the ablative case)> when hiding is denoted.' e.g. *upādhyāyāt antardhatte chāttraḥ*.

[28] A 5.2.6 *yathāmukhasaṃmukhasya darśanaḥ kha*, '*kha* after the nominal bases *yathāmukha* "face to face" and *saṃmukha* "facing" in the meaning of seeing.' The output would be, according to commentaries the forms *yathāmukhīnaḥ/ saṃmukhīnaḥ*, 'looking straight/ face to face' said e.g. of a mirror.

of the affixes previously taught in various meanings, when designating an inhabited country. If the derivation were founded on the combination of formatives, namely *pañcālānāṃ nivāsaḥ*, when this combination is absent, i.e., when the denoted country cannot be described as the settlement of Pañcāla warriors, there should also be non-perception of the derived form. But in fact, the questioned name for this country may still exist and be used as a conventional name. In this rule, *adarśana*, used as a *nomen rei actae* is implicitly opposed to a stronger, and ontologically prior absence. If the combination of words *pañcālānāṃ nivāsaḥ* does not match with the reality, it does not exist, eventhough it is correct from a purely grammatical point of view. This risks entailing the impropriety (*adarśanam*, i.e., the not seeing in the correct usage of language) of the derived form *pañcālāḥ* as the name of a certain country, which is nevertheless still used.

Thus, Pāṇini's usage seems to exploit many ambiguities and potentialities of the term. Some other derivates of the verbal base *dṛś*, above all the passive verbal form *dṛśyate*, are on the contrary used in a more specific, almost technical meaning. The expression *api dṛśyate* is found a number of times always referring to linguistic units (mostly affixes but also sounds) which are to be seen or also occur (meaning c/d) outside the context set by a preceding rule.[29]

1.1.3 Later systematisation of the term a-darśana*: A (non)-perception above and before ontological considerations*

The term is then liberally used by Kātyāyana, while Patañjali uses it only while commenting on Kātyāyana's occurrences: *adarśana* appears in the context of several comments on nine different rules, and eight times out of these nine, it is first used in one or more *vārttikas*.[30] In the ninth case Patañjali is, in fact, quoting the term *adarśana* from the relevant *sūtra*.[31] The term seems thus to belong almost exclusively to Kātyāyana's lexicon and to be only passively used by Patañjali.

[29] The relevant rules are A 3.2.75, 101, 178; 3.2, 130; 5.3.14; 6.3.137; 4.73; 7.1.76. The formula is never to be found in the negative. The passages have already been discussed in Cardona 2004 who shows how these rules specifically account for linguistic variation in domains that cannot be fully determined. In all these cases the observation of current correct speech is used to decide on the correctness of the targeted forms.

[30] The vt. are M 1.134 l. 13 vt. 2 *ad* A 1.1.56; 158 l. 21 vt. 4 *ad* A 1.1.60; 162 l. 1 vt. 4 and l. 4 vt. 5 *ad* A 1.1.62; 227 l. 198 vt. 2 e l. 23 vt. 3 *ad* A 1.2.51; 387 l. 14 vt. 6 *ad* A 2.1.35; M 2.315 l. 4 vt. 1 and l. 7 vt. 2 *ad* A 4.3.101; p. 358 l. 2 vt. 1 and l. 6 vt. 2 *ad* A 5.1.72; p. 359 l. 12 vt. 1 *ad* A 5.1.80.

[31] M 2.440 l. 7 *ad* A 5.4.76.

Kātyāyana's occurrences may be roughly divided into whether the term is used with direct reference to the meaning in A 1.1.60 or not. These last occurrences show a tendency towards a specialization of the term in the sense c) of *nomen rei actae* even though the meaning b) of *nomen actionis* is rarely ruled out completely. The syntagms themselves where the term occurs are frozen: *tasyādarśanāt* 'because of its non-perception', *tatrādarśanāt* 'because of the non-perception in that meaning/context'. A few examples should suffice.

While discussing the purpose of rule

> A.1.1.56 *sthānivad ādeśo 'nalvidhau*, 'A substitute has the status of its substituend (*sthānivat* "[behaves, is treated] in the same manner as a substituend") except in respect of an operation that depends on an original sound (*analvidhau*).' (tr. Cardona 1997, p. 58)

Kātyāyana questions the assumption that the rule is taught to block the otherwise natural extension of rules from the placeholder to the substitute, in the case of rules concerning sounds [of the place-holder]:

> *alvidhau pratiṣedhe 'viśeṣaṇe 'prāptis tasyādarśanāt //2// alvidhau pratiṣedhe 'saty api viśeṣaṇe samāśrīyamāṇe 'sati tasmin viśeṣaṇe 'praptir vidheḥ / pradīvya prasīvya/ kiṃ kāraṇam / tasyādarśanāt / valāder ity ucyate na cātra valādiṃ paśyāmaḥ.*
> In the case of the prohibition in rules concerning sounds, the rule does not apply, in absence of the qualifier, because of the non-perception of this [vt. 2]. Even if there were no prohibition for rules concerning sounds, in the case of [a rule] founded on a qualifier, if there were no such qualifier, the rule would not apply, just like in *pradīvya* and *prasīvya*. Why? Because of the non-perception of this. The rule says 'before [an affix *ardhadhātuka*] beginning with a consonant or a semivowel (excluded *y*)' and here we do not find something beginning with a consonant or a semivowel (excluded *y*).

Let us note what could at first sight be considered an odd anticlimax – yet the same occurring in A 1.2.55, see before – in the reasoning that puts the absence of a given qualifier (*'sati tasmin viśeṣaṇe*) before its non-perception (*tasyādarśanāt*). It reminds us that the usage of the term *adarśana* is consistently and consciously used to identify an absence at the level of linguistic perception, with no ontological assumptions. One of the effects of the absence of a certain feature in a given linguistic context, let us say, to stay with this example, with a consonant or a semivowel with the exception of *y* at the beginning, is that it is not perceived in that context and thus cannot trigger the application of a rule conditioned by the feature. In this sense, non-perception is crucial, even more than non existence.[32]

This perception is always restricted to a specific domain, the domain of correct, shared linguistic usage. This is particularly evident in the occurrences of *tatrādarśanāt,* a formula that identifies the non-perception of a linguistic unit in a given meaning. A 5.1.72 teaches the affix *ṭhaÑ* after the verbal bases *pārāyaṇa* 'recitation' *turāyaṇa* (n. of a sacrifice) and *cāndrāyaṇa* 'fasting regulated by the moon' with the meaning 'it performs [them]'. Yet, the actual usage of the term is more restrictive: even though both the pupil and the teacher may be said to perform a recitation only the student may be called *pārāyaṇika* and similarly, even though both the sacrificer and the institutor of the sacrifice are present at the sacrifice, only the institutor is a *taurāyanika.* vt. 1 raises this point:

> *tadvartayatīty anirdeśas tatrādarśanāt //1//* [...] *pārāyaṇaṃ ko vartayati? yaḥ parasya karoti / turāyaṇaṃ ko vartayati? yaś carupuroḍāśān nirvapati / tatrādarśanāt / na ca tatra pratyayo dṛśyate // iṅyajyoś ca darśanāt //2// iṅyajyoś ca pratyayo dṛśyate / yaḥ pārāyaṇaṃ adhīte sa pārāyaṇika ity ucyate/ yas turāyaṇena yajate sa taurāyaṇika ity ucyate // yaś caivādhīte yaś ca parasya karotīty ubhau sau vartayataḥ / yaś ca yajate yaś ca carupuroḍāśām nirvapaty ubhau sau vartayataḥ // ubhayatra kasmān na bhavati? anabhidhānāt.*
>
> "It performs them" is a meaningless instruction because it is not seen in this meaning' [vt. 1] [...] Who performs a recitation? He who does it for another. Who performs the *turāyaṇa* sacrifice? The one who presents the *caru* oblation. Yet the affix is not seen in this sense. 'And it also is seen in the meaning of [the verbal bases] *i-* and *yaj-* [vt. 2]. And the affix is also seen in in the meaning of [the verbal bases] *i-* 'to study'[33] and *yaj-* 'to sacrifice'. He who studies the recitation is a *pārāyaṇika.* He who sacrifices with the *turāyaṇa* sacrifice is called a *taurāyaṇika.* But both, the one who studies and the one who does it for another, both 'perform'. And the one who

[32] This same shade of meaning is seen in some occurrences of the positive term *darśana.* Extremely significant from this respect is the passage where Kātyāyana and Patañjali discuss the nature of the sounds. The vt. 12 *yugapac ca deśapṛthaktvadarśanāt* affirms that we can be sure that there are multiple sounds also 'because they are perceived simultaneously in different places'. The usage of the term here focuses again on what is perceived beyond and irrespective of what is in reality. So much so that the discussion continues showing that there are some objects/ phenomena that can be perceived simultaneously in different place and yet are unique, like the sun: *yadi punar ime varṇāḥ ādityavat syuḥ / tad yathā / eka āditya 'nekādhikaraṇastho yugapad deśapṛthaktveṣūpalabhyate* 'Let us say that these sounds are like the sun. For example: one single sun residing in many substrata can be perceived (*upalabh-*) contemporaneously in different places.'

[33] Indeed the prefixed verbal base *adhi-i* has the meaning 'to study' as found in the following example.

institutes a sacrifice and the one who presents the *caru* oblation both perform. Why is [the suffix] not taught in both meanings? Because it does not mean this.

Kātyāyana uses *adarśana* (and even more frequently *darśana*) in this meaning of 'perception (of a word)' in context very similar to those in which Patañjali, generally uses the term *prayoga* 'usage'. This perceived word is the real cause and guide for the speakers' linguistic choices, more authoritative than any information coming from grammatical or broader linguistic analysis. Twice in almost identical passages Kātyāyana attributes authoritativeness to the perceived usage of a given word to this at the expense of the awareness of its meaning conditions (*kāraṇa*), i.e. its reconstructed analytical meaning. In other words, the perceived usage of a word plays the role of cause for the application of the word itself (*darśanaṃ vai hetuḥ*). For example, confronted with the (somehow extreme) hypothesis that *bhrātṛ* 'brother' could also be used in the meaning of *svasṛ* 'sister' because the two of them, brother and sister share the same condition, Kātyāyana answers:

> But the perception is the cause [for using some word]. And one does not see the word brother (*bhrātṛ*) in the meaning of sister (*svasṛ*). If it is said that the perception is the cause, it is equivalent [vt. 2]. If it is said that the perception is the cause, it is equivalent: one should see the world *bhrātṛ* also in the sense of 'sister' because the meaning condition [of the two] (*kāraṇa*) is equivalent. This is not how [the two words] are understood in everyday usage; certainly in everyday usage when someone says 'Bring the brother' the sister is not brought.[34]

Leaving aside the freerer occurrences of the term (*a)darśana*, it is now time to focus on the occurrences strictly linked to the term used in A 1.1.60 to express the meaning of *lopa*. In those occurrences, the commentaries show the need to somehow specify this term, to set some limits in its usage. The most interesting passage in this context is Kātyāyana and Patañjali's discussion on the rule A 1.2.51 *lupi yuktavad vyaktivacane* and its purpose. The vt. 1 says that, since elsewhere it is the gender and number[35] of

[34] M 1.250 ll. 20-5 *ad* A 1.2.68, 70 and 71 vt. 2: *darśanaṃ vai hetuḥ / na hi svasari bhrātṛśabdo dṛśyate / darśanaṃ hetur iti cet tulyam //2// darśanaṃ hetur iti cet tulyam etad bhavati / svasary api bhrātṛśabdo dṛśyatām tulyaṃ hi kāraṇam / na vā eṣa loke saṃpratyayaḥ / na hi loke bhrātā nīyatām ity ukte svasā nīyate.* Cf. also M 1.433 ll. 2-7 vt. 11 *ad* A 2.2.29. See Candotti and Pontillo 2010, §§ 1.2-3.

[35] Kātyāyana already reads the compound *vyaktivacane* as meaning 'gender and number'. For a discussion on this rule see Pontillo 2010.

the denoted object that is taught, the rule is meant to precise the different behaviour in the case of *luP*. That is, in the case of *luP* the gender and number are like those of the derivational base.[36] This explanation is questioned by an objector on the basis of the fact that a non-perception cannot receive gender and number by extension:

> *lupo adarśanasaṃjñitvād arthagatir nopapadyate //2// lubnāmeyam adarśanasya saṃjñā kriyante na cādarśanasya liṅgasaṃkhye śakyete atideṣṭum / lupo 'darśanasaṃjñitvāt arthagatir nopapadyate // na vādarśanasyāśakyatvād arthagatiḥ sāhacaryāt //3// na vaiṣa doṣaḥ / kiṃ kāraṇam / adarśanasyāśakyatvāt / adarśanasya liṅgasaṃkhye aśakye atideṣṭum iti kṛtvādarśanasacārito yo 'rthasya gatir bhaviṣyati sāhacaryāt // yogābhāvāc cānyasya //4// adarśanena ca yogo nāstīti kṛtvādarśanasahacarito yo 'rthasya gatir bhaviṣyati sāhacaryāt.*
> Because the object termed by *luP* is a non-perception, one does not obtain the comprehension of the object [vt. 2]. This very *luP* is made as the technical name of a non-perception and gender and number cannot be extended to a non-perception. And because of *luP* having a non-perception as its meaning, one does not obtain the desired meaning. Or it is not so. Because of the impossibility (of extension) for the non-perception, the desired meaning will be obtained through association [vt. 3]. There is no such a defect. Why? because of the impossibility for the non-perception. Once one has realised that gender and number cannot be extended to a non-perception, there will be comprehension of the object associated to the non-perception, because of the principle of association. And because any combination with something else is absent [vt. 4]. Having realised that there is no combination with a non-perception, there will be comprehension of the object associated to the non-perception, because of the principle of association.

The object obtained by association is the affix zeroed by *luP*. In a technical meaning the principle of *sāhacarya* or 'association' is a condition to activate the conveyance of specific meanings of a word in the presence of another word in the same phrase, see the often quoted example of the compound *rāmalakṣmanau* where the name Lakṣmaṇa triggers the desired meaning for the polysemic personal name Rāma.[37] Yet Patañjali's usage of the term is looser; the principle is advocated for all the the possible 'associations' triggered by a given word, be it with its own meaning or with its synonyms.[38] Thus, the non-perception taught by

[36] E.g. Pañcālāḥ 'place of residence of the Pañcāla warriors'.

[37] Cf. NPbh 103: *sahacaritāsahacaritayoḥ sahacaritasyaiva grahaṇam.*

[38] See M 1.176 l. 24 *ad* A 1.1.68 vt. 4: *mantrādisahacarito yo 'rthas tasya gatir bhaviṣyati sāhacaryāt*; P 1.517-8 *ad* A 1.1.67 [=68] vt. 1: *agner ḍhag ityādau tv arthasya pratyayena paurvaparyāsaṃbhavāt sāhacaryāt sarvasya tadvācinaḥ saṃpratyayaḥ syād*

A 1.1.60 cannot be interpreted as an absolute non-perception, as something almost equivalent to non existence. The zeroed element is somehow always in the background of the linguistic non-perception and grants the possibility of some grammatical rules, here for example the possibility of extension.

Both in Pāṇini and in his commentators, the usage of the term *adarśana* seems thus to be specifically limited to those cases where there is no ontological assumption and there should not be. This is very clearly in the occurrences, to be found already in Pāṇini, with a meaning of *nomen actionis*, where it is clearly the lack of sight/perception from the agent that is focused. Yet the same shade of meaning is also implied in the *nomen rei actae*: it is a lack of cognitive content independently from ontological considerations. Only the further specializations of the term, such as the fact of 'showing up, appearing' must be ruled out from the picture of terminological usage in early commentators. Kātyāyana's usage of the term is extremely consistent and unequivocally distinct from the usage of the term *abhāva*. Patañjali, on the other hand, only quotes the term when used by Kātyāyana but is not eager to use it on his own account: it may be that the intrinsic ambiguity of the term and its shift towards a more 'ontological' dimension made it less fit for this specific usage.

It may seem strange to find such an ambiguous and polysemic term in what should be a technical context such as the metarule A 1.1.60. Yet this may be explained if we pay due attention to some features of Pāṇinian metalanguage and practice. First of all, the rule is not a definition but a name-giving rule (*saṃjñāsūtra*). The purpose of the rule is not to define the concept of *lopa* in the most unambiguous way, but rather to attribute the proper *denotatum* (*saṃjñin*) to the name *lopa*, namely non-perception, just as the name *vṛddhi* is attributed to the sounds *ā*, *ai*, *au*. Moreover, here whatever is playing the role of the *denotatum* of a technical term, is supposed to be used in a common and worldly meaning, with all its ambiguities and semantic density. The real import and scope of this non-perception is not to be derived from A 1.1.60 alone but from this, together with the other metarules concerning *lopa* and all the rules where *lopa* is applied. The concept of *lopa* is to be derived by the totality of the Pāṇinian system of which it is a crucial device. In the following paragraphs we shall see that this is exactly how commentaries try to integrate the different pieces of information coming from the whole text into their interpretation of A 1.1.60.

iti sūtrārambhaḥ; M 2.218 ll. 14-5 *ad* A 4.1.48 vt. 3: *caturbhiḥ prakārair atasmin sa ity etad bhavati tātsthyāt tāddharmyāt tatsamīpyāt tatsāhacaryād iti.*

1.2 A perceptible non-perception [vt. 1]

Pāṇini's term *adarśana* is commented upon by Kātyāyana and Patañjali who both aim to progressively limit the purport of this 'non-perception'. The first step of this process is to be found in vt. 1 which recalls two previous *vārttikas* giving some general rule on the interpretation of names (*saṃjñā)* to determine the specific extension of the name *lopa*:

> M 1.158 l. 5 vt. 1 *ad* A 1.1.60 *lopasaṃjñāyām arthasator uktam*, 'As regards the name *lopa*, it has already been stated that [it is a name] of a meaning and of something existent.'

The two *vārttikas* recalled are vt. 3 *ad* A 1.1.44 (M 1.102 l. 3) as far as the mention of *artha* is concerned and vt. 9 *ad* A 1.1.1 (M 1.40 l. 26) for *sat*. These two *vārttikas* respectively account for the fact that *lopa* denotes the meaning of *adarśana* i.e. 'non-perception' – and not its pure form as is most common for grammatical names[39] and for the fact that the term does not create its own *denotatum,* once again the (already) existent non-perception. Then this second point raises a problem that should have been considered as already solved with the very first definition (and the very first *sūtra*) of the A. The flaw consists in the possibility of there being mutual dependence between the name (*vṛddhi* in the first rule and *lopa* in our case) and the named (respectively the actual sounds *ā, ai* and *au* and the "non-perception"). In other words, the name runs the risk of ending up in the void, before its object is actually named. The name *lopa* is given to a non-perception, which must therefore exist previously, but it is also what, in applicative rules, brings about this non-perception. Naming *lopa* and enjoining it are therefore known as mutually dependent operations, and these never work[40]. The solution proposed in vt. 9[41] for the term *vṛddhi* resorted to the permanence (*nityatva*) of words including the sounds *ā, ai* and *au* and consequently to the obvious priority of the existence of these sounds compared with the assignment of the name. When Pāṇini enjoins the name *vṛddhi* in some verbal or nominal base, for example, he is not creating any new entity in the world's language, he is

[39] Cf. M 1.158 l. 6 *ad* A 1.1.60 vt. 1: *arthasya tāvad uktam / itikaraṇo 'rthanirdeśārtha iti*, "With regard to meaning, this much has been stated (in vt. 3 *ad* A 1.1.44). '*Iti* is stated in order to point out the meaning.'"

[40] M 1.158, ll. 2-4 *ad* A 1.1.60: *itaretarāśrayaṃ ca bhavati / ketaretarāśrayatā / sato'darśanasya saṃjñayā bhavitavyaṃ saṃjñayā cādarśanaṃ bhāvyate tad etaditaretāśrayaṃ bhavati / itaretarāśrayāṇi ca na prakalpante.*

[41] M 1.40 ll. 26-28 *ad* A 1.1.1 vt. 9: *siddhaṃ tu nityaśabdatvāt //9// siddhaṃ etat / katham / nityaśabdatvāt / nityāḥ śabdāḥ / nityeṣu śabdeṣu satām adaicāṃ saṃjñā kriyate na saṃjñayādaico bhāvyante.*

simply accounting for what is already there. This answer became the reference-model of all cases of mutual dependence.[42] Adapted to the needs of the rule, the solution will thus run as follows: "words are permanent: the name will be created for a non-perception which exists (*satoḥ adarśanasya*) in permanent words and the non-perception is not created by the name".[43] Permanent whole words used in everyday language thus offer a frame for the interpretation of the status, role and meaning of the linguistic parts.

But why here in A 1.1.60 is an already solved problem tackled once again? Certainly, neither Kātyāyana nor Patañjali bring up the problem anytime they come across the attribution of a name to some linguistic entity or concept. In fact if we have a look at the different occurrences where the two authors feel the need to re-examine the problem of mutual dependence, we may see that there is definitely a rationale behind their choices. Let us begin with some figures: the problem of mutual dependence is tackled 17 times in the M but only twice is the reference to the solution given in A 1.1.1, is both explicit and sufficient: these may be called the cases of "trivial" mutual dependence. The other cases require more complex solutions and sometimes are explicitly defined as being different from the trivial one[44].

Thus, the two occurrences referring to A 1.1.1 are thus easily checked. The first one is the first vt. *ad* A 1.1.8: *mukhanāsikāvacano 'nunāsikaḥ*, the definition of the technical term *anunāsika* as that which is pronounced in the mouth and in the nose. Of course the solution is that of the pre-existence of nasal sounds before the name *anunāsika* itself[45]. The reason for discussing this point again here is not explicitly stated, one may only guess that the reason lies in the special status of an *anunāsika* sound, which does not pertain to the original enunciation of the *Śivasūtra*.[46]

The second passage is our passage on A 1.1.60. Both Kātyāyana and Patañjali extremely laconically delegate the solution here, to

[42] See Candotti 2004; Candotti 2006, §§ 4.4.1-3.

[43] M 1.158 ll. 6-8 *ad* A 1.1.60 vt. 1: *sato 'py uktam / siddhaṃ tu nityaśabdatvāt / nityāḥ śabdāḥ / nityeṣu ca śabdeṣu sato 'darśanasya saṃjñā kriyate na saṃjñayādarśanaṃ bhāvyate.*

[44] Cf. M 1.112 ll. 6-7 *ad* A 1.1.45 vt. 3: *naiṣa doṣaḥ itaretarāśrayamātram etac coditam / sarvāṇi cetaretarāśrayāṇy ekatvena parihṛtāni siddhaṃ tu nityaśabdatvād iti / nedaṃ tulyam anyair itaretarāśrayaiḥ.*

[45] M 1.60 l. 20 vt. 1 *ad* A 1.1.8: *anunāsikasaṃjñāyām itaretarāśraya uktam*; l. 21 *ad* A 1.1.18 vt. 1: *kim uktam / siddham tu nityaśabdatvād iti / nityāḥ śabdā nityeṣu ca śabdeṣu sato 'nunāsikasya saṃjñā kriyate na saṃjñayānunāsiko bhāvyate.*

[46] *anunāsika* sound, together with *anusvāra, visarjanīya, jihvāmūlīya, upadhmānīya* and *yama* are classed by Patañjali (cf. M 1.28 ll. 16-9 *ad akṣarasāmāmnāya* 5 vt. 5) among *ayogavāha* sounds, defined as sounds which are heard without being taught (*na kvacid upadiśyante śruyante ca*).

the one proposed in A 1.1.1. In all these three occurrences the "real" words used in everyday life (*nitya śabda*) are the only frames where the permanent relationship between form and meaning is guaranteed.

Another passage may be added to this very short list, but it is partly different from the paradigmatic ones. In fact, it is by invoking the permanence of linguistic forms (*nityaśabdatva*) – at the core of A 1.1.1's solution – that Kātyāyana's and Patañjali's commentaries on A 1.3.1 (M 1.257 ll. 20 e 22) solve the defect of mutual dependence which is raised when the exclusion of reference to the Dhātupāṭha's list in the definition of a verbal base is accepted, as indirectly proposed by vt. 8.[47] In the case of a purely semantic definition of a verbal base, the mutual dependence occurs between the injunction of an affix conditioned by this semantic feature of the base and the fact that the same semantic condition is brought about only provided the affix is already there:

> 'And there is mutual dependence as there is the denotation of "being" (*bhāva*) only when the affix follows and the affix itself [is taught] [precisely] after that.' [vt. 9] And there is mutual dependence. Which mutual dependence? The denotation of 'being' (*bhāva*) is understood only when the affix follows and the affix is [precisely] taught after a base which is identified through its denoting 'being'. Only once the affix has arisen, the expression of 'being' is comprehended and the same affix is due to arise after [an item] expressing 'being'. This is mutual dependence. And mutually dependent actions do not succeed.'[48]

Thus this occurrence is different from the preceding ones since the mutual dependence is not between a rule attributing a given *denotatum* to a technical name and rules enjoining that same *denotatum* through the technical name. Rather, the conflict here is between a rule establishing a semantic definition for a given linguistic unit and rules using that same semantic value as a condition for the same linguistic unit to receive the desired output. Yet the solution is very similar to the preceding ones:

[47] The whole commentary *ad* A 1.3.1 revolves around the possibility of giving a pure extensional definition of a verbal base (*dhātu*) through a reference to the Dhātupāṭha's list (vtt. 1b-7) or by resorting to a semantic definition of a verbal base as 'what expresses "being" (vtt. 8-13)'.

[48] M 1.257 ll. 19-22 *ad* A 1.3.1 vt. 9: *itaretarāśrayaṁ ca pratyaye bhāvavacanatvaṁ tasmāc ca pratyaya //9// itaretarāśrayam ca bhavati / ketaretarāśrayatā / pratyaye bhāvavacanatvaṁ tasmāc ca pratyayaḥ / utpanne hi pratyaye bhāvavacanatvaṁ gamyate sa ca tāvad bhāvavacanād utpādyaḥ / tadetaretarāśrayaṁ bhavati / itaretarāśrayāṇi ca na prakalpante.*

> 'But this is solved: since words (*śabda*) are permanent, the affix [takes place] without resorting to the expression of "being".' [vt. 10] This is solved. How? Words are permanent and, within these permanent words the affix arises without resorting to the expression of "being".[49]

If we stay with Kātyāyana, therefore, we find that he refers back to A 1.1.1 only twice, i.e. with the definition of *anunāsika* and with the definition of *lopa*, and once, in a more indirect way, in the case of an – only tentative – semantic definition of a linguistic segment. Therefore, it seems that he tackles the problem again when he considers that the situation is somehow different from the one already described in A 1.1.1: when the *denotatum* is a sound not recited in the Śivasūtra, which is heard but not taught, or a linguistic unit not included in a list. What is lacking here is the warranty coming from a closed list not open to change, and thus *nitya* to a certain degree.

Here in A 1.1.60, what is so strange about asking for a new discussion of mutual dependence? Certainly there is no list of 'non-perceptions' to be found in language: yet, the commentaries answer, they are included in the words of everyday language which are permanent, and as such they are non-perceptions which exist (*sato 'darśanasya*) whatever is intended with this oxymoron.

1.3 Non-perception asks for being delimited [vtt. 2 and 3]

The continuation of Kātyāyana and Patañjali's commentary on A 1.1.60 is to be connected to the solving of the mutual dependence problem, although it deals with the discussion of another *doṣa*, namely the risk of over-application of the term *lopa.*

> M 1.158 l. 9 vt. 2 *ad* A 1.1.60 *sarvaprasaṅgas tu sarvasyānyatrādṛṣṭatvāt*, 'But there is the potential involvement [of the name] with anything since nothing is perceived elsewhere.'[50]

[49] M 1.257 ll. 23-5 *ad* A 1.3.1 vt. 10: *siddhaṁ tu nityaśabdatvād anāśritya bhāvavacanatvaṁ pratyayaḥ // 10 // siddham etat / katham / nityāḥ śabdāḥ / nityeṣu ca śabdeṣv anāśritya bhāvavacanatvaṁ pratyaya utpadyate.*

[50] The compound *sarvaprasaṅga* is used in the case of *lopa*, to convey the meaning of 'the potential involvement of whatever rule'. It also occurs in three other *vārttika*s, i.e. in M 1.120 ll. 15-6 vt. 1 *ad* A 1.1.50; 1.291 l. 1 vt. 2 *ad* A 1.3.67; 3.152 l. 8 vt. 5 *ad* A 6.3.34, regularly referred to a possible overextension of a technical name (respectively the single names of *ādeśa*s such as *guṇa* and *vṛddhi*, *ātmanepadam, strī*) to more than one *denotatum*, so that this technical name - included in operational rules – could determine undesired operations. Patañjali's analysis (M 1.291 l. 2 *ad* A 1.3.67 vt. 2) of the compound *sarvaprasaṅga* is *sarvatra prasaṅgaḥ*, 'that which is possibly involved everywhere'. For a survey of the vt. and M occurrences of the terms *prasaṅga* and *prasakta*, partly discussed

What is meant by this 'elsewhere' is explained by Patañjali by highlighting what is, conversely, the appropriate place for a word, namely its specific domain of usage (*prayogaviṣaya*): 'In fact no linguistic form is perceived elsewhere from its/ own domain of usage.'[51]

To state it plainly, the defect of over-application of the name *lopa* comes from the fact that, as there is no list of linguistic non-perceptions, any non-perception of a given item, even outside its own domain of usage, could qualify for the name *lopa*. Thus, once solved the problem of mutual dependence, that is, the problem of having no already existing object to which the name can be applied, vt. 2 points to the need to find a criterion to choose the specific *denotatum* of *lopa* from among all the unlimited available objects candidates. Definitively, both nothing and anything must be discarded as *saṃjñins* of *lopa*.

The following *vārttika* then looks for the actual drawbacks of this lack of delimitation in the *denotatum*. Kātyāyana identifies a major one in the fact that it obliges the elimination of rule A 1.1.62 *pratyayalope pratyayalakṣaṇam* which transfers all the operations concerning an affix to the cases of non-perception (*lopa*) of that affix:

> M 1.158 l. 13 vt. 3 *ad* A 1.1.60 *tatra pratyayalakṣaṇapratiṣedhaḥ*, 'In this case, the prohibition of the specific operations concerning the affix [is requested].'

If any absence of an affix even outside its domain of usage were termed *lopa*, all the operational rules pertaining to all affixes non perceived in a given form should be extended to that form through A 1.1.62.

Both the examples quoted by Patañjali before and after the vt. 2 start from the possible use of the term *lopa* as conveying the meaning of non-perception referred to whatever affix is not perceived after a given nominal stem. The two nominal stems chosen as examples are *trapu-* 'tin' and *jatu-* 'lac'. Since the affix *aṆ* is not perceived after either of the two stems, this non-perception of *aṆ* is supposed to be termed as *lopa*.[52] As a consequence, according

on occasion of several preceding inquiriesy shared by M.P. Candotti and T. Pontillo, see now also Freschi and Pontillo 2012 § 3.3, where the translation adopted here for *prasaṅga* as 'potential involvement' is explained on the basis of the survey itself.

[51] M 1.158 l. 11 *ad* A 1.1.60 vt. 2: *sarvo hi śabdo yo yasya prayogaviṣayaḥ sa tato 'nyatra na dṛśyate.*

[52] M 1.158 l. 12 *ad* A 1.1.60 vt. 2: *trapu jatv ity atrāṇo 'darśanaṃ tatrādarśanaṃ lopa iti lopasaṃjñā prāpnoti.*

to the example mentioned by Patañjali,[53] the *vṛddhi*-replacement taught by A 7.2.115 (*aco ñṇiti*, '[*vṛddhi*] instead of the final vowel [of the pre-affixal base] before an affix with marker *Ñ* or *Ṇ*') is potentially involved in the stems *trapu*- and *jatu*-, merely because of this non-perception of *aṆ*. Nevertheless, this first example is easily discarded because rule A 7.2.115 includes the term *aṅga* 'pre-affixal base' as a condition for applying the *vṛddhi*-replacement. The stems *trapu*- and *jatu*- cannot be defined as pre-affixal bases for the affix *aṆ* which has never been taught after *trapu*- and *jatu*-.[54]

The second potential involvement which is discussed, deals with the non-perception of the affix *KVIP* after the same nominal stems.[55] In this case the *āgama -t* is taught for whatever *kṛt* suffix with *anubandha P* by A 6.1.71 (*hrasvasya piti kṛti tuk*), i.e., by a rule which does not restrict in any way or by any device the base of the affixation. Thus this is a *doṣa* which might remain unsolved, unless the restriction explained in vt. 4 blocks the application of this rule in a different way – as we will see below.

1.4 Non-perception of something that is otherwise necessary [vt. 4]

1.4.1 Looking for a linguistic definition of a necessary unit

Therefore the final interpretation of rule A 1.1.60 begins by stating that not any existing non-perception is the *denotatum* of the term *lopa*, but rather it is that the term, each time it is used, signifies a specific non-perception, precisely the 'non-perception of an otherwise necessary element', or, more precisely of an element automatically/potentially involved in a given domain (*prasakta*):

> M 1.158 l. 21 vt. 4 *ad* A 1.1.60: *siddhaṃ tu prasaktādarśanasya lopasaṃjñitvāt*, 'This is established because *lopa* is the name of the non-perception of something that is automatically/ potentially involved [there].'

Yet, even this crucial specification is not sufficient according to Patañjali and the *denotatum* of *lopa* remains too vast (M 1.158 l. 22 – p. 159 l. 1 *ad* A 1.1.60 vt. 4):

> *yadi prasaktādarśanaṃ lopasaṃjñaṃ bhavatīty ucyate grāmaṇīḥ senānīḥ atra vṛddhiḥ prāpnoti / prasaktādarśanaṃ lopasaṃjñaṃ bhavati*

[53] M 1.158 ll. 14-5 *ad* A 1.1.60 vt. 3: *aco ñṇitīti vṛddhiḥ prāpnoti.*

[54] M 1.158, ll. 15-7 *ad* A 1.1.60 vt. 3: *naiṣa doṣaḥ / ñṇiti aṅgasyāco vṛddhir ucyate / yasmāt pratyayavidhis tadādi pratyaye 'ṅgaṃ bhavati / yasmāc cātra pratyayavidhir na tatpratyaye parataḥ / yac ca pratyaye parato na tasmāt pratyayavidhiḥ.*

[55] M 1.158 ll. 17-8 *ad* A 1.1.60 vt. 3: *kvipas tarhy adarśanaṃ / tatrādarśanam lopa iti lopasamjñā prāpnoti.*

> *ṣaṣṭhīnirdiṣṭasya / yadi ṣaṣṭhīnirdiṣṭasyety ucyate cāhalopa evety avadhāraṇe* [A 8.1.62] *cādilope vibhāṣā* [63] *ity atra lopasaṃjñā na prāpnoti / atha prasaktādarśanaṃ lopasaṃjñaṃ bhavatīty ucyamāne katham evaitat sidhyati / ko hi śabdasya prasaṅgaḥ / yatra gamyate cārtha na ca prayujyate / astu tarhi prasaktādarśānaṃ lopasaṃjñaṃ bhavatīty eva / katham grāmaṇīḥ senānīḥ / yo 'trāṇaḥ prasaṅgaḥ kvipāsau bādhyate.*
> If it is said that 'the non-perception of something that is automatically/ potentially involved [there] gets the name *lopa*', [then] in *grāmaṇīḥ, senānīḥ* there should be the *vṛddhi*-replacement [of vowel of the verbal base *nī*-]. – The non-perception of something potentially involved provided it is mentioned with the 6th ending gets the name *lopa*. – If it is said 'of something mentioned with the 6th ending' [then] in the rules A 8.1.62 '<The first verbal pada is not all *anudātta*> when there is the zero replacement (*lopa*) of *ca* and *āha* and the particle *eva* is used in the sense of restriction' and A 8.1.63 'And marginally when there is the zero replacement of units of the list beginning with *ca*', in these rules the name *lopa* would not apply. – But [even] if we say that 'the non-perception of something which is potentially involved gets the name *lopa*' how can this [usage of *lopa*] be realized? – What indeed is a potential involvement (*prasaṅga*) for a word? It is where its sense is intended although it is not employed. Then, let us stay with 'the non-perception of something which is potentially involved gets the name *lopa*'. – How about *grāmaṇīḥ* and *senānīḥ*? – Here this possible involvement of *aṆ* is blocked by *KviP*.

The passage is dense and complex and asks for some commentary. Let us follow Patañjali's reasoning step by step. The discussion begins with an opponent stating that the definition of *lopa* as 'the non-perception of something that is potentially involved' is too vast. For, what are the elements automatically/ potentially involved in a given domain? For example, all the elements enjoined by a general rule, such as *aṆ* (in A 3.2.1), in the domain of its exception rules, e.g. in *grāmaṇīḥ, senānīḥ*, where A 3.2.61 teaches the affixation of *KviP* as an exception to the affixation of *aṆ*. Should the term *lopa* merely conveys the meaning of non-perception of a potentially involved element, a stem such as *grāma-ṇī-* or *senā-nī-* could act as a pre-affixal base with reference to (at least) two potentially involved affixes, namely the affix *aṆ* enjoined by the general rule A 3.2.1 and the affix *KviP* actually enjoined by one of the exception rules to the affix *aṆ*, i.e. by A 3.2.61. In the first case, as a consequence, the *vṛddhi*-replacement taught by A 7.2.115 (*aco ñṇiti*) would be applied once again to the mentioned stems (***grāma-ṇai-* and ***senā-nai-*). The reference to an "automatically involved unit" would thus not enable one to distinguish between a place-holder (*sthānin*) and an element taught in a general rule (*utsarga*) both being, in the opponent's view, expected in the contexts where their substitutes (*ādeśa*) and exceptions (*apavāda*) appear.

To rule out such cases, Patañjali proposes a further restriction, namely that the *prasakta* element must be enunciated in the sixth ending: *prasaktādarśanaṃ lopasaṃjñaṃ bhavati ṣaṣṭīnirdiṣṭasya.* In other words, the element that has the chance to apply must be a *sthānin,* a substituend which is enunciated with the 6th ending in grammar and, through this 6th ending is bound to its substituend. No such relation is to be found between an affix taught generally and its exceptions as both are taught with nominative endings.

Yet Patañjali cannot accept this restriction, because it does not account for some rules such as A 8.1.62-63, where we find some zeroed elements, acting as conditions, whose *lopa* has not been taught by means of a 6th ending and in no other way, and thus are outside of the substitution frame. Which is, by the way, far from surprising: since it deals with words, such as *ca* and *aha,* rather than with suffixes, it is obvious that their use is merely determined by the meaning intended by the speaker, rather than by some rules that enjoin them.

Therefore, Patañjali ends up with a broader definition of *lopa* so that it also encompasses the cases of the zero of words that are not dependent on grammatical rules nor in any competing analytical string. To do this, Patañjali elaborates a different definition of "the involvement" of a word in a given linguistic context: 'What indeed is a potential involvement (*prasaṅga*) for a word? It is where its sense is intended although it is not employed.' Thus, Patañjali proposes to come back to the interpretation of *lopa* as being the name of the non-perception of a unit/ word which is potentially involved, provided this involvement is interpreted as happening a context where the meaning of the unit/ word is intended although the linguistic unit itself is not employed. At the same time Patañjali rejects the drawback quoted at the beginning of the discussion of vt. 4, i.e. the potential involvement of *aṆ* (taught with a general rule or *utsarga*) when *KviP* is enjoined by an exception (*apavāda*). In fact, he says, the potential involvement of the affix *aṆ* is blocked by the very usage of *KviP.* This is by no means a categoric answer, which is in fact hinting at a well-known – even though higly disputed – position concerning the relationship between an *utsarga* and its *apavāda* that can be condensed in Patañjali's stance that, even if there is no explicit statement in Pāṇini's grammar on the fact that an exception rule is bound to block a general one, nevertheless we can assume that such a principle is at work in grammar in the same way as we can recognise it in some everyday's life examples (*laukiko dṛṣṭānta*): 'In the world even if there is the possibility of applying both rules there is the blocking [of the general one]. e.g. "Give curds to the brahmins, buttermilk to Kauṇḍinya." Even if there is the possibility of offering curds [to Kauṇḍinya], the offering of buttermilk forestalls it.'[56]

1.4.2 Conclusions: lopa *is a specific kind of substitution [A 1.1.56]*

One of the most striking points in the just concluded discussion on rule A 1.1.60 is the proposal of singling out the *prasakta*-element by the usage of the 6th ending to express it in the rules. In fact this seems to allude to a crucial vt. concerning the general rule of substitution (M 1.138 l. 6 vt. 17 *ad* A 1.1.56): *siddhaṃ tu ṣāṣthinirdiṣṭhasya sthānivadvacanāt,* which proposes to limit the *sthānivadbhāva* (i.e., the rule-extension from a substituend to its substitute) to the cases where the substituend is expressly mentioned with the 6th ending.

In fact, in the context of A 1.1.56 (vtt. 15-17) we find a sort of wider and better argued discussion on the necessity of finding an unambiguous way to determine what a *prasakta*-unit exactly is in each single context. The discussion begins with a provisional assumption of a sort of overlap between two mechanisms that respectively account for the relationship within the pairs *sthānin/ ādeśa* and *utsarga/ apavāda*:

[56] M 1.115 ll. 2-4 *ad* A 1.1.47 vt. 1: *loke hi saty api saṃbhave bādhanaṃ bhavati / dadhi brāhmaṇebhyo dīyatāṃ takraṃ kauṇḍinyāyeti saty api saṃbhave dadhidānasya takradānaṃ nivartakaṃ bhavati.* This way of thinking of the relation between a general rule and its exceptions has later on been crystallized in various *paribhāṣās*. Nāgeśa (U 1.480 *ad* A 1.1.59 [=60] vt. 4) in our passage quotes NPbh 63, which nevertheless amounts, as the author points out, to negating the possible involvment of the general rule in the exception: *parihṛtya cāpavādaviṣayam ity nyāyena prasaṅga eva nāstīti bhāvaḥ,* 'By the metarule (*nyāya*) "Having put aside the domaine of the exceptions..." it is the potential involvement itself that does not occur; this is the meaning.' Although in Pāṇini there is not an explicit teaching on the relationship between general and specific rules, a general principle blocking general rules in case of specific ones is for sure at work in the *Aṣṭhādhyāyī.* Moreover it seems also to be implicitly assumed in some rules whose aim is in fact to limit it, e.g., in A 3.1.94 *vāsarūpo 'striyām* that teaches as optional the affixes taught in the section beignning with A 3.1.91 (provided they do not have an identical shape and they are not used to form feminine derivatives) thus showing that, in other sections of the *Aṣṭādhyāyī* an affix taught as en exception supersedes an affix taught in a general way. See also Patañjali's commentary on this rule (M 2.81 ll. 3-4 *ad* A 3.1.94 vt. 10) *ime 'rhe kṛtyā vidhīyante te viśeṣavihitāḥ sāmānyavihitaṃ tṛcaṃ bādheran,* 'These *kṛtya*-affixes taught in the meaning of "worthy of" being prescribed in a specific way should block [the affix] *tṛc* which is prescribed in a general way.' On the assumption that this principle governing the relationship between *utsarga* and *apavāda* as something which 'was recognized in pre-pāṇinian times', see Cardona 2007, pp. 702-3, who also underlines the importance of this *paribhāṣā*: *nyāyair miśrān apavādān pratīyāt,* 'One should understand exceptions combined with general rules' (*Ṛgvedaprātiśākhya* 1.53).

M 1.138 l. 1 vt. 15 *ad* A 1.1.56: *apavādaprasaṅgas tu sthānivattvāt*, 'There is indeed a potential involvement (of the corresponding *utsarga*) with the *apavāda*, because of this *sthānivat* condition ('like a *sthānin*').'

Patañjali explains this through an example according to which the features of the affix *aṆ* taught by the general rule A 3.2.1 could be transferred to the affix *Ka* taught as an exception by A 3.2.3 because the affix *aṆ* could be considered to be equivalent to a substituend (*sthānivattvāt*).[57]

Now the opposition between the affix *aṄ* (enjoined by a general rule) and the affix *KviP* (enjoined by one of its exceptions) discussed in M *ad* A 1.1.60 is for sure to be interpreted against this same background. Also in A 1.1.60, we can assume that the discussion is about the possible overlap between the mechanism of generalization and that of substitution, eventhough the very special kind of substitution, namely that is *lopa*, and that what Patañjali is referring to in A 1.1.60, is a solution Kātyāyana had already given in this specific context of A 1.1.56.[58]

vt. 17 (quoted above) allows the two mechanisms to be neatly distinguished – eventhough they share the basic reference to the *prasaṅga* as a potential involvement – by strictly combining the mechanism of substitution with the metalinguistic usage of the 6th ending. Thus the automatic involvement of a word/ linguistic unit is governed in at least two different ways according respectively

a) to the arrangement of rules through the mechanisms mainly conveyed by the *anuvṛtti* and essentially based on the dichotomy between *utsarga* and *apavāda*,
b) and according to the substitution schema, including its metalinguistic lore.

Patañjali (M 1.138 ll. 7-9 *ad* A 1.1.56 vt. 17) takes a further step and allows the restriction to the 6th ending in A 1.1.56 directly through the *anuvṛtti* of the term *ṣaṣṭhī* from A 1.1.49: *ṣaṣṭhī sthāneyogā*, 'A sixth ending has to be connected with "in place of".'[59]

[57] M 1.138 ll. 1-2 *ad* A 1.1.56 vt. 15: *apavāda utsargakṛtaṃ ca prāpnoti / karmaṇy aṇ* (3.2.1) *āto 'nupasarge kaḥ* (3.2.3) *iti ke 'py aṇi kṛtaṃ prāpnoti / kiṃ kāraṇam / sthānivattvāt.*

[58] For some other passages where this same comparison is put forward by Patañjali, see Freschi and Pontillo 2012 § 3.3.4.

[59] M 1.138 ll. 7-9 *ad* A 1.1.56 vt. 17: *tat tarhi ṣaṣṭhīnirdiṣṭagrahaṇaṃ kartavyam / na kartavyam / prakṛtam anuvartate/ kva prakṛtam / ṣaṣṭhī sthāneyogā iti.*

The specificity of the last part of the M commentary on A 1.1.60 consists in the special attention paid to the proper definition of what a *prasakta*-unit is. In M *ad* A 1.1.56 the restriction to the unit taught with the 6th ending was sufficient to unambiguously identify the object of the substitution and to rule out the object taught in a general rule. Commenting on A 1.1.60, however, Patañjali needs to account for *lopa*s that are nowhere taught by explicit grammatical rules; thus their matching *prasakta*-units cannot be singled out through the metalinguistic usage of the 6th ending. The zeroing of words such as *ca* and *aha* occurs in everyday language and speakers are aware of it, since these zeros are aimed at expressing some meaning. Nevertheless the grammar does not teach these operations. The second definition of the *prasakta*-unit given by Patañjali, i.e., where the meaning is understood and the form is not perceived, is compulsory to account for these last cases. While substitution in general may be considered purely dependent upon the specific Pāṇini methodological choice, the zeroing also includes a more spontaneous side of this phenomenon.

To sum up, Patañjali overtly aims at putting zero in the specific domain of substitution: zero is the substitute and the zeroed element is the substituend. If we stay with the strictly *śāstric* side of the phenomenon, zero is something which appears and by appearing, blocks what would otherwise (in the absence of the substitution-rule) take place, as happens elsewhere. Typically, the zero of sounds is well represented inside this *śāstric* frame. The main reason to consider a given sound as a unit potentially involved in a given context is because there is a rule teaching its substitution.
Exactly the opposite is the case of whole words which are almost never replaced by zero through grammatical rules and which are nevertheless expected in a given context because their meaning is apprehended. Both frames seem to be equally important to account for the pertaining phenomena as regards the zero of affixes. In fact, the zero of affixes is regularly taught in their relevant context. At the same time they are also expected, because their meaning is apprehended. *Lopa* thus becomes a device to account for the cases of dissymmetry between meaning and linguistic input, about which see below § 3.3.

This inclusion of *lopa* in the domain of substitution would not have been so obvious at Kātyāyana and Patañjali's time, given that Patañjali himself discusses and refuses the view attributed to an opponent who denies it (M 1.164 ll. 20-3 *ad* A 1.1.62 vt. 14):

ādeśaḥ sthānivad ity ucyate na ca lopa ādeśaḥ / lopo 'py ādeśaḥ / katham / ādiśyate yaḥ sa ādeśaḥ / lopo 'py ādiśyate / doṣaḥ khalv api syād yadi

lopo nādeśaḥ syāt / ihācaḥ parasmin pūrvavidhau ity etasya bhūyṣṭhāni lopa udāharaṇāni tāni na syuḥ.
It is stated that a substitute (*ādeśa*) is as if it were the place-holder (*sthānin*), and *lopa* is not a substitute. – *Lopa* is also a substitute. – How is it possible? A substitute is that which is specifically instructed (*ādiśyate*) and *lopa* is specifically instructed too. Moreover, should *lopa* not be a substitute, surely there would be some shortcomings. [For instance] here, [where it is stated]: '*acaḥ parasmin pūrvavidhau*' (A 1.1.57), the numerous examples of this [rule] which are [examples which occur] in the case of *lopa* would not be there.

In other words, to counter the opponent objection on the status of *lopa* Patañjali points out that Pāṇini's practice itself hints at *lopa* being a kind of substitute. And it is most likely that this interpretation, may safely be attributed to Pāṇini too. Contemporary research on the *Aṣṭādhyāyī*, speaking of 'zero replacements' for describing the various *lopa* phenomena, also seems to favour this.[60] Furthermore, even though not explicitly defined as an *ādeśa* – at least if we accept the traditional interpretation according to which *ādeśa* is not continued in A 1.1.60 from 1.1.56 – *lopa* behaves as an *ādeśa*. An important piece of evidence besides the nominative + genitive pattern, which is regularly followed in the rules of *lopa*, is the fact recalled by the commentator himself, that some *lopa*s are mentioned among the exceptions to A 1.1.56.[61]

2 Zero in the Wider Context of Substitution

2.1 The linguistic place (sthāna) of substitution [A 1.1.49]

We have already reconstructed in the preceding paragraphs a kind of double frame used by Patañjali in order to account for

[60] See e.g. Cardona 1997 § 79.

[61] Just to quote one among these examples, see M 1.146 ll. 1-2 *ad* A 1.1.57: *paṭayati laghayatīti ṭilope kṛte 'ta upadhyāyāḥ iti vṛddhiḥ prāpnoti / sthānivadbhāvān na bhavati*, '[When it is said] *paṭayati* makes sharp', *laghayati* 'makes light' (causative forms where the causative affix *ṆiC* is introduced after a nominal stem – here *paṭu-* 'sharp' and *laghu-* 'light', to name an action after that which the action realizes as its effect – here the fact to make something else sharp or light, by force of vt. 6 *ad* A 3.1.26), when *lopa* of *ṭi* (i.e. *lopa* of *u* in *paṭu-* or *laghu-*) applies (*ṭi* is the part of an unit which begins with the last vowel according to vt. 1 *ad* A 6.4.155 according to A 1.1.64), a *vṛddhi*-replacement of the penultimate short vowel *a* (A 7.2.116) risks being applied. This does not happen because of the condition of behaving [of the *ādeśa*] as if it were the *sthānin* (according to A 1.1.57).' In fact if the *ṭi* portion of *paṭu* (which is subject to *lopa*) were to be considered as if it were there, *a* of *paṭu* would not be the penultimate sound and as a consequence, it would not be subject to the *vṛddhi*-replacement.

lopa as a replacement of a unit, which is expected in a given place

a) either because its matching *artha* is apprehended there,
b) and/or because the unit itself would actually occur there, if *lopa* did not apply there, i.e., insofar as it is "potentially involved" (*prasakta*) there.

This frame hinted at by vt. 4 will be further elaborated by later commentaries in strict connection with the general rule teaching the metalinguistic value of genitive as expressing the relationship between a place-holder and its substituend, namely A 1.1.49 *ṣaṣṭhī sthāneyogā*, 'The sixth ending is combined with *sthāne* "in the place [of]"' and, more precisely, in connection with the meaning of the word *sthāna* there used. Yet, it is important to stress the fact that, in Patañjali, it is in the occurrence of A 1.1.60 that the problem is tackled and by no means in the context of the general frame of substitution where, at most, Patañjali seems to favour the second interpretation:

> (M 1.126 ll. 16-7 *ad* A 1.1.51 vt. 3): *kiṃ vaktavyam etat / na hi / katham anucyamānaṃ gaṃsyate / sthāna iti vartate sthānaśabdaś ca prasaṅgavācī*, 'Has this [word *sthāne*] to be explicitly mentioned? No, indeed. How shall that which is not said be understood? There is *anuvṛtti* of "*sthāne*". And the word *sthāna* is an expression for *prasaṅga*.' [62]

As Kahrs 1998, pp. 248-9 already highlighted, it is from Kaiyata onwards[63] that the double frame for the interpretation of substitution consolides, taking grounds on an interpretation of the noun *sthāna* either

> 'as *bhāvasādhana*, that is to say, as an action noun formed with the suffix *LyuṬ* (*-ana* with presuffixal accent) by A 3.3.115 *lyuṭ ca*' or alternatively as *adhikaraṇasādhana*, 'that is to say, as a noun denoting a locus, in this case formed with *LyuṬ* by A 3.3.117 *karaṇādhikaraṇayoś ca*.'[64]

[62] Therefore *sthāne* is taken twice, so that M 1.126 l. 19 *ad* A 1.1.51 vt. 3 concludes: *uḥ prasaṅge 'ṇprasajyamāna eva raparo bhavati*, 'As *aṆ* is potentially involved when there is the potential involvement of *ṛ*, it is followed by *r*'. For some further details about the context of this passage see Freschi and Pontillo 2012b § 3.4.1.

[63] In Bhartṛhari the opposition is rather between an interpretation of sthāna as meaning *artha* 'meaning' or *kāla* 'time'. For a translation and commentary of the passage see Kahrs 1998, pp. 250-5.

[64] On this point Kahrs 1998, pp. 248-9 relies on the *Pradīpa* of Kaiyaṭa on the Mahābhāṣya at A 1.1.1 and A 1.1.49 as regards the first analysis and on the interpretation of Jinendrabuddhi's *Nyāsa* on the *Kāśikā* at A 1.1.49 and Nāgeśa's

Under the second alternative, of *sthāna* as a place where a given unit "stays", e.g. Kaiyaṭa on the M at A 1.1.1 suggests a particular *locus*, that is the meaning (*artha*) of speech units.[65] Under the first alternative – *sthāna* meaning 'the act of staying/ a standing' – the commentators propose some particular meanings for the term *sthāna*, among which *prasaṅga*.

The two alternatives have as an apparent distinct consequence the interpretation of substitution rules as aiming to respectively enlighten either the substitute, which is said to occur in the meaning of the place-holder, or the place-holder, missing where the substitute appears. In other words, according to the *artha*-interpretation, a substitution teaches that "possibly a Y *ādeśa*" appears, i.e., a Y unit with the same meaning as the *sthānin* can replace it, while according to the *prasaṅga*-one, a substitution rule teaches that "possibly an X *sthānin* appears" meaning that the X place-holder would automatically appear in the given context were it not for the presence of its *ādeśa*.[66]

Laghuśabdenduśekhara as regards the second one. However precisely with regard to this specific kind of substitution, namely the zero-replacement of some padas, Pāṇini seems to assume it as a linguistic phenomenon that does not need to be expressly taught in the grammar. In fact – as quoted above in § Ø (3) and 1.4.1 – the rules A 8.1.45; 62; 63, mention *lopa* of some *padas* such as *ca* or *kiṃ* as a condition for the accentuation of the first verbal *pada* in the relevant sentence, even though no rule accounts for thi specific case of substitution. Moreover A 1.4.105 and 2.3.14 teach two morpho-syntactic rules which apply, provided that the meaning of some additional word is evident from the complex meaning of the relevant sentence, i.e. provided that a certain *pada* is involved as a *sthānin*. It deals with the so-called "natural ellipsis" or better with the the zero-replacement of some words whose meaning is nevertheless to be postulated to account for the complex meaning of a syntagm – cf. Deshpande 1981, pp. 179-83; Kiparsky 1982, pp. 24-5; 37-51; Deshpande 1985, pp. 33-60; Bronkhorst 1987a; Deshpande 1989; Benson 1990, pp. 134 f. However precisely with regard to this specific kind of substitution, namely the zero-replacement of some *padas*, Pāṇini seems to assume it as a linguistic phenomenon which does not need to be expressly taught in the grammar. In fact – as quoted above in § Ø (3) and 1.4.1 – the rules A 8.1.45; 62; 63, mention *lopa* of some *padas* such as *ca* or *kiṃ* as a condition for the accentuation of the first verbal *pada* in the relevant sentence, even though no rule accounts for thi specific case of substitution. Moreover A 1.4.105 and 2.3.14 teach two morpho-syntactic rules which apply, provided that the meaning of some additional word is evident from the complex meaning of the relevant sentence, i.e. provided that a certain *pada* is involved as a *sthānin*. It deals with the so-called "natural ellipsis" or better with the the zero-replacement of some words whose meaning is nevertheless to be postulated to account for the complex meaning of a syntagm – cf. Deshpande 1981; Kiparsky 1982, pp. 24-5; 37-51; Deshpande 1985, pp. 33-60; Bronkhorst 1987a; Deshpande 1987.

[65] P 1.170 *ad* A 1.1.1 vt. 9 [=7]: *sthānaśabdo 'rthavācī / tiṣṭanty asmiñ śabdā iti sthānam.*

[66] Cf. also the use of the term *avakāśa* as the specific place of a specific unit, employed as a quasi-synonymous word for *prasaṅga* e.g. in M 2.444 ll. 1-2 *ad*

Kahrs seem to suggest a possible overlapping between the two interpretations relying on a quotation from Abhayanandin,[67] but this opinion perhaps must be dated back even to Patañjali, at least as regards what is specifically affirmed for *lopa* in M *ad* A 1.1.60 vt. 4 quoted above. Moreover Patañjali seems to hint at the fact that *prasaṅga* can also be interpreted as a noun denoting a *locus* when, discussing the risk of *sarvaprasaṅga* in M 1. 158 l. 11 *ad* A 1.1.60 vt. 2 quoted above, he introduces the concept of *prayogaviṣaya* 'a specific usage-domain for each linguistic unit/ word (*śabda*)'.[68] With regard to the *lopa* of meaningful units,[69] the coincidence of the meaning or function conveyed by the units taught by the concurring rules (*prasaṅgas*), i.e. the coincidence of the meaning of *sthānin* and *ādeśa* is of course a compulsory condition, which makes the substitution possible. *Sthāna* thus results as being the "well established place" where two or more rules are potentially applied, that which indirectly gives an answer to the tackled problem of the contradiction of *lopa* with the close relationship between the linguistic unit as an input (a cause) and sense as its output (effect) which is currently professed by grammarians.

3 Symmetry and Dissymmetry in Linguistic Phenomena

To clearly understand the import of the description of *lopa*-phenomena in early pāṇinian tradition we first of all must place it against the wider frame of how this same tradition interpreted the relationship between linguistic units (*śabda*) and meanings (*artha*) and lastly try to discern the ideological background of this frame.

A 5.4.154: *vibhaṣā kab yadā na kap so 'vakāśah / kapaḥ prasaṅga ubhayaṃ prāpnoti paratvāt kap prāpnoti*, 'Marginally when there is *kaP*, this is not the specific place for *kap*. If there is a potential involvement of *kaP*, both are obtained but only *kaP* is obtained because it follows (the other one)'.

[67] Kahrs 1998, p. 262

[68] A strictly similar statement is found in VP 3.14.583: *yaḥ śabdaś caritārthatvād atyantaṃ na prayujyate. viśaye 'darśanāt tatra lopas tasyābhidhīyate*, 'Where a word is not used because of its meaning being understood, one speaks of its *lopa* as it is not seen in its specific domain.'

[69] Less obviously when the *lopa* of sounds is enjoined by mentioning the morphological context of these sounds, i.e. when *lopa* consists in an *ekādeśa* 'partial substitution', the meaning of the *arthavat* unit to which the sounds subjected to *lopa* pertain has to be the same both when *lopa* is applied and when it is not applied. Nevertheless this coincidence of *artha* is not a condition for evoking the *prasaṅga*-mechanism. Rather since no change of meaning can be determined by the sounds alone, the meaning itself is however indifferent to the zeroing of one sound or more. See below § 3.2.

3.1 The biunivocal relationship between forms and meanings works at different linguistic levels

There is at least one clear stance in Pāṇinian tradition on how the verbal communication of meaning works. The addresser needs to employ words, e.g. to utter them, in order to arouse the desired mental image in the mind of the addressee. The mere existence of a word (or of any linguistic unit) is not sufficient to bring about meaning, if the word is not actually employed (e.g. uttered) as the input that brings about the desired meaning in the mind of the addressee. This is very succinctly recalled in Patañjali's aphorism on the nature of word (M 1.18 ll. 19-20 *ad* Śivasūtra 1 vt. 12):

> *śrotropalabdhir buddhinirgrāhyaḥ prayogeṇābhijvalita ākāśadeśaḥ śabdaḥ*, 'Becoming perceptible through the ear, to be grasped by the mind, enlightened by usage and residing in ether: this is the word (*śabda*).'

From the point of view of the speaker, it is the word-meaning the speaker intends to convey that impells the usage of that same word like – to use Bhartṛhari's metaphor – the churning sticks that kindle a flame through their inner fire (VP 1.46):

> Just as the light residing in the churning sticks is the cause for (kindling) other flames, in the same way also the word residing in the mind is the cause for the separate audible words.[70]

Seen the other way round, from the point of view of the hearer, words, lighted up by usage, become perceptible by the ear and are grasped by the mind of the addressee that transforms, so to say, this phisical perception into a concept (VP 1.56):

> *viṣayatvam anāpannaiḥ śabdair nārthaḥ prakāśyate // na sattayaiva te 'rthānām agṛhītāḥ prakāśāḥ* //56//
> The meaning cannot be illuminated by words that haven't attained the condition of object [of perception]. It is not by mere being (*sattā*) that they can illuminate the objects of meaning without being grasped [themselves].

As a consequence, since word forms (*śabda*) are considered as causes giving rise to the cognition of objects (*artha*) in the mind of the participants in the communicative event, neither verbal communication should be realizable at all without the physical

[70] VP 1.47: *araṇiṣṭhaṃ yathā jyotiḥ prakāśāntarakāraṇam// tadvac chabdo 'pi buddhistaḥ śrutīnāṃ kāraṇaṃ pṛthak //47//*

perception (*pratyakṣa*) of the word, nor should any single perceptible unit be capable of conveying more than one object at the same time. Uttered word and comprehended meaning deploy themselves at a common pace, as already highlighted by Kātyāyana:

> Because of the fact that word forms apply to their objects one by one (*pratyartham*) there is no denotation (*abhidhāna*) of more than one object (*artha*) through a single word form [vt. 1]. Thus in case of denotation of more than one object there would be more than one word form [vt. 2].[71]

Early grammarians applied this one-to-one relationship – that calls to mind, with some significant differences, what Bronkhorst 1996 called "the correspondence principle" – not only to words but to all meaningful linguistic units.[72] In these cases too, just like in the case of whole words, morphemic linguistic units convey their meaning only if they are actually uttered within the word. Using Patañjali's words, 'in fact there is no understanding of a sense without employing the word-form which denotes that.'[73] Such a parallel between words and sub-units is made by Patañjali in a passage where he is discussing the device of *ekaśeṣa*. *ekaśeṣa* – to cut a long story short – is a device to reduce to one the many occurrences, for example, of words having the same form but different meanings (let us say *akṣa* 'axle, *akṣa* 'die' and *akṣa* 'rosary seed') to obtain the plural form *akṣāḥ*. At a certain point of a very long discussion, Patañjali wonders whether it is necessary for the *ekaśeṣa*-rule to also teach that this single reminder *akṣāḥ* is in the plural. His answer is that it is not necessary to teach it, since it is implicit by the very fact that *akṣāḥ* is one reminder for

[71] M 1.233 l. 16 *vt. 1 ad* A 1 2 64: *pratyarthaṁ śabdaniveśān naikenānekasyābhidhānam*; l. 20 *vt.* 2: *tatrānekārthābhidhāne 'nekaśabdatvam.*

[72] There are nevertheless some striking differences between what we call here the one-to-one relationship and Bronkhorst's "correspondence principle". He (1996, pp. 1) describes as an 'implicit presupposition' stating that 'the words of a statement correspond, one by one, to the things that constitute the situation described by that statement.' Bronkhorst's principle is at the same time narrower than ours, as it applies only to words in sentences, and more compelling as it establishes a one-to-one relation between words and 'things that constitute the situation described by that statement' while we content ourselves with a relation between word forms and meanings/ denoted objects. Moreover, unlike the correspondence principle, this one-to-one relationship is explicitly resorted to by commentators from Kātyāyana onwards. For some other passages discussing the *pratyārtham* principle and its implications s (see Candotti and Pontillo 2010).

[73] M 1.241 l. 1 *ad* A 1.2.64 vt. 29: *na hy antareṇa tadvācinaḥ śabdasya prayogaṃ tasyārthasya gatir bhavati.*

many, and as proof, he makes reference to two *lopa* procedures, where the sense of a *kṛt* affix is understood, even though its form is not used:

> This is realized because of the retention itself of only one form. In fact, there is no understanding of a sense without employing the word-form that denotes this. On the contrary, we see that without employing the word-form that denotes it, there is also understanding of this sense as in the case of *agnicit* and of *somasut.*[74] We consider that it occurs thanks to *lopa*, that is, in these cases there is also an understanding of this sense without employing the word-form that denotes it. In the same way here, it is also realized thanks to *ekaśeṣa* which, because of the retention of only one form, allows the dual or plural meaning to be understood.[75]

We can see here how the same reasoning is applied to whole words and to morphological units even in the somehow extreme case of an apparent flaw in the symmetry frame itself. And it is the apparent absence of a morphological unit, accounted for by the highly formalised mechanism of *lopa* that is used as an argument to explain the presence of a similar mechanism in case of words. On the contrary, in cases where the symmetry between forms and meanings seems well established, the reasoning goes the other way round taking grounds on evidences from upper linguistic segments (be them words or synthagms/ phrases).

Patañjali (M 1.219 ll. 19-25 *ad* A 1.2.45 vt. 9) plainly expounds the grammatical process on which this presupposed one-to-one symmetry between the semantic and the phono-morphological level of language is based. It deals with the abstraction of linguistic units, realized through two complementary systematic actions, i.e. the so-called *anvaya* lit. 'association' and *vyatireka*, lit. 'distinction', aimed respectively at catching what is the continuity and discontinuity among different compared units:

> Indeed [the meaning of verbal base etc.] is well established by force of association and distinction [vt. 9]. – It is well established. – How? – By force of association and distinction. – What is this association or what is distinction? Commonly if one says *vṛkṣaḥ* 'a tree' (sing. nom.) a certain linguistic unit is heard, i.e., the linguis-

[74] With *lopa* of the affix *KviP*.

[75] M 1.240 l. 27-241 l. 5 *ad* A 1.2.64 vt. 29: *tat caikaśeṣakṛtam / na hy antareṇa tadvācinaḥ śabdasya prayogaṁ tasyārthasya gatir bhavati / paśyāmaś ca punar antareṇa api tadvācinaḥ śabdasya prayogaṁ tasyārthasya gatir bhavatīti agnicit somasud iti yathā / te manyāmahe lopakṛtam etad yenātrāntareṇāpi tadvācinaḥ śabdasya prayogaṁ tasya arthasya gatir bhavatīti / evam ihāpy ekaśeṣakṛtam etad yena atraiko 'yam avaśiṣyata ity anena dvyarthatā bahvarthatā vā bhavati.*

> tic unit *vṛkṣa* with ist final sound *-a* and with the flexional ending *-s*. A certain meaning is understood, namely the object (*denotatum*) which is endowed with roots, a trunk, fruits, leaves and a singular number. If one says *vṛkṣau* 'two trees' (du. nom.), a certain linguistic unit is left behind, another arises and another remains. The sound *s* is left behind, the sound *au* arises and the linguistic unit *vṛkṣa* with its final sound *-a* remains. At the same time, a certain meaning is left behind, another arises and another remains. The singular number is left behind, the dual number arises and the object which is endowed with roots, a trunk, fruits and leaves remains. As a consequence we consider that the meaning which is left behind pertains to the sound which is left behind, the meaning which arises pertains to the sound which arises and the meaning which remains pertains to the sound which remains.[76]

3.2 Phones and morphemes, both parts of whole words, are similar to each other

The same kind of reasoning can be applied even when the presence/ absence of single, meaningless, sounds is at stake. In fact, commentators often hint at the closeness between morphemes and phones, as far as their contribution to building the significant wholes is at stake. Particularly telling from this respect is the well-known debate concerning the question of whether pure sounds are meaningful or not. A question which is itself startling from a Western perspective, which nevertheless finds its place in the theoretic frame of Pāṇinian commentators. Among the possible arguments in favour of the meaningfulness of sounds there are two particularly interesting ones for our topic. Sounds are meaningful:

> Also because there is comprehension of anothe meaning when there is a change in sounds. [vt. 10][77]
> And since there is no understanding of the meaning, if there is no perception of the sound.[vt. 11] [78]

[76] M 1.219 ll. 19-25 *ad* A 1.2.45 *vt*. 9: *siddhaṃ tv anvayavyatirekābhyām // 9 // siddham etat / katham/ anvayād vyātirekāc ca / ko 'sāv anvayo vyatireko vā / iha vṛkṣa ity ukte kaścid cchabdaḥ śruyate vṛkṣaśabdo 'kārāntaḥ sakāraśca pratyayaḥ / artho 'pi kaścid gamyate mūlaskandhaphalapalāśavān ekatvā ca/ vṛkṣāv ity ukte kaścic chabdo hīyate kaścid upajāyate kascid anvayī / sakāro hīyate aukāro upajāyate vṛkṣaśabdo 'kāránto 'nvayī / artho 'pi kaścid dhīyate kaścid upajāyate kascid anvayī / ekatvā hīyate dvitvam upajāyate mūlaskandhaphalapalāśavān anvayī / te manyāmahe yaḥ śabdo hīyate tasyāsāv artho yo 'rtho hīyate yaḥ śabda upajāyate tasyāsāv artho yo 'rtha upajāyate yaḥ śabdo nvayī tasyāsāv artho yo 'rtho 'nvayī.*

[77] M 1.30 l. 7 vt. 10 *ad akṣarasāmāmnāya* 5 *varṇavyatyaye cārthāntaragamanāt*. The well known examples are *kūpa* 'well', *sūpa* 'soup' and *yūpa* 'post'.

[78] M 1.30 l. 13 vt. 11 *ad akṣarasāmāmnāya* 5 *varṇānupalabdhau cānarthagateḥ*. The examples are those of couples of words such as *vṛkṣaḥ* 'tree' ≠ *ṛkṣaḥ* 'bear', only distinguished by a single phone.

Patañjali emphasises the link between the absence of sound and the absence of meaning by interpreting the negative compound *anarthagati* as if it were *atadarthagati* 'no understanding of the sense of that (word)' and Bhartṛhari goes even further in equating the function of sounds to that of morphemic units: as examples, he first proposes some morphemic ones (*pibati* vs. *vipibati* and *pratiṣṭhate* vs. *tiṣṭhati*) and ends with the canonical phonetic example *ṛkṣa/ vṛkṣa.*[79]

Nevertheless this somehow striking perspective seems to derive consistently from the general frame of these grammatical works. Actually, they aim to justify the words of everyday language, which are permanently used with a precise meaning, rather than to construct complex linguistic units starting from their minimum components. Even these components themselves, just like pure linguistic sounds, only derive from this kind of comparative abstraction and somehow they become active and contribute to determine the linguistic meaning only if they are part of whole inflected words (*pada*s). Only the fully inflected words are the permanent frame inside which the linguistic units play their role: it is sufficient on this point to remember the persistence shown by Patañjali in always referring to the whole words when bringing judgement on the permanence of linguistic units as already shown above.[80]

The vitality of linguistic segments strictly depends on their joining in meaningful inflected words, just as branches, leaves and fruits which are alive while they are linked to their trees. Patañjali uses exactly this metaphor to illustrate the part-whole relationship of linguistic units, thrice in an identical formula: *vṛkṣaḥ pracalan sahāvayavaiḥ pracalati*, 'A tree when it shakes, shakes with its parts'.[81] Once this example is included in a discussion about the status of a linguistic element of which only a part has undergone substitution. Another occurrence is specifically devoted to discussing a proposed addition regarding the general rule on substitution (A 1.1.56). The addition should specify that

[79] D 2.32 ll. 14-9 vt. 11 *ad akṣarasāmāmnāya* 5: *varṇānupalabdhau cānarthagateḥ //5//* (vt 11 *ad Śivasūtra* 5). *ihārthavato 'nupalabdhau so 'rtho na gamyate // yathā pibati vipibati iti* […] *evaṁ pratiṣṭhate tiṣṭhatīti / iha ca vṛkṣa iti vakārānupalabdhau mūlādisamudāyo na gamyate.*

[80] See § 1.2. The limits of a purely mechanic composition building from the minimum units to higher ones were very clear for Sanskrit grammarians, see on this point Candotti and Pontillo 2010. Moreover such a framework is perfectly consistent with some parallel reflections on the final aim of grammar, especially Houben's idea of 'preliminary statements' in the mind of the user to be refined through grammatical competence (see. Houben 2003, p. 161).

[81] For the analysis of all occurrences of this formula, see Candotti and Pontillo 2007.

an element only partly modified by substitution (*ekadeśavikṛta*) is as if it were not modified, just as the substitute is as if the placeholder were still there. The traditional example is that of the verbal forms *pac-a-tu, pac-a-ntu* which are derived from *pac-a-ti, pac-a-nti* through substitution of the *-i* of *-ti* with *-u*. Patañjali's aim is to refute the proposed addition, by proving that it is not necessary. In fact, there is a kind of implicit interpretation-rule which also recurs elsewhere in the M, sometimes even with the same examples,[82] stating that

> That which has undergone a change in regard to one of its parts, is by no means (in consequence of this change) something else.[83]

In this regard, Patañjali also mentions this mundane example:

> Like this: when a dog has an ear or tail cut off, it remains a dog indeed. It does not become a horse or a donkey.[84]

Forcing the passage quoted above within a perspective which is self-evidently beyond the scope of the example quoted by Patañjali, we could even propose the meaning that dog's absent parts (such as the cut off ear or tail) are merely non present as active causes of manifestation. They cannot be effectively perceived but they are nevertheless present as expected parts of a dog, i.e. as parts which are potentially involved in the perceptible manifestation of the whole living being which is identified as 'dog'.[85] And from this specific perspective it is true that a given phoneme (such as the *v* at the beginning of *vṛkṣa*) is not less expected (and necessary in order to convey the desired meaning) than a morpheme such as *vi* in *vipibati*.

3.3 Wholes are the permanent frames upon which the symmetry is established

On the other hand this pattern opens the way to the well-known difficulty relating to the permanence of words. If words were to lose or modify some of their parts like dogs losing an ear or a tail, they would not be considered as permanent. In fact,

[82] Cf. e.g. M 1.501 l. 25 *ad* A 2.4.85 vt. 10; see Candotti and Pontillo 2007.

[83] M 1.136 l. 8 vt. 10 *ad* A 1.1.56: *ekadeśavikṛtam ananyavat*. It corresponds to NPbh. 37.

[84] M 1.136 ll. 9-10 *ad* A 1.1.56 vt. 10: *tad yathā / śvā karṇe vā pucche vā chinne śvaiva bhavati nāśvo na gardabha iti.*

[85] Of course the contingent diachronic dimension of cutting off parts of the whole such as an ear or the tail of a dog is to be excluded.

elsewhere grammarians tend to resort to the substitution of full words (*sarvapadādeśa*) in order to avoid what could otherwise look like 'a change, modification of words'.[86]

Again, it is the whole and undivided that guarantees for the meaning and function of the parts, precisely as only a whole chariot is fit for movement, whereas its constituents, if they are taken apart, are not fit for such. This is the famous example Patañjali propounds in order to explain that 'the combinations (*samudāya*) of sounds have meaning, whereas the parts have not.'[87]

This partly coincides with the equally famous, probably contemporary, *Milindapañha* dialogue denying the ontological existence of every individual specifically meant as an entity which is independent from its components and which at the same time is nothing outside them.[88] In fact, as Buddhists unanimously agree, there is no whole independent of its parts nor do wholes exist at all. Furthermore through the long history of the Buddhist *dharma*-theory, only a limited number of *dharmas* came to be accepted as the really self-existing entities[89] and, as is well known, their existence is merely momentary according to the majority of Buddhist schools.

Precisely in order to avoid the judgement of momentariness for sounds, words and sentences, the Sarvāstivādin School postulated – probably for the first time – the self-existence for two linguistic *dharmas*, namely the *vyañjanakāya* and the *nāmakāya/padakāya*, i.e. sound and word.[90] Patañjali also considers word and sound as the

[86] M 1.75 ll. 13-4 *ad* A 1.1.20 vt. 5: *sarve sarvapadādeśā dākṣīputrasya pāṇineḥ / ekadeśa vikāre hi nityatvaṃ nopapadyate.*

[87] M 1.220 ll. 22-4 *ad* A 1.2.45 vt. 10: *yathā tarhi rathāṅgāni vihṛtāni pratyekaṃ vrajikriyāṃ praty asamarthāni bhavanti tatsamudāyaś ca rathaḥ samartha evam eṣāṃ varṇānāṃ samudāyā arthavanto 'vayavā anarthakā iti.* Cf. also M 1.1 ll. 6-13: *atha gaur ity atra kaḥ śabdaḥ / kiṃ yat tat sāsnālāṅgūlakakudakhuraviṣāṇy artharūpam sa śabdaḥ,* 'Now, when it is said "*gauḥ*", what is the word? Is it that which consists in the object possessing a dewlap, tail, hump, hoofs and horns? is this the word?'.

[88] (Mil 25) *nāhaṃ bhante nāgasena mus bhaṇāmi, īsañca paṭicca akkhañca paṭicca cakkāni ca paṭicca rathapañjarañca paṭicca rathadāḍakañca paṭicca ratho 'ti saṅkhā samaññā paññatti vohāro nāmamattaṃ pavattatī 'ti,* 'Revered Nāgasena, I am not telling a lie: it is depending on the pole, on the axle, on the wheels, on the body of a chariot, on the flag-staff of a chariot, on the yoke, on the reins, and on the go*ad* if "chariot" exists as a denotation, appellation, designation, as a current usage, as a name.' For an *alaṃkāra*-perspective of this special attention paid to the whole-part relationship see Boccali and Pontillo 2010, pp. 128 ff.

[89] These *dharmas* are "classified abstractly by distinctive intrinsic nature" (*svabhāva*): cf. Cox 2004, p. 553.

[90] By contrast the Vaiśeṣika-*darśana* does not conceive the word but only the sound as a stable entity, even though on the other hand it elaborates a strategic answer to the dangerous Buddhist thesis about the whole-parts relationship, by avenging the ontological existence of constituents (namely their harmonical coexistence with the wholes, which as a consequence are treated

only two self-existing autonomous linguistic entities. As pointed out and reconstructed by Bronkhorst 1987, they could match with the two expressions *padasaṃghāta* and *varṇasaṃghāta*, merely employed as examples in M 2.104 ll. 2-3 *ad* A 3.2.49 vt. 3 but likely derived by means of the agent affix *aṆ* (A 3.4.67) in the sense of 'what collects sound/-s' and 'what collects word/-s' respectively,[91] i.e. as 'individual word' and 'individual sound', both to be considered as indivisible and independent entities in the real language.

Consistently, the sole morphological unit which is considered self-existent by Patañjali is the inflected *pada*, whose autonomy is never questioned. The different treatment of morphological entities, described in the grammar as somehow originating dependently, reveals the illusory autonomy of sub-units of words - with the regular highlighting of the dependence – relationship between morpheme and morpheme in a *pada* or between *pada* and *pada* in a compound.

3.4 lopa *is a means to restore symmetry in language*

The strain of the early pāṇinian tradition to maintain symmetry between the phonic aspect of a word and its semantic content is evident from this general picture of verbal communication. This symmetry is impaired at every level, but deviances from the standard can be identified and accounted each time within the general pattern and accounted for. *Lopa* is a major device to account for instances of dissymmetry between form and meaning, particularly at the level of phones and morphs; at the level of full words, one will rather find other procedures, above all *ekaśeṣa* or 'the single remainder'.

The interpretation of *lopa* in the wider frame of substitution is crucial to restore the symmetry between form and meaning: it establishes a link between the absence of a signifier and another linguistic form perceived elsewhere. Staying with the examples at the very beginning of this paper, the zeroed sound *ti* in *viṃśaka* 'bought by twenty [coins]' (ex. 1b) is linked to *ti*-sounds such as those perceived in *viṃśati* 'twenty' and *viṃśatitama* 'twentieth'. Similarly and even more cogently, *jambu* meaning the fruit of the *jambū* tree shows zero for the elsewhere realized affix *aṆ*, above all in the concurrent form *jāmbava*.

Such a link, as we have seen, is far from arbitrary, as it has been established with a form that would otherwise be expected

as composite objects).

[91] They should not be thus derived by means of *GHaÑ* (A 3.3.18) in the sense as "collection of sounds" and "collection of words" respectively.

in that position, should the specific rule of substitution not have been there. This transforms what could have been absolute non-existence in the absence of a specific signifier leaving a trace behind, the *sthāna* or the well-established place for two concurrent rules to apply. In other words, *lopa* is absence in the form of an empty case, a blank specified in terms of position and boundaries and, in the case of morphs, capable of prompting meaning like any other signifier.[92]

4 *The Cause-Effect Pattern and its Linguistic Import*

4.1 *Words as causes*

It is now possible to take a further step backwards and try to place and interpret this need for establishing, as far as possible, biunivocal relations between form and meaning in a wider background. We have already in § 3.1 seen how the conveyance of meaning is interpreted within a cause-and-effect frame: inner words are the "cause" (*kāraṇa*) for audible words and audible words are compulsory to comprehend the intended meaning. Yet in the case of words the picture is somehow more complex. In fact, from a purely gnoseological point of view, words are peculiar objects which, through one and the same communicative act, arouse two different types of knowledge: a perceptive knowledge concerning the form of the word and a linguistic/ mental knowledge concerning its meaning. This requires an explanation as it seems to deny the otherwise accepted postulate that a single cause is at the origin of one and only one effect.

This point is mostly explicitly stressed by Bhartṛhari. In the Paspaśā, the introductory chapter of M, Patañjali looks for a definition of what the word (*śabda*) is and, after several other tentatives, he comes up with two answers, among which the one that interest us is that a word, such as the word *go* meaning 'a cow', is that which, 'once uttered (*yenoccaritena*) there is knowledge (*saṃpratyayo bhavati*) of an animal with a dewlap, tail, hump, hoofs and horns'. Patañjali is thus content to highlight the necessary relationship between the perceptible phenomenon on the one hand and the aroused mental cognition on the other.[93] By contrast, Bhartṛhari focuses on Patañjali's expression *yenoccaritena* 'once ut-

[92] Analogously, the gnoseological reflection on the concept of 'non perception' (*anupalabdhi*), both in Buddhist schools and in brahmanical *darśanas*, often focused on its being an intrinsically composite judgment, formed by the concomitant awarness of a presence and of an absence.

[93] M 1.1 ll. 10-1: *kas tarhi śabdaḥ / yenoccaritena sāsnālāṅgūlakakudakhuraviṣā ṇināṃ saṃpratyayo bhavati sa śabdaḥ.*

tered', to go deeper into the analysis of linguistic perceptive objects. There is more than one view (*atrānekaṃ darśanam*)On how a word, one uttered can convey a meaning, Bhartṛhari says, on how a word, once uttered, conveys a meaning there is more than one view (*atrānekaṃ darśanam*). Two out of the three mentioned views fit well into what Houben 1995, p. 69 called a 'two-level model':

a) the word uttered is an inferior (*avara*) kind of word, whose only aim is to make its own form known. Therefore, it cannot at the same time, make something else, i.e. its meaning, known. Only the word residing in the mind has the capacity of bringing about meaning. [94]
b) the word once uttered discloses the *jāti* (the genus) of its own form (e.g. *vṛkṣa* once uttered communicates to the listener the fact of being the word *vṛkṣa*) and then this *jāti* conveys the outer meaning, i.e. tree.[95]

Let us notice that both these solutions *de facto* reinstate the one-to-one relationship between cause and effect; yet they second one introduces a succession in the process of communication (first the own form of an uttered word is apprehended and then this concept gives rise to the comprehension of the meaning) that does not fit with the overall grammatical interpretation of communication acts. The other solution c) – considered by Houben as a stance of the 'two capacity model' is to assume that words, like lamps, have a double capacity, namely that of manifesting themselves and at the same time manifesting the objects around them (D 1.3 ll. 19-20):

> *anye manyante / dviśaktiḥ śabda ātmaprakāśane 'rthaprakāśane ca samarthaḥ / yathā pradīpaḥ ātmānaṁ prakāśayan nidhyarthān prakāśayatīti.*
> Others think: a word has two powers, it is capable of revealing itself (*ātmaprakāśana*) and its meaning (*arthaprakāśana*). Just like a lamp while revealing itself illuminates also the objects in the receptacle.

Thus far beyond the well-known theme of the need of a physical input to cause verbal cognition, this passage, which is a straightforward addition by Bhartṛhari to Patañjali's text, makes us aware of a restricted number of cases where, at least in the opinion of

[94] D 1.3 ll. 13 ff.: *kecid manyante / yo vāyam uccāryate kramavān avaraḥ / kaścid anyaḥ akramaḥ śabdātmā buddhisto vigāhate / tasmād arthapratipattiḥ.*
[95] D 1.3 ll. 15 ff.: *anye manyante / yathā varṇeṣu varṇaturīyā bhāgā varṇajātiṁ vyañjayanti evaṁ varṇā vākyantareṣu ye kramajanmānaḥ ayugapatkālās te taṁ padasthām varṇajatim abhivyañjayanti/ vṛkṣaśabdo vṛkṣatvam/ jater arthasya pratipattiḥ.* tatm

some, the assumed one-to-one relationship between causes and effects have to be dismissed. Therefore both lamps, which can at the same time illuminate themselves and illuminate things around them, and words, which manage to contemporaneously communicate their form and convey their meaning are advanced as, provisional, exceptions to the mentioned principle.

Yet, this example of the lamp, self-evident and intuitive as it may seem, is dense of wider implications and has been discussed at length also in openly gnoseological contexts, which aim to confute the assumed identity of the cognition with its object, such as it was maintained e.g. by the Mādhyamika Buddhist Śūnyavāda, which entailed the impossibility of any reliable knowledge of the phenomenal word. Similar instances are easily found in *darśana*-litterature, e.g. NS 2.1.19 where well-established means of valid cognition are compared with the light of a lamp (*pradīpaprakāśasiddhivat*), precisely because they do not need a second lamp to make themselves known.[96] Analogously in the Mīmāṃsā-commentary of Śabara, which might have been earlier or contemporary with Bhartṛhari. The argument is put in the mouth of the opponent (*pūrvapākṣa*) merely in the sense that even the *siddhāntin* cannot deny the factshould agree that a notion while making the other objects known, must itself be known, as the lamp which both is itself seen and renders other things visible.[97]

As Houben 1995, pp. 72-5 points out it is difficult to discern Bhartṛhari's favoured position between the two-level and the two capacity model, as both models are frequently mentioned in various contexts, especially in the VP.[98] On the other hand, it is likewise difficult to imagine that Bhartṛhari was not aware of the important theoretical implications of both models, as his keen commitment to some strictly related topics will clearly show. In fact, if assuming the existence of two simultaneous cognitions (that of the cognition itself and that of the cognised object) somehow saves the reality and independence of phenomenal

[96] Cf. *Nyāya-Sūtra* 5.1.10: *pradīpopādānaprasaṅganivṛttivat tadvinivṛttiḥ*, 'As it is not necessary to bring a (second) lamp to see the (first) lamp (which people who desire to see things bring to see them), in the same way is not necessary for the instance (which is stated in order to make known a thing that is not known).'

[97] ŚBh *ad* MS 1.1.5: *utpadyamānaivāsau jñāyate jñāpayati cārthāntaraṃ pradīpavad.* The conclusion specifies that notions cannot be the direct object of sense/perception, but rather they depend on inference. Therefore the notion is inferred without a form, whereas the object is perceived with a form.

[98] For a collection and comment on some further Bhartṛhari's reflections on this subject see Houben 1995, pp. 66-75.

word, on the other hand it exposes whoever professes it to the risks of self-reference and circularity. Bhartṛhari was perfectly aware of that risk, so much so that he is the first, at the best of our knowledge, to tackle the so-called Liar Paradox and other paradoxes founded on the flaw of self-reference.[99] His final answer is that a cognition and its object, even though they may be grasped simultaneously, are ontologically distinct, and a cognition cannot become the object of (another) cognition without losing its own nature (VP 3.1.106):

> *yathā jyotiḥ prakāśena nānyenābhiprakāśyate / jñānākāras tathānyena na jñānenopagṛhyate //*
> Just like a light is not illuminated by another lamp, in the same way that which has the form of a cognition is not grasped by another cognition.

Accordingly, with regard tof we now come back to the domain of words and linguistic usage, the same statement is paraphrased this way in VP 3.3.26:

> *na ca vācakarūpeṇa pravṛttasyāsti vācyatā / pratipādyaṃ na tat tatra yenānyat pratipādyate //*
> Indeed there is no condition of being signified even for what proceeds in the form of a signifier, since that by which something else is expressed cannot not being able to; it cannot be expressed in that same context (*tatra*) that by which something else is expressed.

This means, if we come back to the D passage we started from, that, despite the similar terms used for both the effects of an uttered words, namely the revelation of the word itself (*ātmaprakāśane*) and the revelation of the intended object (*arthaprakāśane*), the terms refer to two different functions: words denote intended objects but cannot denote themselves without loosing their very capacity of being signifiers, just like when the signifier *agni* denotes the pure word form *'agni'*.

As a consequence, every cognition has a phenomenon (and not another cognition) as its substratum[100] and every uttered

[99] Bhartṛhari's treatment of this kind of paradoxes have been discussed by Herzberger and Herzberger 1981, Houben 1995, pp. 213-33 and Houben 1995a.

[100] *na hy ajñāte 'rthe kaścid abuddhim upalabhate / jñātetv anumānād avagacchati ...tasmād apratyakṣā buddhiḥ ...akārāṃ eva hi buddhiṃ anumīmīmaha sākāraṃ cārthaṃ pratyakṣaṃ evāvagacchāmaḥ tasmād arthālambanaḥ pratyayaḥ*, 'None is able to acquire a notion before the object has been known. It is only after the object has become known that one comes to know of that (= the notion) and this is through inference. Therefore the notion cannot be an object of sense-perception. In fact, when we infer a notion, we infer it without a form, whereas when we

word conveys the intended meaning, not itself as a signifier: the dreaded lack of substance of phenomena is in some way banned. Thus, if words at some level seem to dismiss the symmetry between cause and effect it is only to reinstore on even firmer grounds the necessary relation between form and meaning.

4.2 Causes with more than one effect and effects without causes

Once again *lopa* phenomena seem to impair the neat elegance of the whole picture. Somehow they must have effectively somehow looked like a derangement, by no means the only one, of the naturally expected cause-effect sequence, upon which other branches of wisdom and speculative sciences also reflected at length. For instance, in the most ancient tradition of Mīmāṃsā-*darśana*, precisely in MS, which might have been contemporary Kātyāyana's vtt. and consequently antecedent to M, we find statements which emphasize the one-to-one relationship, respectively between *śabda* as an injunction and *karman* as an object of the injunction i.e. as a ritual enjoined act[101] and between the mention of a distinct result and the injunction of a distinct *karman.*[102]

On the other hand, Jaimini teaches some devices as exceptions to this general pattern, namely with regard to the subsidiary rites, which can help several main rites to achieve their purposes, avoiding repetitions. There are some extension (*atideśa*) procedures granting more than one effect for a single cause. For example the preliminary offerings as a subsidiary act are performed only once and are effective for each main act of the same complex ritual performance of the same day and place.

Chapters 11 and 12 of MS are entirely devoted to these specific procedures of transference as exceptions to the symmetry between cause and effect, including some occurrences of the device called *prasaṅga* '[extension by] involvement' which is used to designate a procedure according to which a subsidiary rite joins in another subsidiary rite proper to a different main performance, by sharing some implements with it. *Kalpasūtras* also show some specific kinds of *atideśa* which are termed as *prasaṅga* and they are often result as being inserted in a closely technical

directly come to know of a perceptible object, we perceive it with a form. Therefore the conception of ideas has its substratum in the object.' (ŚBh *ad* MS 1.1.5)

[101] e.g. MS 2.2.1-2: *śabdāntare karmabhedaḥ kṛtānubandhatvāt // ekasyaivaṃ punaḥ śrutir aviśeṣād anarthakaṃ hi syāt.*

[102] e.g. MS 2.2.25: (*pūrvapākṣa*) *phalaśrutes tu karma syāt phalasya karmayogitvāt.* For a comparable *Nyāya*-semantic principle according to which all words must be without a reference and for the risk of rulelessness (*aniyama*) of a supposed non-entity (absence) see Chakrabarti 1997, pp. 211-45.

scheme of ritual description aimed at avoiding repetitions and as a consequence, at overcoming a one-to-one relationship between cause and effect, between injunction and performance.

Chapter 3 of Freschi and Pontillo's contribution, included in the present volume, is entirely devoted to the analysis of these occurrences. As explained there, the opposition between the *prasaṅga*-principle and the *tantra*-one is, fully presented in the most ancient extant commentary on MS, i.e. in the *Śabarabhāṣya*, dating back to the 5th century CE. Yet, what we find there is not a thoroughly/ unprecedented and overtly disrupting innovative technical point of view, considering as there are some more ancient hints at this opposition.[103] The event of the *prasaṅga* assumes the form of a possible extended function of a secondary ritual element already introduced for another main performance, provided that this function is explicitly and autonomously enjoined for the further secondary element. *tantra* is a procedure of extended application, according to which some subsidiary rites can be shared as subordinate by more than one primary act, on condition that they are not prescribed for each primary act separately, according to a specific time and place.[104] Śabara chooses two simple and intriguing examples from common life to illustrate these two procedures: the *prasaṅga*-procedure is compared with 'the spreading of light also on the public road by a lamp placed in a palace'[105] and the *tantra*-one directly [106] with 'a lamp placed in the midst of many brāhmaṇas'.[107]

Kātyāyana and Patañjali use both the terms *prasakta* and *prasaṅga* and *tantra* and *atantra*[108] quite straightforwardly, without feeling the need either to define or to comment on them. In particular they might have employed the term *prasakta ad* A 1.1.60, being effectively certain that this term would be immediately understood immediately. We suppose that they relied on an

[103] See Freschi and Pontillo 2012, specifically § 4.1.2.

[104] MS 11.4.1: *codanaikatvād rājasūye 'nuktadeśakālānāṃ samavāyāt tantram aṅgāni*. For the use of the technical term *tantra* in Vyākaraṇa and Mīmāṃsā tradition, see also Pontillo 2008.

[105] *yathā pradīpasya prāsāde kṛtasya rājamārge 'py ālokakaraṇam* (ŚBh on MS 12.1.1).

[106] When, regarding commenting MS 12.1.3, Śabara again wonders what the difference between *prasaṅga* and *tantra* is, this detail is given special emphasis: on the one hand the metaphor sfocuses on a function, the making of light, which is the help rendered by the subsidiary act, on the other hand it directly deals with a lamp as a standard of comparison, namely the subsidiary rite itself: *tatrāṅgam eva sādhāraṇam iha tv aṅgakṛta evopakāraḥ*.

[107] *yathā bahūnām brāhmaṇānāṃ madhye kṛtaḥ pradīpaḥ* (ŚBh on MS 11.1.1).

[108] See Freschi and Pontillo's contribution §§ 2.4 and 3.4.

otherwise well-known procedure, i.e. a shared knowledge. Nevertheless, to the best of our knowledge, Bhartṛhari is the first grammarian who uses both terms *tantra* and *prasaṅga*, putting them side by side as two kinds of extension devices (*atideśa*). For example in VP 2.77, we find both principles mentioned (among others) in a *kārikā* confuting where the indivisibility of the meaning of a sentence is confuted: if the individual word and its meaning are denied any existence, certain current mundane and *śāstra*-principles like *prasaṅga* and *tantra* would be suspended.[109]

Indeed, Bhartṛhari's crucial passage on this technical terminological pair is a reinterpretation of a M discussion on the double function of the *gaṇas*, supposed, at the same time, to list some relevant words and to teach the correct pronunciation of sounds.[110] M explains how there are also causes which serve two purposes (*dvigatā hetavaḥ*), by using the specific ritual act performed by pouring water onto the roots of mango trees to satisfy the *pitṛ*s as an example.[111] Bhartṛhari, on the other hand, is not contented with the mere assertion (there are causes triggering more than one effect) but looks for an explanation of this apparent exception to the rule. In fact he finds at least two principles that can account for the phenomenon. The first one (D 1.37 ll. 5-11 *ad* vt. 18) is, in Bhartṛhari's words, characterized by renunciation (*tyāgalakṣaṇa*):

> *dvigata-* are [things] reaching two objects. *hetu-* are [things] capable of bringing about effects. In this world it happens that one single cause (*hetu*) is seen to accomplish two goals. The water is only one. The action having this object (= the water) and characterized by renunciation, once performed on the root of a mango tree, it constitutes a single cause which is the same both for satisfying the ancestors Pitṛs and for watering the trees. In other cases this water is certainly not reaching two objects, when Devadatta and Yajñadatta have to be satisfied[112] and mango trees have to be watered from a distant place. Thus, just as when the offering of water takes place, it brings about both goals, provided that one proceeds keeping in mind that the perceptible offering of water is

[109] *prāsaṅgikam idam kāryam idaṃ tantreṇa labhyate / idam āvṛttibhedābhyām atra bādhāsamuccayau* (VP 2.77)

[110] See M 1.13 l. 21 vt. 18: *ākṛtyupadeśāt siddham iti cet saṃvṛtādīnāṃ pratiṣedhaḥ*, 'If it is established that [we can manage to know the desired phonemes, pitch, quantity and nasality of vowels included] [merely] by teaching their generic form, a prohibition of the vowels beginning from the closed ones (should be added).'

[111] M 1.14 ll. 13-4 *ad* vt. 18: *dvigatā api hetavo bhavanti / tad yathā / āmrāś ca siktāḥ pitaraś ca prīṇitā iti.*

[112] I.e. each needs his own amount of water.

capable of accomplishing a not perceptible goal; analogously, the recitation of the *Gargādi* and *Bidādi gaṇa*s is capable of realising both parts and whole, when their operational effect takes place.[113]

The original context of Patañjali's quotation (*āmrāś ca siktāḥ pitaraś ca prīṇitā iti*, 'the mangoes are watered and the manes satisfied') has not been traced and it is somehow venturesome to look for a strict interpretation of this passage. Yet some interesting points can be safely stated, namely that a) one possibility for an action to get more than one result is to be carried out in a religious context aiming at the obtainment of an invisible result b) it is the awareness of the performer, not a capacity residing in the instrument of the action, that grants this;[114] c) the two results are characterized by opposite features: the watering of the mangoes is near and visible while the refreshing of the ancestors is distant and invisible.

Going one step further, Bhartṛhari (D 1.37 ll. 11-6 *ad* vt. 18) opposes an overt *prasaṅga-* interpretation (*prasaṅgalakṣaṇa*) to this metaphysic interpretation of the double effect phenomenon:

> Or the establishment of the goal is characterised by an automatic involvement (*prasaṅga*). If [something] attains a goal through something else, while not prompting the attainment of that goal, it is called '*prasaṅga*'. For example, who desires [food] is an instigator[115] for the [obtainment of] food but he is not an instigator for the putting [of the saucepan] on the fire, like one who eats leftovers.[116] [and hence does not prompt the putting of the saucepan on the fire]. Indeed only someone who would cook again even though there is cooked food still available would be such,[117] (and hence he would prompt the putting of the saucepan on the fire), when [the preparation of] much cooked food is accomplished for his sake. Here, it is the prohibition in the case of [the defects] beginning from the closed phones that is looked for.

113 D 1.37 ll. 5-11 *ad* vt. 18): *dvāv arthau gatāḥ dvigatāḥ. hetavaḥ kāryanirvṛttau samarthāḥ. iha loke eka eva hetur dvayor arthayoḥ prasādhako dṛṣṭaḥ. ekam udakam. tadviṣayā kriyā tyāgalakṣaṇā āmramūle kṛtā pitṛtarpaṇe druseke ca sama eko hetuḥ. anyatra tad evodakaṃ na dvigataṃ bhavati yadā devadattayajñadattau tarpayitavyau bhavataḥ. āmrā api viprakṛṣṭadeśāt sektavyā bhavanti. tatra yathaivodakadānaṃ dṛṣṭam adṛṣṭārthaṃ sādhayituṃ samartham ity evaṃ buddhyā prakramya pravartamānam ubhayaṃ niṣpādayati evaṃ gargādibidādipāṭhaḥ samarthaḥ ubhayaṃ kartum avayavān samudāyaṃ ca kārye pravartamāna iti.*

114 In another context the same water is not capable of refreshing Yajñadatta and Devadatta contemporaneously.

115 The term *prayojaka* is not exclusively Mīmāṃsic, being actually included both in A and in vtts. and in M. See for instance A 1.4.55 and vt. 13 ad A 3.1.26 respectively.

116 And hence does not prompt the putting of the saucepan on the fire.

117 I.e someone prompting the putting of the saucepan on the fire.

> If, in this case, the parts (i.e., the sounds of the *gaṇa*s *Gargādi, Bidādi*, etc.) convey [also] their own form , which is in each case-always qualified by another word which isbeing the first enunciation (*upadeśa*) teaching of (*upadeśa*) the whole, what would the fault be? In this way, the mango trees prompt the watering separately (i.e., on their own); the pitṛs ancestors do not prompt anything. In their case, they experience the offering of water, which is prompted [(by the mango trees]), by means of *prasaṅga*.[118]

There are many striking points of difference in this *prasaṅga* interpretation as opposed to the *tyāga*-one. First of all, there is no question of a distinction here between visible and invisible results. Yet the awareness and aims of the performer are still crucial in determining what the principal action is (getting eatable food) and what is simply associated to it (cooking it) and that therefore can therefore be skipped if it has already been done for other reasons. Similarly the example of the mangoes can be interpreted not as an action principally devoted to the satisfaction of manes, but, on the contrary, prompted by the need of watering the mango trees and then automatically involved in the overall ritual concerning the ancestors.

Finally, Bhartṛhari comes to the *tantra*-interpretation (D 1.37 ll. 17-38 *ad* vt. 18), already presented by Patañjali as being more linguistically oriented (ll. 17-9):

> Analogously, sentences are also commonly seen to have two places [of application]. He tells [us] that this (the fact of having two functions) is not only a property of objects. – Therefore, what is it then? – It is also a property of linguistic units. Among these, there are some linguistic units, which, although single units, are endowed with an accumulated denotative power. Only one part [at a time] of their denotative power is used. [...][119](ll. 21-2) A user

[118] D 1.37 ll. 11-6 *ad* vt. 18: *atha vā prasaṅgalakṣaṇārthasiddhiḥ / yady arthāprayojako' nyadvāreṇārthaṃ pratipadyate sa prasaṅga ity ucyate / yathā bhojanenārthī yaḥ prayojako 'dhiśrayaṇasya ca vighasāśivad aprayojakaḥ / yo hi niṣṭite 'py anne punaḥ pācayet sa evaṃ bhūtaḥ yadā tadarthaṃ bahvannaṃ prasādhitam / saṃvṛtādiṣu pratiṣedhaś codyate / tatra yady avayavāḥ samudāyopadeśaparaśabdena svarūpaṃ sarvatraiva viśiṣṭaṃ pratipādyeran ko doṣa syāt / evam āmrāḥ pṛthak sekasya prayojakāḥ pitaro 'prayojakāḥ / tatra prayuktam udakadānaṃ prasaṅgenānubhavantīti.*

[119] Then only the former M example (*śveto dhāvati*) is repeated in D 1.37 ll. 19-20 *ad* vt. 18. Additionally on the other hand two words each of which expresses two meanings, i.e., *purā* (1) 'formerly'; (2) 'along with', and *ārāt* (1) 'nearby'; (2) 'far off' are premised, as two easier preliminary examples of polysemous (*anekārtha*) words. As a consequence, the topic switches from the M reflection on the polysemous sentences to a more general linguistic phenomenon of polysemy, so that under the definition of *śabdaḥ śaktipracitaḥ* (repeated as *śabdo 'nekaśaktipracitaḥ* at l. 20) 'linguistic unit endowed with an accumulated denotative power' are both sorts of double entendre (*śliṣṭa*), i.e., the so-called *śliṣṭam*

> (= of language, i.e., a speaker) uses [the linguistic unit *śvetaḥ*] [either] by saying *śveto gaur* 'a white ox' [or] by saying *śvā sa ita* 'this dog has gone': the receivers (i.e. the listeners) understand their meaning according to the part of the denotative power [which is used]. These two linguistic units (e.g. the two *śvetaḥ*) have been pronounced with a different object. [120]

Here the multiple function of the recitation of *gaṇas*, which simultaneously discloses both wholes and parts, is thus confirmed by Bhartṛhari, who exemplifies it once again by a comparison with a lamp, closely comparable with the above mentioned ŚBh example:

> Like a lamp, proceeding through centralised application (*tantra*) t operates according to the intended object of people who are in need of it or, even when it is just one who is desirous to see, through [that same *tantra*-principle], it brings about knowledge and other effects even though it is just one who is desirous to see.[121]

Through this lamp-image Bhartṛhari actually points out two different patterns of centralised application (*tantra*) in the domain of linguistic signification. As the illuminating function of a single lamp can be extended to more than one people or to more than one exigency of the same user, similarly a single linguistic unit pronounced by a single speaker can convey the same meaning to more than one listener and/or more than one meaning even for a single listener, independently from the speaker's intention. This interpretation of a linguistic act sets deliberately aside the possibility of a speaker aiming to convey more than one meaning through the same linguistic unit – precisely as a rhetoric and poetic device. The speaker's side of the action of conveying a meaning results to be strictly unitary. The speaker chooses

abhinnapadaprāyam and the śliṣṭam bhinnapadaprāyam. The first depends on not segmented *padas* (i.e., on homonymous words), the latter on a different syntactic segmentation of the sentence. See Daṇḍin, *Kāvyadarśa*, 2.310: *śliṣṭam iṣṭam anekārtham ekarūpānvitaṃ vacaḥ / tad abhinnapadaṃ bhinnapadaprāyam iti dvidhā*, 'A pun (double entendre) is the desired [expression] having one form but more than one sense. It is of two kinds, depending on its relying on non-segmented *padas* (i.e., on homonymous words) or on segmented *padas* (i.e. on a different segmentation of sentence, which results in heteronymous words)'.

120 D 1.37 ll. 17-9 and 21-2 *ad* vt. 18: *tathā dviṣṭhāny api vākyāni dṛśyante / etat kathayati / na kevalam arthadharma evāyam / kiṃ tarhi / śabdadharmo 'pi / iha kaścid eka eva śabdaḥ śaktipracitaḥ / tasya kevalaṃ śaktyavacchedamātraṃ kriyate /* [...] *śveto gaur iti / śvā sa ita iti prayoktā prayuṅkte / pratipattāraḥ yathāśaktyavacchedenārthaṃ pratipadyante / arthāntareṇa dvāv etau śabdāv uccāritau.*

121 D 1.37 ll. 22-3 *ad* vt. 18: *yathā pradīpas tantreṇa pravartamāno 'rthināṃ yathābhipretam arthaṃ nirvartayati / ekasyaiva vā vidyādikā didṛkṣoś ca tantreṇa nirvartayati.*

to say either "white" or "the dog is gone" and the listener has to catch the correct option. Analogously, according to VP 2.298-9, a word that also conveys meanings connected to yet different from the meaning to convey which it was used, is compared with a lamp (*dīpa*) that, through proximity (*sāṃnidhyāt*), reveals in an object other things than that for the illumination of which it was employed (*pra-yuj-*).[122]

The final effect of *tantra* on linguistic units is described as a sort of process of multiplying the single sentence of a speaker which lastly produces more than one sentence through a single utterance:

> It is just like in the case of linguistic units: [a linguistic unit brings about] such an action by which the movement (*parispanda*) of a separated linguistic unit (*karaṇa*) is effected so that two linguistic units are indeed uttered by means of the simultaneous centralised extension (*tantra*) [of the linguistic unit itself].[123]

In this long D passage we thus find for the first time *prasaṅga* (the key term in A 1.1.60 commentaries) side by side with *tantra* and *tyāga* in an explicitly linguistic context concerned by explaining how a given linguistic utterance may perform more than one duty, i.e. may convey more than what is expected. The difference between the *prasaṅga*- and the *tantra*- procedure is here clearly highlighted as the difference between the unsystematic involvement of an element in a context different from its own where its function is needed (*prasaṅga*) and the centralisation of functions in one and same unit through proximity (*tantra*).

4.3 Conclusions

Earlier Kātyāyana and Patañjali, who show that they have a knowledge of these two procedures, without however opposing them to each other, apparently resorted to the *prasaṅga*-terminology and to the *atideśa*-procedures technically elaborat-

122 VP 2.298-9: *ghaṭādiṣu yathā dīpo yenārthena prayujyate / tato 'nyasyāpi sāṃnidhyāt sa karoti prakāśanam // saṃsargiṣu tathārtheṣu śabdo yena prayujyate / tasmāt prayojakād anyān api pratyāyayati asau.*

123 D 1.37 ll. 24-5 *ad* vt. 18: *evaṃ śabdeṣu tadṛśīṃ kriyām āpāditakaraṇaparispandāṃ yathā tantreṇa dvāv eva śabdāv uccaryate.* The *tantra*-principle seems here seems here directly connected with what, in VP, is traditionally referred to as the Bheda 'differentiation' view, which assumed as much statements as the meanings to be conveyed. The same link between Bheda view and the *tantra*-principle is found in VP 2.474-5: *atyantabhinnayor vā syāt prayoge tantralakṣaṇaḥ / upāyas tatra saṃsargaḥ pratipattṛṣu bhidyate // bhedenādhigatau pūrvaṃ śabdau tulyaśrutī punaḥ / tantreṇa pratipattāraḥ prayoktrā pratipāditāḥ.*

ed by the *Kalpasūtras*, in order to solve the tackled problem of the contradiction of *lopa* with the close relationship between a linguistic unit as an input (a cause) and sense as its output (effect). Their specific further step consists in linking the already technical *prasaṅga*-context to the highly formalized substitution-pattern, thus granting the capability of operating through the substitute to the substituendum.

Looking at things from this angle, *lopa* which is generally considered the borderline case of replacement – the so-called zero-replacement – seems vice versa to assume the role of the paradigmatic case of replacement, where the *śabda* as a cause is not perceived, although its *artha* as an effect is conveyed through a *prasaṅga*-procedure but is not replaced by anything else with regard to its phonic feature. Therefore this *śabda* as an input does exist (it is *adarśana* and not *abhāva*) and it can be perceived elsewhere according to an asymmetrical but consistent relationship between cause and effect and more generally between what is empirically perceived (*pratyakṣa*) and what can be defined as existing, that is, pertaining to the real world.

Thus both Patañjali and Bhartṛhari might have been interested in distinguishing the non-perception (*adarśana*) from the inexistence (*abhāva*) for the same reason which brought Śabara to devote such a long discussion to confuting the thesis of the identity between cognition and its object, and, as a consequence, the inconsistency and vacuity of Cognition, especially according to the Mādhyamika Buddhist Śūnyavāda. The image of the two powers of a lamp which we have quoted above, as in the case of *lopa*, was possibly aimed at maintaining the possibility of having direct perception of the cause even when it is *in absentia*, i.e. when it is perceived elsewhere from a spatial (and not temporal) point of view. Analogously, the Mīmāṃsā-example of the making of light also on the public road by a lamp placed in a palace, as an extended function of this lamp which is not perceived by whoever is on the road, can be considered as an answer to the speculative request of being perceptible, which is compulsory for whatever cause according to the classical *darśanas*. The exigency of restricting *lopa* to a determinate negation, precisely a negation of perception (*prasaktasya a-darśanam*) seems to be consistent with the explicit Nyāya-Vaiśeṣika exclusion of any absolute negation, such as by contrast it is at least confronted with the determinate one, for instance in Plato's philosophical the controversy over non-being.[124] Naiyāyikas maintain that a negative entity is not

[124] For a sketch of this comparison between Plato's and Nyāya-Vaiśeṣika theories of negative entities see Chakrabarti 1978, p. 129.

an 'independent entity', i.e., it can neither be abstracted from the place from which the negatum is excluded (*anuyogin*) nor prescind from a reference to the negatum (*pratiyogin*)[125]: according to the classical example, we can say 'a jar is not here' both because here we perceive 'a place where there is not a jar' and because we have perceived a jar elsewhere or otherwise, so that on that occasion we were able to say 'here there is a jar'.[126]

Analogously Pāṇini's commentators from Kātyāyana onward, assert that the relationship between the linguistic unit which is potentially involved (*prasakta*) in a specific place (*sthāna*) and its zero-substitute has to be indispensably safeguarded.

Abbreviations

A	*Aṣṭādhyāyī* – Sharma 1987-2003
CLG	- Saussure 1916
D	*Dīpikā* (on the M) 1 – Bronkhorst 1987
	2 – Palsule 1988
EDSHP —	
KātyŚrSū	*Kātyāyana Śrautasūtra* – Thite 2006
M	*Mahābhāṣya* – Kielhorn 1880-1885
Mil	*Milindapañha* – Trenckner 1880
MS	*Mīmāṃsā-Sūtra* – Abhyankar and Jośī 1970-1976
NPBh	Nāgeśa's *Paribhāṣenduśekhara* – Abhyankar 1960-1962
NS	*Nyāya-Sūtra* – Ruben 1928
P	*Pradīpa* – Shastri 1938
PM	*Padamañjarī* – Śastri and Shukla 1983-1885
ŚBh	*Śabarabhāṣya* – Abhyankar and Jośī 1970-1976
U	*Uddyota* – Shastri 1938
VP	*Vākyapadīya* – Rau1977
VPBh	Vyādi's *Paribhāṣāvṛtti* – Wujastyk 1993
vt.	Kātyāyana's Vārttika in M

125 See Chakrabarti 1978, p. 131. For a comparison with the Bhaṭṭa Mīmāṃsā school which accepts absence as a distinct instrument of knowledge see Freschi 2008 and Freschi 2010.

126 For the discussed interpretation of this example as an inferential judgement see Torella 2007, pp. 475-6.

References

Abhyankar, Kashinath Vasudev, ed. (2001). *The Paribhāṣendu-śekhara of Nāgojībhaṭṭa. Edited and Explained by Franz Kielhorn. Part II: Translation and Notes.* 2nd (1st ed. 1960). Poona: Bhandarkar Oriental Research Institute.

Abhyankar, Kashinath Vasudev and Ganesasastri Ambadasa Jośī, eds. (1970). *Śrīmajjaiminipraṇite Mīmāṃsādarśane: Mīmāṃsākakanthirava-Kumārilabhaṭṭapraṇita-Tantra-vārtikasahita-Śābarabhāsyopetaḥ.* Pune: Anandasrama.

Al-George, Sergiu (1967). "The Semiosis of Zero according to Pāṇini." In: *East and West* 17, Nos. 1-2, pp. 115-24.

Bal Shastri, ed. (1938). *Patañjali's Vyākaraṇa Mahābhāṣya with Kaiyaṭa's Pradīpa & Nāgojibhaṭṭa's Uddyota and Bhaṭṭoji Dīkṣita's Śabdakaustubha With the Commentary Abhinava Rājalakṣmī by Acharya Guruprasad Shasti* (Navāhnika Vol. 1). Delhi: Pratibha Prakashan 1938 (rist. 2001).

Benson, James (1990). *Patañjali's Remarks on aṅga.* South Asian Studies Series. Delhi: Oxford University Press.

Bloomfield, Leonard (1933). *Language.* London: Allen & Unwin 1935 [New York 1933].

Boccali, Giuliano and Tiziana Pontillo (2010). "The Background of the *samastavastuviṣayarūpaka* and its importance in early *kāvya*." In: *Pandanus* 4,2 '10, pp. 109-138.

Bronkhorst, Johannes (1987). *Three Problems pertaining to the Mahābhāṣya* (Post-Graduate and Research Department Series, 30: "Pandit Shripad Shastri Deodhar Memorial Lectures", 3rd Series). Poona: Bhandarkar Oriental Research Institute.

Bronkhorst, Johannes, ed. (1987a). *Mahābhāshya-Dīpikā of Bhartṛhari.* Fascicule IV, Āhnika I. Critically edited. Poona: Bhandarkar Oriental Research Institute.

Bronkhorst, Johannes, ed. (1987b). "Review of Deshpande 1985." In: *Indo-Iranian Journal* 30, pp. 296-301.

Bronkhorst, Johannes (1996). "The Correspondence Principle and its Impact on Indian Philosophy." In: *Indo-Shisôshi Kenkyû* 8, pp. 1-19.

Brough, John (1951). "Theories of General Linguistics in the Sanskrit Grammarians." In: *Transactions of the Philological Society* 1951, pp. 27-46. Repr. in: *A Reader on the Sanskrit Grammarians,* ed. J.F. Staal. Cambridge 1972, pp. 402-413.

Candotti, Maria Piera (2004). "Come dire che 'il vasaio sta modellando il vaso' senza cadere in contraddizione: origine grammaticale di un dibattito filosofico." In: *Atti dell'Undicesimo Convegno Nazionale di Studi sanscriti, Milano 22 Novembre 2002.* Ed. by Oscar Botto, Giuliano Boccali and Victor Agostini. Torino: s.n. (Ciriè: Essegrafica), pp. 55-67.

Candotti, Maria Piera (2006). *Interprétations du discours métalinguistique dans la tradition grammaticale indienne. La fortune du sûtra A 1 1 68 chez Patañjali et Bhartṛhari.* Firenze: Firenze University Press.

Candotti, Maria Piera and Tiziana Pontillo (2004). "Substitution as a Descriptive Model in Pāṇini's Grammar: towards an Opposition between Phonological and Morphological Level?." In: *Atti del Secondo Incontro Genovese di Studi Vedici e Pāṇiniani* (Genova, 23 luglio 2003 – 15 ottobre 2003). Ed. by R. Ronzitti and G. Borghi. Recco, Le Mani, pp. 1-45.

Candotti, Maria Piera and Tiziana Pontillo (2007). "The (In)separable Parts of a Plant in the *Mahābhaṣya* Imagery i.e. How Nature May Inspire a Grammarian." In: *Pandanus '07*, pp. 43-63.

Candotti, Maria Piera and Tiziana Pontillo (2010). "The Autonomous Process of Denotation: Kātyāyana and Patañjali on the Limits of Analysis." In: *Tīrthayātrā. Essays in Honour of Stefano Piano.* Ed. by P. Caracchi, A.S. Comba, A. Consolaro and A. Pelissero. Alessandria: Edizioni dell'Orso, pp. 41-61.

Candotti, Maria Piera and Tiziana T. Pontillo (2012). "Interpreting Forms with Markers: the Morphological Approach." In: *Proceedings of 12th World Sanskrit Conference* (Section 5: *Vyākaraṇa*, Helsinki, 13-18 July 2003). Motilal Banarsidass. pp. 61-82.

Candotti, Maria Piera and Tiziana Pontillo (forthcoming). "Conceptualizing Absence: Interpretations of Zero in Pāṇinian Grammarians." In: *Proceedings of ICHoLS XI Workshop "The Indian Traditions of Language Studies"*, Potsdam, 28th Aug.-2nd Sept. 2008.

Cardona, George (1997). *Pāṇini. His Work and Its Traditions.* 1. *Background and Introduction.* Delhi: Motilal Banarsidass.

Cardona, George (2004). "Pāṇinian Sūtras of the Type *anyebhyo 'pi dṛśyate.*" In: *Jambū-jyoti (Munivara Jambūvijaya Festschrift).* Ed. by M.A. Dhaky J.B. Shah. Ahmedabad: Shresthi Kasturbhai Lalbhai Smarak Nidhi, pp. 91-107.

Cardona, George (2007). "On the Position of Vyākaraṇa and Pāṇini." In: Preisendanz 2007, pp. 693-710.

Chakrabarti, Kisor Kumar (1978). "The Nyāya-Vaiśeṣika Theory of Negative Entities." In: *Journal of Indian Philosophy* 6, No. 2, pp. 129-44.

Chakrabarti, Arindam (1997). *Denying Existence. The Logic, Epistemology and Pragmatics of Negative Existentials and Fictional Discourse* ("Synthese Library" Studies in Epistemology, Logic, Methodology, and Philosophy of Science, ed. by Jaakko Hintikka, 261). Dordrecht: Kluwer Academic Publishers.

Cox, Collett (2004). "From Category to Ontology: the Changing Role of Dharma in Sarvāstivāda Abhidharma." In: *Journal of Indian Philosophy* 32, Nos. 5-6, pp. 543-97.

Debrunner, Albert (1954). *Altindische Grammatik.* 2.2. *Die Nominalsuffixe.* Göttingen: Vandenhoeck & Ruprecht.

Deshpande, Madhav M. (1981). "Sanskrit Gerund Constructions: Some Disputations." In: *Indo-Iranian Journal* 23, No. 3, pp. 167-85.

Deshpande, Madhav M. (1985). *Ellipsis and Syntactic Overlapping: Current Issues in Pāṇinian Syntactic Theory.* Poona: Bhandarkar Oriental Research Institute.

Deshpande, Madhav M. (1989). "Ellipsis in Modern Linguistics and Pāṇini." In: *Annals of Bhandarkar Oriental Institute* 70, pp. 103-24.

Freschi, Elisa (2008). *Abhāvapramāṇa and Error in Kumārila's Commentators.* In: *Nagoya Studies in Indian Culture and Buddhism: Saṃbhāṣā 27,* Department of Indian Studies, Nagoya University, pp. 1-29.

Freschi, Elisa (2010). "Facing the Boundaries of Epistemology: Kumārila on Error and Negative Cognition." In: *Journal of Indian Philosophy* 38, No. 1, pp. 39-48.

Herzberger, H. and R. Herzberger (1981). "Bhartṛhari's Paradox." In: *Journal of Indian Philosophy* 9, pp. 1-17.

Houben, Jan E.M. (1995). *The Sambandha-samuddeśa (Chapter on Relation) and Bhartṛhari's Philosophy of Language.* Groningen: Egbert Forsten.

Houben, Jan E.M. (1995a). "Bhartṛhari's Solution to the Liar and Some Other Paradoxes." In: *Journal of Indian Philosophy* 23, No. 4, pp. 381-401.

Kahrs, Eivind (1998). *Indian Semantic Analysis : the nirvacana Tradition.* Cambridge, U.K. – New York: Cambridge University Press.

Kastovsky, Dieter (1969). "Wortbildung und Nullmorphem." In: *Linguistiche Berichte* I, 2, pp. 1-13.

Kielhorn, Franz, ed. (1880-1885). *The Vyākarana-Mahābhāshya of Patañjali,* 3 vols. Bombay [Osnabrück. 1970].

Kiparsky, Paul (1982). *Some theoretical problems in Pāṇini's grammar* (Post-graduate and Research Department Series n° 16 "Professor K.V. Abhyankar Memorial Lectures", 2nd Series). Poona: Bhandarkar Oriental Research Institute.

Palsule, G.B., ed. 1988. *Mahābhāshya-Dīpikā of Bhartṛhari.* Fascicule V, Āhnika II. Critically edited, Poona.

Pontillo, Tiziana (1999). *Allomorfi e morfema "zeromorfi" in Pāṇini: sostituzione di morfemi con zero fonico* ("Dottorato in Glottologia e Filologia" XII Ciclo 1996-1999). Italy: Faculty of Arts and Humanities of the University of Milan.

Pontillo, Tiziana (2003). "Il prototipo e le regole specifiche della letteratura rituale come modello della tecnica di sostituzione di Pāṇini: il verbo *lup-* e il sostantivo *lopa-* nei *Kalpa-Sūtra*." In: *Annali della Facoltà di Lettere e Filosofia dell'Università degli Studi di Cagliari*, n.s. XXI, LVIII (2004), pp. 5-42.

Pontillo, Tiziana (2010). "Once Again on *vyakti-vacane* in *Aṣṭādhyāyī* I.2.51: *śravaṇaḥ/ śravaṇā*." In: *Rivista di Studi Sudasiatici* 4, pp. 97-126.

Preisendanz, Karin, ed. (2007), *Expanding and Merging Horizons. Contributions to South Asian and Cross-Cultural Studies in Commemoration of Wilhelm Halbfass* (Österreichische Akademie der Wissenschaften. Philosophisch-Historische Klasse Denkschriften, 351. Band, Beiträge zur Kultur- und Geistesgeschichte Asiens Nr. 53). Wien: Austrian Academy of Sciences Press.

Rau, Wilhelm, ed. (1977). *Vākyapadīya of Bhartṛhari*. Wiesbaden.

Ruben, Walter, ed. (1928). *Die Nyāyasūtra's. Text, Übersetzung, Erläuterung und Glossar.* (*Abhandlungen für die Kunde des Morgenlandes* XVIII, 2). Nandeln: Kraus Reprint (1966) [Leipzig 1928].

Saussure, F. De (1916). *Cours de linguistique génerale*, publié par Ch. Bally et A. Sechehaye, avec la collaboration de A. Riedlinger. Paris: Librairie Payot et Cie (here quoted according to the edition of 1922 (*Recueil des publications scientifiques de F. de Saussure*, ed. C. Bally and L. Gautier. Lausanne and Geneva: Payot) [Lausanne – Paris 1916].

Scharfe, Hartmut (1965). "*vacana* 'Numerus' bei Pāṇini?." In: *Zeitschrift für Vergleichende Sprachforschung* 79, pp. 239-46.

Sharma, Rama Nath (1987-2003). *The Aṣṭādhyāyī of Pāṇini*, 6 vols. New Delhi: Munshiram Manoharlal.

Śastri, S.D.D and K.P. Shukla, ed. (1983-1985). *Nyāsa or Pañcikā Commentary of Ācārya Jinendrabuddhipāda and Padamañjarī of Haradatta Miśra on the Kāśikāvṛtti [Commentary on the Aṣṭādhyāyī of Pāṇini*] of Vāmana-Jayāditya critically edited by Śastri – K.P. Shukla, 6 vols. Varanasi: Sudhi Prakashan.

Thite, Ganesh Umakant, ed. (2006). *Kātyāyana-śrautasūtra: text with English translation and notes.* Delhi: New Bharatiya Book Co.

Torella, Raffaele (2007). "Studies on Utpaladeva's Īśvarapratyabhijñāvivṛti Part I: Anupalabdhi and Apoha in a Śaiva Garb." In Preisendanz 2007, pp. 473-90.

Trenckner, Vilhelm, ed. (1880), *Milindapañha* (Pali Text Society). London: Luzac 1962 [1880].

Whitney, William Dwight (1875). *The Life and Growth of Language.* London: D. Appleton and Company.

Paolo Corda

The Infinite Possibilities of Life: Interpretations of the śūnyatā *in the Thinking of Daisaku Ikeda*[*]

The concept of *śūnyatā* (Skt.)/ *suññatā* (Pāl.) ('emptiness') is, as known, one of the cornerstones of Buddhist thought. The term (and its related adjective *śūnya* [Skt.]/ *suñña* [Pāl.] ['empty, void']),[1] which appears both in the Pāli Canon[2] and in the most ancient Mahāyānic *sūtras*,[3] finds its highest expression in the

[*] I would like to thank my dear friend Marialuisa Cellerino for her precious support in translating this paper, and the Italian Buddhist Institute Soka Gakkai for giving me access to the English translations of Ikeda's works in its head office in Florence. All possible mistakes and omissions in this paper are, of course, my responsibility only.

[1] Both probably derive from the Sanskrit root √*śū*, weak form of *śvi*, which etymologically means 'to swell', 'to grow', 'to increase', I suppose with reference to the dilatation of an empty cavity, i.e. an empty space susceptible of being filled (see Pokorny 1959-1969, 1, pp. 592-4). In the Pāli Canon the term *suñña*(-*tā*) is strictly related to the concept of *anattā* (Skt. *anātman*) and to the practice of *samādhi* (meditation); for textual references on this point, see below; also Rhys Davids and Stede 1921-1925, s.v.

[2] See in particular MN 3.104 (*Cūḷasuññatasutta*); MN 3.109 (*Mahāsuññatasutta*); SN 3.140 (*Pheṇa*); SN 4.54 (*Suñña*); and Sn 1116-9 (*Mogharājamāṇavapucchā*), which attests that the term was already used in the early phases of Buddhism: *suññato lokaṃ avekkhassu mogharāja sadā sato* (Sn 1119). On the dating of *Suttanipāta*, see Cicalò 2002, pp. 13-6; Norman 1983, pp. 63-4. For an examination of the concept of emptiness in early Buddhism, see Choong 1999.

[3] See e.g. the significant passage in the *Śālistambasūtra*: *yaḥ kaścid-bhadanta śāriputremaṃ pratītyasamutpādaṃ bhagavatā samyak praṇītam-evaṃ yathābhūtaṃ samyakprajñayā* [...] *asatas-tucchato ṛktato 'sārato rogato gaṇḍataḥ śalyato 'ghato 'nityato duḥkhataḥ śūnyato 'nātmataś-ca samanupaśyati* (Śāl, pp. 70-1). In accordance with Ross Reat's hypothesis, a similar sequence can also be found in the Canon, but the passage he gives for reference (i.e. SN 2.112: *aniccato ... dukkhato ... rogato ... bhayato passanti*; see Śāl, p. 71) is only partially similar to the above-

sūtras of mature Mahāyāna (particularly in the *Prajñāpāramitā* literature)[4] and in the works of Nāgārjuna (2nd-3rd c. CE) and his school.[5] Daisaku Ikeda (1928-), a contemporary Buddhist philosopher, peacebuilder and educator,[6] during the last thirty years has developed an interpretative point of view on the *śūnyatā* as potentiality[7] placing it in relation to the concept of 'life'.[8]

quoted one. Instead, a closer similarity can be detected in a passage that occurs in MN 1.435-6 and 500: *so yad-eva tattha hoti rūpagataṃ vedanāgataṃ saññāgataṃ saṅkhāragataṃ viññāṇagataṃ te dhamme aniccato dukkhato rogato gaṇḍato sallato aghato ābādhato parato palokato suññato anattato samanupassati* (the same passage also occurs several times in AN 2.128 and 130, 4.422-6; an analogous passage in SN 3.167-8; a similar and wider sequence, with *rittato* and *tucchato*, in Nd[1] 53, 56, 277, 427, Nd[2] 127); the strong similarity between the sequences of the two passages, to the best of my knowledge, has gone unnoticed until now. On the antiquity of the *Śālistambasūtra*, its correspondences to the Pāli Canon and its significance for the reconstruction of the conceptual framework of the earliest Buddhism, see Ross Reat 1993. On the three *lakṣaṇas* or 'marks of existence' (i.e. *anitya, duḥkha, anātman*), see Conze 1962, pp. 34-46. On the responsibility of the Sarvāstivādins in adding the term *śūnya* to the three *lakṣanas*, see Streng 1967, p. 47, n. 3.

[4] For an overview on *Prajñāpāramitā* literature, its origin and development, and its ontology, see Conze 1978; Conze 1967, pp. 123-47; Conze 1953.

[5] On Nāgārjuna's works and *Madhyamaka* literature, see Lindtner 1987; Ruegg 1981; Ruegg 2010, pp. 13-36. For a preliminary introduction to Nāgārjuna's philosophy and to his main work, the *Mūlamadhyamakakārikās*, see Kalupahana 1991; Westerhoff 2009.

[6] For an introduction to Ikeda's life and works, his philosophical thinking and his commitment for peace and education, see Kimura 2002; Giaiero 2008; Urbain 2010; Ikeda 2001. Also his official website, http://www.daisakuikeda.org/.

[7] The term 'potentiality' should not be intended here in the sense of a material indeterminate principle or substance, i.e. as a sort of *prakṛti* or as a *dravya*. Conze's specification (1962, p. 61) quoted by Streng (1967, p. 77) seems to be largely surpassed nowadays (see e.g. Oh 2000). It is a fact that the early Chinese translations of Buddhist *sūtras* were influenced by Taoist technical terminology, but from Kumārajīva (according to Sengzhao, 344-413 CE) onwards the *geyi* method (i.e. the method of matching the meaning of Buddhist and Taoist concepts) was abandoned in favour of more 'critically' based methodologies (on *geyi*, see Kürcher 2007, p. 184; T'ang 1951; see also Ikeda 2009b, pp. 53-5), so that e.g. – as Inada states – the Chinese had been able, through Buddhist influence, 'to understand the true import of *śūnyatā* and incorporate it into their own Taoist concept of *wu*' (Inada 1994, pp. 33). *Śūnyatā* as potentiality should rather be intended, in accordance with Westerhoff's examination of the concept of *svabhāva* in Nāgārjuna's work, not as a substance-*svabhāva* but instead as an absolute-*svabhāva*, i.e. the essence-*svabhāva* of *pratītyasamutpāda* (on this concept see below, n. 37), as Buddhapālita defines it, the uneliminable specific quality of the causal process (see Westerhoff 2009, pp. 19-52, in particular n. 16). Intended this way, the *śūnyatā* constitutes thus the *conditio sine qua non*, the condition of possibility of the arising of phenomena (i.e. conditioned beings), in accordance with its probable etymological meaning.

[8] As we will see, Ikeda uses at least three different strictly related acceptations of the concept of 'life': biological, phenomenological, and organicistic.

1 The Concept of 'Life' in Ikeda's Thought and its Relation to śūnyatā

The reference to the concept of 'life' has deep roots in the thinking of Ikeda: it goes back to an insight of his Buddhist master Jōsei Toda (1900-1958), who mused at length about the meaning of the *Saddharmapuṇḍarīkasūtra*[9] and other scriptures in his cell during his imprisonment,[10] in particular on what is considered in the Far East the prologue of the former, i.e. the *Anantanirdeśasūtra*[11] (無量義經, Jpn. *Muryōgikyō*). In this last scripture there is a portion in verses that says:

> [H]is body[12] [is] neither existing nor not existing,
> neither caused nor conditioned, neither self nor other,
> neither square nor round, neither short nor long,
> neither appearing nor disappearing, neither born nor extinguished,
> neither created nor arising, neither acted nor made,[13]
> neither sitting nor lying down, neither walking nor standing,
> neither moving nor turning, neither idle nor still,[14]

[9] For a preliminary introduction to the *Saddharmapuṇḍarīkasūtra*, which text was gradually composed probably between the end of the 1st c. BCE and the end of the 2nd c. CE through successive additions to the original *gāthās* and short prose passages, see Kern 1884, pp. ix-xxxix; Meazza 2001, pp. 3-39. For a preliminary introduction to Kumārajīva's Chinese translation of the text done in 406 CE (T 262: 妙法蓮華經, Jpn. *Myōhōrengekyō*), of great historical and literary importance, see Watson 1993, pp. ix-xxix; Katō et al. 1975, pp. xiii-xviii. For an examination of Kumārajīva's translating methods applied to the *Madhyamaka* literature, see Robinson 1976, pp. 71-95. For an account of the different manuscripts of the *sūtra*, see Jamieson 2002.

[10] In 1943 Toda and his master, the pedagogist Tsunesaburo Makiguchi (1871-1944), were arrested and imprisoned for their opposition to the war and to the Japanese militarist government. The elderly Makiguchi died in prison, while his disciple was released on July 1945, shortly before the end of the war. Ikeda talks of these events in his biographical and autobiographical novel series *The Human Revolution*. See also Kimura 2002, pp. 118-20; Giaiero 2008, p. 17; Urbain 2010, pp. 56-7, 61. On Toda's life and commitment for peace, see ibid., pp. 49-73.

[11] Work of uncertain date, translated into Chinese by Dharmajātayaśas probably in 481 CE; see Katō et al. 1975, p. xvii.

[12] The body of the Buddha (i.e. the *dharmakāya*).

[13] Tamura translates 非爲作 as "neither made nor produced" (Katō et al. 1975, p. 6). Both 爲 *wéi* and 作 *zuò* correspond to the derivatives of the Sanskrit root √*kṛ* (see Hirakawa 1997, pp. 799 and 199 respectively) and mean 'to do, to make', but while the former seems to express an action that lasts over time (i.e. 'to affect sthg.', also 'to suffer the effect of some action'; see Morrison 1815-1822, 1-2, p. 566; Mathews 1943, p. 1048), the latter seems to express an action that resolves itself immediately or in a short amount of time (i.e. lit. 'to arise'; see Morrison 1815-1822, 1-1, p. 93; Mathews 1943, p. 996).

[14] Tamura translates 非閑靜 as "neither calm nor quiet" (Katō et al. 1975, p. 7). 閑 *xián* (see Morrison 1815-1822, 1-3, p. 600; Mathews 1943, p. 397: 'bar, barrier, fence') corresponds to the Skt. *vivikta*= 'separated, isolated, solitary' (see Hirakawa

> neither advancing nor retreating, neither in safety nor danger,
> neither right nor wrong, neither gaining nor losing,[15]
> neither that nor this, neither departing[16] nor coming,
> neither blue nor yellow, neither red nor white,
> neither crimson nor purple nor any other sort of color [...] (tr. Watson 2009, p. 7)[17]

But what actually is this indescribable 'body of the Buddha'? In his novel *The Human Revolution,* Ikeda describes in this way the insight of his master Toda:

> Suddenly, the word 'life' flashed through his mind.
> And in that instant, he arrived at a complete awareness of the meaning of the twelve mystic lines[18] [...]
> 'Is not the entity[19] none other than life? When we realize this, then nothing is mystic or mysterious. It is now obvious that the Buddha means life itself.'
> Toda rose to his feet. He did not in the least feel the bitter cold of the cell and was completely unaware of the time. Breathing deeply, with rosy cheeks and glowing eyes, filled inside with a boundless joy, he began to walk back and forth.
> It was a tiny cell. He paced up and down in a self-possessed manner, his emaciated shoulders braced upright and his fists clenched tight.

1997, p. 1198), while 靜 *jìng* (see Morrison 1815-1822, 1-3, p. 657; Mathews 1943, p. 162: 'to be silent, stillness; quiet, peaceful, without motion') to the terms *śānta, śama, śamatha* etc., which have similar meanings like 'tranquil(lity), calm(ness), free from (absence of) passions' (see Hirakawa 1997, p. 1244).

15 Tamura translates 非得失 as "without merit or demerit" (Katō et al. 1975, p. 7). 得 *dé* (see Morrison 1815-1822, 1-2, p. 123; Mathews 1943, p. 888: 'to obtain, to attain, to gain') corresponds to the Skt. *√labh/ pra-√āp* and their derivatives (which express the idea of obtaining sthg.; see Hirakawa 1997, p. 446); 失 *shī* (see Morrison 1815-1822, 1-1, p. 586; Mathews 1943, p. 813: 'to lose, to miss, to err') corresponds to the Skt. *(vi-)√naś,* its derivatives and similar terms (which express the ideas of perishing, deprivation and loss; see Hirakawa 1997, p. 336). I suppose that Tamura's translation also takes account of the meanings that these characters get in the Japanese language (see Nelson 1997, pp. 415 and 293 respectively).

16 Tamura translates 去 *qù* as "going" (Katō et al. 1975, p. 7); the character (see Morrison 1815-1822, 1-1, p. 333; Mathews 1943, p. 227: 'to go [away]') corresponds to the Skt. *√gam/ √i/ √yā* and their derivatives (see Hirakawa 1997, p. 224).

17 其身非有亦非無, 非因非緣非自他, 非方非圓非短長, 非出非沒非生滅, 非造非起非爲作, 非坐非臥非行住, 非動非轉非閑靜, 非進非退非安危, 非是非非非得失, 非彼非此非去來, 非青非黃非赤白, 非紅非紫種種色 (T 276, 385a4-9). See also Katō et al. 1975, pp. 6-7.

18 Traditionally the passage is called 'of the thirty-four negations', the reckoning depending on the occurrencies of the negative particle 非 *fēi,* but in fact the negatives are forty-five.

19 Here it refers to the 'body of the Buddha' (i.e. the *dharmakāya*). On this concept, see e.g. Cornu 2003, entry 'kāya', p. 301, where the author defines the first aspect of *dharmakāya* (i.e. the *svabhāvakāya*) as the dimension of emptiness of enlightenment (*bodhi*), pure potentiality free from characteristics (*alakṣaṇa*), in which there is no duality and in which the discursive or conceptual thought (*vikalpa*) disappears.

'Buddha is both life itself and an expression of life. It does not exist outside ourselves, but within our lives. No, it exists outside our lives as well. It is the life of the entire universe! Everyone inherently possesses Buddhahood.[20] And we can tap it by chanting daimoku[21] to the Gohonzon.'
He wanted to cry out – to anyone, to everyone. In that instance, his narrow cell seemed to expand infinitely. (Ikeda 1986b, pp. 8-9)[22]

As Ikeda states, Toda wanted to perceive, to experience that entity (i.e. the *dharmakāya*) with his whole life, because he was never satisfied with abstract understanding (i.e. with discursive thought; Ikeda 1995, p. 29). The *dharmakāya* – Ikeda claims – can only be described through a series of negations, its reality not being satisfactorily containable by any definition; but although it can be said that it transcends the descriptive possibilities of language, and that after all it dwells in the state of *kū* (i.e. *śūnyatā*),[23] these explanations are still unsatisfactory (ibid.), obviously because of their abstractness.

[20] Here it refers to the Buddha-nature (*tathāgatagarbha*). For an examination of this concept in Indian and Chinese Buddhism, see Brown 1991; Lai 1982. For a general sketch on this point in relation to the development of Chinese Buddhism, also Lai 2002. On the *tathāgatagarbha* as Absolute in Mahāyānic thought, see Takasaki 1966, pp. 26-31. For an examination of Tiantai Zhiyi's (538-597 CE) conception of the Buddha-nature in relation to *Madhyamaka* philosophy, see Ng 1993, pp. 62-89.

[21] Lit. 'title (of the Lotus Sūtra)', i.e. the fundamental religious practice of Nichiren Buddhism consisting in the repetition of the *mantra* 南無妙法蓮華經 (Jpn. *Nam-myōhō-renge-kyō*, 'Praise to the Lotus Sūtra of the True Law') in front of the *maṇḍala* (Jpn. *Go-honzon*, lit. 'The object of worship', being 御 *GO* an honorific prefix) written by Nichiren Daishōnin (1222-1282) in 1279. It should be noted that the lotus flower in Tiantai-Nichiren hermeneutics represents the simultaneity of cause and effect, therefore from a doctrinal perspective this *mantra* refers not to a mere title but instead to the Law, i.e. the *Dharma*, of causal process, i.e. of *pratītyasamutpāda*, which is described as *sad-*, i.e. 'good, true'. Kumārajīva translates *sad-* with the Chinese character 妙 *miào* which lit. means 'beautiful, excellent, wonderful, mysterious, subtle' (see Morrison 1815-1822, 1-1, p. 613; Mathews 1943, p. 627).

[22] For further details on Toda's reflections in his cell about the concept of the 'body of the Buddha', the Thirty-four Negations, the significance of the concept of 'life' as interpretative tool of Buddhist doctrine in modern times, and the meaning of the *Saddharmapuṇḍarīkasūtra*, see Ikeda 1986b, pp. 3-11. See also Ikeda 1995, pp. 27-38.

[23] The Chinese character 空 (Chn. *kōng*, Jpn. *KŪ*) that translates the related Sanskrit words *śūnya* and *śūnyatā* (and also *rikta* and *ākāśa*; see Hirakawa 1997, p. 908), covers the semantic ambit of the concepts of 'void (space)', 'empty' (see Morrison 1815-1822, 1-2, p. 803; Mathews 1943, p. 547; Nelson 1997, p. 816); moreover, as Ikeda states, it must be distinguished from the mere nothingness (無 Chn. *wú, mó*; Jpn. *BU, MU*; see Morrison 1815-1822, 1-2, p. 543; Mathews 1943, p. 1065; Nelson 1997, p. 695; it corresponds to the Skt. *abhāva, asat, nāstitva*; see Hirakawa 1997, p. 752); see Toynbee and Ikeda 2007, p. 255.

Indeed, Ikeda explains that the state of *kū* (i.e. *śūnyatā*), a void permeated by potentiality, is something real[24] though it is not phenomenally manifest;[25] and although it seems to resemble the non-being (i.e. the mere nothingness), it is quite different from this because, under proper conditions, it can become manifest in perceivable forms (i.e. phenomena, conditioned beings),[26] so it cannot be conceived either as being (i.e. *bhāva*) or as non-being (i.e. *abhāva*; Toynbee and Ikeda 2007, p. 255), simply, it transcends both.

It should be noted that Toda's insight came from a real life situation, from his relation to the lived reality of a harsh detention, from his effort to go beyond that situation, in which physical constraint only left the freedom of the spirit intact, which he knew how to cultivate through reflection and meditation. The knowledge that he gained then was precisely that 'Buddha is life itself'.[27]

Ikeda states:

> *Life* is a straightforward, familiar word we use every day. But at the same time it is a word that can express the most profound essence of the Buddhist Law, a single word that expresses infinite meaning. All human beings are endowed with life, so this word has practical, concrete meaning for everyone. In this way, Mr. Toda's realization made Buddhism comprehensible to all.
> Life also has enormous diversity. It is rich and full of energy. At the same time, it operates according to certain laws and has a defined rhythm. The doctrine of a single life-moment possessing three thousand realms (*ichinen sanzen*)[28] describes this harmony

[24] In the sense of a fact, not of a physical being (a phenomenon, i.e. a finite, conditioned being), which would obviously be contradictory because the *śūnyatā*, as known, is not a thing, a conditioned being.

[25] The state of emptiness is not directly visible or perceptible as it is not a phenomenon among phenomena, but the 'source' of them (i.e. it lies underneath them not as substance but as condition of possibility). On the *śūnyatā* as substratum that can, under proper conditions, cause activity in the visible superstratum (i.e. the phenomenal reality), see Ikeda 1982, p. 55. 'Substratum' means here, I think, not a substance but the causal structure operating through the principle of *pratītyasamutpāda* that lies underneath the above perceptible structure of phenomena.

[26] According to the principle that 'nothing comes from nothingness'. As Ikeda states elsewhere, nothing can be produced from nothingness, but from the *śūnyatā*, which is an infinite potentiality, anything and everything can be produced depending on the causes involved (Ikeda 2009a, p. 148); the sense of this passage is that the *pratītyasamutpāda*, being empty, i.e. *śūnya*, is infinitely productive.

[27] See Ikeda 1995, p. 30.

[28] 一念三千. This doctrine had been developed by Tiantai Zhiyi (539-597 CE) in his main work *Great Concentration and Insight* (摩訶止観, Chn. *Mohe Zhiguan*, Jpn. *Maka Shikan*). The concept of *ichinen* (Chn. *yinian*) is related to the Sanskrit

> in diversity, and one who has perceived the essence of this principle is a Buddha.
> Life is also free and unfettered. It is an open entity in constant communication with the external world, always exchanging matter and energy and information. Yet while open, it maintains its autonomy.[29] Life is characterized by this openness to the entire universe and a harmonious freedom. (Ikeda 1995, p. 31)

Considered not as a mere word or abstract conceptual category, but as a complex set of phenomena imbued with a constant dynamic, life is in itself impermeable to language, indefinable, because both language and discursive thought, by their nature discriminative, cannot embrace or exhaust its infinite richness;[30] they can only express partial aspects of it from time to time, being themselves after all manifestations of the fundamental reality of life, and therefore of the *śūnyatā.* Toda – Ikeda explains – believed that the true nature of life does not flow or stand still, but rather is analogous to the empty space (Ikeda 1995, p. 38), that must be understood not as a mere physical space characterized by the absence of objects (in accordance with the container-contents model), but as a situational context fraught with possibilities, from which the multiple manifestations of life arise;[31] and this is precisely the *śūnyatā,* as we have already noted.

2 *Nāgārjuna, Emptiness and the Dynamic of Life*

A use of negation analogous to that in the above passage of the *Anantanirdeśasūtra* can be found in the well-known *incipit* of

word *kṣana* and its derivatives (see Hirakawa 1997, p. 14) but its meaning is wider than that of the latter (see EBDC 2002, entry 'ichinen', pp. 299-300). For an examination of Tiantai metaphysics, see Liu 2006, pp. 3-14. For an introduction and a translation of the first chapter of Zhiyi's above-mentioned work, see Donner and Stevenson 1993.

29 Here Ikeda seems to use a biological meaning of the concept of 'life'. For an interesting examination of life from a biological point of view, see Maturana and Varela 1994. On the autonomy of biological life, see also Varela 1979.

30 *Śūnyatā* – Ikeda states – means that nothing has a fixed existence because all phenomena are fundamentally empty, i.e. undifferentiated potentiality, and this potentiality might be explained as the energy that causes both natural (like the blossoming of flowers) and human phenomena (like the language; Huyghe and Ikeda 2007, p. 170), where 'energy' is not to be understood in the sense of modern physics but rather as the potential through which life can manifest and individualize itself (see Toynbee and Ikeda 2007, pp. 246-7). On the limits of language and discursive thought, see Ikeda 2004, pp. 45-6; Ikeda 2010, pp. 38-9.

31 Referring to the reflections and studies on physical space from classical Greece to modern science, Ikeda notes that space is different from the mere void because it is able to influence physical objects and, depending on conditions, even to produce matter (Toynbee and Ikeda, p. 268).

Nāgārjuna's *Mūlamadhyamakakārikās*, which supposedly has no evident historical connection with the former:

> I honour him, the most excellent amongst the speakers, who, fully enlightened, taught the dependent co-arising (*pratītyasamutpādam*), (which is) the blissful[32] cessation of conceptual constructions, i.e. of the proliferations of discursive thought (*prapañca-upaśamaṃ śivam*),[33] without destruction (*anirodham*) nor production (*anutpādam*),[34] without annihilation (*anucchedam*) nor permanence (*aśāśvataṃ*), without identity (*anekārtham*) nor diver-

[32] Also 'propitious' to the reaching of final Liberation, i.e. *Nirvāṇa*. Here it can also be referred to *pratītyasamutpāda* (see below). For an alternative translation, see Kalupahana 1991, p. 101.

[33] In translating *śiva* (which essentially means 'auspicious, kind, blissful') Kumārajīva used the Chinese character 善 *shàn*, which means 'good, virtuous, gentle, mild' (see Morrison 1815-1822, 1-1, p. 404; Mathews 1943, p. 777), although he had other characters at his disposal. According to Robinson (1976, p. 83) the use of that character does not convey the meaning of the word *śiva*, but I suppose that Kumārajīva's choice was due to the fact that he interpreted this word 1. as an attributive qualifier referred to the *samāsa prapañca-upaśama*, and 2. as also expressing in the sentence the meaning of 'kind, benign', which the original Sanskrit word actually has. It is a fact, anyhow, that the term *śiva* may be interpreted as either a noun (in this case, in accordance with Monier-Williams' *Dictionary*, it might mean 'liberation, emancipation') or an adjective (in this case it can be referred to either *pratītyasamutpādam* or *prapañca-upaśamam*), and that the expression *prapañcopaśamaḥ śivaḥ* recurs only once more (MMK 25.24: *sarvopalambhopaśamaḥ prapañcopaśamaḥ śivaḥ | na kvacitkasyacitkaściddharmo buddhena deśitaḥ*; see MMK[V], p. 236; MMK[P], p. 538; according to Kalupahana 1991, p. 152, there might be a third occurrence of the expression in the form of the synonym *draṣṭavyopaśama śiva* in MMK 5.8, see below, n. 39), in the final verses of the twenty-fifth chapter of MMK, which concerns the examination of *Nirvāṇa*. In this case too the word *śiva* might be interpreted as either a noun (according to Kalupahana 1991, p. 369) or an adjective referring to the immediately foregoing words *sarvopalambhopaśamaḥ prapancopaśamaḥ* (according to Inada 1993, p. 159), but it is indisputable that Nāgārjuna's use of this term precisely in this chapter is not accidental; it should be noted though that the *samāsa prapañca-upaśama* also recurs only twice in the MMK (in the *incipit* and in the verses quoted above), so that it seems that in the context of MMK the expression *prapañcopaśamaḥ śivaḥ* may form a whole concept. It is interesting to observe also that a grammatical Indian source (*Uṇādisūtra* 1.153) relates the word *śiva* to the root √*śī* 'to lie', so that its meaning would be 'in whom all things lie,' and also that it is perhaps related to the root √*śvi*, the same to which the word *śūnya* is related. *Prapañca* means lit. 'expansion, development, manifestation'; Kalupahana (1991, p. 101) translates it as 'obsession', and *upaśama* as 'appeasement', in accordance with the Canon (see Kalupahana 1980, pp. 83-4), emphasizing in this way, I think, the emotional aspect of these concepts and giving them thus a sense which is more related to meditation and more psychological rather than analytical.

[34] Kalupahana (1991, p. 101) translates *anirodham* and *anutpādam* as 'non-ceasing' and 'non-arising', Inada (1993, p. 39) as 'non-extinction' and 'non-origination', but in this case I prefer to translate more literally.

sity (*anānārtham*),[35] without coming (into existence) (*anāgamam*) nor going (out of existence) (*anirgamam*).[36]

This eightfold negation referred to the Buddhist principle of *pratītyasamutpāda*[37] (with which, in Nāgārjuna's philosophy, the concept of emptiness is identified) should not be intended in a restrictive sense (i.e. as limited only to the above eight concepts) – Ikeda claims – because 'it is through this process of negation of every possible concept that one arrives at an understanding of the *śūnyatā*' (Ikeda 2009a, p. 147). But although one arrives at it through a process of negation, this emptiness 'is not the same as mere "nothingness" [...]: we have negated all the possible characteristics or predicates that might ordinarily be used to describe it, but it is totally different in its essential nature from the kind of nothingness that is customarily associated with nihilistic thought[38] [...]; such a mere nothingness or non-being, which is the opposite of being, would of course in Nāgārjuna's thought be negated along with all other concepts,' because ultimately the *śūnyatā* 'transcends both non-being and being' (ibid., pp. 147-8).[39] The Middle Way (i.e. the *madhyamāpratipad*) – Ikeda

[35] The word *nānā* means both 'different' and 'various', the latter implying a plurality, so I prefer to translate *anānārtham* as 'non-diversity' rather than 'non-difference'.

[36] My translation. MMK(V), p. 4; MMK(P), p. 11: *anirodhamanutpādamanucchedamaśāśvataṃ | anekārthamanānārthamanāgamamanirgamaṃ || yaḥ pratityasamutpādaṃ prapañcopaśamaṃ śivaṃ | deśayāmāsa saṃbuddhastaṃ vande vadatāṃ varaṃ.* I partly followed the readings of Gnoli's translation (2001-2004, 2, p. 587), and Inada's (1993, p. 39). For an alternative translation of and a brief introduction to this passage, see Kalupahana 1991, p. 101. Kumārajīva's version of this passage: 不生亦不滅, 不常亦不斷, 不一亦不異, 不來亦不出, 能說是因緣, 善滅諸戲論, 我稽首禮佛, 諸說中第一 (T 1564, 1b14-17). For a translation, see Robinson 1976, p. 83; Ikeda 2009a, pp. 146-7.

[37] As known, the theory of dependent co-arising (i.e. the *pratītyasamutpāda*) - as Ikeda states – means that every phenomenon, either natural or social, is strictly connected to every other one, therefore nothing can exist in isolation because all phenomena are interrelated (Ikeda 2004, p. 5; Ikeda 2010, p. 7). According to this theory – Ikeda explains elsewhere – 'no beings or events exist entirely separate in the world; all are linked to other beings and other events through the chain of causation [i.e. the causal process of *pratītyasamutpāda*]' (Ikeda 2009a, p. 148).

[38] Mahāyāna Buddhism – Ikeda claims – places the *śūnyatā* in a philosophical framework in which reality is conceived as an eternal flux, i.e. the ceaseless and dynamic flowing of life itself, which differs from a nihilistic, and therefore static, understanding (Ikeda 2004, p. 6; Ikeda 2010, p. 7; also Ikeda 1982, p. 138).

[39] See, e.g., MMK 5.8: *astitvaṃ ye tu paśyanti nāstitvaṃ cālpabuddhayaḥ | bhāvānāṃ te na paśyanti draṣṭavyopaśamaṃ śivaṃ* (MMK[V], p. 54; MMK[P], p. 135). On the transcendence of the concept of *śūnyatā* compared to those of being and non-being, see Ikeda 1982, p. 54, where the Author states that if one tries to think of the *śūnyatā* as existent, it does not exist, while if one tries to think of it as non-existent, it does exist, albeit on a non-ordinary plane.

concludes – 'consists of a process of perpetual negation [...:] it is an attempt to describe the interdependence of potentiality and [takes] place by continually postulating what it is not' (ibid., p. 149).

According to him, there are two fundamental reasons for which negations are used to express the *śūnyatā*: the first is that, as we saw above, it defies positive description (Ikeda 1982, p. 56); the second is the need of overcoming preconceptions and avoiding conventional value judgements (ibid.).[40]

About the problem of the limits of discursive thought and language, it can be further specified that while discursive thought 'tends to reify and crystallize the reality' (i.e. our experiences; see Ikeda 2004, pp. 45-6),[41] similarly language 'tends to fix and imprison phenomena' into words and conceptual schemes (Ikeda 2004, p. 46). According to Nāgārjuna – Ikeda notes – the words only have an instrumental value:[42] 'the absolute reality of all phenomena, in fact, goes beyond the language and cannot be defined by it' (ibid.; my translations). The great Indian philosopher wishes to point out 'that we must not allow ourselves to become the prisoner of mere words such as *dependent origination* and *non-substantiality*[43] [i.e. emptiness; ...] rather they are ideals to be realized and made concrete through the unceasing

[40] On this subject, see the passages of the *Vimalakīrtinirdeśasūtra* that tell about Śāriputra (whose vicissitudes in the text represent the culmination of the critique of conventional thinking), in particular VN 3.3-4 ('The silence of Śāriputra'; see Lamotte 1962, pp. 142-5; Thurman 1976, pp. 24-5; Watson 1996, p. 37); VN 5.1-5/9-10 (see Lamotte 1962, pp. 242-7, 249-52; Thurman 1976, pp. 50-2; Watson 1996, pp. 75-8); VN 6.7-15 (see Lamotte 1962, pp. 271-83; Thurman 1976, pp. 58-63; Watson 1996, pp. 86-92). For a brief introduction to and a translation of the Tibetan version of the *sūtra*, see Thurman 1976; of Kumārajīva's Chinese translation (T 475), see Watson 1997. For a more specialized treatment of the text based on the Tibetan version and Xuanzang's (Hsüan-tsang, ca. 600-664) Chinese translation, see Lamotte 1962. For a brief account of Prof. Takahashi's (Taishō University) recent discovery of the original Sanskrit of this text, see Steinkellner 2004, p. 24. For Ikeda's interpretation of the above-quoted passages, see Ikeda 2009a, pp. 103-8.

[41] I mainly follow the Italian translation of this work, because it was carried out directly on the Japanese original text and encompasses the complete passage, while some parts of it are missing in the English translation.

[42] See MMK 24.10: *vyavahāramanāśritya paramārtho na deśyate* | *paramārthamanāgamya nirvāṇaṃ nādhigamyate* (MMK[V], p. 216; MMK[P], p. 494). See also the well-known 'simile of the raft' in MN 1.134-5 (*Alagaddūpamasutta*), where the Buddha states that the Teaching, i.e. the *Dharma*, is like a raft which, being built for the purpose of crossing an expanse of water, should be abandoned without attachment once reached the other shore (for a translation of this passage, see Ñāṇamoli and Bodhi 1995, pp. 228-9).

[43] See MMK 13.8: *śūnyatā sarvadṛṣṭīnāṃ proktā niḥsaraṇam jinaiḥ* | *yeṣāṃ tu śūnyatā dṛṣṭistānasādhyān babhāṣire* (MMK[V], p. 108; MMK[P], p. 247).

practice of the Way of the Buddha,' so that the philosophy of Nāgārjuna 'should therefore be properly understood not as a system of intellectual terms and concepts but as a program for action' (Ikeda 2009a, p. 150).[44]

Clinging to the words and abstract concepts, trying to harness reality with them, while losing sight of the essential: this is the error of those who do not actively perceive the *śūnyatā*, an attitude that inevitably leads to withdrawing into the narrow boundaries of the prearranged and of the conventional, and to losing the momentum toward life and the unlimited possibilities it constantly offers. Stopping the flow of reality with words – Ikeda concludes in this regard – means destroying the dynamic osmosis between completeness and incompleteness and creating the illusion that a temporary stability of phenomena is eternal[45] (Ikeda 2004, p. 46; Ikeda 2010, p. 39). Life, however, as we know, is a continuous pulse, a constant oscillation between being and non-being, a continuous fluctuation of phenomena that now appear emerging from the rich substratum of the *śūnyatā* by causality and soon disappear retreating in the state of latency (i.e. of pure possibility), ready to emerge again when the right conditions are present. This is the rhythm of life according to Ikeda and, from his point of view, according to Buddhism. Besides, such a complex set of phenomena as life cannot be understood by examining it from a single fixed point of view (Ikeda 1982, p. 49).[46] So this would explain the reason behind the long list of negations in the *Anantanirdeśasūtra* (and similarly, in the *Madhyamakakārikās*): it is the complete negation of all ordinary conceptions and even of the common, conventional negation itself (although the recognition of the instrumental value of words and abstract concepts does not mean absolute negation of their function and utility, as Nāgārjuna himself states;[47] ibid., p. 56). A clever expedient (an *upāya-kauśalya*,[48] it could be said), therefore, to lead the ordinary person as well as the scholar to an elevated attitude of openness of mind and heart to life and its innumerable and polyhedric objectual and situational realities.

[44] Indeed, as Ikeda suggests immediately after, most of Nāgārjuna's writings 'were in fact the product of actual debates he held with his contemporaries' (Ikeda 2009a, p. 150). On the work of Nāgārjuna as intended to criticize the doctrinal views of both Sautrāntikas and Sarvāstivādins, see Kalupahana's (1991) introduction to and analysis of the MMK.

[45] I think he is referring here to a *śaśvatavāda*-like position.

[46] A similar and wider comment on the same subject in Ikeda 1982, p. 63.

[47] See MMK 24.10-11 (MMK[V], p. 216; MMK[P], pp. 494-5).

[48] For a preliminary introduction to this important Buddhist concept, see Pye 2003; Federman 2009. On this concept in Nāgārjuna's thought, see Schroeder 2000.

3 'Non-duality', Discriminative Thought and Individual Inner Transformation: The Role of śūnyatā *in the Twenty-first Century*

Among the dialectical couples that belong to ordinary and discriminative thought refuted by the Buddhist 'doctrine of non-duality' (*advayadharmamukha*),[49] according to Asaṅga (4th c. CE), there is primarily that of being/not-being (or existence/non-existence, i.e. *bhāva*/*abhāva*).[50] This couple, according to Buddhism, is only applicable to perceptible and phenomenal reality, because the fundamental reality, the ultimate reality of the *dharmas*[51] (i.e. *tathatā*), transcends both categories. From Ikeda's interpretative point of view, phenomenal life and death are part of the endless cycle of cosmic life that embraces and surpasses both, never reducing itself to either one of them or both.[52] In this the ultimate reality, i.e. the *śūnyatā*, – Ikeda states – is similar to dreams because like dreams it cannot be organized into the common concept of reality, being both the former and the latter independent of the two most important measuring parameters of ordinary reality, i.e. time and space (Ikeda 1982, pp. 47-8).[53]

The spiritual nature of life,[54] i.e. the *śūnyatā*, indeed, – Ikeda claims – goes beyond the ordinary limits and concept of space and time because, by being an everlasting and all-pervasive limitless potential, it breaks the space-time framework, and consequently cannot be confined within the concepts of existence and non-existence (Ikeda 1982, p. 55; Ikeda 2004, pp. 126-7; Ikeda 2010, p. 141).

Toda's insight, therefore, 'was not simply intellectual; it signified a transformation in the innermost reaches of his life itself' (Ikeda 1995, p. 32), and his thesis (i.e. his philosophical viewpoint), according to Ikeda, 'not only informs us on the nature of life but has the power to change our way of thinking [...,] it leads to a sense of hope and practical action in our daily lives' (ibid., p. 34). The world – Ikeda states – is 'not made up of things but of phenomena [i.e. events]' (ibid., p. 40), thereby expressing the need for a shift of current thinking from a materialistic view

49 On this, see VN 8.1-33 (Lamotte 1962, pp. 301-18; Thurman 1976, pp. 73-7; Watson 1996, pp. 104-11).

50 On this subject, see Lamotte 1962, pp. 39-51 and p. 301, n. 1.

51 For a preliminary examination of this concept, see Stcherbatsky 1923.

52 See Ikeda 2004, pp. 126-7; Ikeda 2010, p. 141. On human individual life as a form of cosmic life action, see Ikeda 1982, p. 26. On the universe as a sea of life that potentially comprises infinite possibilities for manifestation, see Toynbee and Ikeda 2007, p. 247.

53 On the chaotic and incoherent nature of dreams, see also Ikeda 1982, p. 46.

54 See Ikeda 1982, p. 54; also ibid., p. 26.

to a more strictly phenomenological one,[55] able to embrace the wholeness and sacredness of individual lives.

Conversely, discriminative thought, which views life and the individual as abstract entities, leads to distortions that end up impoverishing the living entity of his complex inner and relational richness, both at the level of the macrocosm and the microcosm,[56] as far as the depersonalization of the individual and his environment:[57] consider e.g. nationalistic extremism,[58] where the person is no longer conceived as an end in himself but as merely functional to the realization of a totally abstract ideal, which pervasively models both individual and social life until they are dehumanized.

Therefore, it is necessary 'to pay attention not to pursue in an extremist way the illusory hypostatization of an "ideal" project, far from the transformations of reality' (Ikeda 2004, p. 46; my translation), whatever it is, even the noblest.[59]

Ultimately – Ikeda explains – :

> One conclusion from my dialogues with leading thinkers is that the only real solution is for human beings themselves to change, that the sole key lies in 'human revolution.'[60]
> It could further be said that without establishing a correct view of life and death, it is impossible to conquer inner darkness and delusion at the most fundamental level. Without the view of life and death of the Middle Way – a view that rejects the extremes of the doctrine of annihilation [Skt. *ucchedavāda*] and the doctrine of eternity [Skt. *śaśvatavāda*] – true and lasting happiness cannot be achieved.
> The only way for human beings to change is for them to conquer their inner darkness and rediscover the eternal sanctity and dignity within their own lives. (Ikeda 2006, pp. 8-9)

As Ikeda himself says in his foreword to *The Human Revolution*, 'a great human revolution in just a single individual will help achieve a change in the destiny of a nation, and further, will enable a change

[55] In other words, 'a shift from things as static objects to things that have a living story to tell' (Ikeda 1995, p. 41).

[56] On this subject, see Ikeda 1995, p. 38.

[57] On this subject and G. Marcel's concept of 'spirit of abstraction', see Ikeda 2009c.

[58] Ikeda has a vivid memory of the Japanese militaristic nationalism and of the Second World War (which the former contributed to rouse), during which his elder brother Kiichi, to whom he was deeply attached, was killed. He mentions it in Ikeda 1995, pp. 44-5. On this, see also Urbain 2010, pp. 34-7; Kimura 2002, pp. 116-8.

[59] On the United Nations as a project not to pursue in an abstract and extremist way, see Ikeda 2004, pp. 46-7; Ikeda 2010, p. 39.

[60] On this concept, which is central in Ikeda's thought, see Urbain 2010, pp. 97-113.

in the destiny of all mankind' (Ikeda 1986a, p. iv). And the *śūnyatā*, if properly understood and put into practice as an attitude of generous openness to the inexhaustible richness of life, is – according to Ikeda's interpretation – one of the essential elements for achieving this change at both an individual, social and global level.

Abbreviations

AN	*Aṅguttaranikāya* – Morris and Hardy 1885-1910.
DLMBS	Digital Library & Museum of Buddhist Studies (National Taiwan University Library, 2004) – http://buddhism.lib.ntu.edu.tw/BDLM/en/index.htm.
EBDC	The English Buddhist Dictionary Committee.
IKGA	Institut für Kultur- und Geistesgeschichte Asiens (Institute for the Cultural and Intellectual History of Asia), Vienna.
IOP	The Institute of Oriental Philosophy, Tōkyō.
JCP	*Journal of Chinese Philosophy.*
MMK(P)	*Mūlamadhyamakakārikās* – La Vallée Poussin 1903-1913.
MMK(V)	*Mūlamadhyamakakārikās* – Vaidya 1960.
MN	*Majjhimanikāya* – Trenckner and Chalmers 1888-1925.
Nd[1]	*Mahāniddesa* – La Vallée Poussin and Thomas 1916-1917.
Nd[2]	*Cullaniddesa* – Stede 1918.
PEW	*Philosophy East and West.*
PTS	The Pali Text Society, London.
ROS	*Rome Oriental Series,* ed. by G. Tucci.
Śāl	*Śālistambasūtra* – Ross Reat 1993.
SBE	*Sacred Books of the East,* ed. by F.M. Müller.
SN	*Saṃyuttanikāya* – Leon Feer 1884-1904.
Sn	*Suttanipāta* – Andersen and Smith 1913.
T	*Taishō Shinshū Daizōkyō* – Takakusu and Watanabe 1924-1934.
VN	*Vimalakīrtinirdeśasūtra* – Lamotte 1962.

References

Andersen, Dines, and Helmer Smith, eds. (1913). *Sutta-Nipāta.* New edition. London: Pali Text Society.

Brown, Brian E. (1991). *The Buddha Nature. A Study of the Tathāgatagarbha and Ālayavijñana.* Delhi: Motilal Banarsidass.

Choong, Mun-keat (1999). *The Notion of Emptiness in Early Buddhism.* Delhi: Motilal Banarsidass.

Cicalò, Sergio (2002). "La formazione della catena del *pratītyasamutpāda.*" In: *Annali della Facoltà di Lettere e Filosofia dell'Università di Cagliari*, n.s., XVIII (vol. LV), 2000.
Conze, Edward (1953). "The Ontology of the Prajñāpāramitā." In: *Philosophy East and West* 3, No. 2, pp. 117-29.
Conze, Edward (1962). *Buddhist Thought in India. Three Phases of Buddhist Philosophy.* London: George Allen & Unwin. Reprinted with corrections 1983.
Conze, Edward (1967). *Thirty Years of Buddhist Studies.* Oxford: Bruno Cassirer.
Conze, Edward (1978). *The Prajñāpāramitā Literature.* Tōkyō: The Reiyukai.
Cornu, Philippe (2003). *Dizionario del Buddhismo.* Italian edition ed. by D. Muggia. Torino: Bruno Mondadori. First edition: *Dictionnaire Encyclopédique du Bouddhisme.* Paris: Éditions du Seuil, 2001.
Donner, Neal and Daniel B. Stevenson (1993). *The Great Calming and Contemplation. A Study and Annotated Translation of the First Chapter of Chih-i's Mo-Ho Chih-Kuan.* Honolulu: University of Hawaii Press.
EBDC, ed. (2002). *The Soka Gakkai Dictionary of Buddhism.* Tōkyō: Sōka Gakkai.
Federman, Asaf (2009). "Literal Means and Hidden Meanings. A New Analisis of Skillful Means." In: *Philosophy East and West* 59, No. 2, pp. 125-41.
Giaiero, Prisca (2008). *Daisaku Ikeda, maestro di dialogo.* Molfetta: La Meridiana
Gnoli, Raniero, ed. (2001-2004). *La rivelazione del Buddha.* Translations by C. Cicuzza, R. Gnoli, and F. Sferra. 2 vols. Milano: Mondadori.
Hirakawa, Akira (1997). *A Buddhist Chinese-Sanskrit Dictionary.* Tōkyō: The Reiyukai.
Huyghe, René and Daisaku Ikeda (2007). *Dawn After Dark. A Dialogue.* London – New York: I.B. Tauris.
Ikeda, Daisaku (1982). *Life. An Enigma, a Precious Jewel.* Tōkyō – New York – San Francisco: Kodansha International.
Ikeda, Daisaku (1986a). *The Human Revolution.* Vol. 1, No. 1. Los Angeles, CA: World Tribune Press.
Ikeda, Daisaku (1986b). *The Human Revolution.* Vol. 4. Los Angeles, CA: World Tribune Press.
Ikeda, Daisaku (1995). *Conversations and Lectures on the Lotus Sutra.* Vol. 1. London: SGI-UK.
Ikeda, Daisaku (2001). *Soka Education. A Buddhist Vision for Teachers, Students and Parents.* Santa Monica, CA: Middleway Press.
Ikeda, Daisaku (2004). *Un Nuovo Umanesimo. Conferenze in Celebri Atenei di Tutto il Mondo.* Milano: Esperia.

Ikeda, Daisaku (2006). "Attaining Buddhahood in This Lifetime. The Fundamental Purpose of Life and a Source of Hope for Humankind." In: SGI President Ikeda's Study Lecture Series. Lectures on 'On Attaining Buddhahood in This Lifetime.' Lecture 1. *Monthly SGI Newsletter,* No. 6753 (March 1, 2006).

Ikeda, Daisaku (2008). *The Living Buddha. An Interpretative Biography.* Translated by B. Watson. Santa Monica, CA: Middleway Press.

Ikeda, Daisaku (2009a). *Buddhism. The First Millennium.* Translated by B. Watson. Santa Monica, CA: Middleway Press.

Ikeda, Daisaku (2009b). *The Flower of Chinese Buddhism.* Translated by B. Watson. Santa Monica, CA: Middleway Press.

Ikeda, Daisaku (2009c). *Toward Humanitarian Competition. A New Current in History.* Annual peace proposal, January 26, 2009. Online: http://www.daisakuikeda.org/main/peacebuild/peace-proposals/pp2009.html (accessed 23 September 2011).

Ikeda, Daisaku (2010). *A New Humanism. The University Addresses of Daisaku Ikeda.* London – New York: I.B. Tauris.

Inada, Kenneth K. (1988). "The Range of Buddhist Ontology." In: *Philosophy East and West* 38, No. 3, pp. 261-80.

Inada, Kenneth K. (1993). *Nāgārjuna. A Translation of his Mūlamadhyamakakārikā with an Introductory Essay.* Delhi: Sri Satguru Publications.

Inada, Kenneth K. (1994). "The Challenge of Buddho-Taoist Metaphysics of Experience." In: *Journal of Chinese Philosophy* 21, No. 1, pp. 27-47.

Jamieson, R.C. (2002). "Introduction." In: *The Journal of Oriental Studies* 12, No. 3, pp. 165-73.

Kalupahana, David J. (1980). "The Early Buddhist Notion of the Middle Path." In: *Journal of Chinese Philosophy* 7, No. 1, pp. 73-90.

Kalupahana, David J. (1991). *Mūlamadhyamakakārikā of Nāgārjuna. The Philosophy of the Middle Way.* Delhi: Motilal Banarsidass.

Katō, Bunnō, et al., trs. (1975). *The Threefold Lotus Sutra.* Translations by B. Katō, Y. Tamura and K. Miyasaka. Tōkyō: Kōsei Publishing.

Kern, Hendrik, tr. (1884). *The Saddharma-puṇḍarīka; or, the Lotus of the True Law.* Sacred Books of the East 21. Oxford: Oxford University Press.

Kimura, Keiko (2002). *Un portrait de Daisaku Ikeda.* Paris: Editions L'Harmattan

Kürcher, Erik (2007). *The Buddhist Conquest of China. The Spread and adaptation of Buddhism in Early Medieval China.* Third edition with a foreword by S.F. Teiser. Leiden: Brill. First published 1959.

Lai, Whalen (1982). "Sinitic Speculations on Buddha-nature. The Nirvāṇa School (420-589)." In: *Philosophy East and West* 32, No. 2, pp. 135-49.

Lai, Whalen (2002). "Buddhism in China. A Historical Survey." Entry from the *Encyclopedia of Chinese Philosophy*, ed. by A.S. Cua, London – New York: Routledge, pp. 7-19.

Lamotte, Étienne, tr. (1962). *L'Enseignement de Vimalakīrti (Vimalakīrtinirdeśa)*. Louvain: Publications Universitaires.

La Vallée Poussin, Louis de, ed. (1903-1913). *Mūlamadhyamaka-kārikās (Mādhyamakasūtras) de Nāgārjuna. Avec la Prasanna-padā Commentaire de Chandrakīrti. Bibliotheca Buddhica* 4. St. Petersbourg: The Imperial Academy of Sciences.

La Vallée Poussin, Louis de and Edward J. Thomas, eds. (1916-1917). *Niddesa I. Mahāniddesa.* 2 vols. London: Pali Text Society.

Léon Feer, M., ed. (1884-1904). *Saṃyutta-Nikāya.* Index volume ed. by Mrs. Rhys Davids. 6 vols. London: Pali Text Society.

Lindtner, Christian (1987). *Nagarjuniana. Studies in the Writings and Philosophy of Nāgārjuna.* Delhi: Motilal Banarsidass.

Liu, JeeLoo (2006). *Tian-tai Metaphysics vs. Hua-yan Metaphysics. A Comparative Study.* Online version only: http://faculty.fullerton.edu/jeelooliu/Tian-tai%20vs.%20Hua-yan.htm (also in pdf; accessed 16 September 2011).

Liu, Ming-Wood (1985). "The Yogācārā and Mādhyamika Interpretation of the Buddha-nature Concept in Chinese Buddhism." In: *Philosophy East and West* 35,2, pp. 171-92.

Liu, Ming-Wood (1989). "The Early Development of the Buddha-nature Doctrine in China." In: *Journal of Chinese Philosophy* 16, No. 1, pp. 1-36.

Mathews, Robert H. 1943. *Chinese-English Dictionary.* Revised American edition. Cambridge, MA: Harvard University Press. Reprinted 1975.

Maturana, Humberto, and Francisco J. Varela (1994). *De Máquinas y Seres Vivos. Autopoiesis: La Organización de lo Vivo.* Santiago de Chile: Editorial Universitaria.

Meazza, Luciana, tr. (2001). *Sutra del Loto.* With an introduction by F. Sferra. Milano: Rizzoli.

Monier-Williams, Monier (1899). *A Sanskrit-English Dictionary.* Oxford: Oxford University Press.

Morris, Richard and E. Hardy, eds. (1885-1910). *The Aṅguttara-Nikāya.* Index volume by M. Hunt, revised and ed. by C.A.F. Rhys Davids. 6 vols. London: Pali Text Society.

Morrison, Robert (1815-1822). *A Dictionary of the Chinese Language. In Three Parts.* 6 vols. Macao: East India Company's Press.

Ñāṇamoli, Bhikkhu and Bhikkhu Bodhi, trs. (1995). *The Mid-*

dle Length Discourses of the Buddha. A New Translation of the Majjhima Nikāya. Boston: Wisdom Publications.

Nelson, Andrew N. (1997). *The New Nelson. Japanese-English Character Dictionary.* Based on the Classic Edition. Completely revised by J.H. Haig. New edition. Tōkyō: Tuttle Publishing.

Ng, Yu-kwan [Rujun Wu] (1993). *T'ien T'ai Buddhism and Early Mādhyamika.* Honolulu: University of Hawaii Press.

Norman, Kenneth R. (1983). *Pāli Literature. A History of Indian Literature,* ed. by J. Gonda, vol. VII, fasc. 2. Wiesbaden: Otto Harrasowitz.

Oh, Kang-nam (2000). "The Taoist Influence on Hua-yen Buddhism. A Case of the Sinicization of Buddhism in China." In: *Chung-Haw Buddhist Journal* 13, 2, pp. 277-97. Online: DLMBS, http://ccbs.ntu.edu.tw/FULLTEXT/JR-BJ001/93608.htm (accessed 27 September 2011).

Pokorny, Julius (1959-1969). *Indogermanisches Etymologisches Wörterbuch.* 2 vols. Bern und München: Francke.

Pye, Michael (2003). *Skilful Means. A Concept in Mahayana Buddhism.* Second edition. London – New York: Routledge.

Rhys Davids, Thomas W. and William Stede, eds. (1921-1925). *The Pali Text Society's Pali-English Dictionary.* London: Pali Text Society. Reprinted 1966.

Robinson, Richard H. (1957). "Some Logical Aspects of Nāgārjuna's System." In: *Philosophy East and West* 6, No. 4, pp. 291-308.

Robinson, Richard H. (1972). "Did Nāgārjuna Really Refute All Philosophical Views?". In: *Philosophy East and West* 22,3, pp. 325-31.

Robinson, Richard H. (1976). *Early Mādhyamika in India and China.* Delhi: Motilal Banarsidass.

Ross Reat, Noble (1993). *The Śālistamba Sūtra.* Delhi: Motilal Banarsidass.

Schroeder, John W. (2000). "Nāgārjuna and the Doctrine of 'Skillful Means'." In: *Philosophy East and West* 50, No. 4, pp. 559-83.

Seyfort Ruegg, David (1981). *The Literature of Madhyamaka School of Philosophy in India. A History of Indian Literature,* ed. by J. Gonda, vol. VII, fasc. 1. Wiesbaden: Otto Harrasowitz.

Seyfort Ruegg, David (2010). *The Buddhist Philosophy of the Middle. Essays on Indian and Tibetan Madhyamaka.* Boston: Wisdom Publications.

Stcherbatsky, Theodor (1923). *The Central Conception of Buddhism and the Meaning of the Word 'Dharma'.* London: Royal Asiatic Society.

Stede, William, ed. (1918). *Niddesa II. Cullaniddesa.* London: Pali Text Society.

Steinkellner, Ernst (2004). *A Tale of Leaves. On Sanskrit Manuscripts in Tibet, their Past and Their Future.* Amsterdam: Royal Netherlands Academy of Arts and Sciences. Online: IKGA, http://ikga.oeaw.ac.at/Mat/steinkellner_leaves.pdf (accessed 20 September 2011).

Streng, Frederick J. (1967). *Emptiness. A Study in Religious Meaning.* Nashville, TN – New York: Abingdon Press.

Takakusu, Junjirō, and Kaigyoku Watanabe, eds. (1924-1934). *Taishō Shinshū Daizōkyō.* 85 vols. Tōkyō: Daizo Shuppan Company. Online: The SAT Daizōkyō Text Database (Department of Indian Philosophy and Buddhist Studies, Graduate School of Humanities and Sociology, University of Tōkyō, 1998-2008), http://21dzk.l.u-tokyo.ac.jp/SAT/index_en.html (accessed 14 September 2011).

Takasaki, Jikido (1966). *A Study on the Ratnagotravibhāga (Uttaratantra). Being a Treatise on the Tathāgatagarbha Theory of Māhāyana Buddhism.* ROS 33. Roma: Is.M.E.O.

T'ang, Yung-t'ung (1951). "On Ko-Yi, the Earliest Method by which Indian Buddhism and Chinese Thought were Synthesized." In: W.R. Inge et al. (eds.). *Radhakrishnan: Comparative Studies in Philosophy Presented in Honour of His Sixtieth Birthday.* London: Allen & Unwin, pp. 276-86.

Thurman, Robert A.F., tr. (1976). *The Holy Teaching of Vimalakīrti. A Mahāyāna Scripture.* University Park, Pennsylvania: Pennsylvania State University Press.

Toynbee, Arnold, and Daisaku Ikeda (2007). *Choose Life. A Dialogue,* London – New York: I.B. Tauris.

Trenckner, Vilhelm and Robert Chalmers, eds. (1888-1925). *The Majjhima-Nikāya.* Index volume ed. by Mrs. Rhys Davids. 4 vols. London: Pali Text Society.

Urbain, Olivier (2010). *Daisaku Ikeda's Philosophy of Peace. Dialogue, Transformation and Global Citizenship.* London – New York: I.B. Tauris.

Vaidya, P.L., ed. (1960). *Madhyamakaśāstram of Nāgārjuna with the Commentary; Prasannapadā by Chandrakīrti.* Darbhanga: The Mithila Institute.

Varela, Francisco J. (1979). *Principles of Biological Autonomy.* New York: North Holland.

Watson, Burton, tr. (1993). *The Lotus Sutra.* New York: Columbia University Press.

Watson, Burton, tr. (1996). *The Vimalakirti Sutra.* New York: Columbia University Press.

Watson, Burton, tr. (2009). *The Lotus Sutra and Its Opening and Closing Sutras.* Tōkyō: Soka Gakkai.

Weber-Brosamer, Bernhard, and Dieter M. Back (2005). *Die Philosophie der Leere. Nāgārjunas Mūlamadhyamaka-Kārikās*

Übersetzung des buddhistischen Basistextes mit kommentierenden Einführungen. Second revised edition. Wiesbaden: Harrassowitz.

Westerhoff, Jan (2009). *Nāgārjuna's Madhyamaka. A Philosophical Introduction.* New York: Oxford University Press.

Part II

Reflections on Signless Signification in Literature and Arts

Cinzia Pieruccini

Presences and Absences in Indian Visual Arts: Ideologies and Events

Interpretation of the art of the past in subsequent periods depends on the quantity and kind of works that are in effect handed down; obviously, this is a universal issue. Absences result not only from natural wasting away and destruction, but may also be due to specific choices or inclinations of the predecessors, or even to the directions of research being pursued by the moderns. There is always the need to reflect on the relation between presences and absences and what lies behind them if we are to interpret aright the message that earlier civilisations – indeed, all civilisations – meant to convey by means of their visual arts.

With respect to this issue, Indian art offers a somewhat peculiar case. As all scholars are well aware, the figurative and architectural heritage that has come down to us from ancient India represents only a partial comment on the country's long centuries of cultural history. And, obviously, in the case of India, too, there is a limit to the gaps that can be filled. However, it is also true that at times the gaps in Indian art seem to cry out, to the extent that one feels duty bound to delve deeper. On the one hand, there are reasons that seem to have excluded the production of works and monuments in various periods and phases, while on the other, there are the many factors that spelt oblivion for the heritage that had been created. On analysis, the gaps can be pieced together in a broad and significant picture, and it is on this that I wish to dwell here with a few reflections.[1]

[1] These pages address a readership with no specialization in Indian art, and were conceived as a contribution to the Workshop 'Il segno e il vuoto' (Sign and Void), Cagliari, 8-9 April 2011, the proceedings of which are published here.

As we know, Vedic and Brahmanic India left no artistic evidence; in fact, the first signs we have date back to the 3rd century BCE, with the Maurya pillars, renowned for the inscriptions of King Aśoka, which also happen to represent the first documented example of Indian writing. The great Vedic-Brahmanic sacrificial rites took place on altars specially built in the open air, and no need for temples was felt. In the Vedic hymns many divinities, including Indra, Varuṇa and Rudra, are attributed with anthropomorphic features, and on the evidence of textual analysis, attempts have been made in the past to demonstrate that the Vedic-Brahmanic civilizations were already accustomed to the use of divine images;[2] some searching argumentation is already well summarized (and refuted) by Jitendra Nath Banerjea in his classic text on iconography, the final version of which came out in 1956[3]. It is now generally accepted as a fact that the Vedic divinities were not represented in cult images; the sacred word and the rite are held to have sufficed to evoke and conjure up the presence of the gods.[4] And, it is widely held, it is precisely due to the lack of temples and sacred images that we find no artifacts representing this cultural phase.

With such arguments, normally encountered in the historical-artistic literature on India, a number of points are more or less unwittingly taken for granted. In fact, the initial assumption is that the art handed down to us from ancient India is religious art; in the Vedic-Brahmanic phases no need was felt to produce religious buildings and statues, which is why we have no artistic documentation of the period. Actually, it is an a posteriori criterion that is being applied here, an approach dear to scholars of Indian studies – and by no means only to them. To interpret blank or enigmatic phases of Indian culture, scholars often look to subsequent stages, known to them, taking them as keys to interpret the earlier phases of which relatively little is known.

[2] It is worth recalling that in India the earliest (anthropomorphic) images of supernatural beings known to us can be traced back to roughly the 2nd-1st century BCE. In this connection, see the recent study by Rhye Quintanilla (2007). It is also to be recalled that in early Buddhist art the Buddha was not represented in human form but by symbols, 'signs' of his presence. The lack of divine Vedic-Brahmanic images and of anthropomorphism in the early images of the Buddha are all part of the vast and general issue termed Indian 'aniconism', which represents in turn a fundamental chapter in the great question of the 'absences' in Indian art; on this phenomenon, or rather cluster of phenomena, I have offered a few considerations elsewhere (Pieruccini, in press).

[3] Banerjea 1956^2, pp. 36-70.

[4] Cf., for example, Srinivasan 1997, pp. 185-96. The approach taken by Srinivasan is that 'we look at the Vedic ritual as a three-dimensional, living icon whose properties could provide models upon which to construct devotional icons' (Srinivasan 1997, p. 192).

The question that has to be faced at this point is not so much about the legitimacy of the criterion itself, but rather the reliability of the assumption upon which it rests in this case. Can we be sure that it is correct to state that the art of India was a purely religious art? Perhaps we can only define thus the art (and, objectively, not even all of it) that has come down to us, or at least that we are acquainted with. Moreover, we are also attributing – again more or less wittingly – to a presumable art of the Vedic period, characteristics that, as we will see more clearly later on, again fit in very well with subsequent periods. We expect to find art not only in the religious sphere, but also in the patronage of the highest strata of society. In fact, Vedic-Brahmanic religious observance belonged to the élite of a population, the majority of whom presumably followed other cults – cults, moreover, of which we have no direct evidence, since our knowledge of the India of these remote phases is based on the literature produced by the priests of this élite.

The 'religious' label for the art of India is generally taken for granted in the approach adopted in textbooks on Indian art. This applies both to monographic studies, where there are obviously more cogent reasons for denotations like 'Buddhist art', 'Hindu art', etc., and to the more general studies, where headings and chapters generally tend to group together Buddhist, Hindu, Jaina and, possibly, Islamic art.[5] In a valuable book Vidya Dehejia recently pointed out the impossibility of drawing a Western type dividing line in Indian art between the sacred and profane, on the pattern envisaged by Mircea Eliade.[6] One example Dehejia is particularly fond of to illustrate her position is a magnificent and relatively new addition to our understanding of the art of India, having come to light only as from 1986. My reference here is to the Rānī kī Vāv, the 'Queen's Well', built at Patan in Gujarat by Queen Udayamatī of the Solaṅkī dynasty around 1063: it extends over seven underground levels, and in this arid area must have offered extraordinary comfort to the population and travellers in terms of water, shade and shelter.[7] What we have here then is a well, i.e. a civil construction, but with an extremely rich iconographic programme arraying a profusion of images of divinities, depicted with that keen attention to the beauty of the human

[5] For example, we may cite a number of celebrated texts that have constituted fundamental stages in the study of Indian art history, identifying periods and environments with religious definitions in the titles themselves: Brown 1942; Brown 1942a; Rowland 1953; and the more recent, and still indispensable, Huntington 1985.

[6] Dehejia 2009: cf. in particular pp. 16-7.

[7] Dehejia 2009, pp. 103-5.

body characteristic of medieval Indian art, and accompanied by female figures ('nymphs') in turn evoking beauty, sensuality and fecundity. More or less elaborately structured, these stepwells are monuments frequently encountered in Gujarat (and not only there), the sculpture representing religious subjects regularly mingling with a fair proportion of *mithuna*, i.e. of couples, of sensual women, and depictions of everyday events like making butter or fighting.[8]

As for the sacred/profane dichotomy, the two planes clearly intersect here: we have buildings created for "profane" use, and yet covered and embellished, and rendered significant, by extensive figurative decoration of a religious kind, mingling and merging with magnification of the human body, sensuality and beauty, and more besides. There can, however, be no denying that we have here the imagery characteristic of religious architecture finding its way into a building serving civil ends, and not vice versa. We find in the wells the sensuality of gods and nymphs, and more or less the same variety of subjects, as in the great temples of the period – suffice it to recall Khajuraho. In other words, we can sense here the will to "sanctify" a major public work. Of course, the great temples were also "public works" with which the sovereign asserted and consecrated, in the etymological sense of the verb, his power, and which were (and in the south of India still are) used by the population as places for meeting, festivities, entertainment and everyday activities. In short, the great dividing line we can trace in the works of ancient India is not, I believe, between sacred and profane, but rather between private and public, official. And what emerges in all evidence is that whatever has been conserved of historical India only belongs to the latter typology.

In concrete terms, the prime factor behind the conservation of monuments and works was the use of material able to stand up to the weather, the effects of overgrowing tropical vegetation, or too easy deliberate destruction. With its blazing summers and months of oppressive monsoon humidity, the Indian climate has played a decisive part in precipitating the natural decay of works and monuments (and manuscripts), while fires were also a frequent scourge. The excellent quality of the fired bricks used in urban architecture in the proto-historic Indus Civilization, together with the desertification of vast areas, represented the right conditions for the conservation of the remains of a city like Mohenjo Daro. In historical India the turning point was definitively marked by the use of stone, the first finds of which are, as

8 Jain-Neubauer 1981, pp. 69-76.

we have seen, to be dated as from the 3rd century BCE. On the evidence of the most ancient stone monuments, and not only the most ancient, it can be seen quite clearly that the structures had been conceived on the basis of building experience acquired with wood architecture. The most eloquent example of this is to be seen in the railings of the ancient *stūpas* dating back to the 2nd century BCE-1st century CE, constructed in stone as exact copies of wooden fencing (Fig. 1). We must therefore conclude that what remains had been preceded by a period characterized by wooden buildings, long since lost.

Of course, stone is a demanding material, involving high quarrying and transport costs and skilled workmanship. Only wealthy communities, such as in some phases the Buddhist community or certain mercantile guilds, and above all such important figures as sovereigns, members of royal families and ministers, could afford to commission its use. Inevitably this entailed the consequence that stone was to be used only for major works and, given the central role of religious thought throughout Indian civilization, first and foremost – much as was the case, for example, with the cathedrals of medieval Europe – for monuments associated with the faith and worship. Concentrating their efforts in these works, those who commissioned them sought other-worldly credit and, as we have seen, exercised their power, consolidating it in this world with sacred semblances. By lavishing superior material, superior merit was gained: it is '100 times more meritorious to give a brick temple than a thatched temple; 10,000 times more meritorious to give a stone than a brick temple' (*Mahānirvāṇa Tantra,* XIII 24, 25).[9] And note that this does not apply to architecture alone, for sculpture, of course, has from the outset been an integral part of religious buildings, on the walls, within the cellae and so forth. Metal, too, has a place in this context, for metalwork also involves considerable skill and expense, and again such resources were reserved for cult images. The huge investments going into religious art called for the best of the designers and workmen available; in short, this art always saw a concentration of excellence also in terms of technical and expressive expertise.

There were some exceptions. For example, the Mauryan pillars, marking the beginnings of Indian art, are not a religious but an imperial monument, and similar inspiration is behind the statues of the Kuṣāṇa kings of Mathura or Surkh Kotal, or, ultimately, also such medieval public works as the Rānī kī Vāv. With regard to the art of Gandhāra, Kurt A. Behrendt significantly points out that the fact that the mature art of this area appears

[9] Quoted in Kramrisch 1976, vol. 1, p. 113.

only to be religious, i.e. Buddhist, is a direct consequence of the way excavation was conducted. In fact, unlike the investigations into the earlier periods, the excavations on the settlements dating to the period between the 2nd and 8th centuries focused on the religious sites, and not the cities. If Buddhism indeed represented the dominant subject matter of art, the scholar concludes, the fact that it seems to be the sole art ultimately depends on the direction taken by investigation.[10] One tends to find only what one seeks. Undeniably, however, in the evidence that has come down to us thanks to the use of stone and metal – the evidence we are acquainted with – it is religion that decidedly dominates the scene.

As had been the case before, less durable materials – wood, and indeed a fair amount of brick – continued to be used alongside the work in stone. As the great ancient *stūpas* were being raised, the monasteries and temples built beside them were normally still in wood; we find evidence of the forms they took in the well-known reproductions of cave architecture (Fig. 2) as well as in the reliefs on the *stūpas* themselves.[11] Wood and brick must have been the materials used not only for the many religious buildings that have since disappeared,[12] but also for the city walls, the civil dwellings and the palaces of the sovereigns and nobles which, as the literature records, were sumptuous, adorned with rich furnishings, statues and paintings. Interesting depictions of ancient cities can be seen in the reliefs of Buddhist sites, and notably at Sanchi (1st century), while a glimpse of what the royal palaces looked like is offered, in particular, by the wall paintings (end of 5th century) of the Ajanta complex, again Buddhist.[13]

In the following centuries, while still having temples built in stone, the sovereigns continued to build their own palaces in rather less durable materials; indeed, not even the oldest surviv-

[10] Behrendt 2007, p. 19.

[11] For images of *bodhigharas*, i.e. small temples built around the tree of the Buddha's Enlightenment, offered by the reliefs on the ancient *stūpas*, cf. the still valuable study by Coomaraswamy (1991, pp. 22-33). On the architectural issues associated with the caves (and the earliest Indian architecture), see, for example, the recent book by Hardy (2007, pp. 74-87).

[12] Banerjea had already pointed out that the existence of temples and images presumably associated with partly non-Vedic divinities was documented and accepted by the Brahmans themselves in the last phases of Vedic literature (Banerjea 1956^2, pp. 68-70).

[13] For some depictions of cities and palaces in the reliefs of Sanchi and for the associated bibliography, see Pieruccini 2010. On the archaeological remains and some important literary descriptions (*Mahābhārata*, *Rāmāyaṇa*, *Mayamata*) of the ancient royal palaces, a useful summary can be found in Michell and Martinelli 1994, pp. 68-70.

ing palaces of the Hindu sovereigns predate the advent of Islam,[14] and the adoption of more durable materials may ultimately have resulted from the examples offered by the palaces of the new lords and masters.

It is also worth stressing that the first steps in building with stone, *stūpa* railings and Hindu temples – the latter beginning to spread in the Gupta period, in the 4th-5th century – seem to have involved some difficulty. Mention has already been made of the carpentry type joints of the ancient *stūpas*. The earliest Gupta temples are tiny, the architecture uncertain; if we consider the art of the Calukyas and the Pallavas, as from the 6th century on, it emerges in all evidence that in both areas excellence in sculpture predated such quality in architecture, for the cave temples and indeed the monolithic examples in the case of the Pallavas anticipate by some decades at least, and to impressive effect, the examples actually built (Fig. 3). At least eight cave temples are attributed to the first great Pallava sovereign, Mahendravarman (580-630), and in the Sanskrit inscription on the temple believed to have inaugurated the series, in the locality of Mandagappattu, we read, significantly:

> This brickless, timberless, metalless and mortarless mansion... was caused to be made by king Vicitracitta ('Imaginative mind') for Brahmā, Īśvara (Śiva) and Viṣṇu. (*Epigraphia Indica* XVII)[15]

Hence sacred buildings existed in the materials here excluded. According to the chronology commonly accepted for the Pallava works, following the cave temples are the reliefs and the small monolithic temples attributed to the period of Narasiṃhavarman Mahāmalla (630-668) and his second successor Parameśvaravarman (672-700). For the earliest structural temples in stone, on the evidence at least of the surviving examples, we have to wait for the reign of Narasiṃhavarman II known as Rājasiṃha (700-728), when we already have a masterpiece, the Kailāsanātha of Kanchipuram: an example of that sudden and extraordinary maturity that we often seem to encounter – albeit possibly here, too, due to some missing links – in much of the artistic (and no less in the literary) production of ancient India.

With the earliest documented monumental use of stone, the cave works – whether Buddhist or Hindu – in any case reflect the principle of endowing durability to structures that normally (precisely because customarily built in less permanent materials) lack it, again thanks only to a lavish use of resources.

[14] Michell and Martinelli 1994, p. 68.

[15] Srinivasan 1964, p. 47, with slight modifications. I also follow this scholar for the datings of the Pallava sovereigns.

Paintings represent a particular case. We know only too well that this is the most fragile of all the arts; apart from a few special cases, the most striking being the caves of Ajanta, the vegetal or mineral pigments have proved unable to resist decay. In a famous article, A.K. Coomaraswamy offers no fewer than a hundred literary examples attesting to the painting of ancient India.[16] Paintings adorned the walls of palaces or were executed on fabric or wooden panels; of the most significant examples cited by Coomaraswamy and well-known in literary terms, we may mention the *Mahā Ummagga Jātaka*, referring to wall paintings in the palaces, the *Dūtakāvya* attributed to Bhāsa, where a painting on fabric is described which represents the affront suffered by Draupadī in the gambling room of the *Mahābhārata*, and the gallery of the *Uttararāmacarita* by Bhavabhūti, where Rāma and Sītā review the various events in their lives.[17] Portrait painting, although probably highly conventional and with scant attention to the physiognomic features of individuals, appears to have been very widespread, also at the amateur level, to judge by the ways and frequency with which it crops up in Indian classical literature, prompting various narrative or dramatic developments.[18]

A point worth stressing is that the disappearance of painting has, much as has also been the case with the art of classical Greece, drastically changed our perception of the stone monuments that have survived, doubtless originally coloured to a great extent, and embellished with painted parts; traces of stucco work and pigments can still be picked out on many temples and caves. Moreover, we can often make out or must hypothesize – this is a point we will be returning to – more recent painted additions. For example, for the visitors of today, at least some of the fascination of the celebrated cave temples of Badami is owed to the extraordinary warm light of the red sandstone, but noticing the portion of painted ceiling still to be seen in the magnificent n. 3 (dedicated in 578 CE) we cannot help wondering whether people in the past have always shared the same sensations of light and colour (Fig. 3).

To sum up then, first place in the elements determining our perception of Indian art goes to the material which, depending largely on the extent of the investments, has stood up to the test of time. At the same time, we must bear in mind that, given the scant use of binding substances which has always characterized

[16] Coomaraswamy 1930-1932; see also Coomaraswamy 1930-1932a. For an exhaustive bibliography on references to painting in ancient Indian literature, cf. Schlingloff 2000, Vol. II, pp. 193-6.

[17] Coomaraswamy 1930-1932, nn. 17-20, 44, 65.

[18] Cf. Pieruccini 1996.

Indian stone architecture, this has likewise often fallen prey to decay or violence. A major factor behind the destruction and abandonment lies in the constant wars between rival kingdoms and invasions for conquest or plunder, defining a history of devastation of truly disheartening proportions. Over the centuries the most tempting preys were the Buddhists' monastic centres and the medieval temples – great concentrations of wealth accumulated over long periods thanks to the devout, the patronage of kings and the firm, not infrequently rapacious administration of the priests. Alongside the lust for plundering was the iconoclastic pretext for the incursions of the Islamic armies, who brought with them a severe monotheistic vision and the ban on the representation of God, in total contrast with the Indian approach. This came above all at the cost of the temples of northern India, where in fact remarkably few pre-Islamic buildings remain intact. As we know, in the destruction of the ancient heritage there were two crucial phases: the ruinous, predatory incursions made from what is now Afghanistan by Maḥmūd of Ghazni, no fewer than 17 between about 1000 and 1026, and of course the Turco-Afghan conquest and the definitive settlement of these new rulers in the north of India around 1200. We may cite two famous events as emblematic of the havoc wreaked. In the case of Maḥmūd, the worst case of destruction was undoubtedly that of the great and prosperous temple of Somnath in Gujarat (1026), the hollow *liṅga* of which contained, according to the chronicles, immense quantities of gold and jewels. In the account of the contemporaneous and often accompanying al-Bīrūnī, this was the fate of the great *liṅga*:

> He ordered the upper part to be broken and the remainder to be transported to his residence, Ghaznin, with all its coverings and trappings of gold, jewels, and embroidered garments. Part of it has been thrown into the hippodrome of the town, together with the *Cakrasvâmin* (Viṣṇu), an idol of bronze, that had been brought from Tâneshar. Another part of the idol of Somanâth lies before the mosque of Ghaznin, on which people rub their feet to clean them from dirt and wet. (al-Bīrūnī, *Indica*, Ch. LVIII)[19]

A similar case of desecrating 'dismantlement', though also carried out in haste, with the purpose of immediately creating a concrete sign of the new rule, is to be seen in the second famous

[19] Translation taken from Sachau 2000, vol. 2, p. 103. On the destruction of the city of Somnath and the massacre carried out here by Maḥmūd, see also *The Mir'āt-i Aḥmadī (The Political and Statistical History of Gujarat)* of 'Alī Muḥammad Khān (Alí Mohammed Khán) (1761), cap. XII (http://persian.packhum.org/persian/main).

event, connected with the arrival of the Turco-Afghans in India. In 1195, having recently installed himself in Delhi after his final victory over Pṛthīvirāj Cauhān, the Hindu sovereign of Delhi and Ajmer, Quṭb al-Dīn Aibak founded the first mosque of the new conquerors – the mosque that is called to this day Qūwat-ul-Islām. According to an inscription set on a lintel,[20] twenty-seven sacred buildings were demolished to build it, their divine images defaced. The pillars of the temples were set one upon another to attain a greater height, and arranged to create a vast rectangular cloister which was to remain, even through the successive additions, the great ancient heart of this mosque (Fig. 4). As in the case of Somnath, many Hindu 'idols' are probably buried in the floors of the Indian mosques to be ignominiously trampled underfoot. The practice is documented up to the time of Aurangzēb, in turn a major figure amongst the destroyers of temples in the name of faith. Among others around the years 1669-1670 he razed to the ground the temple of Viśvanātha at Varanasi, destroyed for the first time on Aibak's arrival, the reconstructed temple of Somnath, and the most important temple of Mathura, the Vishnuite Keśava Rāi, built a couple of generations before: he had the temple's principal image taken to Agra and buried there under the steps of the Mosque of Jahānārā. He is attributed with the destruction of two hundred and forty temples in Mewar alone between 1679 and 1680.[21] Note that Aurangzēb's initiative aimed not only at ancient works, but also at reconstructions or entirely new constructions, allowance for which was made in more tolerant times; incidentally, some similar initiatives had also been taken by his father, Shāh Jahān. Of the European invaders, the prize for aggressiveness towards local monuments – in this case in southern India – should very likely go to the Portuguese.

Naturally, in the course of history the decline of the various dynasties has often meant that the ancient capital cities were wiped out or transformed into poor villages. Disquieting reflections still arise over the ruthless observations that in the 1970s, V.S. Naipaul

[20] Cf. for example Alfieri 1994, p. 33. It is worth recalling that the Hindu temple and Indian Islam did not lend themselves to the kind of conversion and oscillation that occurred between Islam and Christian churches: compare, for example, Hagia Sophia in Istanbul, the Mezquita of Cordoba and the Cathedral of Seville. In India, the practice, documented by countless examples (Varanasi, Ayodhya, Mathura…), has, rather, been to destroy the temple and build a mosque on the same site, or also vice versa.

[21] Data drawn from *Anecdotes of Auranzib (English translation of Ahkam-i-Alamgiri ascribed to Hamid-ud-din Khan Bahadur), With A Life of Aurangzib and Historical Notes*, by Jadunath Sarkar, 2nd rev. ed., M.C. Sarkar & Sons, Calcutta 1925, Introduction, Chapter 'Aurangzib's Reign in Northern India' (http://persian.packhum.org/persian/main).

dedicated to the ruins and the modern inhabitants of ancient Vijayanagara[22] – this, for a combination of many factors, being the most striking example of such transformation. The city, founded along the river Tungabhadra in a spectacular landscape of hills formed by red boulders that look as if they had been piled up by a giant at play, was for a couple of centuries among the richest and most glorious of Asia, capital of the enormous empire to which it gave its name. In 1565, assailed by a coalition made up of the Muslim states of Deccan and some Hindu princes, it was defeated, plundered and annihilated. What kept the site alive after the devastation, however, was the sacredness of the temple dedicated to Śiva Virūpākṣa, erected by the Vijayanagara kings on the basis of a probably earlier cult and extended in the following centuries, while shepherds and outcasts settled amongst the decaying monuments of the city.[23] Today commonly known as Hampi, lying in its immutable and surreal landscape of stone, the ancient capital now shows a kaleidoscopic combination of monuments protected by the Archaeological Survey of India, pilgrims, Indian and Western tourists with their facilities and shops, and still a considerable number of indigent inhabitants settled in the ruins of the Royal Street.

Throughout the history of India, the factor catalysing and spreading the process was the recurrent tendency of the sovereigns of the major and minor dynasties to move their capitals, hastily building new ones only, in many cases, to abandon them almost at once. This for a great variety of reasons – strategic, economic, or sheer ambition. An outstanding case was the removal, accomplished in 1328 by the Sultan Muḥammad ibn Tughluq, of the capital from Delhi to Devagiri, in the region of present-day Aurangabad in Maharashtra, which had been the capital of the Hindu kingdom of the Yādava and which Muḥammad renamed Daulatabad, i.e. the 'Dwelling of Prosperity'.[24] A great many of the inhabitants of Delhi – at least the court, in any case, the administrative and religious apparatus and part of the army, were driven out in a forced exodus over the roughly 1100 kilometres separating the two cities. The experiment was to prove very short-lived, for Daulatabad was found to offer neither a good supply of water nor a strategic position, and was abandoned by Muḥammad no later than 1335-1336. The most spectacular case, however, was of course the much celebrated Fatehpur Sikri, the

[22] Naipaul 1977.

[23] In the extensive bibliography on the ancient city of Vijayanagara, cf. Michell 1990; Fritz and Michell 2003.

[24] On Daulatabad see for instance Michell 1986, pp. 16-25.

'City of Victory', begun by Akbar in 1571, which in the space of just a score of years was reduced to a fantastic empty shell, various of its splendid buildings and structures still baffling certain interpretation.[25] Actually, thanks to the initiative of mythical rulers, and of Rājpūts, Sultans and Mughals, the entire urban fabric of Delhi derives from an assembly of many 'cities', as such largely obliterated in the modern metropolis.

And in all the cases, countless episodes of destruction resulted from the mere fact that the significance of the long-abandoned monuments, and especially the Buddhist monuments, was forgotten. The ancient building material was often reused until the not so distant past for immediate needs, and ancient sculpted slabs of stone are often to be seen incorporated in the walls of the village dwellings. Moreover, various monuments suffered severe damage at the hands of the early generations of explorers and British authorities. Of the many examples we might mention, a particularly striking case, given the importance of the monument, is the *stūpa* of Amaravati (2nd century BCE-3rd century CE), which was subjected to a long series of debatable official initiatives together with devastating acts of plunder during the 19th century, and indeed the local population even went as far as burning the slabs from the monument to obtain lime.[26] Coming to more recent times, the 1960s saw a substantial part of the Buddhist remains of Nagarjunakonda transferred to be reconstructed a short distance away, since the original site had been submerged subsequent to the construction of a dam on the river Krishna. The opposition that has for some decades been set up against the project for a great system of dams on the bed of the river Narmada is also connected with the chances of survival of the still revered temple sites, doomed to be wiped out by the project.

On the other hand, the very continuity of cult and vitality of the sacred places have also been widespread factors in the modification and re-elaboration of the monumental structures over the centuries. The process can be seen, in fact, as an intrinsic part of the nature and beauty of such places, in many cases adding particular quality and interest to the sites. But this has also entailed mortifying interventions carried out in various (and also recent) periods even on certain temple sites of profound artistic importance, including the addition of bleak containing walls or thick coats of paint, the legacy in crude and gaudy modern colours of the time-honoured practice of painting monuments.

[25] The extensive bibliography on Fatehpur Sikri includes a recent and indeed important study by Petruccioli (2007).

[26] Cf. for example Dehejia 1997, p. 151.

Here, too, there is no end to the cases we might mention; on a recent visit I was particularly struck by the case of the temple of Vīranārāyaṇa at Gadag, associated with the figure of the great poet Kumāra Vyāsa (15th century), who is said to have composed his *Mahābhārata* in Kannada in its precincts; here traces of the original structures attributable to the 12th century can be found only with a painstaking search amid the architectural additions and paint coverings (Fig. 5).

Let me conclude with a few remarks on what seems to me to be the attitude that India in general now takes towards her monuments – remarks based on empirical and by no means systematic observation, which can therefore only be taken as very provisional. On the one hand, the India of the villages continues to use, as it has done for centuries, unattended or ruined ancient monuments for the purposes of dwelling or other everyday activities, the sight of which may move or touch the outside observer, since it seems to manifest a sort of authentic life of the monument, a life that somehow goes on in the face of the evident decay, as if today's inhabitants were perfectly familiar with the past (Fig. 6). On the other hand, over the last few decades the Archaeological Survey of India has fenced in a growing number of important monuments, planting gardens around them and setting up ticket booths. Conservation of the sites is, of course, a vast issue, and we are all truly grateful to the Archaeological Survey for its endeavour. At the same time, however, there can be no denying that some of the new arrangements have detracted from the fascination of the monuments, reining them in, eclipsing scenery and life, forcing them into a single dimension – that of the historical 'monument' – while depriving them of many others. Ultimately, however, this is simply yet another in the series of transformations and, let us face it, obliterations, that we must take into account today in our appraisals of Indian art.

References

Alfieri, Bianca Maria (1994). *Architettura islamica del subcontinente indiano.* Lugano: Edizioni Arte e Moneta.

Banerjea, Jitendra Nath (1956²). *The Development of Hindu Iconography.* New Delhi: Munshiram Manoharlal 1985 (reprint of revised edition).

Behrendt, Kurt A. (2007). *The Art of Gandhara in the Metropolitan Museum of Art.* New York: The Metropolitan Museum of Art, New Haven and London: Yale University Press.

Brown, Percy (1942). *Indian Architecture (Buddhist and Hindu Periods).* Bombay: B. Taraporevala Sons & Co.

Brown, Percy (1942a). *Indian Architecture (Islamic Period).* Bombay: B. Taraporevala Sons & Co.

Coomaraswamy, Ananda K. (1930-1932). "One Hundred References to Indian Painting." In: *Artibus Asiae,* 4, No. 1, pp. 41-57.

Coomaraswamy, Ananda K. (1930-1932a). "Further References to Painting in India." In: *Artibus Asiae* 4, Nos. 2-3, pp. 126-9.

Coomaraswamy, Ananda K. (1991). *Early Indian Architecture. Cities and City-gates.* New Delhi: Munshiram Manoharlal [1930].

Dehejia, Vidya (1997). *Discourse in Early Buddhist Art. Visual Narratives of India.* New Delhi: Munshiram Manoharlal.

Dehejia, Vidya (2009). *The Body Adorned: Dissolving Boundaries Between Sacred and Profane in India's Art.* New York: Columbia University Press.

Fritz, John M. and George Michell (2003). *Hampi.* Mumbai: India Book House.

Hardy, Adam (2007). *The Temple Architecture of India.* Chichester: Wiley.

Huntington, Susan (1985). *The Art of Ancient India. Buddhist, Hindu, Jain.* New York – Tokyo: Weatherhill.

Jain-Neubauer, Jutta (1981). *The Stepwells of Gujarat: Art-Historical Perspective.* New Delhi: Abhinav Publications.

Kramrisch, Stella (1976). *The Hindu Temple,* 2 vols. Delhi – Varanasi - Patna: Motilal Banarsidass [1946].

Michell, George, ed. (1986). *Islamic Heritage of the Deccan.* Bombay: Marg Publications.

Michell, George (1990). *Vijayanagara. Architectural Inventory of the Urban Core.* Volume one: *Text, Maps, Line Drawings*; Volume Two: *Photographs.* Mysore: Directorate of Archeology & Museums.

Michell, George and Antonio Martinelli (1994). *The Royal Palaces of India.* London: Thames & Hudson.

Naipaul, Vidyadhar Surajprasad (1977). *India: A Wounded Civilization.* London: Deutsch and New York: Knopf.

Petruccioli, Attilio (2007). *Fatehpur Sikri. La capitale dell'impero Moghul, la meraviglia di Akbar.* Milano: Electa Mondadori.

Pieruccini, Cinzia (1996). "Pittura di ritratto nel *kāvya.*" In: *Rivista degli Studi Orientali* LXX, 3-4, pp. 441-53.

Pieruccini, Cinzia (2010). "Depictions of Cities on the Great Stūpa of Sanchi." In: *The City and the Forest in Indian Literature and Art,* ed. by D. Stasik and A. Trynkowska. Warsaw: Elipsa, pp. 114-26.

Pieruccini, Cinzia (in press). "Some Remarks on 'Iconism' and 'Aniconism' in the Depiction of Hindu Gods." In: *Papers of the Seminar 'Reflecting on Images'*, Berlin, April 24-26, 2008.

Rhye Quintanilla, Sonya (2007). *History of Early Stone Sculpture at*

Mathura, CA. 150 BCE-100 CE. Leiden – Boston: Brill.
Rowland, Benjamin (1953). *The Art and Architecture of India. Buddhist-Hindu-Jain.* London – Baltimore: Penguin Books.
Sachau, Edward C., ed. (2000). *Alberuni's India,* 2 vols. Abingdon: Routledge [1910].
Schlingloff, Dieter (2000). *Ajanta, Handbuch del Malereien, Handbook of the Paintings. Erzählende Wandmalereien, Narrative Wall-paintings,* 3 vols. Wiesbaden: Harrassowitz Verlag.
Srinivasan, Doris Meth (1997). *Many Heads, Arms and Eyes. Origin, Meaning and Form of Multiplicity in Indian Art.* Leiden: Brill.
Srinivasan, K.R. (1964). Cave-*temples of the Pallavas.* New Delhi: Archaeological Survey of India.

Fig. 1. Sanchi (Madhya Pradesh), Stūpa II, ca. 100 BCE. (Photo: Courtesy M. Cazzamalli)

Fig. 2. Bhaja (Maharashtra), rock-cut monastic complex, 1st century BCE. (Photo: Author)

Fig. 3. Badami (Karnataka), Cave Temple no. 3, dedicated in 578 CE. View of the porch area. (Photo: Author)

Fig. 4. Delhi, Qūwat-ul-Islām Mosque, founded in 1195. Detail of a pillar of the porch. The whole porch has been built through assemblage of dismantled temple pillars. (Photo: Author)

Fig. 5. Gadag (Karnataka), Vīranārāyaṇa Temple, probably founded ca. 12th century CE. Recently painted ancient details of a doorway. (Photo: Author)

Fig. 6. Lakkundi (Karnataka), people cooking in the *maṇḍapa* of a Late Calukya temple of ca. 12th century CE. (Photo: Author)

Mimma Congedo and Paola M. Rossi

Rethinking the Question of Images (Aniconism vs. Iconism) in the Indian History of Art[1]

1. The present paper aims at offering some preliminary reflections on the question of images in India, in order to start a rethinking of these themes, also in relation to the debated interpretation of the history of Indian art in the light of the notions of aniconism and iconism, which may also be taken as a starting point for the following observations.

The very formulation of such categories results as being theoretically problematic. In its broadest meaning, the use of the term aniconic indicates any non-figurative representation, whose referential level cannot be identified in natural and/or real forms. However, in the scholarly tradition of art history it is common to reduce the category of aniconism to the rejection of anthropomorphic images, often connected to a religious frame. In this perspective, if we go back to the original etymological meaning of 'aniconic' as 'imageless or figureless', the category of aniconism results as implying an identification of images with what presents a figurative aspect and especially a human one, thus implicitly entailing a quite extreme and binding understanding of images themselves.

In the Indian scholarly context, the use of these categories retains such problematic fluctuation, inasmuch as aniconism is understood both as the absence of figurative representations, especially in relation to the Vedic tradition, and also as the absence

[1] Part 1 of the present article was written by Mimma Congedo; part 2 was written by Paola M. Rossi.

of anthropomorphic representations, especially in relation to the iconography of the Buddha and Hindu deities. Conversely, iconism is the category used either for any figurative representation or for any anthropomorphic representation. However, both of the categories usually refer to the representation of deities or religious contents. Again, if the etymological implications of the terms aniconic and iconic in this context are taken to their extreme consequences, such categorization brings with it an identification of images with what has a figurative and anthropomorphic aspect.

Such problematic theoretical implications[2] of the use of the terms aniconism and iconism suggests that it would be worth rethinking them. In this perspective, the Indian context itself, which has produced an ample debate on these topics, provides a particularly valuable starting point for reflection.

It is well known that the history of Indian art and religion is commonly interpreted in the frame of a passage from aniconism to iconism, understood, as outlined above, according to the specific context of speculation either in relation to the lack or presence of figurative representations, or in relation to the lack or presence of anthropomorphic representations. It will be enough to recall the transition from the Vedic culture to Hinduism, or from the so-called Buddha's aniconic representation to the iconic one.[3] However, it has recently been demonstrated that iconic and aniconic representations have tended to coexist over the centuries and cannot be considered as necessarily consecutive and mutually exclusive.[4]

In order to solve the linguistic, theoretical and historical problematic issues related to the categories of aniconism and iconism as highlighted above, the present paper proposes – as a working hypothesis which needs further investigation – to use different categories that might result as being useful in relation to the history of art and religion in India.

[2] These problematic theoretical implications are also suggested by Charles Malamoud's considerations on the notion of aniconism in relation to the Vedic context, inasmuch as Malamoud highlights that in such a context, aniconism is not absolute. Cf. Malamoud 1989, pp. 258-60.

[3] The related bibliography is vast. As to the debate on the Vedic period, it is enough to recall the work by Banerjea (1956). As to the Buddhist scholarly tradition, it is well known that the debate on Buddha iconography and image began with the opposite positions of Alfred Foucher (1905) and Ananda K. Coomaraswamy (1926). More recently, there has been an ongoing debate initiated by Susan Huntington (1990), whose position has been questioned by Vidya Dehejia (1991).

[4] Cf. Granoff and Shinohara (2004).

Rather than stressing the lack or presence of figurative or anthropomorphic figures as the distinctive mark of a certain type of religious or artistic image or practice, as happens with the terms aniconic and iconic, we shall focus on the meaning modalities of representation of a given religious or artistic practice. Inspired by Umberto Eco's work on the Middle Ages Western philosophy,[5] we shall refer to the symbolic and allegoric categories in order to indicate the different meaning modalities that can be activated by an object and applied to its fruition. By referring to the symbolic and the allegoric, we shall try to rethink and replace the categories of the aniconic and the iconic.

In this context, the word symbol indicates what is able to condense the transcendence in itself, that which is able to evoke and 'call' the transcendence to itself, by conveying an intuition and epiphany of the sacred. Thus, the symbol is an instrument through which man tends towards the divine: the divine is the absent object of a research that is pursued through the symbol. In this sense, the presence of symbols represents the most creative moment of culture, when the absent divine can be 'attracted' to an object. If we take advantage of Stietencron's categories, we can say that the symbol embodies the charisma.[6]

If we refer to the Vedic context, the ritual is the moment when man aims at the divine presence through an instrument, the ritual performance itself, which is connected to a dynamic and rhythmic dimension scanned by time. The ritual performance, with its symbols, calls for the presence of the divine without taking it for granted, by trying to attract it to a place created for this purpose, which disappears after the performance and leaves no trace, like the remains of the sacrifice, eaten by the participants in the sacrifice itself, as explained by Charles Malamoud (1989, pp. 13-33)·

On the contrary, allegory is a sclerotization of the symbol, the remains of a symbol, that is to say what remains when the transcendence is no longer condensed in an object, but has to be searched for starting from the object itself, since it is assumed in this very object, inasmuch as it is arbitrarily and conventionally established in a classifying code that is culturally shared. In this sense, the presence of the allegory corresponds to a less creative moment of culture, when there is no tension towards an absent deity inasmuch as the divine is already there and taken for granted. Referring once again to Stietencron's analysis, we may state that the allegory embodies the canon.[7]

5 Cf. Eco 1984.
6 Cf. Stietencron 2001.
7 Cf. Stietencron 2001.

In image making and worship, the search for transcendence is thus carried out starting from a sign, an object in which transcendence is taken for granted and whose distinctive feature is permanence: the object is what remains at the end of the production process and what pre-exists and remains at the end of the worship process, being eminently connected to a spatial and static paradigm rather than to a dynamic, rhythmic and temporal one. In Louis Renou's words: 'Le culte des images divines dans l'Inde ancienne dérive [donc] des thèmes mythiques et spéculatifs de l'antique religion védique. L'appel fait aux dieux, sans cesse répété [...] a fini, dans un autre cadre, par porter ses fruits. Le dieu est présent désormais [...]'.[8]

However, it is evident that these two meaning modalities – the symbolic and the allegoric one – cannot be considered as mutually exclusive in a given context or as necessarily consecutive from a chronological point of view; these two modalities can indeed co-exist, as they are the two poles of a dialectical process, unfolding both diachronically and synchronically in the manifestation of culture.

In this perspective, from a general standpoint, we can define image making and worship as an allegoric moment, inasmuch as images are signs; permanent traces of transcendence, something that is always there, statically pointing at transcendence. Yet, even in this allegorical moment, one can find a symbolic meaning modality; in the course of the ritual cult, images actually have to be consecrated in order to fully accomplish their function of mediation between man and the divine: once again, the transcendence has to be attracted, called to the object and, at the end of the ritual cult, the transcendence has to be dismissed, allowing it to withdraw itself from the permanent trace that is left behind it.

As is well known, the ritual practices of attracting and dismissing the deities – *āvāhana* and *visarjana* respectively – do not only concern the anthropomorphic icons, but also the non-anthropomorphic ones, such as the *liṅga*.[9] Such a practice seems to confirm that, in the perception of the image, it is not the presence or lack of the anthropomorphic element that constitutes its distinctive feature, but the meaning modalities that determine the fruition and perception of the image itself. This mechanism is made even clearer in the case of those images that are not permanently consecrated and whose consecration and dismissal rituals define their own existence as worship objects, such as the images prepared for the annual *Durgā pūjā* and then destroyed,

8 Renou 1978, p. 163.
9 Cf. Eck 1981, p. 7.

or the *kṣaṇika liṅga*, the small clay lamp prepared by the worshipper, to which Śiva's presence is attracted and which is thrown away at the end of the ritual.[10]

In this sense the key element is not the art or worship object, the image itself, but rather the meaning modalities it implies, which can transform its own function and perception. As Ananda K. Coomarswamy and Heinrich Zimmer demonstrated a long time ago, the anthropomorphic images (*mūrti* and *pratimā*) and the non-anthropomorphic ones (*yantra*) have the same function,[11] they only differ in the language they use. To this assumption we can add that both the anthropomorphic and the non-anthropomorphic images can activate different meaning modalities according to the contexts in which they appear and are perceived.

As we have seen, on the one hand, in the image making and worship context, which from a general standpoint could be classified as an allegoric phase of culture, a symbolic meaning modality is also present and is activated in order to perform the ritual. On the other hand, in an eminently symbolic phase, such as the ritual sacrificial one, we find the traces of a progressive allegorization, corresponding to the progressive crystallization and codification of the ritual performance: at some point, the ritual sacrifice also begins to leave traces behind it.

In a recent article,[12] Theodore Proferes has outlined most exhaustively the developments and changes in the rite of installation of the sacrificial post in the Vedic liturgy as represented in the Vedic texts, from the Rigvedic *Saṃhitā* (in particular hymn eight of the third *maṇḍala*) to the *Brāhmaṇa*s, and the *Śrautasūtra*s. He points out that 'from the Rigvedic standpoint, there is no connection between Viṣṇu and the post': [13] the Rigvedic passages metaphorically associate the post with Agni, Savitṛ and Uṣas because these ones 'raise their beam of light up in the sky in a manner that reminded the Rigvedic poets of the erection of the sacrificial post.'[14] The connection with Viṣṇu is conversely present in the Yajurvedic *mantra*s; this liturgical development is connected to the new Vedic notion of cosmos: reality is conceived of as a well ordered system, on three vertical levels – earth, atmosphere, heaven -, the cosmos itself; the ritual becomes a cosmological act, involving all of the cosmic levels, and the cosmic taxonomy is founded on the ritual orthodoxy. The sacrificial post is not only the means through which the profane

[10] Cf. Eck 1981, p. 50.
[11] Cf. Coomaraswamy 1934 and Zimmer 1926.
[12] Cf. Proferes 2003.
[13] Proferes 2003, p. 336.
[14] Proferes 2003, p. 336.

wood is metaphorically connoted as Vanaspati, the Lord of the wood, and identified with him, becoming sacred and evoking the divine presence in the sacrifice, but it is also the device for 'climbing up' to heaven: man becomes immortal and substitutes the deities, transcending his mortal condition.

In relation to the present paper, a passage from AiB[15] is very interesting, inasmuch as it states that,unlike in ancient times, it is no longer necessary to throw the whole sacrificial post into the oblation fire at the end of the soma ritual; in fact MS 3.9.4 and KS 26.6[16] also consider such a practice as an ancient and former ritual. The new cosmic ritual prescribes that the sacrificial post is left installed in its own place, as a permanent remaining sign of the sacrifice, and that only one chip is burnt in substitution of the post. The ritual dynamism has been fixed in the static and terrestrial sign of the ritual efficacy: the post/*yūpa*. From the effort to transcend the concrete reality through metaphorical and symbolical processes, we come to the descent into material reality, the objective correlative and allegory of the otherness.

The process of metaphorizing and transcending is exhausted: rewording Renou's expression, the gods are already on the earth. In the Vedic context, attested through the Vedic literature, the meaning process of reality can be represented as a parabola from the ancient eminently metaphorical Rigvedic culture to the late ritualistic culture of the *Brāhmaṇa* and *Śrauta* texts, focused on the obsessive codification of the ritual, more and more formalized and fixed in a canon, whose performing and evoking capacity is in the process of getting lost. Between them, the Yajurvedic-*mantra* culture, based just on the ritual performance itself as a cosmizing act, represents not only the most intensive effort of metaphorizing reality, aimed at reaching the otherness-heaven, but also accomplishes it completely on the earth, starting to leave remains as evidence of such an accomplishment.

Proferes' essay on the developments of the liturgy connected with the sacrificial post offers us a perfect example of such a cultural parabola: he highlights that the ritual shifts correspond to semantic shifts. In fact, in the Rigvedic strophes, the post as a ritual tool is defined through three different terms: *yū́pa, svā́ru* and *vā́naspati*; such a synonymy is enriched by poetical polysemy: *svā́ru* is often equivalent to beams of light, in association with the Dawn or Agni. However, among these three terms, *yū́pa* itself is not semantically restricted to the sphere of the sacrifice: three of the five occurrences of the term *yū́pa* refer to door-posts of a

[15] Proferes 2003, p. 347.
[16] Proferes 2003, p. 345.

more mundane function. The *sváru-yū́pa* relationship is changed in the Yajurvedic texts: *yū́pa* is usually used as 'sacrificial' post, and *sváru* is applied to that chip which must be thrown into the fire at the end of the ceremony, according to the recent development of the ritual.[17] Such a semantic shift is the sign of the passage from one meaning modality of reality to another: from the symbolical one to the allegorical one, or from charisma to canon.

Both in relation to the sacrificial ritual and the anthropomorphic and non-anthropomorphic image making, we can find a mechanism that unveils and reveals the sacred through a dialectic of presence and absence: paradoxically, the sacred is revealed as fully present when its presence is not taken for granted, but evoked to fill an absence; conversely, when the presence of the sacred is taken for granted, it appears as absent, inasmuch as it is inactive and crystallized. In a way, it seems that the divine cannot dwell openly and for a long time in the world of men; the presence of the divine always has to be temporary, temporarily attracted and then dismissed in order to save its power to transform reality.

Such dialectics of absence/presence can be interestingly put in relation with an etymological and philological reconstruction of some terms connected to the semantic field of images.

2. In the light of such a reconsideration of the categories of the aniconic and the iconic, the purpose of this part of the present article is to offer a textual and etymological analysis of one key term belonging to the semantic field of art in Indian culture. The term explored, among the many available, is *pratimā*, which is particularly important in the Hindu context.

This analysis will allow us to understand to what extent such terms may be related to the symbolic-allegoric dialectics outlined here; the 'presence' of absence and tension towards an 'elsewhere', both as the unfolding of a dynamic and rhythmic paradigm – symbol -, and as a crystallization-sclerotization manifestation of presence, the feature of which is permanence, related to a static paradigm – allegory.

It is well known that *pratimā* is one of the main words indicating image in Sanskrit, with particular reference to the "divine image" which, as the object of the iconic worship, is a sign of "presence". Etymologically, Mayrhofer[18] considers *pratimā́* as a compound: it is a feminine gender root-name from the OIA root *mā-*, meaning 'to measure' – from which *mātrā* 'unit of measure' also derives -,

[17] Cf. Proferes 2003, pp. 341-8.
[18] EWA (1994, 2, p. 341).

made up of the prefix *prắti* 'towards, against, in opposition to, in the presence of, in proportion to'. *Pratimā́* thus indicates 'what measures in proportion to', and it is often well translated by "counterpart, countermeasure, projection"; Mayrhofer proposes "copy-double" as meaning 'Abbild', – the Platonic *eidolon.*

In the *Vedas*, occurrences are not frequent:[19] they are found in the texts classified by Witzel as 'mantric', that is belonging to the textual repertoire of the late Rigvedic period (ṚgV 10.130.3), of the Atharvavedic collection (AVŚ 3.10.3; 8.9. 6; 9.4. 2. AVP 16.24.2; 6.2.4; 20.34.3), and the ritual *saṃhitās* (TS 4.2.10.1; 4.3.7.1; 4.4.11.3; 5.2.9.1-2; 5.3.2.4-5; 5.5.3.2; 5.7.2.1; KS 16.3; 16. 17; 17.10; 21.6; 32.4; 34.14; 40.2; MS 1.4.11: 60.9; 2.7.17: 101.17; 2.8.3: 108.11; 2.8.14: 118.12; VS 13.41; 14.18-22; 15.65; 32.3); they can also be found in the *brāhmaṇas* (ŚB 7.5.2.17; 8.3.3.5; 8.7.4.11; 10.4.3.13, 19, 20; 11.1.6.13; 11.1.8.3; 13.2.5.1; AiB 6.18; KB 10.3; TB 3.2.8.8; GB 1.5.10), in the *brāhmaṇa* sections of the *saṃhitās* and in the *upaniṣads* (ŚvU 4. 19).

The occurrence found in ṚgV 10.130.3, which represents a *hapax* in the Rigvedic context, is particularly interesting and provides a valuable starting point for reflection. The Rigvedic hymn 10.130 is considered as a cosmological one: it represents the foundation and re-foundation of sacrifice that, in the late Vedic context, is equivalent to a cosmogonic action. Furthermore, the Vedic sacrificial context offers a privileged standpoint on the rethinking of the iconic-aniconic categories; as is well known, the issue of the presence or lack of representations during the ritual performance is still unsolved[20] and, more generally, Brahmanic ritualism manifests the dialectic absence-presence/ symbol-allegory also in a diachronic perspective.[21]

As to the Rigvedic hymn 10.130, this includes the motif of the foundation of the sacrifice also found in the famous *puruṣasūkta* (10.90). It also has the same enigma structure – characterized by interrogatives – of the very well known hymn 10.121 (*kasūkta*), and the enigma itself sounds like the similar *sát-á-sat* question of hymn 10.129.

[19] All the Vedic texts, except where specified differently, are quoted from the *Titus Text, Thesaurus Indogermanischer Text und Sprachmaterialien,* available at http://titus.uni-frankfurt.de/indexe.htm. All translations, except where specified differently, are mine.

[20] As is well known, Banerjea 1956 concluded that there is no evidence of image worship in the Vedic period; however, in some Vedic rituals, as described in the *brāhmaṇa* texts, objects and tools are manipulated and placed in the ritual space in order to shape a human figure (i.e. the *mahā-vīra* 'Great Man' in the *pravargya* ritual), or an animal figure, such as the bird-altar of the *agnicayana,* the ritual of piling the fire. Cf. the related observations by Malamoud (1986).

[21] Cf. the observations by Theodore Proferes (2003) recalled above.

The motif of the foundation/re-foundation of the sacrifice is expressed through the metaphorical equivalence between the activity of spinning/weaving and the sacrificial action; such a weft/texture maps and defines the sacred space, according to a metaphor already implied in the technical meaning of the OIA root *tan-* 'to extend, to stretch' the sacrifice, with reference to the preparation of the sacrificial space: in this sense the sacrificial space is a texture (*tán-tra*), made of woven threads (*tán-tu*), stretched (*ta-tá*). The sacrifice is thus 'extended-stretched', as stated in the first strophe:[22]

> 10.130.1ab *yó yajñó viśvátas tántubhis tatá ékaśataṃ devakarmébhir ā́yataḥ*
> 10.130.1cd *imé vayanti pitáro yá āyayúḥ prá vayā́pa vayéti āsate taté*
> The sacrifice that is spread out with the threads on all sides, drawn tight with a hundred and one divine acts,
> is woven by these fathers as they come near: 'Weave forward, weave backward' they say as they sit by the loom that is stretched tight.

The metaphor of weaving is expressed through the technical verbs *prá-ve/ápa-ve* (d): they indicate the two opposite movements of weaving, the 'going to and fro' of the shuttle, according to the opposition of the prepositions *prá/ápa*. According to Maggi (1981, p. 56), *prá* indicates 'la processualità in atto, la vivezza dell'attività',[23] thus referring to an unfolding action, to a process, while *ápa* is connected to the progressive fulfilling of the action, preluding the going back to the starting point and/or the undoing of the texture. The binomial *prá-ve/ápa-ve* expresses a 'doing and undoing' of the sacrificial texture, which is both a 'divine act', and an 'act performed by the Fathers', repeated innumerable times: the action of the Fathers must be the repetition of the primordial divine act, the archetypical sacrifice, and in this sense the sacrifice-texture is periodically 'done and undone', re-founding the primordial act. Moreover, the weaving act not only defines and shapes the primordial chaos-*a-sat* into the cosmic space, but it also 'scans' it into the cosmic time, infusing a rhythmic order into the chaos: the rhythmic movement – 'forwards and backwards' – of the shuttle in the weaving/sacrifice founds time. Such a cosmic metaphor is clearly expressed in the second strophe: space is defined through 'pegs', and time is scanned through rhythmic sounds, the 'melodies' made of *ṛ́c*-es, metrically structured strophes.

[22] The Vedic text is after Van Nooten and Holland 1994, the translation is by Wendy Doniger O'Flaherty (1981).

[23] See Maggi 1981, p. 56.

10.130.2ab *púmām̐ enaṃ tanuta út kṛṇatti púmān ví tatne ádhi nā́ke asmín*
10.130.2cd *imé mayū́khā úpa sedur ū sádaḥ sā́māni cakrus tásarāṇi ótave*
The man stretches the warp and draws the weft; the man has spread it out upon this dome of the sky.
These are the pegs, that are fastened in place; they made the melodies into the shuttles for weaving.

However, in the periodic and inexhaustible doing and undoing of the primordial act, the micro- and macro-cosmos are mutually reflected in one another, and the enigma resounds there:

10.130.3ab *kā́sīt pramā́ pratimā́ kíṃ nidā́nam ā́ jyaṃ kím āsīt paridhíḥ ká āsīt*
10.130.3cd *chándaḥ kím āsīt práügaṃ kím ukthám̐ yád devā́ devám áyajanta víśve*
What was the original model, and what was the copy, and what was the connection between them? What was the butter, and what the enclosing wood?
What was the metre, what was the invocation, and the chant, when all the gods sacrificed the god?

Here the Brahmanic myth of the primordial sacrifice is implied: according to the *brāhmaṇa* texts, the sacrifice was founded by Prajāpati,[24] the cosmogonic deity who ejects the entire reality (the cosmos, the gods), becoming 'undone, sacrificed' himself as a sacrificial oblation in order to sustain the cosmos. For instance, in ŚB XI 1.8.2-3, on the occasion of the Full and New Moon sacrifice, it is said:

[…] *tébhyaḥ prajā́patir ātmā́nam prádadau yajñó haiṣām āsa yajño hi devā́nām ánnam // sá devébhya ātmā́nam pradāya / áthaitám ātmánaḥ pratimā́n asṛjata yád yajñaṃ tásmād āhuḥ prajā́patir yajña íty ātmáno hy ètám pratimām ásṛjata*
Prajā́pati gave himself to them [gods]: indeed the sacrifice became theirs, for the sacrifice is the food of the gods. (2) Having given himself to the gods, then he ejected the *pratimā́* of himself that is this sacrifice: therefore it is said 'Prajā́pati is the sacrifice', for he ejected the *pratimā́* of himself as this (sacrifice).

Here the primordial sacrifice performed by the gods is not defined *pramā́*, but the two syllables – *pra* and *mā́* – resound in the whole passage through their iteration in *prajā́pati* – *prā́dadau*, and in *ātmā́nam* – *haiṣām āsa*; however, the replica of the first sacrifice, that is the sacrifice performed 'here' among men, is

[24] Sāyaṇa's commentary also follows the same interpretation.

called '*pratimā́* of Prajā́pati'. On both of these occasions Prajā́pati is identified with the sacrifice; moreover, elsewhere in the same text, Prajāpati himself is also said to be both officer and sacrificer of the cosmic sacrifice.[25] The cosmic multifunctionality of the Brahmanic Prajāpati is one of the answers found by the sacerdotal speculation for the enigma *sat-a-sat/* being-non-being already proposed in the late Rigvedic hymns:[26] does existence come from an unqualified primordial, from an original One or an original duality? Was there originally being or non-being, or is existence a cyclical alternation of being and non-being, where one preludes the other? This is the enigma also brought up in R̥gV 10.130.3 through two key terms: *pramā́* and *pratimā́*.[27]

The term *pramā́* is also a root name from the root *mā́*- 'to measure', like *pratimā́*, but its prefix is different: here we find *pr̥ś* and thus *pramā́* indicates 'the process of measurement' in its doing; it is the very act of measuring, which as such cosmicizes and defines space.[28] In this context, the root *mā́*- acquires a connotation that is not only ritual – the definition of the sacrificial space – but also and mainly cosmic, as the sacrifice is the main cosmogonic act.[29] In this sense *pramā́* is the primordial sacrifice, the paradigmatic performance. As to *pratimā,* it indicates the process of specular measurement – "counter", the specular replica of the act of measuring in its doing. Such a meaning of the prefix *práti* is attested by the Rigvedic occurrences of other derivatives from the root *mā́*- with the same prefix *práti*: the case of *pratimā́na* results as being meaningful. In the late Rigvedic hymns it is quoted 4 times in relation to Indra,[30] as a neuter substantive, literally meaning 'what is counter-measured': from the mythic and cosmogonic context of the occurrences, it clearly results that *pratimā́na* indicates something/ someone "equivalent by measure", "correspon-

[25] Cf. ŚB 11.1.8.4, quoted below. On this topic, cf. also Smith 1984; Malamoud 1986.

[26] Please note that the last strophe of the Rigvedic hymn 10.121, revealing the enigma by mentioning Prajāpati as the Cosmic One, is considered as later: the cult and the myth of Prajāpati are fully developed in the *brāhmaṇas*, especially in the exegesis of the *agnicayana* ritual, the piling of the fire altar.

[27] On the relation *pramā́/ pratimā́* cf. Oldenberg 1919, pp. 114-5.

[28] The same root *mā*- represents the lexical basis of the semantic field of Hindu architecture: terms like *pramāṇa*- 'measure-proportion' and *vimāna*- 'temple' demonstrate that the meaning of the root implies the specific technical acceptation of 'ordering the space on a proportional basis'. Cf. Kramrisch 1976, pp. 129-76.

[29] On the cosmogonic value of the root *mā́* and its derivatives (*mā́yā; mā́trā*) cf. Gonda 1959 and Maggi 1993.

[30] R̥gV 1.32.7; 1.52.12; 1.102.6; 10.111.5.

dent to" inasmuch as it is "in front of, it is opposed to", often as an adversary; such as for instance in ṚgV 1.32.7, where Vṛtra is the *pratimā́na* of Indra, and in ṚgV 1.52.12c, where the Earth is the *pratimā́na* of Indra's strength.[31]

Following such an interpretation, *pratimā́* in 10.130.3 is the equivalent and specular measure of *pramā́*, the replica of the primordial texture/ sacrifice, the double of the prototypic cosmogonic act; it is not clear whether the connotation opposer-adversary is also implied, which might allude to the 'competition-conflict' which according to Jan C. Heesterman is the historical origin of the sacrifice itself.[32] However, it is evident that *pratimā́* somehow already implies the notion of substitute: the sacrificial act of the 'Fathers' is a "replica" of the divine one, by producing a "'substitute"' of it.[33] In Brian K. Smith's words:

> Vedic ritualism [...] is based on substitution. The theology, metaphysics, and ontology created by the Vedic ritualists presume the inaccessibility of transcendent prototypes and the necessity, therefore, of ritual action using counterparts or "symbols" for the "real thing". Indeed, the sacrifice as a whole is a counterpart of the transcendent Cosmic One, Prajāpati or Puruṣa, who has created the ritual as *pratimā* of himself.[34]

However, the category of the 'mantric' texts to which the late Rigvedic hymn belongs, attests a phase of the ritual Vedic formalism that is yet to be fully systematized: the hierarchical structure of the cosmic levels has not been strictly defined yet; in fact 'the victim simultaneously represents the deity and the sacrificer, just as the ritual as a whole mediates between macrocosmos and microcosmos'.[35] The interrogative does not actually put an empha-

[31] ṚgV 1.32.7: *apā́d ahastó apṛtanyad índram ā́sya vájram ádhi sā́nau jaghāna / vṛ́ṣṇo vádhriḥ pratimā́nam búbhūṣan purutrā́ vṛtró aśayad víastaḥ*, 'Handlos und fußlos kämpfe er gegen Indra. (Indra) hat ihm den Vajra auf den Rücken geschlagen. Der Kastrierte, der dem Stier (Indra) ein Maß sein wollte, der Vṛtra lag da, vielfach zerstückelt.'. ṚgV 1.52.12c: *cakṛṣé bhū́mim pratimā́nam ójaso*, 'Du (Indra) hast die Erde zum Gegengewicht deiner Körperkraft gemacht'. Translation after Witzel and Goto (2007).

[32] Cf. Heesterman 1993, pp. 7-44. Such a conflict is evident in the narrative sections of the *brāhmaṇa* texts, where it is said that the sacrifice-*yajña* is the prize for the winner in the contest between gods-*deva* and anti-gods-*asura*. The term *pratimā* is used in a clear conflicting context in AiB 6.18, where two seers-*ṛṣi*, Viśvāmitra and Vāmadeva, rival one another in composing hymns; one seer composes hymns which are the counter-measure of the other's.

[33] As to the notion of 'substitution' see Doniger O' Flaherty and Smith 1989, pp. 189-224, and especially Smith 1989, pp. 73-5; 169-99.

[34] Cf. Smith 1989, p. 176.

[35] Cf. Smith 1989, pp. 176-7. However, Smith claims that there are different grades in substitution; prototype and copy share the same essence, but manifest

sis on the qualitative difference between the 'original' and the 'copy' – as required by Western Platonic tradition -, and it is not even clear whether the projection is a more or less incomplete projection of the prototype. On the contrary, the interrogative highlights that *pramā́* and *pratimā́* have the same cosmogonic function; they cannot actually be distinguished: the key feature lies in the repetition and recursion of the process itself, in the constant rhythm of the binomial *prá/ ápa*. The sacrificial performance is developed through the reference to the presence of being: its being modeled, appearing, being revealed, fulfilling and withdrawing in absence. It is this process itself that becomes the repeated model, *prá/ práti*, the 'doing and undoing': the absence preludes a renewed presence and the latter a renewed 'undoing'.

The sacrifice that is cyclically made, repeating itself as identical to itself, is in the first place a 'model' and in this cyclic process, the original act and its replica-substitute are confused: both of them are just presence and manifestation of *sat*. In this sense *pratimā́* indicates the 'iteration of the manifestation of presence in act'. It has not fully become a ritual 'substitute' yet; it is the 'counter-part' of presence, through which presence itself completely fulfils itself.[36]

The binomial *pramā́-pratimā́* 'paradigm/ replica' in its Rigvedic dialectic tension seems to correspond to the dynamic symbol-allegory. However, with the development of the ritual formalism attested in the *brāhmaṇas*, the rhythmic re-doing as an endless extension of presence, made of micro-/ macro-cosmic correlations and metaphorizations, of replicas of replicas or of substitutes and substitutes, slowly loosens the tension towards the transcendent. *Pratimā́* no longer indicates the symbolization process in its iteration, but either a specific cosmic phenomenon, which is the result of the sacrifice and thus its permanent extension, or a domestic animal, a common object, a tool for the ritual, which is used in the human micro-cosmos.[37] Thus, *pratimā́* is beginning to be fixed in what leaves a trace outside the ritual performance. It starts to fully acquire the role of a ritual substitute, until it becomes the sacrificial substitute *par excellence*, the sacrificial oblation itself.

it differently, as the ritual counterpart does not keep the same completeness of the original. Thus, according to Smith, the very notion of substitution, developed in the *brāhmaṇa* texts and their ritual formalism, forms the basis of the cosmic hierarchy characterizing the Hindu dharmic conception.

[36] Smith also recognizes that the theory of substitution is rooted in the *brāhmaṇas*, and is fully and systematically developed only in the *śrautasūtras*.

[37] The debated question of the rest-*śeṣa* is implied in this process. Cf. Malamoud 1972.

In the mantric texts one can only find some hints of such a sclerotization: this happens when *pratimā́* is identified with a natural phenomenon, an animal or an object, that is, with something that after the ritual materially leaves a trace of itself in the macro- and the micro-cosmos. In this sense we have a first trace connected to the root *mā́-* with the prefix *práti*, which is found in the enigmatic hymn ṚgV 1.164. Strophe 24 is particularly interesting:

> 1.164.24ab *gāyatréṇa práti mimīte arkám arkéṇa sā́ma traíṣṭubhena vākám*
> 1.164.24cd *vākéna vākáṃ dvipádā cátuṣpadā akṣáreṇa mimate saptá vā́ṇīḥ*
> With the *gāyatrī* foot they fashion a hymn; with the hymn, a chant; with the *tríṣṭubh* foot a strophe; with the strophe of two feet or four feet they fashion a speech. With the syllable they fashion the seven tones.

The verb *prati-mā́-* is used here with a clear poetic connotation; all the terms present in this strophe point at the poetic technique of composition, from the names of the rhythmic-metric structures of the strophes, to the hymn (*árka*) made of strophes (*ṛ́c*), and the melody (*sā́man*); the hymn is thus the result of a replication/counter-measurement of a rhythmic model (*chándas*), the scanning of which defines the ritual time, as in ṚgV 10.130.2-3. However, the root *mā́-* with the prefix *práti* is also based on the reproduction of a 'trace' (*padá*); it does not only convey the poetic metaphor according to which, composing a hymn is equivalent to a complex work of rhythmic and sound measurement or to a replica of the rhythmic movement of the 'going to and fro' in weaving. It is actually well known that *padá*, as the neuter redetermination of the masculine root name *pā́d-/ pád-* 'foot',[38] indicates both the trace moving and living beings leave with their feet,[39] and also the linguistic sign, the word:[40] in this case a word which is uttered rhythmically, and which ends up constituting the section of the strophe (*pāda*), the repeated fixed model.[41] It is thus a word inadequate for the profane dimension of the human microcosmos: it is the sign of presence and remains repeated in the mnemonic tradition of the poets starting from the first seers, as a

[38] Cf. EWA, 1996, 2, pp. 77-8.

[39] In his famous essay, Oguibénine 1988 identifies such living beings with cattle, in particular with the sacrificial cow.

[40] The same relation between the root *prati-mā́* and the name *pád-* is found in JB III 319: the soma oblation is the *pador pratimā́*-counterpart of the feet, that is, their 'trace'-*pada*.

[41] Cf. Maggi 1989, particularly p. 90.

double of the primordial path left by the sacrificial animal, along which the divine and the human periodically meet again. Thus in the last strophe of R̥gV 10.130 the work of the poet-seers is equivalent to a circular process (*ā-vŕ̥t-*), in which the beforewards and afterwards conflate in a harmonic continuum, just as in the chariot wheel movement:

> 10.130.7ab *sahástomāḥ saháchandasa āvŕ̥taḥ sahápramā ŕ̥ṣayaḥ saptá daíviyāḥ*
> 10.130.7cd *pū́rveṣām pánthām anudŕ̥śya dhī́rā anvā́ lebhire rathíyo ná raśmī́n*
> The ritual repetitions harmonized with the chants and the metres; the seven divine sages harmonized with the original models (*pramā*).
> When the wise men looked back along the path of those who went before, they took up the reins like charioteers.

In this infinite web of correspondences one can find the connection between the name of the deities and the names of the rhythmic-metric structures (R̥gV 10.130, strophes 4-5), which constitute the strophes of the Rigvedic hymns; such hymns thus become the sign of the divine presence, especially when uttered/ scanned for the ritual performance; the metric word-*padá* is made full of presence, being the vehicle of presence:

> 10.130.4ab *agnér gāyatrí̄ abhavat sayúgvā uṣṇíhayā savitā́ sám babhūva*
> 10.130.4cd *anuṣṭúbhā sóma ukthaír máhasvān bŕ̥haspáter br̥hatī́ vā́cam āvat*
> The *gāyatrī́* metre was the yoke-mate of Agni; Savitr̥ joined with the *uṣṇi* metre, and with the *anuṣṭúbh* metre was Soma that reverberates with the chants. The *br̥hatī* metre resonated in the voice of Bŕ̥haspáti.

> 10.130.5ab *virā́ṇ mitrā́váruṇayor abhiśrī́r índrasya triṣṭúb ihá bhāgó áhnaḥ*
> 10.130.5cd *víśvān devā́ñ jágatī ā́ viveśa téna cākl̥pra ŕ̥ṣayo manuṣyà̄ḥ*
> The *virā́ j* metre was the privilege of Mitra and Varuṇa; the *triṣṭúbh* metre was part of the day of Indra.
> The *jágatī* entered into all the gods. That was the model for the human sages.

The word is "replica-countermeasure" – and thus the image – of the divine, which becomes concrete when it is the object of the "mental" vision and when it is uttered/ scanned in the ritual performance, but which will fade away with the end of the sacrifice:[42]

[42] Cf. R̥gV 10.177.1: *pataṃgám aktám ásurasya māyáyā hr̥dā́ paśyanti mánasā*

10.130.6ab *cākḷpré téna ŕ̥ṣayo manuṣyā̀ yajñé jāté pitáro naḥ purāṇé*
10.130.6cd *páśyan manye mánasā cákṣasā tā́n yá imáṃ yajñám áyajanta pū́rve*
That was the model for the human sages, our fathers, when the primeval sacrifice was born.
With the eye that is mind, in thought I see those who were the first to offer this sacrifice.

However, such a metric structure, modeled on the primordial sacrifice in the *mánas* 'mental stream' of the poets, leaves a trace-*padá*-word, even outside the ritual performance, constituting the *padá*-word of the Vedic collections (*saṃhitā́s*), and fixed in a textual repertoire forming the Vedic *corpus*. It is well known that such a *corpus* has been transmitted through sophisticated mnemotechnics, among which 'recitation word by word', the *padapāṭha*: a word continuously repeated for educational purposes, a pure sound trace which, considered outside the performative context, remains 'inactive'-empty of presence, thus no longer an actual manifestation of presence or an effective ritual counterpart.

Thus among the Atharvavedic occurrences of *pratimā́*, the most meaningful is AVŚ VIII 9.6, summing up all of the elements highlighted above: it has a clear cosmogonic connotation and suggests the relation between the rhythmic-metric-scanned word and the divine, between the word-trace and the sacrificial cow. According to Whitney[43] it is actually a "mystic" hymn, devoted to *virāj*, which is equivalent here to the cow-mother and the word-metre. Strophe 5 sounds as follows:

8.9.5ab *bṛhatī́ pári mā́trāyā mātúr mā́trā́ dhi nírmitā*
8.9.5cd *māyā́ ha jajñe māyā́yā māyā́yā mā́talī pári*
bṛhatī the measure was fashioned forth out of a measure [as] out of a mother; illusion was born from illusion, Mātalī out of the illusion.

Thus the phonetic play of the syllable *mā* 'to measure' is apparent, inasmuch as it is obsessively repeated, being the semantic base both of *māyā*, illusion, and the *nomen agentis mā́tṛ* 'measurer'; the latter is also the homophonic double of *mātṛ* 'mother'.[44] The

vipaścítaḥ / samudré antáḥ kaváyo ví cakṣate márīcīnām padám ichanti vedhásaḥ, 'The wise see in their heart, in their spirit, the bird anointed with the magic of the Asura. The poets see him inside the ocean; the sages seek the footprints of his rays.' Cf. also ṚgV 10.129.4.

[43] Cf. translation by Whitney 1905, vol. 2, p. 507. The Vedic text is after Roth and Whitney 1924.

[44] Cf. Ronzitti 2001, p. 26.

strophe itself is a *pratimā́*: it is an accumulation of phonetic doubles able to fulfill the polysemic process. The following strophe reveals the enigma by presenting the term *pratimā́*, referred to Agni-Vaiśvānara: the fire-womb is produced in the measurement, connected to *māyā*, and thus to a cosmic counterpart-*pratimā́*: the day sky (*dyaú*) reached by the sacrificial prayers and oblations. It is not only the manifestation process of the ongoing presence, but also the final result of such a process; the sky only exists thanks to the periodic sacrificial oblations.

8.9.6ab *vaiśvānarásya pratimópári dyaúr yā́vad ródasī vibabādhé agníḥ*
8.9.6cd *tátaḥ ṣaṣṭhā́ d ā́múto yanti stómā úd itó yanty abhí ṣaṣṭhám áhnaḥ*
Vaiśvānara's counterpart [is] the sky above, as far as Agni forced apart the two firmaments; from the sixth yonder come the *stomas*; up from here they go unto the sixth of the day.

As to the other Atharvavedic occurrences, one is referred to Indra, defined as "the counterpart of the waters" (AVŚ 9.4.2),[45] with allusion to the cosmogonic myth of the liberation of the waters imprisoned by Vṛtra, while another one is referred to the night (*rātri*), which as a counterpart of the year (*saṃvatsara*) must ensure prosperity (AVŚ 3.10.3).[46] The term *pratimā́*, if connected to the notion of time, can be equivalent to a manifestation process of the ongoing presence; however, the same strophe is also quoted in TS V 7.2.1,[47] where it must accompany the piling of a series of bricks with which the fire altar is built in the *agnicayana* ritual: in the play of the ritual equivalences, the night-*pratimā́* is represented by the bricks themselves. It does not only represent the process of the piling of the bricks, but it is also crystallized in the bricks themselves.

Likewise, four of the occurrences of the term *pratimā́* in the *Śatapathabrāhmaṇa* (10.4.3.13, 19, 20; 11.1.6.13) are referred to the notion of time. In the section describing the Full and New-Moon sacrifice, the equivalence between Prajāpati, sacrifice and year is declared: ŚB 11.1.6.13:

sá aikṣata prajā́patiḥ imaṃ vā ātmánaḥ pratimā́m asṛkṣi yát saṃvatsaram íti tásmād āhuḥ prajā́patiḥ saṃvatsara íty ātmáno hy ètám pratimām ásṛjata yádv eva cáturakṣaraḥ

[45] *apāṃ pratimā́*: same expression in AVP 16.24.2a.

[46] The expression *saṃvatsarasya pratimā́* becomes formulaic in the *Gopathabrāhmaṇa*: it is repeated many times in 1.5, the exposition of the *sattra* of the year, especially in 1.5.10 with the formula *sahasrasaṃvatsarasya pratimā-* 'counterpart of a thousand years'. As to the two occurrences in AVP 6.2.4; XX 34.3, they result as being quite obscure.

[47] Also in KS 40.2.

> Prajāpati reflected: 'I have emitted the counterpart of myself, that is, the year'. And therefore they say: 'Prajāpati is the year', for he emitted it as a counterpart of himself, that is, made up of four syllables [like Prajāpati].

The relation between cosmic time and the rhythmic scanning of the word – already present in the *saṃhitā* texts – is thus apparent: the Prajāpati-*saṃvatsara* equivalence is grounded in the fact that they have the same number of syllables.[48] The other three occurrences of the term *pratimá* (ŚB X 4.3.13, 19, 20) form part of a section of the *agnicayana* ritual; here the term *pratimá* denotes a concrete object of the ritual, thus losing its fluid connotation of processuality: it begins its crystallization in the stones placed around the circular altar (*gārhapatya*), around the other fire altars, *dhiṣṇya* e *āhavanīya*, and in the bricks constituting the three altars. These quotes are included in a passage dealing with immortality: once proven that the year, and thus time, are the sign of man's mortal condition, the passage proposes a solution for overcoming time-death. The sacred act – the piling of the fire altar – ensures the return to life after death, that is, immortality (ŚB 10.4.3. 9-10). Once again the process of the ritual act implies a permanence in being; it is not only the action itself that ensures immortality, but also the objects employed in the act: the stones constituting the circle of the sacrificial altar, the same stones that are said to represent the year. The stones are thus the counterpart of the nights (*rātri*) (ŚB 10.4.3.13), the bricks are the counterpart of the days (*ahan*), the half-months (*ardhamāsa*),[49] the months (*mā́sa*) (ŚB 10.4.3.19) and the hours (*muhūrta*) (ŚB 10.4.3.20): through these, immortality is reached or, better, 'time is defeated'. This passage actually represents a sophisticated time scanning founded on a complex numerical scale of multiples and submultiples; we can read Eggeling's[50] rendering in its famous translation:

> Thus the enclosing-stones, supplying the place of nights, are made the (means of) gaining the nights, they are the counterpart of the nights: there are three hundred and sixty of them, for there are three hundred and sixty nights in the year. Of these, he lays twenty-one round the *gārhapatya*, seventy-eight round the *dhiṣṇya* hearths, and two hundred and sixty-one round the *āhavanīya* (13). All these [the bricks of the five layers] make three

[48] In ŚB 12.3.2.1ss.: *saṃvatsara* is the sacrificer-*yajamāna* for the same reason: both the terms are made up of four syllables.

[49] The same expression, *ardhamāsānām pratimā*, is found in ŚB 12.2.5.1 on occasion of the *aśvamedha*, the horse sacrifice.

[50] Eggeling 1897.

> hundred and ninety-five. Of these, three hundred and sixty, supplying the place of days, are made the (means of) gaining the days, they are the *counterpart of the days*: there are three hundred and sixty of them, for there are three hundred and sixty days in the year. And for thirty-six (additional days) which there are the filling of the earth (counts as) the thirty-sixth; twenty-four thereof, supplying the place of half-moons, are made the (means of) gaining the half-moons, they are the *counterpart of the half-moons*. And the (remaining) twelve, supplying the place of months, are made the (means of) gaining the months, they are the *counterpart of the months*. And, lest the Seasons should be wanting, these (twelve bricks), by two and two (taken) together, supply the place of seasons (19). As to the Lokapr̥ṇā (space-filling bricks), supplying the place of the *muhūrta* (hours), they are made the (means of) gaining *muhūrtas*, they are the *counterpart of the muhūrtas*: there are ten thousand and eight hundred of them, far so many *muhūrtas* there are in the year. Of these, he lays down twenty-one in the *gārhapatya* (altar), seventy-eight in the *dhiṣṇya*-hearths, and the others in the *āhavanīya*. So many, indeed, are the (different) forms of the year: it is these that are secured for him (Prajāpati, the Year), and are put on him (20).

It is evident here that time is hierarchically structured: the repeated piling of stones and bricks is the repetition of a time scanning/ measurement, thus a 'counter-measure', but the stones and the bricks used in the ritual acquire the role of substitutes of the same sections of time, inasmuch as they are material and concrete objects, in which the time process itself is crystallized. Likewise, for space: the altar-bricks are 'pieces' of 'measured' cosmos, that is, structured in a spatial order, through the iteration of the ongoing measuring process; they are not only *pratimā́s*, but also 'substitutes' of the parts of the cosmos itself. Thus the formulaic *mantra*,[51] *yajñasya tvā pramayābhimayonmayā pratimayā parigr̥hnāmi*, 'I take possession of you with the fore-measure, the upon-measure, the up-measure, the counter-measure of the sacrifice', is referred both to the performance in its unfolding-doing, and to the concrete piling of the altar: the *brāhmaṇa* prose itself in KS 13.1 suggests this interpretation. And again in the TS 5.5.3.2, the same section of the *agnicayana* ritual, the following *mantra* is said: *váyasāṃ vā eṣá pratimā́yā cīyate yád agnír*, 'This, the fire, is indeed piled through the counterpart of birds'.[52] One of the fire altars is actually shaped like an enormous greatly winged bird, flying towards the east, made up of seven layers of piled bricks. The term *pratimā* is also used here in the instrumental case: it is evident that it does not only indicate an ongoing ritual process – the pil-

[51] KS 32.4, 34.14; MS 1.4.11:60.9; also in ApŚrSū 4.5.4, AśvŚrSū 3.13.15.

[52] Text after Weber 1873; the translation is mine.

ing of the altar equivalent to the flying bird – but also a concrete element of the ritual, the altar-bird-bricks (object-animal).

However, the *agnicayana*,[53] i.e., the most sophisticated ritual in the sacerdotal tradition, which fulfils the perfect cosmos-sacrifice correspondence, is only systematically analyzed in the *brāhmaṇa* texts, where it is specified that during this ritual various kinds of fire altars are piled (*gārhapatya, dhiṣṇya* and *āhavanīya*), but especially the bird-altar: the whole ritual and in particular the piling of the bird-altar represent Prajāpati himself, the Cosmic One-Sacrifice. The whole ritual is equivalent to the creative primordial act, as always proceeding, and progressively shaping space and time, brick by brick: all the micro- and macro- cosmic elements are listed as emanations of the ritual procedures, they are *pratimās* 'counter-measures'.

Thus in TS 4.3.7.1[54] one can find the *mantras* accompanying the piling of the fourth layer of bricks of the fire altar during the *agnicayana*: they constitute a list of elements of the meso-macro-micro-cosmic ritual, each of which is defined as the *chandas*-metric-rhythmic structure. The whole cosmos comes out of the process of rhythmic scanning/measurement, a progressive extension/expansion starting from *mā́-* 'to measure':

> 4.3.7.1 *mā́ chándaḥ pramā́ chándaḥ pratimā́ chándo 'srīvíś chándaḥ panktíś chánda uṣṇíhā chándo bṛhatī chándo 'nuṣṭúp chándo virā́ṭ chándo gāyatrī chándas triṣṭúp chándo jágatī chándaḥ pṛthivī chándo 'ntárikṣaṃ chándo dyaúś chándo sámāś chándo nákṣatrāṇi chándo mánaś chándo vā́ k chándaḥ kṛṣíś chándo hiraṇyaṃ chándo gaúś chándo 'jā́ chándo 'śvaś chándaḥ /*
> *Mā* is metre, *pramā́* is metre, *pratimā́* is metre, *asrīvís* is metre, *panktí* is metre, *uṣṇíh* is metre, *bṛhatī* is metre, *anuṣṭúbh* is metre, *virāj* is metre, *gāyatrī* is metre, *triṣṭúbh* is metre, *jágatī* is metre; earth is metre, atmosphere is metre, sky is metre, seasons are metre, constellations are metre; mind is metre, word is metre, ploughing is metre, gold is metre, cow is metre, female goat is metre, horse is metre.

However, in the *brāhmaṇa* prose section (TS 5.3.2.4-5), one can find the explanation that each *chandas*-metre corresponds to a brick that has to be placed at a specific cardinal point, and thus the whole ritual of the altar piling consists of a rhythmic spatial-temporal expansion; such expansion is the result of the progressive iteration of the piling of each brick, each being *mā́/pramā́/pratimā́/* etc. In this sense every brick is *pratimā*, but also the whole altar resulting from the piling of the bricks is *pratimā*: the manifestation process of being in its iteration is fulfilled brick

[53] Cf. Staal et al. (1983).
[54] Also in KS 26.3; MS 2.8.3: 108.11; VS 14.18-22.

by brick, so that each of them is defined *tanū*-body, etymologically "subtle essence'", the result of *tan*-extending-stretching being.[55] Likewise, the same *mantra* quoted in VS 14.18-22 is explained in *Śatapathabrāhmaṇa* (8.3.3.5):

> *mā́ chánda iti ayaṃ vaí loko mā́yaṃ hí lokó mitá iva pramā́ chánda íty antarikṣaloko vaí pramāntarikṣalokó hy asmā́ l lokāt prámita iva pratimā́ chánda íty asau vaí lokáḥ pratimaiṣa hy ántarikṣaloke prátimita iva* [...] '*Mā* is metre': this world is indeed 'measure', for this world is, as it were, measured; '*pramā́* is metre': the middle-world is indeed 'fore-measure', for the middle-world is, as it were, measured forward from this world; '*pratimā́* is metre': that world is indeed 'counter-measure', for it is, as it were, counter-measured in the middle world [...].

In the *brāhmaṇa* text the process of cosmicization is more and more sophisticated, as the ritual process is more and more meticulously structured: the fire altar is piled layer by layer, with different kinds of bricks, according to their position; we are dealing here with the *chandasya*-bricks, or 'metre-bricks'. The phonetic play of the syllable *mā* – already in AV III 9. 5-6 – is made more intense, and its echo is unfolded in the world, through the atmosphere, up to 'that world', the sky, which is thus *pratimā́*; the echo corresponds to the cosmic expansion.[56] In this phase of the ritual development the term *pratimā́* stands not only for the ritual processuality, but also for two antinomial realities; the concrete object of this world and the macrocosmic correspondent in the 'other' world.

Such realities are mutually connected through the ritual performance, that is, the process of unfolding of the presence in progress, but outside the ritual context, they are disconnected and one can be considered as the substitute of the other one only thanks to their ritual correspondence. This antinomial relationship is fully accomplished in the sacrificial victim, which represents the counter-measure of the primordial sacrificial oblation *par excellence*; once more, according to the Brahmanic tradition, Prajāpati himself. However, what is offered during the sacrifice becomes a counter-part and counter-measure only in the ritual context, whereas outside it, in the human micro-cosmos, the oblation is something else (animal, vegetable, object);

[55] On the relation bricks-metres-bodies, cf. Malamoud 1986, pp. 77-98, and Malamoud 2002, pp. 19-28.

[56] The same phonetic play and cosmogonic value of the root *mā* are found in the funeral hymn AVŚ 18.2, in the formulas 39-44 and in the prose section 45: 'to measure the measure' (*mā- mātrā-*) means to finish the terrestrial life and to attain the sky.

it enters the ritual context as a substitute, allegorically representing the sacrificed deity. In particular, the dialectic symbol-allegory tension seems to fade away in a sclerotization of presence when the counter-measure is man himself (*puruṣa*), the sacrificer (*yajamāna*): either the human sacrifice is accepted, or one cannot but use a substitutive oblation, the substitute of *pratimā*, the sacrificer who promotes the iteration itself of the ongoing presence.[57]

Thus the *mantra* quoted in VS 13.41 refers to the sacrificial fire, commonly defined embryo (*garbha*), able to acquire manifold forms, flowing in its tongues, expanding everywhere in its sparks: *ādityáṃ gárbhaṃ páyasā sám andhi sahásrasya pratimāṃ viśvárūpam*, 'With milk anoint you the infinite embryo, counterpart of thousand, which has every shape'.[58] The *brāhmaṇa* prose in ŚB 7.5.2.17 includes this *mantra* in the ritual of the piling of the altar, in particular in the description of the foundation of the bird-altar itself (7.4.1). First of all a lotus-leaf is placed: it is considered as the birth-place for the fire-Agni-embryo; then, something shining (*rukma*), a golden plate, is deposed on it. Above the latter a *puruṣa* is placed, that is, a golden figure of a man, which is said to be equivalent to the sacrificer (*yajamāna*), to the fire-Agni, and the deity of sacrifice, Prajāpati. It should be a small idol representing a man with upstretched arms, so as to extend its body, with its head facing east (7.4.1.15-45). Afterwards the brick-layers are piled. In 7.5.1-2 the fire enters the ritual scene in a fire-pan (*ukhā*): the heads of each sacrificial victim are placed on the pan one after the other, starting from the *puruṣa*'s head, after anointing the fire with milk.

Which *puruṣa* are we dealing with in this context? The sacrificer himself or the golden man? It is stated that through this formula man, in this case the sacrificer, obtains life for a thousand years, suggesting a relation with Prajāpati. Given the above-mentioned equivalence between victim and sacrificer in Prajāpati, it becomes evident that the sacrificial victim and the sacrificer are one the counterpart of the other: victim and sacrificer are mutually measured, the one 'counters' the other, aiming at doubling themselves endlessly. And again in ŚB 11.1.8.4, on the occasion of the above mentioned Full and New-Moon sacrifice, it is stated that the sacrificer offers himself-*ātmānam* to the gods, like the prototypic Prajāpati, thus being oblation for the gods – *havir hy èṣá devā́nām.*

[57] As the original violent act gets more and more quenched in the ritual, according to Heesterman's theory, the substitute becomes necessary.

[58] Also in TS 4.2.10.1 (TS 5.2.9.1-2 is the *brāhmaṇa* explicative prose); MS 2.7.17: 101.17; KS 16.17.

Therefore the oblation is the counterpart of the sacrificer, but the golden man in the *agnicayana* ritual is not only a counterpart of the sacrificer: it is also its substitute, as the oblation/victim itself. The *mantra* in VS 15.65:[59] *sahásrasya pramā́ asi sahásrasya pratimā́ asi sahásrasyonmā́ asi*, 'You are the fore-measure of a thousand, you are the counter-measure of a thousand, you are the up-measure of a thousand', included in the *agnicayana* section of the *Śatapatha* (ŚB 8.7.4.11), is referred not only to the fire-Agni and the sacrificer, but also to the golden man placed on the ground under the fire altar. The officer recites it bestrewing both the fire-Agni and the sacrificer with golden chips, as explained in 8.7.4.9:

> *yā́vān agnir yā́vaty asya mā́trā tā́vataivā̀sminn etád amŕ̥taṃ rūpám uttamáṃ dadhāti sahásreṇa sárvaṃ vaí sahásraṃ sárveṇaivā̀sminn etád amŕ̥taṃ rūpám uttamáṃ dadhāti*
> As great as Agni is, as great as is his measure; with so much he thus bestows upon him immortality, that highest form: with a thousand; a thousand means everything: with everything he thus confers upon him immortality, that highest form.

Micro-meso- and macro-cosmos are evoked here and mutually connected: the man-sacrificer is the unit of measure on which the bird altar is built (*taṃ vā údbāhunā púruṣeṇa mimīte / púruṣo vaí yajñas ténedaṃ sárvam mitaṃ* [...], 'He measures it by the man with upstretched arms; indeed, the sacrifice is the man and everything here is measured by him', ŚB10.2.2.6). The fire altar is able to increase exponentially – 'thousandfold' – such a measure, being the counter-measure that is itself fully accomplished in immortality and elsewhere already identified with the 'sky' or 'that world', 'the other world'.

The dialectic symbol-allegory reaches its climax, yet the balance is already broken: *pratimā́* is no longer the processuality in its unfolding, since it is fully identified and sclerotized in an object, a material substitute of the three cosmic levels – man-fire-sky. The golden *puruṣa* is a real thing and not a simple counter-measure, or better, by virtue of the counter-measure – the ritual performance - it can be considered as a substitute. Thus a chain mechanism is being initiated: the victim-substitute can itself be substituted by other kinds of oblations (animals, vegetable cakes),[60] according to a hierarchical perspective, the same perspective which is also developed in parallel with the ritual formalism. Thus, on the one

[59] Also in TS 4.4.11.3; KS 17.10; 21.6; MS 2.

[60] Cf. TB 13.2.8.8 and KB 10.3. According to Smith 1989, p. 180-1, it can be considered a 'double substitution':.

hand the sacrifice of man (*puruṣamedha*) represents the highest grade of the sacrificial scale – allowing the attainment of immortality, like Prajāpati – while on the other hand, in the chain of substitutions of the sacrificial victims, the sacrifice slowly loses its effectiveness: the *pratimā* 'counter-measure' can no longer ensure immortality, the latter being understood as processuality of the ritual action per se. In this sense the same *mantra* of VS 32.3 (*ná tásya pratimā́ asti yásya nā́ma mahád yáśaḥ*), quoted in *puruṣamedha*, is also found in an Upanisadic context (ŚvU 4.19) in a very different sense:

> *nainam ūrdhvaṃ na tiryañcaṃ na madhye parijagrabhat / na tasya pratimā asti yasya nāma mahad yaśaḥ*
> No one will catch hold of him from above, from across, or in the middle. There is no *pratimā* of him, whose name is Immense Glory.

In the Upanisadic context, immortality is the overcoming of the sacrificial action (*karman*), and thus the overcoming of the iteration of the vital process of man himself, bringing man to doubling himself in the offspring (*prajā*): the very value of *pratimā* is denied.

However, it is especially in the *śrautasūtra* texts, where the ritual formalism is made extreme, that the 'permanently' doubled model becomes sclerotized as a repetition, as an immanent trace related to a static paradigm: in these texts we find actual established substitution criteria, the first of which is resemblance (*sāmānya*).[61] The dichotomical symbol-allegory tension is definitely loosened, and the value of *pratimā* fades away with it; *pratimā* begins to indicate an object-'image', by virtue of a 'likeness-resemblance'.

Thus, the term *pratimā* mainly belongs to the ritual lexicon and represents the core of the semantic field of ritualism: it fully expresses its dichotomic tension between symbol and allegory. In a synchronic perspective, it represents the meso-cosmos itself, being shaped and existing only in the ritual context. Once the performance is accomplished, the dialectic tension between micro-macro cosmos is also exhausted, leaving a trace/ appearance/ likeness of the permanence of being. In a diachronic perspective, it follows the development and the parabola of the Vedic ritualistic culture: once the performative tension is exhausted, it becomes a sclerotized paradigm, indicating that material object-image which in the Hindu conceptualization is only animated on the occasion of a specific religious ceremony.[62]

[61] Cf. Smith 1989, pp. 183-4.

[62] Cf. above pp. 2-4.

Abbreviations

AiB	*Aitareyabrāhmaṇa*
ĀpŚrSū	*Āpastambaśrautasūtra*
ĀśvŚrSū	*Āśvalāyanaśrautasūtra*
AVŚ	*Śaunakīyātharvaveda*
AVP	*Paippalādātharvaveda*
EWA	Mayrhofer 1986-2000
GB	*Gopathabrāhmaṇa*
JB	*Jaiminīyabrāhmaṇa*
KB	*Kauśītakibrāhmaṇa*
KS	*Kauśītakisaṃhitā*
MS	*Maitrāyaṇīsaṃhitā*
ṚgV	*Ṛgveda*
ŚB	*Śatapathabrāhmaṇa*
ŚvU	*Śvetāśvataropaniṣad*
TB	*Taittirīyasaṃhitā*
TS	*Taittirīyasaṃhitā*
VS	*Vājasaneyisaṃhitā*

References

Banerjea, Jitendra Nath (1956). *The Development of Hindu Iconography. Second Edition (Revised and Enlarged).* Calcutta: University Press, 1956[2].

Coomaraswamy, Ananda K. (1926) "The Origin of the Buddha Image". In: *Journal of the American Oriental Society* 46, pp. 165-70.

Coomaraswamy, Ananda K. (1934). *The Transformation of Nature in Art.* Harvard University Press: Cambridge.

Dehejia, Vidya (1991) "Aniconism and the Multivalence of Emblems". In: *Ars Orientalis* 21, pp. 45-66.

Doniger O'Flaherty, Wendy, ed. (1981). *The Rig Veda. An Anthology.* London: Penguin Books.

Doniger O'Flaherty, Wendy and Brian K. Smith (1989). "Sacrifice and Substitution: Ritual Mystification and Mythical Demystification". In: *Numen* 36, pp. 189-224.

Eck, Diana (1981). *Darsan. Seeing the Divine Image in India.* New York: Columbia University Press.

Eco, Umberto (1984). *Semiotica e filosofia del linguaggio.* Turin: Einaudi, pp. 199-254.

Eggeling, Julius (1897). *Śatapatha-Brāhmana, according to the Text of the Mādhyandina School* (the *Sacred Book of the East*, ed. by F. Max Müller, vol. 43). Oxford: Clarendon Press Oxford.

Foucher, Alfred (1905). *L'art gréco-bouddhique du Gandhara: étude sur les origines de l'influence classique dans l'art bouddhique de l'Inde e de l'Extrême-Orient.* Paris: Ernest Leroux.

Gonda, Jan. "The 'Original' Sense and the Etymology of Skt. *Māyā*". In: *Four Studies in the Language of the Ṛgveda*. The Hague: Mouton, pp. 119-94.

Granoff Phyllis and Koichi Shinohara, eds. (2004). *Images in Asian Religions*. Vancouver: UBC Press.

Heesterman, Jan C. (1993). *The Broken World of Sacrifice*. Chicago: The University of Chicago Press 1993.

Huntington, Susan L. (1990). "Early Buddhist Art and the Theory of Aniconism". In: *Art Journal* 49, No. 4, pp. 401-8.

Kramrisch, Stella (1976). *The Hindu Temple*. Delhi: Motilal Banarsidass.

Maggi, Daniele (1981). "Il motivo della tela fatta e disfatta tra epos e ideologia". In: Tristano Bolelli (editor), *Studi vedici e medio-indiani* (Pisa: Edizione Giardini 1981, pp. 49-86).

Maggi, Daniele (1989). "Idee linguistiche nell'India vedica". In: *Annali dell'Istituto Orientale di Napoli* 11, pp. 63-114.

Maggi, Daniele (1993). "Viṣṇu, il centro e la misurazione dello spazio agrario nell'India del Ṛgveda". In *Studi e Saggi Linguistici*, 33, pp. 105-25.

Mayrhofer, Manfred (1986-2000). *Etymologisches Wörterbuch des Altindoarischen*, Heidelberg: Carl Winter.

Malamoud, Charles (1972). "Observations sur la notion de 'reste' dans le brahmanisme". In: *Wiener Zeitschrift für die Kunde Südasien* XVII, pp. 6-26.

Malamoud, Charles (1986). "Briques et mots. Observations sur le corps des dieux dans l'Inde védique". In: *Le Corps des dieux*, edited by Charles Malamoud and Jean-Pierre Vernant. Paris: Gallimard, pp. 77-98.

Malamoud, Charles (1989). *Cuire le monder, rite et pensée dans l'Inde ancienne*, Paris: Malamoud, Charles (1994). *Cuocere il mondo.* Milan: Adelphi Édtions La Découverte

Malamoud, Charles (2002). "A Body made of Words and Poetic Metres". In *Self and Self Transformation in the History of Religions*, edited by David Shulman and Guy G. Stroumsa. Oxford – New York: Oxford University Press.

Oguibénine, Boris (1988). *La déesse Uṣas. Recherches sur le sacrifice de la parole dans le Ṛgveda*. Louvain – Paris: Peeters.

Oldenberg, Hermann (1919). *Vorwissenschafliche Wissenschaft: Die Weltanshauung der Brāhmaṇa Texte*. Gottingen: Vandenhoeck und Ruprecht.

Proferes, Theodore N. (2003). "Poetics and Pragmatics in the Vedic Liturgy for the Installation of the Sacrificial Post". In: *Journal of the American Oriental Society* 123, No. 2, pp. 317-50.

Renou, Louis (1978). "Les images des dieux dans la littérature de l'Inde ancienne". In: *L'Inde fondamentale. Etudes d'indianisme* réunies et présentées par Ch. Malamoud. Paris: Hermann, pp. 157-63.

Ronzitti, Rosa (2001). *Campi figurali della 'creazione' nel* R̥gveda. Alessandria: Edizioni dell'Orso.

Roth, Rudolf and William Dwight Whitney (1924). *Atharva Veda Sanhita.* 2nd ed., edited by M. Lindenau, Berlin: Dümmlers [Berlin 1856].

Van Nooten, Barend A. and Gary B. Holland, eds. (1994). *Rig Veda. A Metrically Restored Text.* Harvard University Press: Cambridge, Massachusetts.

Smith, Brian K. (1984). "Sacrifice and Being. Prajapati's Cosmic Emission and its Consequences". In *Numen* 32, pp. 71-85.

Smith, Brian K. (1989). *Reflections on Resemblance, Ritual, and Religion.* New York – Oxford: Oxford University Press.

Staal, Frits et al. (1983). *Agni. The Vedic Ritual of the Fire Altar.* Berkeley: Asian Humanities Press, 2 vols.

von Stietencron, Heinrich (2001). "The Dynamics of Legitimization and Innovation in Indian Religions". In: *Charisma and Canon: Essays on the Religious History of the Indian Subcontinent,* edited by Vasudha Dalmia, Angelika Malinar, and Martin Christof. New Delhi: Oxford University Press, pp. 14-38.

Weber, Albrecht, ed. (1872). *Die Taittirīya-Saṃhitā.* Leipzig: Brockhaus.

Whitney, William Dwight, tr. and comm. (1905). *Atharva-Veda Saṃhitā.* Cambridge, Massachusetts: Harvard University.

Witzel, Michael and Toshifumi Goto, eds. (2007), *Rig-Veda. Das heilige Wissen. Erster und zweiter Liederkreis.* Frankfurt am Mein – Leipzig: Verlag der Weltreligionen.

Zimmer, Heinrich (1926). *Kunstform und Yoga im Indischen Kultbild.* Berlin: Frankfurter Verlags – Anstalt.

Patrizia Mureddu

Denotation in absentia *in Literary Language: The Case of Aristophanic Comedy*

1 'Defective Communication' in the Strategies of Comedy

While studying the degrees and modalities of comedy in Aristophanes over the last few years, I have often come across a mechanism which seems to me to be common to the comedy of every age and which, for lack of a generally accepted definition, I shall call 'defective communication'. By this I mean that body of allusions, metaphors, puns, which can only work if they refer to an implicit network of information from which the listener or spectator is able to freely extract the necessary data to trigger the comic level of the message.

This particular aspect of ancient comedy[1] has attracted scarce attention over the last fifty years, perhaps due to the strong influence of Bakhtin's remarks about carnivalesque[2] in the field of study on the ancient theatre. It is quite easy to understand why scholars are especially impressed by those manifestations of comic which seem to be more remote or belonging to "another" culture: elements from the Dionysian cult, "gastronomic" topics[3],

[1] Süß 1920 was the first to attempt a systematic study on comedy and Witz in the ancient world; later important contributions were made by Plebe 1952; Plebe 1956; Thierfelder 1979; Halliwell 2008.

[2] Bakhtin 1965. On the importance of Bakhtin's studies for the understanding of Aristophanes' comic, see Carrière 1979; Rösler 1991; Platter 1993; von Möllendorff 1995.

[3] Degani 1990; Degani 1991; Wilkins 2000; Bowie 2002.

obscenities[4], aischrologia[5], iambic invective[6]. At the same time I believe that it could be just as enlightening to observe, in cultural contexts so different to ours, the utilization of strategies that still work and whose persistence could count for something in defining the very concept of "comedy".[7]

To give a better idea of the topic in question, I should like to quote an anecdote from fifty years ago. The episode is well known to all Italians of my generation since it generated a great deal of criticism.

During an official ceremony, the then President of the Republic, perhaps due to a somewhat over-zealous official, missed the proffered chair and almost tumbled to the ground. This laughable event involving such a distinguished character was broadcast live into the homes of nearly half the Italian population by the only existing TV channel of the time. Ugo Tognazzi and Raimondo Vianello, the two presenters of the popular *Uno, due, tre!* programme, hinted to the episode in a one might say "subliminal sort of way"; one of them pretended to fall off his chair, at which the other jokingly said: 'Hey, but who do you think you are?' This joke went down well with the audience who were able to grasp the cryptic allusion: so much so that the programme was accused of nothing less than 'public outrage of the head of state'.

Similar cases can be found in Greek comedy right from its very beginnings; in fact, one of the greatest difficulties in the complete understanding of the comic Aristophanes can be attributed to the fundamental role played by a vast array of innuendos.

All teachers faced with a class of students and embarking on the reading of an ancient comedy are obliged to provide not only the translation but also a set of often complex information. Thus, for example, the comment made by one of the two servants who introduce the *Knights*, regarding the quotation from Euripides' *Hippolytus* (vv. 18 f.):

> ΝΙ. πῶς ἂν σύ μοι λέξειας ἁμὲ χρὴ λέγειν;
> ΔΗ. μή 'μοιγε, μή 'μοί, μὴ διασκανδικίσῃς
> Nikias: *How can I make you say what I should say?*
> Demosthenes: Oh no, please, I beg you, *don't chervil me!*

would be a real brainteaser, unless we recall a well-known

[4] Henderson 1991².

[5] Rösler 1993.

[6] Moulton 1979; Rosen 1988; Degani 1988; Degani 1993; Treu 1999; Mastromarco 2002.

[7] See Mureddu-Nieddu 2009 for a more detailed analysis of this topic and a more comprehensive bibliography.

catchphrase that describes Euripides as the son of a greengrocer. The author only needed to mention the σκάνδιξ ('chervil', a herb which was probably in greater use then than it is today) to bring the matter up again – through the *impromptu* creation of the verb διασκανδικίζω – and the conciseness of the allusion will have had not a minor part in the successful outcome of the comic remark. Today, guiding a modern reader along this path means irreparably losing the original comic potential.

I have no intention of undertaking an explanation of the psychological processes that make people laugh in these cases: probably, feelings of complicity or a sense of belonging have a certain role to play,[8] and perhaps even the production of a heuristic type of pleasure – the very one that is the problem solvers' wholly intellectual 'reward'.

It is however well known that the success of this strategy is subject to a particular set of circumstances: the actual sharing of the implied information, a correct evaluation of the quantity of the explicit data[9] and finally, as all comic actors or tellers of jokes know, accurately chosen timing. The short pause has to be just long enough to set off the necessary synapses and make your audience or public laugh.

2 *'Artistic Language' in Literary Comedy*

Although there are a myriad of possibilities regarding the applications of the above-mentioned strategies, I shall only consider some modes of expression peculiar to the *artistic language* of Aristophanes.

Even though there is indeed a general tendency – in the wake of a well known Aristotelian definition[10] – to describe the lan-

[8] In his recent and important paper, Halliwell 2008, pp. 19-30, in mentioning the 'playful' side of laughter, comments: 'We might characterize playful laughter provisionally, then, as a cooperative, reciprocally pleasurable form of behavior... Playful laughter is a badge and unifying agent of friendship'. However, the comic game that unites a group can also have (as can be seen in political satire of every age) an aggressive side towards enemies or mere strangers: 'Accordingly, the dividing line between play and actual aggression – between the autonomous give-and-take of the former and the consequential animus of the latter – is thin' (ibid.). Cf. also Halliwell 1991, pp, 283-5; Aloni 1995, p. 76; Rapallo 2004, pp. 27 ff.

[9] For Banfi 1995, pp. 40-7, one of the comic motifs is to be found in the attempt at contravening the first of the laws that – according to Grice 1978 – are at the basis of every communicative interaction: provide exactly as much information as required. However, he only considers cases in which the infraction goes in the opposite direction to our analysis: not 'defective' but 'excessive communication'.

[10] *Poet.* 5 (1149a 32 ff.)

guage of comedy referring to colloquial, familiar, direct categories, in short, to stylistically 'low' language, we cannot forget that even the latter (just like every literary language) undergoes processes of elaboration and stylization; even more so in the case of a creative, imaginative and ingenious author like our great Athenian writer.[11] This choice also delimits the scope of my research. In fact I shall only take into consideration phenomena of a phonetic, lexical, morphological or syntactic kind that can be attributed to the creativity of Aristophanes himself – or from the whole of Attic comedy – excluding those shared by all the Greek language, or typical of one of its dialectal divisions.

Let me give a simple example. In a way that is still similar to today, Attic used to denominate the various market areas by using elliptical expressions referring to the goods on sale: ἐν βιβλίοις, ἐν στεφάνοις, ἐν ἰχθύσι (literally: 'in the books', 'in the garlands', 'in the fish') which corresponded respectively to the more complete wording of 'at the book stall', 'at the garland stall', 'at the fish stall',[12] clearly named "*in absentia*". Our Comic however did not invent these and consequently, similar phenomena will not be dealt with here.

3 Comic Metaphor

I shall avoid to be led astray by the myriad of Aristophanes' metaphors,[13] even if I realize that I am robbing myself and you of a sure source of entertainment. This does not mean that I am not aware of how much, from this point of view, the instruments of the comic poets are dissimilar in quality and function from those of their tragic counterpart. I have elsewhere observed how, in Aristophanes, the use of images mainly causes a breach in communication, 'per includere nel tessuto del discorso un grumo di materia estranea, attingendolo dalla più triviale quotidianità'.[14]

As a consequence of its 'distorting' effect, when this material is inserted in the midst of lengthy enumerations, it adds its own

[11] Far fewer studies have been dedicated to Aristophanes' linguistic inventiveness compared to those on the same subject relating to other lyrical or tragic authors. We have to go as far back as Uckerman 1871 for a comprehensive study. Albini 1997, pp. 87-98; Noël 1997; Kloss 2001 partly dealt with the matter; Bonanno 1987, Ghiron-Bistagne 1989, Olson 1992, Andrisano 2002, Ercolani 2002, Willi 2003, Kanavou 2011, dealt with a particular aspect of Aristophanes' linguistic creativity ('talking nouns').

[12] *Poll.* 9, 47: cf. Aristoph. *Nub.* 1065; *Av.* 13, 1288; *Vesp.* 789; *Thesm.* 448; *Eccl.* 303.

[13] Please refer to the exhaustive researches by Taillardat 1962, Komornicka 1964, Newiger 2000[2].

[14] Mureddu 2006, pp. 220-2.

peculiar flavor to the comic mechanism of the accumulation of words.[15] I shall quote, as the only example of this process, Strepsiades' keynote tirade (*Nub.* 445 ff.) when he wishes to become, thanks to the teachings of Socrates, a complete and utter scoundrel:

εἴπερ τὰ χρέα διαφευξοῦμαι
τοῖς τ' ἀνθρώποις εἶναι δόξω
θρασύς, εὔγλωττος, τολμηρός, ἴτης,
βδελυρός, ψευδῶν συγκολλητής,
εὑρεσιεπής, **περίτριμμα δικῶν,**
κύρβις, κρόταλον, κίναδος, τρύμη,
μάσθλης, εἴρων, γλοιός, ἀλαζών,
κέντρων, μιαρός, **στρόφις**, ἀργαλέος,
ματιολοιχός.
...just to save my skin,
so let the people call me
bold, tongued, reckless, impudent,
despicable, lie paster, windbag,
trial's waste, law tablet,
castanets, fox, drill, horsewhip,
hypocrite, clingy, cheat,
duster, miserable, **pulley**, heavy,
plate licker.

The translation does not pay justice to the expressive vitality of the Greek (let alone the impossibility of reproducing the rhythm of a *pnigos* in anapaests) and above all is unable to account for the fact that alongside the various adjectives we find a *pot pourri* of all kinds of different objects (περίτριμμα, κύρβις, κρόταλον, τρύμη, μάσθλης, κέντρων, στρόφις),[16] which only assume the attributive role required by the syntax thanks to their position in the sequence. The very fact that their presence is not "normalized" by the intervention of any syntactic or morphological element, allows them to deploy their whole comic potential. Apart from κίναδος, 'fox', none of these nouns – at least as far as we can see – is normally used in the metaphoric sense required in this context. Consequently, to make their meaning clear, interpreters are obliged to substitute them with adjectives in the target language: which obviously leads to an evident impoverishment of the final comic effect.

As regards the metonymy in itself, and its possible comic value, I shall only consider a few cases which up till now (as far as I know)

[15] About this characteristic comic strategy cf. the useful survey of Spyropoulos 1974.
[16] Albini 1997, pp. 87 ff.

have been overlooked by scholars of ancient comedy, where this stylistic-rhetoric figure is used to substitute a complex set of information. In the comedies in our possession, in at least two cases this information is contained in the preceding verses, which allows us to have a clear idea of the process used by the author.

In the first scene of *Lysistrata*, the main character announces her friends that she has devised a plan to bring peace to the Greek cities. The women are delighted; Myrrhine, a young and provocative newly-married Athenian woman, proclaims, that she would be willing to divide herself in two just to see this happen, even if she had to become a sole (vv. 115 f.):

ἐγὼ δέ γ' ἂν κἂν ὡσπερεὶ ψῆτταν δοκῶ
δοῦναι ἂν ἐμαυτῆς παρατεμοῦσα θἤμισυ

But when she learns that the price to be paid is withholding sexual privileges – and thus complete abstinence from the joys of love – she, just like all the other women, immediately changes her mind and bursts out with an exclamation of utter refusal (ἀλλ' ὁ πόλεμος ἑρπέτω '...let the war carry on whatever!') which causes Lysistrata to retort (v. 131):

ταυτὶ σὺ λέγεις, ὦ ψῆττα;
And you're the one to say something like that, you *sole*?

In the last part of *Peace*, the farmer Trygaeus, after bringing back the goddess Peace to man, is tormented by a stream of wicked scoundrels, who are only interested in turning things to their own advantage. The priest Hierocles also arrives, worried about losing all the benefits he had enjoyed during the war in his position as a diviner and oracle monger. He claims the right to oversee the sacrificial celebrations, quoting in support of his assertion a weird rigmarole referring to Bacides, a very popular author of oracles at the time (v. 1070 f.):

εἰ γὰρ μὴ νύμφαι γε θεαὶ Βάκιν ἐξαπάτασκον
μηδὲ Βάκις θνητούς, μηδ' αὖ νύμφαι Βάκιν αὐτόν -
If only the nymphs had not tricked Bacides,
and Bacides man, and then again the nymphs Bacides...

After having put up with this annoying character for a short while and when the latter tries to make off with the roast meat, Trygaeus decides to send him packing with a good thrashing (v. 1119) shouting

ὦ παῖε παῖε τὸν Βάκιν
Come on, let *Bacides* have it, let him have it!

In the two quoted passages, the nouns ψῆττα and Βάκις take the place of an extensive turn of phrase, meaning in one case 'you who said you wanted to become a sole', and in the other 'this man who tormented us with the oracles of Bacides'. Both cases make use of an extremely succinct metonymy, which forces the listener to bring to mind a complete section of the comedy, making him/her become actively involved in the comic mechanism.

4 Towards "Zero": A Work of Gouging Out

Commonly found in Greek was a nexus where an adverbial determination accompanied by the verb 'to see' moved as it were the *focus* from the observed object to the quality of one's gaze. Thus just as in many of today's modern languages, expressions like βλέπειν, ἰδεῖν κακῶς do not mean 'to *see* badly', but rather 'to *frown*', in other words, to gaze with a hostile demeanour.

The nexus was already productive in the Homeric period, as shown by its presence in formulary systems (τὸν δὲ ὑπόδρα ἰδῶν προσέφη 'And *frowning* he replied...'), and with greater stylization, in lyrical poetry (Pind. *Ol.* 9, 111: ὁρᾶν ἀλκάν 'to *radiate* courage') and in tragedy (Aesch. *Sept.* 498 φόβον βλέπων 'with a gaze that strikes terror'). It must also have been widely used in popular and colloquial language: βλέπειν ταυρηδόν, for example, 'with the gaze of a bull', referred perhaps to a haughty stance, became the distinctive mark[17] of Socrates' 'mask' evoking his gaze both insolent and sly. Continuing along these lines, Aristophanes attempts something more daring, gradually subtracting from the connective structure, as if he is gouging out, conjunctions and morphemes, until he almost touches on the limits of semantic obscurity.

Indeed, in *Vesp.* 900 (κλέπτον βλέπει 'he really has the gaze *of a thief!*') and in *Pl.* 424 (βλέπει γέ τοι μανικόν τε καὶ τραγῳδικόν 'she has the gaze *of a lunatic, of a tragedy*'), the recourse to an adverbial determination has to be considered part of the norm. On the other hand, in the cases of βλέπειν βαλλήναδε (*Ach.* 233: 'with a gaze as to *Ballene*'[18]) and of βλέπουσα θυμβροφάγον (*Ach.* 254: 'with the gaze of someone who eats *bitter herbs*', i.e.: 'being all compunction'), the allative *-de* ending and the clear adjectival structure of the compound make both of them nothing more than comic 'variations of the theme'. But elsewhere Aris-

[17] As shown by the convergence of Platonic evidence with that of Aristophanes.

[18] That is: 'someone who wants to throw stones': the play is based on the overlapping of the name of the town of Pallene with the verb βάλλω, 'to throw, to hit'.

tophanes pushes forward his creativity, resorting to *empty* morphological marks, which on the contrary, result as being *full* of meaning.

Starting from expressions like βλέπειν ἀστραπάς[19], βλέπειν πυρρίχην[20], βλέπειν σκύτη[21] – a comic counterpart of the afore mentioned Pindaric and Aeschylean ὁρᾶν ἀλκάν and φόβον βλέπων – we find expressions in his comedies where the verb βλέπω is simply determined by the apposition of a multicolored series of nouns taken from daily life. In fact, in the various βλέπειν νᾶπυ (*CAv.* 631), βλέπειν κάρδαμα (*Vesp.* 455), βλέπειν ὀρίγανον (*Ran.* 604), βλέπειν ὑπότριμμα (*Eccl.* 292), we find the description of a person's gaze or demeanor, minus any morphological or syntactic intervention, with the mere evocation of bitter herbs or spices or spicy sauces: cress, mustard, oregano, garlic pesto. Here we find a particularly refined use of the usual nexus, which takes on a strong comic connotation just because of the formal absence of elements of reference.

The boldness of this construction can be gauged as regards the amount of difficulty in finding a translation that closely mirrors the model.

A classic quote from *Eccl.* 289 ff. sees the women, after having 'rehearsed' an oratory meeting and opportunely dressed up as men, set off boldly towards their destination:

χωρῶμεν εἰς ἐκκλησίαν, ὦνδρες· ἠπείλησε γὰρ
ὁ θεσμοθέτης, ὃς ἂν
μὴ πρῴ πάνυ τοῦ κνέφους
ἥκῃ κεκονιμένος,
στέργων σκοροδάλμη,
βλέπων ὑπότριμμα, μὴ
δώσειν τὸ τριώβωλον.
Let's go *men*, forward to the assembly! Because the archon
has threatened to whosever not arrives
before dawn, still in the dark,
all covered in dust, desperately fond
of garlic sauce, with a *mustard-gaze*
to not give him the triobolon. [22]

[19] *Ach.* 456: 'emanating lightning from his gaze', referred to the warmonger Lamachus.

[20] *Av.* 1169: 'with the gaze of a war dance', that is, in a state of alert, said of the sentry of the Kingdom of Birds.

[21] *Vesp.* 642: 'emanating leather', i.e. 'with the gaze of one who has tasted the whip'.

[22] The word play is exalted by the apparent parallelism between στέργων σκοροδάλμη and βλέπων ὑπότριμμα in which two different syntactic constructions are hidden.

5 *Compounds as Puzzles*

From the Homeric ῥοδοδάκτυλος ἠώς right down to the most daring constructions of the lyric poets of the late V century (Tim. *Pers.* 31: σμαραγδοχαίτας πόντος 38: μαρμαροπτύχοις κόλποις Ἀμφιτρίτας, 80: ἀγκάλισμα κλησιδρομάδος αὔρας, 88: σύρτις μακραυχενόπλους) compounds rule supreme in archaic Greek poetry.[23] On the other hand, in a literary language characterized by the frequent recourse to invented words, verbal or nominal compounds represented the most simple and effective method for coining new terms. Not by chance, Aristotle, seeing their evident ornate function, prohibited their excessive use in prose, considering them to be a disproportionate and "frigid" rhetorical instrument.[24]

The comic poet did not move away from the norm,[25] undertaking composition more or less according to the well-tried analogical mechanisms which made the relationships between constituents perspicuous, resorting to semantic marks such as the arrangements of the parts, accentuation, the use of binding vowels and the presence of suffixes and adjectival endings.

In this common system, Aristophanes inserts an anomalous category of creations – produced with a pure and simple jumble of terms in the total absence of any phono-morphological indications – whose complex meaning the user has to understand on his own. Let us see a number of illuminating examples, which I shall order in terms of increasing complexity:

Eq. 89
ΔΗ. κρουνοκυτρολεραῖος εἶ
You are a **springjugchatterbox**
(i.e.: 'drinking so much spring water has made you speak in vain'?)

Ran. 246 ff.
ΧΟ. ἢ Διὸς φεύγοντες ὄμβρον
ἔνυδρον ἐν βυθῷ χορείαν
πομφολυγοπαφλάσμασιν
Or when we avoid Zeus' rain
in a dance in the depth
with **boilingbursting**
(i.e.: 'with loud squawks which are transformed into a whirl of bursting bubbles'?)

[23] Sommer 1948 is still the most complete work on the history and mechanisms of Greek nominal composition (with interesting comparisons with similar formations of ancient Indian).

[24] *Rhet.* III 3 (1405b-1406a).

[25] His procedures for 'assembling' and 'disassembling' words are precisely listed by Beta 2007.

Nub. 331 ff.
ΣΩ. πλείστους αὗται βόσκουσι σοφιστάς,
θουριομάντεις, ἰατροτέχνας, σφραγιδονυχαργοκομήτας
κυκλίων τε χορῶν ᾀσματοχάμπτας, ἄνδρας μετεωροφένακας.
They feed many intellectuals:
diviners from Thuri, charlatans,
ringsnailsidlerlonghaired,
singers in cyclic choirs, meteor scoundrels.
(i.e.: 'young idle men with rings, who take great care of their nails and long hair'?)

Vesp. 218 ff.
ΒΔ. ὡς ἀπὸ μέσων νυκτῶν παρακαλοῦσ' ἀεί,
λύχνους ἔχοντες καὶ μινυρίζοντες μέλη
ἀρχαιομελισιδωνοφρυνιχήρατα.
Indeed, they came to call him right until midnight
with lanterns and humming
ancienthoneysidonphryniclovable melodies.
(i.e.: 'in the old fashioned way of Phrynichos: coming from Sidone, all honey, lovable'?)

Vesp. 503 ff.
ΒΔ. ταῦτα γὰρ τούτοις ἀκούειν ἡδέ', εἰ καὶ νῦν ἐγώ,
τὸν πατέρ' ὅτι βούλομαι τούτων ἀπελλαχθέντα τῶν
ὀρθροφοιτοσυκοφαντοδικοταλαιπώρων τρόπων
ζῆν βίον γενναῖον ὥσπερ Μόρυχος, αἰτίαν ἔχω
ταῦτα δρᾶν ξυνωμότης ὢν καὶ φρονῶν τυραννικά.
This is what they like to hear; and now I, for the fact
that I wish to free my father from these
gettingupatdawnsycophantjudgemiserable habits
and let him live the easy life of Moricus, am accused
of acting as a conspirator, aiming at tyranny.
(i.e.: 'of whom gets up early to attend the tribune like a miserable sycophant'?)

Vesp. 1355 ff.
ΦΙ. νέος γάρ εἰμι. καὶ φυλάττομαι σφόδρα
τὸ γὰρ υἵδιον τηρεῖ με, κἄστι δύσκολον
κἄλλως κυμινοπριστοκαρδαμογλύφον.
I am young and under strict control,
my boy watches over me, a terrible person,
and a **splittercuminsesamecutter** too.
(i.e.: 'a miser, capable of splitting a cumin in two, of cutting a sesame seed')

Lys. 456 ff.
ΛΥ. ὦ ξύμμαχοι γυναῖκες, ἐκθεῖτ' ἔνδοθεν,
ὦ σπερμαγοραιολεκιθολαχανοπώλιδες,
ὦ σκοροδοπανδοκευτριαρτοπώλιδες.
οὐχ ἕλξετ', οὐ παιήσετ' οὐκ ἀράξετε;
οὐ λοιδορήσετ', οὐκ ἀναισχυντήσετε.
Women, allies, run out of your houses,

Come on, **graininsquareherbvegsellers**,
Come on, **garlicinnkeeperbakers**,
here, to drag, stamp, rip, insult, fill with shame.
(i.e.: 'sellers of seeds, herbs and vegetables in the square, garlic sellers, innkeepers, bakers')

*Eccl.*1168 ff.
ΧΟ. τάχα γὰρ ἔπεισι
λοπαδοτεμαχοσελαχογαλεοκρανιολειψανοδριμυποτριματοσιλφιο-
παραλομελιτοκατακεχυμενοκιχλεπικοσσυφοφαττοπεριστεραλεκτρυον-
οπτοπιφαλλιδοκιχλοπελειολαγῳοσιραιοβαφητραγανοπτερυγών.
The **trayfulslicefishcatrabbitcranegravycrushedgarlicsilfiocheese-honeypouredthrushpigeoncushatroastedonionwagtaildove-haresalmiscrustgame** has already been served. (i.e.: ????)

All these compounds appear as puzzles made up of fragments of images set alongside each other but missing several essential pieces,[26] which the listener (or reader) has to find and put in the right place, if he/she wishes to grasp the whole concept.

6 Conclusion

As can be seen in this brief look at a number of cases, the lack of explicit determination is part of the game, of the challenge that the comic author proposes to his audience: the recipient has to find the correct arrangement of the syntactic relations, the key to understanding the compounds and the metaphors or metonyms – and the laughter (or at least the smile) that results, serves as recognition of the author's expertise, but perhaps derives also from the interpreter complimenting himself on his own perspicacity.

Abbreviations

Ach.	Aristophanes, *Acharnenses*
Av.	Aristophanes, *Aves*
Eccl.	Aristophanes, *Ecclesiazusae*
Eq.	Aristophanes, *Equites*
Nub.	Aristophanes, *Nubes*
Lys.	Aristophanes, *Lysistrata*
Ol.	Pindarus, *Olympia*
Pax.	Aristophanes, *Pax*
Pers.	Timotheus, *Persae*

[26] See Albini 1997, p. 90, with quotes from *Alice in Wonderland* by Lewis Carroll and from Rabelais' *Gargantua and Pantagruel.*

Pl.	Aristophanes, *Plutus*
Ran.	Aristophanes, *Ranae*
Rhet.	Aristotheles, *Rhetorica*
Vesp.	Aristophanes, *Vespae*

References

Edition: Wilson, Nigel G. (2007). *Aristophanis Fabulae.* Oxford: University Press.

Albini, Umberto (1997). *Riso alla greca. Aristofane o la fabbrica del comico.* Milano: Garzanti.

Aloni, Antonio (1995). "Strategie del comico nella Lisistrata di Aristofane." In *Sei lezioni sul linguaggio comico.* Ed. by E. Banfi, Trento: Università di Trento, pp. 73102;

Andrisano, Angela M. (2002). "Empusa, nome parlante (Ar. Ran. 288ss.)?". In: *Spoudaiogeloion. Form und Funktion der Verspottung in der aristophanischen Komödie.* Ed. by A. Ercolani ('Drama' 11). Stuttgart/Weimar: Metzler, pp. 204-23.

Bakhtin, Michail (1965). *Tvorčestvo Fransua Rable i narodnaja kul'tura Srednevekov'ja i Renessansa,* Moskva: Izd. Chudož (tr. it. *L'opera di Rabelais e la cultura popolare. Riso, carnevale e festa nella tradizione medievale e rinascimentale.* Torino: Einaudi, 1968).

Banfi, Emanuele (1995). "Morfologia del linguaggio comico: tra pragmatica e strategie linguistiche." In: *Sei lezioni sul linguaggio comico.* Ed. by E. Banfi. Trento: Università di Trento, pp. 17-70.

Beta, Simone (2007). "Giocare con le parole." In: *Diafonie. Esercizi sul comico. Atti del seminario di studi, Venezia, 25 maggio 2006.* Ed. by A. Camerotto. Padova: Sargon, pp. 13-43.

Bonanno, Maria Grazia (1987). "Metafore redivive e nomi parlanti (sui modi del *Witz* in Aristofane)." In: *Studi offerti a F. Della Corte.* Urbino: Quattroventi, pp. 213-28.

Bowie, Ewen (2002). "Ionian Iambos and Attic Komoidia: Father and Daughter, or Just Cousins?". In: *The Language of Greek Comedy.* Ed. by A. Willi. Oxford: University Press, pp. 33-50.

Carrière, Jean Claude (1979). *Le Carnaval et la Politique. Une introduction à la Comédie Grecque.* Paris: Les Belles Lettres.

Degani, Enzo (1988). "Giambo e commedia." In: *La polis e il suo teatro/2.* Ed. by E. Corsini. Padova: Editoriale Programma, pp. 157-79.

Degani, Enzo (1990). *La poesia gastronomica greca* (I). Bologna: 'Alma Mater Studiorum' 3, No. 2, pp. 33-50.

Degani, Enzo (1991). *La poesia gastronomica greca* (II). Bologna: 'Alma Mater Studiorum' 4, No. 1, pp. 164-5.

Degani, Enzo (1993). "Aristofane e la tradizione dell'invettiva personale in Grecia." In: *Aristophane : sept exposés suivis de discussions. Proceedings of the conference held in Vandoeuvres-Genève, August 19-24, 1991.* Ed. by J.M. Bremer and E.W. Handley (*Entretiens Hardt*, 38), pp. 1-36.

Ercolani, Andrea (2002). "Sprechende Namen und politische Funktion der Verspottung am Beispiel der Acharner." In: *Spoudaiogeloion. Form und Funktion der Verspottung in der aristophanischen Komödie.* Ed. by A. Ercolani ('Drama' 11). Stuttgart – Weimar: Metzler, pp. 225-54.

Fauth, Wolfgang (1973). "Kulinarisches und Utopisches in der griechischen Komödie." In: *Wiener Studien*, n.f., 7, pp. 39-62.

Ghiron-Bistagne, Paulette (1989). "Jongleries verbales sur les anthroponimes dans les comédies d'Aristophane." In: *Thalie. Mélanges interdisciplinaires sur la comédie* ('Cahiers du GITA' 5). Montpellier: Groupe Interdisciplinaire du Théâtre Antique, pp. 89-94.

Grice, Herbert Paul (1976). "Logica e conversazione." In: *Gli atti linguistici*, ed. by M. Sbisà. Milano: Feltrinelli, pp. 199-219.

Halliwell, Stephen (1991). "The Uses of Laughter in Greek Culture." In: *The Classical Quarterly*, 41, pp. 279-96.

Halliwell, Stephen (2008). *Greek Laughter, A Study of Cultural Psychology from Homer to Early Christianity.* Cambridge: University Press.

Henderson, Jeffrey (1991²). *The Maculate Muse. Obscene Language in Greek Comedy.* New York – Oxford: Oxford University Press [Yale 1975].

Kanavou, Nikoletta (2011). *Aristophanes' Comedy of Names. A study of Speaking Names in Aristophanes.* Berlin – New York: De Gruyter.

Kloss, Gerrit (2001). *Erscheinungsformen komischen Sprechens bei Aristophanes.* Berlin – New York: De Gruyter.

Komornicka, Anna M. (1964). *Metaphores, Personifications et Comparaisons dans l'oeuvre d'Aristophane.* Wroclaw – Warszawa – Krakow: Zakład Narodowy im. Ossolińskich.

Mastromarco, Giuseppe (2002). "'Onomastì komodein' e 'spoudaiogeloion'." In: *Spoudaiogeloion. Form und Funktion der Verspottung in der aristophanischen Komödie.* Ed. by A. Ercolani ('Drama' 11). Stuttgart – Weimar: Metzler, pp. 204-23.

Moulton, Carroll (1979). "The Lyric of Insult and Abuse in Aristophanes." In: *Monuments Historiques* 36, pp. 23-47.

Mureddu, Patrizia (2006). "Metafore tragiche, metafore comiche: il gioco delle immagini." In: *ΚΩΜΩΙΔΟΤΡΑΓΩΙΔΙΑ. Intersezioni del tragico e del comico nel teatro del V secolo a.C.* Ed. by E. Medda, M.S. Mirto and M.P. Pattoni. Pisa: Edizioni della Normale, pp. 193-224.

Mureddu, Patrizia (2006a). "Introduzione." In: *Comicità e riso tra*

Aristofane e Menandro. Ed. by P. Mureddu and G.F. Nieddu. Amsterdam: Hakkert, pp. 1-18.

Mureddu, Patrizia and Gian Franco Nieddu (2009). *L'ingegno proteiforme di Aristofane: verso la costruzione di un comico letterario.* In: *Poikilia. Variazioni sul tema.* Ed. by E. Berardi, F.L. Lisi and D. Micalella. Acireale – Roma: Bonanno, pp. 107-66.

Newiger, Hans-Joachim (2000^2). *Metapher und Allegorie. Studien zu Aristophanes.* Stuttgart – Weimar: Metzler.

Noël, Marie Pierre (1997). "Mots nouveaux et idées nouvelles dans les Nuées d'Aristophane." In: *Ktema* 22, pp. 173-84.

Olson, S. Douglas (1992). "Names and naming in Aristophanic Comedy." In: *The Classical Quarterly* 42, pp. 304-19.

Platter, Charles (1993). "The Uninvited Guest: Aristophanes in Bakchtin's 'History of Laughter'." In: *Arethusa* 26, pp. 201-16.

Plebe, Armando (1952). *La teoria del comico da Aristotele e Plutarco.* Torino: Pubbl. della Facoltà di Lettere e Filosofia.

Plebe, Armando (1956). *La nascita del comico nella vita e nell'arte degli antichi Greci.* Bari: Laterza.

Rapallo, Umberto (2004). "L'umorismo tra antichità e tardoantico: una prospettiva interdisciplinare." In: *Orpheus* 25, pp. 22-63.

Rösler, Wolfgang (1991). "Michail Bachtin e il 'Carnevalesco' nell'antica Grecia." In: *Carnevale e utopia nella Grecia antica.* Ed. by W. Rösler and B. Zimmermann. Bari: Levante.

Rösler, Wolfgang (1993). "Über Aischrologie im archaischen und klassischen Griechenland." In: *Karnevaleske Phänomene in antiken und nachantiken Kulturen und Literaturen.* Ed by S. Döpp. Trier: Wissensch. Verlag, pp. 57-97.

Rosen, Ralph M. (1988). *Old Comedy and the Iambic Tradition* (American Classical Studies,19). Atlanta: Scholars Press.

Sommer, Ferdinand (1948). *Zur Geschichte der griechischen Nominalkomposita.* München: Bayerischen Akademie der Wissenschaften.

Spyropoulos. Ēlias S. (1974). *L'accumulation verbale chez Aristophane (Récherches sur le style d'Aristophane).* Thessaloniki: *paper.*

Süß, Wilhelm (1920). "Das Problem des Komischen im Altertum." In: *Neue jarbücher für das klassische Literatur* 45, pp. 28-45.

Taillardat, Jean (1962). *Les images d'Aritophane.* Paris: Les Belles Lettres.

Thierfelder, Andreas (1979). "Die antike Komödie und das Komische." In: *Würzburger Jahrbücher,* n.f., 5, pp. 7-24.

Treu, Martina (1999). *Undici cori comici. Aggressività, derisione e tecniche drammatiche in Aristofane.* Genova: Università di Genova.

Uckerman, Wilhelm (1871). *De Aristophanis comici vocabulorum formatione.* Harburg: Elwert.
von Möllendorff, Peter (1995). *Grundlagen einer Ästetik der Alten Komödie. Untersuchungen zu Aristophanes und Michail Bachtin.* Tübingen: Narr.
Wilkins, John (2000). *The Boastful Chef. The Discourse of Food in Ancient Greek Comedy.* Oxford: University Press;
Willi, Andreas (2003). *The Languages of Aristophanes. Aspects of Linguistic Variation in Classical Attic Greek.* Oxford: University Press.

Ruben Fais

The Birth of the Buddha in the Early Buddhist Art Schools

In the earliest Indian Buddhist art, the Buddha is represented without ever actually depicting the person, who is replaced by symbols referring both to his presence and to the so-called Great Miracles.[1] In the sculpted decoration of the *stūpas* of Bhārhūt, Sāñcī and Bodh Gayā, the tree represents the Reawakening, the wheel the First Sermon at Benares, and the *stūpa* the death of the Blessed One or *Parinirvāṇa*, which occurred at Kuśināgarā.[2] However, the miracle of the birth has yet to find a corresponding symbol that is unanimously accepted by scholars. James Ferguson and Alexander Cunningham, among the first to take an interest in ancient Buddhist art, failed to identify a symbol corresponding to the first moment of the Buddha's life. Towards the mid 1930s, in his essay *On the Iconography of the Buddha's Nativity*, Alfred Foucher identified the lotus as the symbol of the Nativity, also linking to this miracle the figurative theme of the woman aspersed by two elephants, known as *abhiṣeka*. The last iconography had formerly been interpreted by Cunningham and Ferguson as a depiction of the Hindu goddess Śrī-Lakṣmī, included in an aspersion scene.[3] Ananda K. Coomaraswamy, in his *Elements of Buddhist Iconography*, re-proposed the latter thesis and thus identified the female figure as Lakṣmī and the lotus as the goddess' emblem.[4]

[1] Linrothe 1993, pp. 241-56; Tanaka 1998, pp. 62-76.

[2] Foucher and Marshall 1940; Coomaraswamy 1935a, pp. 40-7; Coomaraswamy 1956; Bénisti 1952, pp. 30-5; Bénisti 1981; Snodgrass 1985, pp. 12-66, 163-377.

[3] Foucher 1934, pp. 1-27; cf. Ferguson 1873, pp. 100-20; Ferguson 1876, p. 116; Cunningham 1879, pp. 117, 22, pl. XXIII.

[4] Coomaraswamy 1935.

The figurative theme of the lotus, hitherto interpreted as a decorative and auspicious element, thus becomes a motif with a specific iconographic significance.[5] The two texts, published in the same period, led to the well-known debate between the two authors. One significant consequence was that research on the problem of the symbolic depiction of the Nativity, which was powerfully influenced by the ideas of great scholars such as Foucher and Coomaraswamy, was stalled and no further interpretations were proposed. In more recent studies, the hesitation between these two theses, both accepted as possible, is a symptom of the status of the question which thus remains without any definitive answer.[6] The primary objective of the present research is thus to endeavour to ascertain whether the miracle of the birth can reasonably be represented by the lotus flower and its iconographic variants, and also to verify whether the aspersion of the female figure is related to the birth of the Blessed One or not, and lastly what meaning the lotus flower and the *pūrṇaghaṭa* have in Buddhist semiotic-religious code. The comparative analysis of Foucher's and Coomaraswamy's contribution nevertheless represents an essential premise on which to base any further research on the topic of the birth.

1 Alfred Foucher: The Birth Rediscovered

Alfred Foucher observed at Sāñcī, as in the later *stūpas* of Mathurā and Amarāvatī, the insistent depiction of the lotus flower, also associated with the conspicuous presence of the other three symbols, the wheel, the tree, the *stūpa*, which already at the time had been unanimously identified with three of the four Great Miracles. This led the scholar to infer that the lotus was the expression of important meanings and was linked to the Great Miracles.[7] The origin of the lotus in water, in particular in mud, which was in contrast with the purity of the flower, became the symbol of a miraculous, immaculate birth in India. Taking this into consideration, Foucher, therefore interprets the lotus flower, on its own, with the vase, or accompanied by other iconographic elements, such as the elephant, as the representation of the birth of the Blessed One, *Jāti*, the missing miracle.[8] Confirmation of this seems to emerge from the Buddhist texts extolling the absolute purity of the birth of the Buddha, of which the flow-

[5] Cunningham 1879, pp. 47, 116.

[6] Srivastava 1983, pp. 120-1; Sudhi 1993, p. 39; Malla 2000, pp. 63-72.

[7] Foucher 1934, pl. IV.

[8] Foucher 1913; Foucher 1934, p. 10. On the symbolic complex of the vase, see Gairola 1953, pp. 210-3.

er is the perfect symbolic image.[9] Foucher postulates that the woman on the lotus depicted in the relief denoted as *abhiṣeka* is not Lakṣmī, but is actually Māyādevī, the Blessed One's mother, and that the scene is therefore a representation of the miracle of the birth.[10] The two elephants bathing the woman with a liquid from their trunks, are thought to signify the bathing of the new-born, the invisible presence of whom is indicated by the parasol, the latter being cited in the episodes relating to the birth narrated in the Buddhist texts. The dual meaning of serpent and elephant expressed by the term *nāga* and, I add, the water, the element to which they belong as well as the treasure both these beings guard and dispense, allows the elephants to perform the bathing in the place of the serpents mentioned in the Buddhist texts, without creating confusion in the worshippers' minds. The purely formal contradiction does not exist at the symbolic level.[11]

2 *Ananda Coomaraswamy: The Lotus in Vedic Literature*

For his part, A.K. Coomaraswamy analyses the aniconic Buddhist symbols, interpreting them in the light of the ancient Vedic and Brāhmaṇic texts. The cosmic lotus, blossoming from the dark chthonian waters, illuminated and fertilized by the light of the sun, is closely linked to the primordial amniotic waters, the source of life, the womb from which all forms of existence spring.[12] On the basis of this legend, the researcher thus postulates that the values of the lotus, the waters and the earth from which the waters themselves emerge, are embodied in the figure of the universal mother, of whom all the female Vedic divinities personify individual aspects. The aniconic Buddhist image of the lotus, either simple or emerging from a water-filled vase, is the visualization of the *Magna Mater* archetype. Coomaraswamy (1971, Part II, p. 61) goes as far as to state: 'It may be that the vase alone should be regarded as an aniconic symbol of an equivalent to the goddess herself.'[13] Also the *abhiṣeka* scene depicts Lakṣmī, Viṣṇu's bride, as

9 Jones 1949, Vol. II, p. 5; Foucaux 1884, pp. 44, 49, 71.

10 Foucher 1934, p. 3; Foucher and Marshall 1940, Vol. I, pp. 97, 99 -171, 176-7, 183-6, 197.

11 For the aspersion see Walshe 1987, p. 204 (Chap. 14, § 128); Homer 1959, p. 168 (Chap. 123); Foucaux 1884, p. 78 (Chap. VII); Foucher 1934, pp. 3-5; cf. Vogel 1926, pp. 95-97; Banerji 1980, pp. 106-13; Zimmer 1946, pp. 59-60, 63, 66, 105-6; Cummings 1982, pp. 95-103.

12 Coomaraswamy 1935, pp. 19-21; Coomaraswamy 1971, Part I, pp. 56-64. Cf. Barua 1934, pp. 32, 47; Zimmer 1946, pp. 34, 46-7, 59-60, 90-102; Rau 1954, pp. 505-13; Gupta 1971; Tucci 1971, pp. 533-67; Scialpi 1976, pp. 120-9; Srivastava 1979.

13 Cf. Al-George and Rosu 1957, pp. 243-54; Scialpi 1976, pp. 145-50, 155-60.

the hypostasis of the universal mother aspersed by the fertilizing rain falling from heaven, a maternal image that ontologically assimilates all the female divinities, including Māyā.[14]

The researcher extends his survey and completes the significance of the flower with elements that will prove useful to our analysis.

Even though Coomaraswamy attributes a female nature to the lotus depicted in ancient Buddhist art, he also points out that in the *Vedas* the flower is also a solar symbol, the son of the sun and of its space-creating light. The flower is the celestial sphere, i.e., the cosmos, its petals are the four cardinal points, i.e., space, every world illuminated and thus created by the sun.[15] These peculiarities render it akin to other important universal symbols, such as the cosmic tree, the pillar of the world, the axle of the sun's chariot and the wheel, with which it shares the function of world support, the creation of space, the image of all the states of being. These elements all share a fire-like energy and display the same solar and masculine nature. Owing to these equivalent characteristics, the lotus can replace the tree as a plant that, at the beginning of the life cycle, sinks its roots into the centre of the cosmos represented by the navel of the supreme being lying over the primordial waters.[16]

In the *Brāhmaṇas* the lotus, in the *Rājāsūya* ceremony, also represents 'the sensible operation, virility, temporal power, *indriyam, vīryam, kṣatram*'.[17] The flower also takes on a generative male valence. The lotus thus reveals its dual igneous and aquatic nature just as the multiple nature of its symbolic valences.[18]

Coomaraswamy points out that the Vedic divinities, like the Buddha, are equated to the above-mentioned symbols representing them. This is not a metaphoric parallelism or allegory, but rather an identity. The presence of the feet at the base of the

[14] Coomaraswamy 1929; Coomaraswamy 1935, pp. 19-24, 59, 71, n. 41; cf. 'Mais ce pourrait être un abhiṣeka de la mère du Bouddha, si on assimile Māyādevī à la Magna Mater ou à la Terre-Mère, et le Bouddha à Agni.' Coomaraswamy 1935a, pp. 46-7; 'puisque Māyādevī ne peut être distinguée de Śrī-Lakṣmī, la Déesse Universelle' (Coomaraswamy 1956, p. 83). Cf. Foucher 1934, p. 23; Banerjea 1956, pp. 135-7, 167-8, 374-5; Bhattacharya 1958, pp. 217-20; Bosch 1960, pp. 81-2, 110, 112-24; Mallman 1963, pp. 183-6; Agrawala 1965; Scialpi, 1976, p. 120; Malla 2000, pp. 63-72.

[15] Coomaraswamy 1935, pp. 17-9; Auboyer 1949, p. 102; Rosu 1961, pp. 167, 178; Snodgrass 1985, p. 80.

[16] Coomaraswamy 1935, p. 8; Coomaraswamy 1971, Part II, pp. 2-3, 19-37; Viennot 1954; Randhawa 1958; Bosch 1960, pp. 56, 60-2; Sengupta 1965; Sinha 1979; Malla 2000, pp. 7-8, 25-6.

[17] Coomaraswamy 1935, pp. 21, 66 n. 15.

[18] Coomaraswamy 1956, p. 82; Bénisti 1952, pp. 5-6, 7.

artistic representations of the tree or the fire pillar at Sāñcī and Amarāvatī, indicates that these images are the equivalent of the actual body of the Buddha. [19]

While there is no doubt that Coomaraswamy's conception seems somewhat forced as it tends to attribute Brahmanic origins or meanings to the Buddhist symbols, it is nevertheless clear that the cosmological emblems themselves used in the Vedas to describe the *Brahman*, are also used later to represent the metaphysical image of the Buddha.

3 Buddhist Sources

In order to assess the above theses, it would appear to be necessary to make a further examination of the Buddhist texts, and to try and verify in greater depth whether, in the so-called aniconic art, depictions exist that could be interpreted as symbols of the birth of the Buddha. Considerable significant evidence exists to support this. One first group of passages refers to Queen Māyā and the son she bears in her womb.

Among these the *Mahāvastu* affirms:

> [...] the best of men is the jewel, his mother is the casket.
> Just as though a gem of beryl in a crystal casket were placed in her curving lap, so does his mother see the Bodhisattva like a body of pure gold illumining her womb.[20]

The *Nidānakathā* goes on to state:

> [...] a womb in which a future Buddha has dwelt, like a sacred relic shrine, can never be occupied by another.[21]
> The future Buddha left his mother's womb [...], unsoiled by any impurities from contact with his mother's womb, pure and fair, and shining like a gem placed on fine muslin of Benares.[22]

And further the *Lalitavistara*:

> Là, où est le fortuné (Bôdhisattva, comme) est placé dans un vase convenable le plus précieux joyau, (toi qui es) le plus précieux des joyaux, ô intelligence sans tache, verse sur le Djamboudhvadja la pluie (de l'amrita)![23]

[19] Coomaraswamy 1935, pp. 7-17, 32-3, 69, n. 33; Verardi 1988, p. 1539.
[20] Jones 1949, Vol. 2, p. 15.
[21] Rhys Davis 1888, p. 65.
[22] Rhys Davis 1888, pp. 66-7; Walshe 1987, p. 204 (Chap. 14, § 121); Homer 1959, p. 168, (Chap. 123).
[23] Foucaux 1884, p. 14 (Chap. 2 v. 20)

De même que Mâyâ est un vase convenable, de même aussi l'être vénérable brille souverainement. On pourra voir ainsi deux êtres doués de qualités supérieures: le fils et sa mère Mâyâ.[24]
Douée de qualités, elle est tout à fait digne d'être la mère du plus grand de tous les hommes. Comme une pierre précieuse est placée dans un beau vase, c'est la reine qui est ce vase pour le dieu des dieux![25]

The text describes to us the child as a jewel, the most precious stone, and, as such, he must be placed in a suitable container, a casket, a coffer, a vase, or in precious coloured Benares muslin. For this purpose the womb of a queen of great virtue and beauty is chosen, who is worthy of being the mother of the greatest of all men. Māyā thus appears as the suitable vase for containing him who is above all the gods. It therefore does not seem unjustified to postulate the vase as the container *par excellence*, the womb of Māyā, Queen Māyā herself. The child is instead likened to an emerald. The precious stone inside the vase is the equivalent of the child inside his mother's womb. The embryo is green like an emerald, like a plant, like water: green is indeed a colour associated with generation, the potentiality of life. However we know that in the reliefs the vase contains lotus flowers.

It is thus advisable to go back and query the sources, and see what they tell us in connection with this flower or, more in general, about other plants and their relationship with the Buddha.

The *Mahāvastu* says:

She, the consort of the king is about to give birth to that peerless offspring who is bright like the flower of the blossoming lotus. [...]
His body is untouched by the impurities of the womb, even like the exquisite lotus that is born in the mud of pools.[26]
His body is proportioned like the banyan tree.[27]
Thou, moreover, o Lotus-eyed One, will become the bourne of men and devas. Thus, at the time and on the occasion of the departure of him whose eyes were bright like the hundred petalled lotus [...].[28]
Again, immediately after the Bodhisattva was born there appeared amid the four million continents a twig of the holy fig tree, the very finest of earth's produce.[29]
His body is untouched by the impurities of the womb, even like the

[24] Foucaux 1884, p. 29 (Chap. 3 v. 18).
[25] Foucaux 1884, p. 49 (Chap. 5, v. 50).
[26] Jones 1949, Vol. 1, p. 176 (§ 221); Vol. 2, p. 21 (§§ 23-24).
[27] Jones 1949, Vol. 1, p. 181(§ 225); Vol. 2, p. 26 (§ 29).
[28] Jones 1949, Vol. 2, p. 4 (§ 4).
[29] Jones 1949, Vol. 2, p. 20 (§23)

exquisite lotus that is born in the mud of pools. Beautiful as the newly risen sun he excels the immortals in Brahamā's heaven.[30]

In this regard, the *Lalitavistara*, states:

Bhâgavat était détaché de tout, comme le lotus sur lequel glisse l'eau.[31]
Lotus des grands hommes.[32]
Et la nuit même où le Bôdhisattva entra dans le sein de sa mère, cette même nuit, s'élevant de la masse des eaux inférieures, en ouvrant le grande terre [...], un lotus s'éleva jusqu'au monde de Brahmâ.[33]
Le Bôdhisattva, aussitôt sa naissance, descendit à terre. Et aussitôt que le Bôdhisattva Mahâsattva y fut descendu, un grand lotus perçant la terre, apparut.
Et lui, se tenant sur le grand lotus, regarda les dix points de l'espace, avec le coup d'oeil du lion, avec le coup d'oeil du grand homme.[34]
Un lotus d'une beauté merveilleuse naquit partout où, sur ses deux pieds embellis de la marque d'une roue, se tint le guide par excellence.[35]
Puisque le monde est sans trouble, puisque le grand lotus est apparu, sans nul doute, rempli d'une grande splendeur, il sera la guide du monde.[36]

Māyā's vase-womb thus encapsulates an exceptional being, far beyond all normal human experience. The *Bodhisattva* is described in terms of splendour, purity, perfection in his proportions and of peerless beauty, and he is constantly compared with two well-defined elements, the lotus flower and, to a lesser degree, with a tree.

The relationship with the lotus is further strengthened by the extremely important, even miraculous, events that accompany

[30] Jones 1949, Vol. 2, p. 218 (§ 24). This is the same concept as is evidenced in the *Majjhimanikāya* 123 (Homer 1959, p. 68) and the *Nidānakathā* (Rhys Davis 1888, pp. 66-7) with reference to Māyā and her son, who are likened to an emerald and muslin, which are not soiled or contaminated as they are both pure.

[31] Foucaux 1884, p. 4 (Chap I), cf. *Saṃyuttanikāya* 3.140. Already in the *Vedas* the lotus is used as a metaphor to represent the detachment of the *Puruṣa* from the reality of *saṃsāra*. In the *Upaniṣads*, its leaves or petals are not moistened by water drops, just as the wise man who lives in the world does not belong to the world, *Chādogyopaniṣad* 4.14.3. The *Ātman* itself is likened to a drop on a lotus leaf which does not become attached to it, *Maitryupaniṣad* 3.2.

[32] Foucaux 1884, p. 10 (Chap. 2).

[33] Foucaux 1884, p. 63 (Chap. 6).

[34] Foucaux 1884, p. 78 (Chap. 7).

[35] Foucaux 1884, p. 85 (Chap. 7, v. 27).

[36] Foucaux 1884, p. 88 (Chap. 7, v. 49).

the birth. In the very moment in which the *Bodhisattva* enters his mother's womb, the cosmic lotus emerges from the obscure depths of the lower waters. Splitting the earth, it rises up to heaven where the gods reside, as far as the world of Brahmā. At the same time as the Blessed One, a branch of the sacred *Ficus Religiosa* is born, a tree which extends throughout all the worlds. The above texts thus confirm the close links between the Buddha and the lotus or the tree.

Let us read on in the *Lalitavistara*, which presents both the vase and the lotus to us.

> Et la nuit même ou le Bôdhisattva entra dans le sein de sa mère, cette même nuit, s'élevant de la masse des eaux inférieures, en ouvrant la grande terre.., un lotus s'éleva jusqu'au monde de Brahmâ. Et personne ne vit ce lotus, excepté le meilleur des hommes leur guide, ainsi que le grand Brahmâ qui commande à un million d'êtres. Et tout ce qu'il y a ici-bas, dans la substance élémentaire des trois mille grands milliers de mondes de force, d'essence ou de quintessence, tout cela fut rassemblé dans le grand lotus en goutte de miel. Le grand Brahmâ, l'ayant mise dans un beau vase de lapis-lazuli la présenta au Bôdhisattva. Le Bôdhisattva l'ayant prise, la but par bonté pour le grand Brahmâ. Il n'y a pas un être dans la multitude des êtres, par lequel cette goutte d'élixir étant bue, elle puisse être aisément digérée, à l'exception d'un Bôdhisattva qui est à sa dernière existence et qui a rempli toutes les (conditions des) terres d'un Bôdhisattva.[37] Dans les demeures des régions des trois mille grands milliers des mondes après les avoir traversées s'est élevé le lotus de Gouṇâkâra, contenant la goutte d'élixir. Ce (lotus) qui a l'éclat de la pureté s'étant, le septième jour, élevé au monde de Brahmâ, Brahmâ, après l'avoir pris, en retira la goutte d'élixir, pour la porter au Bôdhisattva.[38]

The *Nidānakathā* describes the instant of conception:

> Holding in his silvery trunk a white lotus flower, and uttering a far-reaching cry, he entered the golden mansion, and thrice doing obeisance to his mother's couch, he gently struck her right side, and seemed to enter her womb.[39]

These passages from the *Lalitavistara* refer to several events immediately preceding or simultaneous with the *Bodhisattva*'s descent upon the Earth.

They tell us that no one sees the cosmic lotus emerging from the depths at the time of the conception except the *Bodhisattva*

37 Foucaux 1884, p. 63 (Chap. 6)

38 Foucaux 1884, p. 70 (Chap. 6, vv. 27-8)

39 Rhys Davis 1888, p. 63.

and Brahmā. The god fills the great lotus with a drop of honey, *madhu,* in which the essence of the worlds is concentrated. He uses honey since in the Vedas this food, like milk and butter, is deemed to be a founding principle, a source of life and immortality, as is likened to the fertilizing seed of the ocean, a symbol of abundance and the benevolence of the gods. Brahmā takes the lotus and places it inside a lapis lazuli vase, which he then hands to the *Bodhisattva* so that he might drink the drop of elixir. Only a *Bodhisattva* that has attained his ultimate existence can drink and digest such an elixir; by drinking it he will never again suffer the constraint of being incarnate and reborn. The *saṃsāra* chain is broken. This beverage is none other than *amṛta.* Gonda (1965, pp. 47-70) emphasizes: '[…] it's the essence of all vegetable saps and believed to confer mental and physical power on those who drink it, to cure their diseases, to enhance their generative force and, last but not the least, to lengthen their life time. It's the elixir of life, indispensable for men and gods.'[40]

Indeed with reference to the Blessed One, the *Lalitavistara* states:

> C'est le roi des médecins, dispensateur du remède de l'amrita.[41]

The Buddha, from Māyā's womb, heals the illnesses of those who touch the queen:

> Revenus à la santé, sans être changés, ils s'en vont, chacun à sa demeure, parce que, devenu le remède, le roi des médecins est entré dans le sein d'une mere.[42]

Concerning the Buddha himself, after his birth, it is said that:

> Après avoir fait sept pas, celui qui a la voix de Brahmâ fit entendre la meilleure des proclamations: Je serai le meilleur de tous les médecins, le destructeur de la maladie et de la mort.[43]

The Blessed One is the king of medicine, he who brings and dispenses the *amṛta,* the remedy against death. The *amṛta* contained in the lotus is none other than the teaching of the Buddha, his word, his path, his truth, which can illuminate all worlds; in the final analysis, the Buddha himself. On the other hand, the close link between honey and the word, light and truth, is confirmed by the invocations of the *Atharvaveda*:

[40] Cf. Bosch 1960, pp. 62-4.
[41] Foucaux 1884, p. 5 (Chap. 6, v. 5).
[42] Foucaux 1884, p. 71 (Chap. 6, v. 40).
[43] Foucaux 1884, p. 85 (Chap. 7, v. 27)

> O ye Açvins, Lords of beauty! Anoint me with the honey of bees, that I may speak brilliant words among the people. (VI,69,2)[44]

> Let those creatures, without exception together yield fruit to us: the honey of speech, o earth, do thou assign unto me. (XII,1,16)[45]

> What I speak, rich in honey, I speak it. (XII,1,58)[46]

The Buddhist sources are thus in agreement in representing Māyā as a vase worthy of containing the *Bodhisattva* incarnate in her. It should be noted in this connection that the identification of Māyā as a vase worthy of containing the future Buddha, seems to have been underestimated by Foucher or even to have escaped his attention. He actually attributes the meaning of *pūrṇaghaṭa* to the vase, the symbol of well wishing and abundance, without appreciating its symbolic equivalence with Māyā's womb, as clearly stated in particular by the *Lalitavistara.* Indeed, with reference to the good fortune enjoyed by the vase and lotus, he asserts: 'The reasons for the manifest success of this new development are not far to seek; not only by its elegant disposition did it gratify the strong decorative sense of the old image-carvers, but it also possessed in their eyes the advantage of combining with the symbol of the lotus another emblem of great auspiciousness, since, for an Indian, the sight of a brimming water-vessel (*pūrṇaghaṭa)* is a most propitious omen'.[47]

It is essentially in the lotus that he sees the representation of the Nativity, and not without good reason, although this perhaps leads him not to delve deeper into another significant element as is represented by the vase. Compared with Foucher, Coomaraswamy, rightly lays greater stress on the vase-womb correspondence, although he too does not seem to have taken into consideration those Buddhist texts in which Māyā is likened to the perfect vase for containing the Buddha. For the Indian scholar, the *pūrṇaghaṭa* remains a prosperity-wishing icon; it is a symbol of universal and metaphysical generation, not specifically linked to the 'historical' birth of Siddhārta. Indeed, in the light of the Vedic myth of the cosmic lotus emerging from the waters, he does not seem to separate the lotus from the vase, interpreting both as a single image of that primordial maternal womb, and therefore both as symbols of female fertility as embodied in the universal mother. It is essentially this view that leads this scholar

44 Whitney 1962, p. 333.
45 Whitney 1962, p. 664.
46 Whitney 1962, p. 671.
47 Foucher 1934, p. 11.

to overlook the solar nature of the lotus, and therefore not to associate the flower with the Buddha, for whom indeed he had considered other Vedic symbols, depicted in the ancient Buddhist *stūpas*. However, although fundamental, the Vedic basis proved to represent only a starting point for a Buddhist reinterpretation of those symbols.[48] In accordance with the Vedic tradition, both Foucher and Coomaraswamy link the lotus to the meaning of birth, of the Buddha, in the case of the first, and of the whole creation, for the second. However, neither associates the lotus with the physical being of the Buddha. This linkage would actually allow the flower to be upgraded from a generic symbol of generation, to an emblem of the Great Miracle of the Nativity of the Blessed One, able to indicate simultaneously, not only the event of the birth, but the true presence of the Buddha.

In order to evaluate these hypotheses it is necessary again to focus attention on the lotus, following the texts. The latter do not explicitly state that the lotus is the Buddha, as in the case of equating Māyā to the vase, although everyone is constantly extolling the virtues of this flower, which is repeatedly indicated as the perfect symbol of all the physical, spiritual, ontological and cosmogonic characteristics of the Blessed One.[49] The Great Miracle of Śrāvastī is perhaps the event that best confirms the equating of the lotus with the Buddha.[50]

In order to defeat the proponents of the adverse doctrines, the Buddha performs several miracles, including that of emanating from his own body an infinite number of lotus flowers, on each of which is seated a Buddha. It seems that his very nature allows him to multiply himself by blossoming into innumerable flowers. In this episode and in the representations thereof, the complementary nature of the *Tathāgata* as cosmic man and lotus of the world, becomes apparent. Moreover, the texts tell us that during the night in which the Blessed One entered his mother's bosom, there was no agitation in the world as the great lotus had appeared, the world's guide, the men's lotus.[51] The lotus is born out of dark muddy waters, a phenomenon that is viewed as prodigious and

[48] 'Cependant, si le bouddhisme se trouve hériter un fonds indivis de croyance et de traditions manifestées des la fin du *Veda* et des *Brâhmaṇa*, nous devons signaler dans le Bouddhisme des premiers siècles de notre ère une certaine transformation, en ce qui concerne le lotus, dans le sens du miraculeux, du sublime, comme si le nouveau dogme avait cru nécessaire d'ajouter du merveilleux à la valeur cosmique du symbole'" Benisti 1952, pp. 7-8.

[49] The texts instead indicate more clearly the identity between the Buddha and the *amṛta* contained in the lotus donated by Brahmā. Foucaux 1884, p. 5 (Chap. 6); 71 (6, v. 40); 85 (7, v. 27); Bosch 1960, pp. 220-30.

[50] Ferguson 1873, pp. 147-84; Brown 1984, pp. 73-95; Rao 1994, pp. 12, 26.

[51] Foucaux 1884, p. 10 (Chap. 2); p. 88 (Chap. 7, v. 49).

that is therefore likened to the birth of the Buddha into the world. Brahmā's gift of the precious vase, which may be compared to the *pūrṇaghaṭa,* is an action that recapitulates the event, the modality of and the reasons for the birth of the *Tathāgata.*[52] The flower that contains the *amṛta* may be likened to the Buddha who is bringing the elixir with him, and the vase with queen Māyā, from whose womb the *Bodhisattva* will be born into the world of men.[53]

It thus does not seem inappropriate to interpret the *pūrṇaghaṭa* as a symbol of the event of the Buddha's birth.

In the Vedic myth, the cosmic lotus is not only the generative organ of the waters, but it is also possible to interpret it as a son, the fruit of the union of the female element, the waters, which is fertilized by the male element, the sun. The lotus 'is the first product of the creative principle, gold in token of its incorruptible nature.'[54]

The *pūrṇaghaṭa* may therefore justifiably be considered as a representation of the mother with her son, as the generation of every existence.[55]

The lotus is the son of the sun; indeed it is at once the sun and a virile act. It is the power of generation, endowed with fiery, solar and masculine energy. The flower therefore may represent the son, namely, the one which is generated, but at the same time performs also the function of the generating male principle.[56] In Indian philosophy, *Ātman* at the beginning of the creation gives life to the worlds, which are none other than parts of *Ātman* himself; he who generates is identical to him who is generated. As Zimmer (1946,109) writes: 'Son, in the language of myths and symbols, means "double", "alter ego", "living copy of the father", "the father essence in another individualization".' The act of generation increases both the father and the son through the mother. The *Ṛgveda* (VII, 101, 3) states that:

[52] Foucaux 1884, p. 63 (Chap. 6).

[53] The equating of the vase to the maternal womb is evidenced also by a seal from Harappā depicting a goddess from whose genitals springs a plant. Marshall 1931, pl. XII, p. 52.

[54] Zimmer 1946, p. 90.

[55] 'The womb of the individual and the universal mother giving birth to the child is symbolised as the lotus growing in water" Sudhi 1993, p. 38; "Le lotus est un symbole de la naissance du Buddha comme il est le symbole de toutes les naissances miraculeuses ou divines.' Bénisti 1952, p. 9.

[56] The identity of the generator and the generated, as already pointed out by Maria Spagnoli, symbolized by the tree depicted in a Borobuḍur relief showing the Buddha's Nativity, is also expressed by the lotus flower depicted in the reliefs of the aniconic schools inasmuch as it is the equivalent of the tree. Spagnoli 1976, pp. 179, 187, n. 25. I wish to thank Maria Spagnoli for her invaluable advice on the present article.

> The Father's juices grasped the Mother, thereby are increased both Father and Son.[57]

The Buddha is none other than his own son; he is self-generated, self-incarnate through Māyā. The principle that enters Māyā is exactly the same as what leaves her. The lotus of the *pūrṇaghaṭa* represents this dual identity. If Māyā is the vase, as stated in the texts, the lotus may be equated with the generating and the nascent Buddha. The aniconic image of the elephant bearing a lotus in its trunk, which represents the conception, seems to confirm the hypothetical identity of the Buddha as a lotus. The *Tathāgata* descends in the form of a white elephant, a regal and solar animal, a cosmic and transcendent symbol of the universal intellect, while the lotus is his immanent image.[58]

The *pūrṇaghaṭa* thus appears as an archetypal image of the union between male and female.

This thus seems to support Alfred Foucher's hypothesis that, in the earliest *stūpas*, the lotus is to be interpreted as the symbol of the Buddha's birth, as well as of universal fecundity. The flower furthermore is constantly present in the Vedic myths as a medium for divine births. [59]

I also consider that Foucher's proposed interpretation, identifying the female figure in the representation of the *abhiṣeka* as Māyā and the entire scene as a Nativity, is the most plausible. Even though a specific image representing the conception exists, in which Māyā is lying down and the elephant penetrates her side, the capacity for symbolic expression of the ancient Buddhist schools of art, creates an iconography that can condense into the single scene of the *abhiṣeka*, not only a specific instant but the entire birth cycle.[60]

[57] Coomaraswamy 1935, p. 72, n. 45.

[58] Rhys Davis 1888, p. 63. 'In the *Vedas*, the elephant is a symbol of regal splendor, ... and the Buddha is more than once still called an elephant' Zimmer 1946, p. 103, n. 1. 'In the great epic, the *Mahābhārata*, the six-tusked elephant symbolizes the sun, whose course in to the sky is run during a year with six seasons' Cummings 1982, p. 112. For the conception, see Walshe 1987, pp. 203-4 (Chap. 14, §§ 117-21); Homer 1959, pp. 163-9 (Chap. 123); Rhys Davis 1888, pp. 62-5; Jones 1949, Vol. 2, pp. 8-14 (§ 9); Foucaux 1884, pp. 49-65 (Chap. VI); Cowell 1894, pp. 4-5 (Chap. I, §§ 20-22); Coomaraswamy 1956, pl. XXIV, Fig. 61.

[59] Bénisti 1952, p. 5; Rao 1994, pp. 79, 83-5; Malla 2000, p. 43.

[60] 'At Bhārhūt, the method of continuous narration that presents different moments in the same story in a single relief, is very widespread. The criterion of association is the meaning of the various episodes rather than their temporal succession. This method of narration necessarily slow down the viewer's reading of the scene and forces him to seek out that series of relationship between the various figurative elements, used by the artist to link together different moments in an organic and coherent vision' Spagnoli 1970, pp. 330-1.

The vase, the lotus, the woman and the elephants narrate the conception, the birth, the bathing. Here, the elephants perform a two-fold task: they remind us of the moment of purification, fertilization and conception of Māyā. At the same time they suggest the lustral bathing of the child, and are indicative of their close and ancient links with serpents, which personify the waters. Through the aspersion performed by the *nāgas*, the Buddha is purified and invested with the dominion over all possibilities of being, and thus of the legitimate sovereignty over the created world.[61] The elephants also suggest the themes of prosperity and abundance, of well-being and happiness. These representations of the *abhiṣeka* will then form the basis of the iconography of Laṣkmī in the Gupta period.[62]

The various interpretations of the iconological significance of the lotus expressed by Foucher and Coomaraswamy, although apparently mutually exclusive, stem from the choice each makes among the many ontological valences of the flower. Like the tree, the lotus is born out of the chthonian waters, the essence of which is ubiquitous. However, the vegetal element in India combines two factors, *agni* and *soma*, fire and water, *prajāpati* and *nārāyana*, a duo of opposite forces present in the *hiraṇya garbha*, the primordial bud from which divine plants originate.[63] This bud, despite its duality, is unique in its essence and comprises the primitive base from which all creation originates. The golden bud, the cosmic plants and the Buddha himself, who is equated to them, thus display this dual ontological nature, and subsume all the polarities of the universe: male and female, sun and moon, heat and cold. All the aniconic symbols of the Reawakened One, which is more clearly displayed by the lotus and the tree, are thus characterized by a sexual ambivalence.[64] Marie Thérèse De Mallmann remarks on the lunar and female nature specific to the blue lotus and the male nature of the pink lotus.[65] The Buddha

[61] Zimmer 1946, p. 67; Scialpi 1976, pp. 130-41; Spagnoli 2001, pp. 189-204.

[62] Sudhi 1993, p. 39.

[63] *Atharvaveda*, 7.7-8; 4.4; Bosch 1960, pp. 60-1; Coomaraswamy 1971, Part I, pp. 19-22; Scialpi 1976, pp. 120-2; Verardi 1988, pp. 1533-48.

[64] Coomaraswamy 1971, Part I, pp. 28-36; Spagnoli 1976, pp. 189-91. This bivalence is also found in the waters themselves; like the woman, they represent the element to be fertilized but at the same time are the fertilizing male semen, as stated in the *Aitareya Upaniṣad* 1.2.3 *'The waters became semen, and entered the virile member.'* Cf. Scialpi 1976, pp. 152-3.

[65] 'Le lotus bleu est tant aussi fréquemment associé à la lune que le lotus rose au soleil, il est généralement dévolu aux dieux qui portent cet astre dans leur coiffure. Associé au soleil, le lotus rose est l'attribut de toutes les divinités a caractère intégralement ou partiellement solaire' Mallmann 1963, pp. 262-4; cf. Mallmann 1948, pp. 267, 274.

is represented in Gandhāran art with flames emerging from the shoulders and water flowing from the feet, an iconography that expresses the coexistence in the Blessed One of the opposites. This is the first miracle performed by Śākyamuni at Śrāvastī.[66] Giovanni Verardi (1988, p. 1541) writes that: 'This is indeed a transfiguration and more exactly the assumption by the Buddha of his archetypal characteristics.'[67] The lotus is thus simultaneously the generating male principle and the female womb, both fundamental, undeniable truths, by virtue of the coexistence in all things of *agni* and *soma.* Despite this sexual bivalence, one of these two characters may predominate, as in the case of the lotus which, in the ancient artistic schools of art is associated with the Buddha whose essence and values it expresses.

4 Conclusions

The search for an aniconic emblem that, with a sufficient degree of certainty, may be considered to correspond to the miracle of the Nativity, has raised the need to reappraise the longstanding and well-known discussion of this topic between A. Foucher and A.K. Coomaraswamy. In the light of the evidence produced by the two scholars and thanks to the reinterpretation of the various versions of the Buddha's birth described in the texts, it seems possible to suggest an answer to this problem. This answer is in agreement with Foucher's hypothesis that the lotus flower and the *pūrṇaghaṭa* motif, in keeping with traditional Indian thought, represent the miracle of a supernatural and immaculate birth. However, it has been documented that the equating of the vase with Māyā's womb, although stated in the texts, does not seem to have been acknowledged by the French scholar. The *pūrṇaghaṭa* is a motif that is inextricably bound up with the context of the birth of the Blessed One, a hypothesis confirmed in the passage of the *Lalitavistara,* in which the vase with the flower containing the *amṛta* is mentioned, donated by the god Brahmā to the Buddha. Though this text is much later than the aniconic reliefs, it may furnish an indication as far as the scene is concerned. The iconographic theme of the vase and the lotus is thus raised to the status of appropriate emblem of the Miracle of the Buddha's Nativity. By means of Coomaraswamy's important analysis of the meaning of the lotus in Vedic thought, it was possible to shed light on the fact that this flower

[66] Brown 1984, p. 81, Fig. 3.

[67] Verardi 1988, p. 1541 'Si tratta effettivamente di una trasfigurazione, e più esattamente dell'assunzione da parte del Buddha dei suoi caratteri archetipici.'

is an element with a fiery male solar character, which places it in close contact with the emblems generally and unquestionably associated with the Buddha, such as the pillar, the wheel and the tree. These symbols, even in their specific context, are closely linked in Vedic literature to the gods, in particular to Agni, just as they are linked to the Perfect One in Buddhism, links that are converted into an identity. The lotus may thus be considered not only the symbol of the birth of the Blessed One, but the actual image of the Buddha himself. The flower emerging from the vase represents not only the son but also the father, the generator, who fertilizes the mother and is born into life from the latter; a powerful cosmogonic symbol linked to the concepts of fertility and generation. Furthermore, Foucher's interpretation of the motif denoted as the *abhiṣeka* of Lakṣmī can be considered an allegory of the birth of the Buddha. The elephants aspersing water on the female figure subsume the episodes of the conception and the aspersion, and underlie the moment of the birth, thanks to the parasol indicating the presence of the invisible new-born beside the woman who is none other than Māyā. The scene is thus able to subsume the entire cycle of the birth into a single framework. The woman and the elephants are indeed the only figures appearing in the scene of the conception expressed by the earliest Buddhist art schools: they therefore seem to bear witness to an iconographic continuity linking the scene of the *abhiṣeka* to the context of the birth of the Blessed One. The lotus, like all cosmological elements, is an emblem characterized by gender bivalence. It has both a female and a male nature at the same time. The widespread association of the lotus with a female divinity thus seems to be acceptable in the light of these characteristics, although it is not the most relevant as far as the flower represented in the aniconic *stūpas* is concerned. It may be assumed that, in those reliefs, the lotus, the *pūrṇaghaṭa* and the *abhiṣeka* are linked to the figure of the Blessed One. This thus seems to confirm the fact that these figurative motifs identify the Nativity and complete the series of representations of the Four Great Miracles during the aniconic phase of Buddhist art.

References

Al-George Sergiu and Arion Rosu (1957). "Pūrṇaghaṭa et le symbolisme du vase dans l'Inde." In: *Arts Asiatiques,* IV, 4, pp. 243-54.

Auboyer, Jeannine (1949). *Le trône et son symbolisme dans l'Inde ancienne.* Paris: Presses Universitaires de France.

Agrawala, Prithvi Kumar (1965). *Pūrṇa Kalaśa or The Vase of*

Plenty (Indian Civilization Series, vol. 3). Prithvi Prakashan: Varanasi.

Bhattacharya, Kamaleswar (1958). "Abhiṣeka de Lakṣmī." In: *Arts Asiatiques* V, 3, pp. 217-20.

Banerjea, Jitendra Nath (1956). *The Development of Hindu Iconography*. New Delhi: Munshiram Manoharlal 1985 (reprint of revised edition).

Banerji, Sures Chandra (1980). *Flora and Fauna in Sanscrit Literature*. Calcutta: Naya Prakash.

Barua, Beni Madhab (1934). *Bhārhūt, Stone as a Story Teller*. Calcutta and Patna: Indological Book Corporation [1934].

Bosch, Frederik David Kan (1960). *The Golden Germ: an Introduction to Indian Symbolisme*. The Hague: Mouton.

Brown, Robert L. (1984). "The Śrāvastī Miracles, in the Art of India and Dvāravatī." In: *Archives of Asian Art*, XXXVII, pp. 73-95.

Bénisti, Mireille (1952). *Le medaillon lotiforme dans la sculpture indienne de III siècle avant J.C. au VII siècle après J.C.* Paris: Publications du Musée Guimet, pp. 30-5.

Bénisti, Mireille (1981). *Contribution a l'étude du stūpa bouddhique indien: les stūpa mineurs de Bodh-Gayā et de Ratnagiri*. Paris: Publications de L'Ecole Francaise d'Extrême Orient, vol. 125.

Coomaraswamy, Ananda K. (1929). "Śrī-Lakṣmī." In: *Eastern Art, a Quarterly* I, 3, pp. 175-89.

Coomaraswamy, Ananda K. (1935). *Elements of Buddhist Iconography*. Cambridge (Mass.): Harvard University Press.

Coomaraswamy, Ananda K. (1935a). "La sculpture de Bodhgayā." In: *Ars Asiatica* XVII, pp. 40-7.

Coomaraswamy, Ananda K. (1956). *La sculpture de Bhārhūt* (Annales du Musèe Guimet, n.s., 6). Paris: Vanoest.

Coomaraswamy, Ananda K. (1971). *Yākṣas*. New Delhi: Munshiram Manoharlal.

Cowell, Edward Byles, transl. (1894). *Buddhist Mahāyāna Texts*, part I. *Buddha-Karita of Aśvaghoṣha* (Sacred Books of the East, vol. 49). Delhi: Motilal Banarsidass.

Cummings, Mary (1982). *The Lives of Buddha in the Art and Architecture of Asia*. Ann Arbor, MI: University of Michigan.

Cunningham, Alexander (1879). *Stūpa of Bhārhūt: a Buddhist Monument*. Varanasi: Indological Book Corporation.

Ferguson, James (1873). *Tree and Serpent Worship*. London: India Museum, W.H. Allen and Co.

Ferguson, James (1876). *History of Indian and Eastern Architecture*. London: John Murray.

Foucher, Alfred (1913). "Les images indiennes de la Fortune." In: *Mémoires concernant l'Asie orientale (Inde, Asie Centrale, Extrême-Orient)*, I, pp. 123-28.

Foucher, A. (1934). "On the Iconography of the Buddha's Nativity." In: *Memoirs of Archaeological Survey of India* 46, pp. 1-27.
Foucher A. and J. Marshall (1940). *The Monument of Sāñcī*, 3 vols. Delhi: Archeological Survey of India.
Gairola, K. (1953). "Évolution du pùrṇa ghaṭa (vase d'abondance) dans l'Inde et l'Inde Extèrieure." In: *Arts Asiatiques* I, 3, pp. 210-3.
Gonda, Jan (1965). *Change and Continuity in Indian Religion.* The Hague: London – Paris: Mouton.
Gupta, Shakti M. (1971). *Plant Myths and Traditions in India.* Leiden: Brill.
Foucaux, Philippe Edouard (1884). *Le Lalita Vistara* (Annales du Museé Guimet, 6). Paris: Leroux.
Linrothe, Rob (1993). "Inquiries in to Origins of the Buddha Image." In: *East and West* 43, Nos. 1-4, December, pp. 241-56.
Hanneder, Jürgen (2002). "The Blue Lotus. Oriental Research between Philology, Botany and Poetics?". In: *Zeitschrift der Deutschen Morgenlandische Gesellschaft* 152, 2, pp. 295-308.
Horner, Isaline Blew, transl. (1959). *Majjhima Nikāya the Middle Length Sayings.* London: Pali Text Society.
Jones, J.J., transl. (1949). *The Mahāvastu*, 3 vols. London: Luzac.
Lal Malla, Bansi (2000). *Trees in Indian Art And Folklore.* New Delhi: Aryan Books.
Mallmann De, Marie Thérèse (1948). *Introduction a l'étude d'Avalokiteçvara* (Annales du Musée Guimet, 57). Paris: Civilization du Sud.
Mallmann De, M.T. (1963). *Les enseignements iconographique de l'Agni Purāṇa.* Paris: Presses Universitaires de France.
Marshall, John (1931). *Mohenjo Daro and the Hindus Civilization.* London: Asian Educational Services.
Rhys David, Thomas William, transl. (1880). *Buddhist Birth Stories: Jātaka Tales.* Vol. I, *Nidāna Kathā.* London: Pali Text Society.
Randhawa, Mohinder Singh (1958). *The Cult of the Tree and Tree Worship in Buddhist-Hindu Sculpture.* New Delhi: All India Fine Arts & Crafts Society.
Rao, Manjushri (1994). *Sāñcī Sculptures, an Aesthetic and a Cultural Study.* New Delhi: Akay Book Corps.
Rau, Wilhelm (1954). "Lotusblumen." In: *Asiatica, Festschrift Friedrich Weller.* Leipzig: Harrassowitz, pp. 505-13.
Rosu, Arion (1961). "Pūrṇaghaṭa et le symbolisme du lotus dans l'Inde." In: *Arts Asiatiques* VIII, pp. 182-8.
Scialpi, Fabio (1976). "Aspetti della tematica dell'acqua nel *Śatapatha Brāhmaṇa.*" In: *Rivista degli Studi Orientali* V, 1-2, pp. 105-77.

Sengupta, Sankar (1965). *Tree Symbol Worship in India.* Calcutta: Folklore Society.

Sinha, Binod Chandra (1979). *Tree Worship in Ancient India.* New Delhi: Books Today.

Snodgrass, Adrian (1985). *The Symbolism of the Stūpa.* Delhi: Seap Publications (1992 ed.).

Spagnoli, Maria (1970). "Relationship between the Perspective and Compositional Structure of the Bhārhūt Sculptures and Gandhāran Art." In: *East and West* 20, No. 3, pp. 327-47.

Spagnoli, Maria (1976). "A proposito di un rilievo di Borobuḍur." In: *Rivista degli Studi Orientali* V, 1-2, pp. 179-95.

Spagnoli, Maria (1986). "Mara a Bhārhūt. A proposito di un rilievo di incerta interpretazione." In: *Rivista degli Studi Orientali* LX, 1-4, pp. 213-35.

Spagnoli, Maria (2001). "Le nozze del serpente." In: *Rivista degli Studi Orientali* LXXV, 1-4, pp. 189-204.

Srivastava, A.L. (1983). *Life in Sāñcī Sculpture.* New Delhi: Abhinav Publications.

Srivastava, M.C. (1979). *Mother Goddess in Indian Art, Archaeology and Literature.* Delhi: Agam.

Sudhi, Padma (1993). *Gupta Art, a Study from Aesthetic to Canonical Norms.* Delhi: Galaxy.

Tanaka, Kanoto (1998). *Absence of the Buddha Image in Early Buddhist Art: Toward its Significance in Comparative Religion.* New Delhi: D.K. Printworld.

Tucci, Giuseppe (1971). "Earth in India and Tibet." In: *Opera Minora, II, Studi Orientali,* vol. VI. Roma: Bardi.

Verardi, Giovanni (1988). "Tematiche indiane di alcune iconografie gandhāriche. Il Buddha, Agni, i Lakṣaṇa, il miracolo di Śrāvastī e altri problemi." In*: Orientalia Iosephi Tucci Memoriae Dicata,* vol. III. Roma: IsMEO, pp. 1533-46.

Viennot, Odette (1954). *Le culte de l'arbre dans l'Inde ancienne.* Paris: Presses Universitaires de France.

Vogel, Jean Philippe (1972). *Indian Serpent Lore.* Varanasi: Prithivi Prakashan [London 1926].

Walshe, Maurice, transl. (1987). *Dīgha Nikāya, Thus Have I Heard.* London: Wisdom Publications.

Whitney, William Dwight, transl. (1962). *Atharva Veda Saṃhitā,* 2 Vols. Delhi: Motilal Banrasidass.

Zimmer, Heinrich (1946). *Myths and Symbols in Indian Art and Civilization.* New York: Campbell.

Fig. 1. Lotus flower. Bhārhūt. (After Coomaraswamy 1956)

Fig. 2. Pūrṇagaṭa. Sāñcī. (After Foucher 1934)

Fig. 3. Abhiṣeka. Sāñcī. (After Foucher 1940)

Fig. 4. Abhiṣeka. Bhārhūt. (After Foucher 1934)

Fig. 5. Elephant with lotus. Sāñcī. (After Foucher 1940)

Fig. 6. The dream of Māyā. Bhārhūt. (After Coomaraswamy 1956)

Prema Bhat, Paolo Bravi and Ignazio Macchiarella

Untranslatable Denotations: Notes on Music Meaning Through Cultures

1 A Few Starting Points [I. M.]

It is commonly said that music is a preferential tool (or "the" preferential tool) for inter-cultural communication. It is a sort of commonplace that nourishes a rich and diversified amount of activities within the largest cultural contexts. Radio and tv broadcasting, press articles, internet sites, scholastic syllabi, and so on: (the supposed) efficacy of music to cross "cultural borders" is declared as if it were an apodictic fact. This topic is also at the basis of the discourse accompanying the so called "world music", an ubiquitous phenomenon of the present day that essentially 'participates in shaping a kind of consumer-friendly multiculturalism, one that follows the market logic of expansion and consolidation' (Feld 2000, p. 168). Such kinds of "popular beliefs" come from an equivocal concept of music.

In actual fact, it is a very complex question: music sounds can transcend boundaries among world people but some scholarly notions are very useful to understand how music works (and maybe even to facilitate it). Firstly, the nature of what we call music. Due to its ephemerality (Leonardo da Vinci dealt with 'the unfortunate music that dies immediately after its occurrence') music is not a collection of objects. It is the pervasive presence of instruments for the recording/reproduction of sound, with the mass media and musical industry, that makes one think 'of music as a thing – an identifiable art object that can owned by its creator though copyrights and purchased by consumers' (Torino 2008, p. 24). But the essence of music is "a making"; it is a ritualized process of interactions among socio-culturally situated men and women. Based on more or less detailed "shared traces" (written signs like Western scores, mnemonic outlines, the memory of previous listening, etc), music making is always different at every performance, depending on the people who take part in it (both performers and listeners), on their collective and inter-individual relationships, intentionality, ability, on the gathering circumstances etc.

In other words, it is a fallacy to think of music in terms of a "work" or opus; when it is produced (not reproduced as it is when one plays a record), music is a process. It is 'the entire process of conceptualization, realization and evaluation of music. Each performance re-creates, re-established or alters the significance of singing and also of the persons, times, places and audiences involved. It expresses the status, sex and feeling of the performers, and it brings these to the attention of the entire community, which interprets them in a variety of ways' (Seeger 2004, p. 65)

As a collective and shared experience, music represents differences among cultures and groups: it is a manifestation of a variety in choices in sound and organization patterns, in collective behaviour, in conceptualizations and transmission of meanings and values. Far from being a "universal language" (a very trivial formula often reiterated by the mass media which is shared by performers of different cultures like a "commonplace"), music gives immediate representations of a different construction of cultural identities based on inclusion/exclusion mechanisms. These mechanisms concern both musical sounds in themselves, and (above all) what these sounds mean. Combinations among intervals, scales, rhythmical patterns, timbres, all the perceptible elements, identify different virtual (never objectively or definitely bounded) "musical fields"; each of these is regarded as "their very own music" by one more or less large (and more or less open) human group (including both music makers and listeners) – often beyond "traditional" cultural diversities and territorial boundaries, within the complex and ineffable multicultural, contemporary, social scenarios.

Music, unlike language, cannot be "translated"; it has the 'contradictory attributes of being at once intelligible and untranslatable', according to a very well-known verbal formula by Claude Lévi-Strauss (1964, p. 18). Making music takes forms and sense within specific human groups, being individually experienced by its members on the basis of shared cultural backgrounds. Every group attributes specific meaning to its selected sounds and to the performative acts that produce them: very complex meanings, articulated on different levels.

Certainly music expression "always means something", but its meanings are not immediate and, above all, they are not univocal, retaining unutterable and indefinable elements which are different according to every group convention, and individually experienced within it. As a matter of fact, beyond the view of a single music culture for the diversity of human cultures, it is impossible to assign a universal set of meanings to music. Even the same sound sequence could have different meanings: just like a monoplanar system, there are peculiar denotative mechanisms related to music whose codes are masked. To a certain extent, paraphrasing the topic of this meeting, one could say that music works like a particular type of "denotation" ... *in absentia* of denotation, e.g. it always means something that has no precise and fixed signification; in other words, it is a denotation that does not refer to a denotative meaning of signifiers but varies in unlimited ways. And what counts is that these meanings are not necessarily inherent to the original ones elaborated by the cultural group where a music expression was born.

Music expressions easily cross cultural boundaries, acquiring new and original meanings that could be very different from the original ones. Indeed 'music can be more readily appreciated across cultural boundaries than language when there is no translation (...) when the listener hears foreign sounds of which they have little or no previous experience. Of course, it is by no means guaranteed that a listener from one culture will appreciate the music of another. However, the salient fact is that such a thing can occur. (...) one can perceive structure and significance in unfamiliar music even if one's parsing of the music is not the same as a native listener's. The fact that this can occur suggests that there is an aspect of musical meaning that is purely formal (...) music can have meaning for a listener simply because of its perceived sonic logic, without knowledge of the context that gave rise to the music or of an insider's understanding of its cultural significance' (Patel 2008, pp. 302-3).

Thus, musical expression (including music making) could go beyond cultural-linguistic boundaries, possibly acquiring new meanings and original performative scenarios, fostering the will to know other peoples etc. The emotive, motive, evocative stimuli of 'humanly organized sounds' (according to the well-known definition of music by John Blacking, 1973) could be a very salient ingredient in inter-cultural dialogue, since the immediate power of music is a pondered tool to develop the meeting of people with different backgrounds – this is an ace that ethnomusicologists may support on the basis of their knowledge.

In our small way, this is what Paolo Bravi and I tried to do in Cagliari thanks to the happy (and lucky) circumstance of Prema Bhat's stay in our town, dialoguing with her about Carnatic music and more generally about music, about our different perspectives on music.

We did not consider Prema as a sort of ambassador of the "Indian Carnatic musical world". For us, she is a helpful performer and teacher with a peculiar curriculum (including interestingly a long experience as a teacher of Indian Classical music in US Universities), coming from a specific background rooted in the music *milieu* she was educated in (see later).

In a different context we dealt with our theoretical knowledge and different conceptualizations about music structures: this meant focusing on sound patterns and furthermore different cultural meanings and values of the "organized sounds" within social life. Above all, we tried to develop a dynamic didactic activity involving our students from the *Conservatorio di Musica* and Cagliari University's Faculty of Arts (Facoltà di Lettere e Filosofia).

Of course, Prema's relatively short stay in our city did not give us the possibility to adequately develop the topics we have identified, but our goal was not to "say something new about" them, rather to experience them and to establish human relationships *sub musicae speciae.*

At Maria Piera Candotti and Tiziana Pontillo's request, we presented a short account of our experience (including a short practical demonstration by Prema on ālāpanā, a *rāga* improvisation) within the April 8th meeting *"Il segno e il vuoto". Spunti sulla denotazione in absentia dalla riflessione tecnica, speculativa ed estetica dell'India e della Grecia antiche*, in accordance with the interdisciplinary approach proposed by the organizing committee. In the same perspective, here we report an excerpt of our tiny "inter-cultural experience" which has been elaborated for non-musicologist readers. It concerns various subjects in an unsystematic way, from general technical topics to the theme of the meaning of music.

We have avoided proposing a roughly basic introduction to Indian music (the non-specialist reader could profitably use common musical dictionaries, such as *The New Grove Dictionary of Music and Musicians* – Sadie 2001), preferring to focus on particular topics that we hope could be interesting for the comprehensive purposes of the present volume. Of course, our different theoretical and practical points of view are meaningfully contradictory on different points, starting from the basic one concerning the "universality of music": we juxtapose our statements without any attempt to reach a synthesis, also leaving some open questions that call for a more thorough analysis.

2 *A Very Intense Experience [Pa. Br.]*

In Spring 2011, a group of Italian ethnomusicologists – including Ignazio and myself – organized a seminar in Cagliari on *Carnatic Music and Singing* at Cagliari's *Conservatorio di Musica.* The seminar was held by Prema Bhat, an excellent Indian vocalist who was in Cagliari in that period for private reasons. She spent about 9 months in our city, between September 2010 – May 2011. By virtue of her long-standing stay and teaching activity in the USA, Prema had a vast experience in teaching Indian singing to non-Indian students.

The seminar was part of the didactic activities of the Ethnomusicology course offered by the *Conservatorio*, but its attendance was also open to anyone who was interested in the topic. The number of participants was about 15/20 for every session. The audience comprised attendees with different cultural backgrounds and musical attitudes: some had a general interest in Indian culture, some were singers and musicians aiming to expand their artistic experience and musical skills, some were students in Ethnomusicology. All of them had little or no previous experience in Indian music.

The seminar was both theoretical and practice-oriented; on the one hand giving some essential notes on the theory, history and musical forms of Indian Carnatic music and on the other, allowing the participants to attempt the very basic practice of singing short traditional Carnatic compositions set in different *rāgas* and *tālas*.

After the seminar, Prema Bhat held a solo concert, accompanying herself on the *tambūrā*, in the *Conservatorio*'s Auditorium, which attracted hundreds of spectators.

In our perspective, Prema's seminar represented a valuable means of expanding the experience of music (and music learning) for our students of the Ethnomusicology course. This course is mainly devoted to Sardinian music, whose repertories are highly recognised for their richness and complexity. They are directly known – at different levels and with a variety of degrees of familiarity – by the majority of the students. By and large, teachers could take it for granted that students have at least a general idea of what "music making" means – in terms of its functions, its main features, its social values and meanings – in the Sardinian *milieu*. Of course, our study plan includes theoretical widening of the main ethnomusicological subjects, both in musicological and anthropological approaches, with a special regard to the contemporary condition of music making (including the secondary orality transmission – Ong 1982).

In this perspective, the experience of learning and practising a music which is virtually unknown for Western students and neglected in the ordinary musical curricula, was intended to be something different from offering them just a new and exciting experience, or, worse still, a way to explore the hazardous quicksand of "exoticism". Instead, it was a challenging occasion to experience at first hand whether and/or to what extent and/or under what conditions and limitations (and risks!) sharing a musical experience could be a ploy to bring about – as has been widely speculated – communication among peoples, and maybe even a kind of a "Trojan horse" capable of breaking cultural boundaries and overcoming divisions and prejudices.

The seminar was an engaging and enlightening experience for all of us who – in our different roles – took part in it. Besides being an opportunity to learn basic notions about Carnatic music, it was an occasion to experiment, in the climate of confidence created by Prema, and with her unusual (for us) methods of teaching music, to check our capacity to adapt to different patterns of sound organization and to test our potential willingness (or, conversely, to bring out our latent reluctance) to get outside the fence of our well-established notions and practices regarding music.

3 My Musical Background [Pr. Bh]

My earliest memory of Indian classical music goes back to waking up to the sound of an early morning music called "Suprabhātam" (which literally means an auspicious morning) broadcast on the radio every Saturday morning as an opening program. I must have been 3-4 years old and I was drawn to the music and the musician's voice, which was completely in tune with the *śruti* (pitch) accompaniment by the string instrument (*tambūrā*). While I was too young to understand the meaning of the song, I still remember the peaceful feeling that I experienced from that music. I wanted to sing like that. A few years later, I started to learn classical music in the South Indian tradition (Carnatic music) under the guidance of Mr. Kanchna Narayana Bhat for 10 years. I practiced for years using various exercises, songs and improvisation techniques taught by my teacher. While studying, I also learned a lot by listening to other students (from beginners to the advanced). It was a good way to learn so many things by listening for hours (I was able to sing many songs without being taught). Later I performed a lot. For the next few years, I studied with my second teacher Mr. Shrinatha Marate, who taught me and polished my improvisational skills while teaching me many different songs by different composers.

Years later, I moved to the USA and I had to find my way in a whole new culture, which had very little resemblance to what I did back home in India. Here I found a whole new audience who knew very little about Indian Classical music. Whenever I mentioned the word Indian Classical music, people associated it with Sitar Maestro Pandit Ravi Shankar (who popularized it through his association with the Beatles), but they knew very little about Indian Classical voice and other instruments. I made it a point, through my concerts, lecture demonstrations and radio shows and teaching in the University classrooms, that the voice is the basis for all instrumental and Classical dance in India. I had to teach them the basics of a *rāga* (melody), *tāla* (rhythm), *bhāva* (emotions), the different ornaments and embellishments used in Indian classical music, the two classical traditions practised in India, namely Carnatic (South Indian classical tradition) and Hindusthani (North Indian classical tradition), their similarities and differences, the role of composers in the Carnatic traditions (similar to the European Classical tradition), the role of improvisation in Indian Classical music, and the role of music and dance in the everyday life of people in India, etc.

Let me give some ideas about Indian Classical music especially the Carnatic tradition which I practice. Music in India has its origin in the *Vedas*, dating back to about more than 1000 years before Christ. Music was used in the form of chants or hymns in the temples to worship God. All sounds are believed to have their origin in the word "OM". Our ancestors used music as a vehicle for self-realization. During the Vedic time, three notes were used in the hymns, namely Sa, Ri and Ni. Over a period of time, more notes were discovered, using the string instrument Veena, resulting in the seven notes that we use today in Indian classical music, which are Sa, Ri, Ga, Ma, Pa, Dha and Ni. The first and the fifth notes (Sa and Pa) always remain the same whereas the remaining 5 notes Ri, Ga, Dha and Ni have 3 variations each and the fourth note Ma has two variations resulting in 16 notes. Slowly, music became an independent art form. In Carnatic music there are 72 major *rāgas* or melodies (*rāgas* with all the seven notes) and hundreds of minor *rāgas* that are derived from the major *rāgas*.

rāga (melody), *tāla* (time measure) and *bhāva* (emotion or sentiment) are the basis for Indian classical music. A *rāga* is a melody or a group of notes in an ascending and descending order but it also expresses various emotions (or moods), a certain time of the day and night or the seasons. Our ancestors believed that a *rāga* presented at an appropriate time, brings balance in nature. So there are *rāgas* for the morning, afternoon, evening and night. Certain combinations of notes express certain feelings. For example, Bhaulī, a morning *rāga*, could express a meditative feeling (many people in India start their day with yoga and meditation or a simple prayer). Whereas an evening *rāga* called Hindola could bring majesty, *rāga* Madhuvantī could express sadness, *rāga* Nīlāmbarī could induce sleep (best played in the night, not while driving a car).

Students of Indian classical music spend years training their voice to sing within the śruti or pitch (a combination of the first and fifth notes) using the string instrument called *tambūrā*, which provides the drone sound when plucked. Musicians choose a śruti, which is suitable for their individual voice; sometimes it could be a quarter pitch higher or lower than the chromatic pitch used in the Western chromatic system.

tāla is a time measure, displayed by using the right hand with a clap and counting of the fingers and flipping of the hand. In Carnatic music, various *tāla*s are used and every composition is set to a particular *tāla*.

The one thing that I have learned in my experience of performing and teaching Carnatic voice over so many years (both to Indians and Westerners), is that music is a universal language. Even though people may not always understand the words in a song, they do feel the sentiment or emotions it expresses, especially when a *rāga* is improvised, as in *alāpanā* (an improvisational form and an elaboration of the *rāga*, within the limits of a scale, presented before a song), where the sound is used instead of words and a listener has to rely solely on the emotions presented skillfully by the musician. The time theory may not make much sense to a Westerner (actually a great musician could create the morning time in the evening and vice versa) but they definitely understand the variety of emotions (*bhāva*) expressed by the musician.

It is interesting to note that, in the past twenty-five years, the number of Westerners becoming more familiar with Indian classical music has increased. Carnatic music has significantly attracted many Westerners as well, partly due to the systematic organization of the *rāga* and the *tāla* theory and its practical use in Carnatic music has helped more Westerners to better understand the Carnatic tradition. This has resulted in a rise in the number of people going regularly to Southern India to attend the annual music festivals and also to learn the Carnatic tradition, with a subsequent number of books written by Westerners on Carnatic music. While fusion concerts are increasingly becoming popular, traditional concerts have also attracted a great number of Westerners as well. The Western violin was successfully adapted to the Carnatic style more than 250 years ago. In the past fifty years or so, the saxophone, clarinet and mandolin have been successfully Indianised and more recently the cello has made its way to Southern India.

For centuries, music was patronized in India by the kings and wealthy people. Often the kings themselves were great musicians and wrote books extensively on music and musicology. While music is still connected to religion, it does not always depend on religion to flourish, especially after India became independent in 1947; since there were no longer any kings to support classical music and dance, they had to depend on the common people, music organizations, radio and television to support the art form.

4 A Polyphonic Discussion [Pr. Bh.] [Pa. Br.] [I. M.]

After the lectures, we used emails and Skype to discuss both the results of the seminar and the meaning of this short "intercultural" experience. Here are some scattered excerpts of our conversations, focused on some questions to Prema.

[Pa. Br.] When one is engaged in briefly presenting a complex musical and poetical tradition like the Carnatic one to people who do not have any specific experience and training and did not grow up in that country, one has to face the problem of whether or not to assume a "pure" musicological approach by focusing exclusively on the musical structures, or to approach the issue from a socio-cultural perspective by trying to make learners aware of the social practices, the aesthetic values, the historical evolution of the genre. Prema, what approach did you choose to adopt in your seminar in Cagliari?

[Pr. Bh.] As always, I ask myself these questions, 'What would I want to know, if I had no understanding of Indian Classical music?' 'What would I like to know about Indian Classical music?' First of all, I just explain the meaning of the basic terms used in Indian classical music with a demonstration, such as what a *rāga* (melodic scale), *tāla* (time measure) and *bhāva* (expression) are, using very simple words and also explaining the historical or cultural importance associated with this topic, which helps the students a lot.

[Pa. Br.] Some participants at the seminar "translated" the Indian musical notions (names of the notes, rhythmic structures etc.) in terms of the corresponding notions of Western classical music, possibly in order to try to shorten the learning process. Do you (Prema) think it is best for Western musicians and music students to enter into a musical tradition like the Indian Carnatic one through this translation into well-known, widely practised and strictly categorized Western musical notions or would it be better to start a completely renewed learning process, on a – let's say – a new "mental path"? In other words, can we apply a foreign language teaching method to this kind of musical (re)training, namely not to try and translate the verbal expressions from their mother-tongue language but rather to build original sentences ex-novo by using the linguistic structures of the new language one is studying?

[Pr. Bh.] Initially it may help to translate a few things into the other musical tradition but it is important to learn this art form as it is, the way it is learnt in India under the guidance of an established teacher and also to understand the cultural and historical background in that tradition. What I am trying to say is that, unlike Western music where the music is presented through notations and symbols, Indian music is taught orally and is mainly *rāga* based, with a variety of emotions, that are expressed through the *rāga* using various embellishments, ornaments, glides etc, that cannot be written (even though the notations can be written), so one has to learn them through a teacher for many years, and acquire knowledge; then and only then, can one learn on one's own.

[I. M.] Prema, as regards the *absentia* concept, from an ethnomusicological point of view, a very fashionable aspect of the general Indian concept of music is the lack of a concept of "note" (like a fixed sound point) analogous to the Western one.[1] Of course, for you Indian musicians and listeners, it's not a lack (that is, we Westerners lack your concept of sound), but inevitably, it is felt like something missing by Western practitioners. Beyond technical aspects, this sound variability (at least, in our opinion) has something to do with the transmission of emotions, with the meaning of music. Could it be useful to go over the mere teaching of sound combinations? Do you experience this particular aspect during your lectures?

[Pr. Bh.] I teach that there is a fixed sound or a point of reference for all the notes in Indian classical music that can be played on a piano or other Western instruments. As I have mentioned before, we use different forms of embellishments in our music, in order to express certain emotions. Depending on the *rāga*, certain notes are presented with a wave called a *gamaka* (where a particular note swings between two notes) while some other notes are held straight, whereas some notes may have glides. This helps to distinguish one *rāga* from the other (especially with those *rāgas* that have similar scales with minor differences). This is one of the biggest differences in Indian and Western Classical music. In Indian classical music, the instrument follows the voice. Whatever

[1] A very interesting inter-cultural dialogue on technical aspects about Indian Classical system is in Widdess 2000 (1994).

is sung, can be played on the instruments as well. So the mere learning of a combination of notes is not enough to be a Carnatic vocalist. One has to have a teacher (Guru) to understand these and many other concepts.

[Pa. Br.] Instrumental analysis can give useful insights into this matter. I have carried out some preliminary research on this aspect of the performance by analyzing the frequency distribution and some melodic profiles of Prema's singing in her Cagliari Concert. The first two songs of this concert ('Gajānanam' and 'Parvatī Nāyaka') were based on the *rāga* Bhaulī. The structure of this *rāga* can be seen in Fig. 1, upper panel). As the tonagram in Fig. 1, middle panel, displays, the second degree of the scale (in Indian-Carnatic terms, the *śudda* Ri), seems to have a weak presence in this song in terms of the overall distribution of the frequencies throughout the performance.[2]

The rounded rectangle superimposed on the graph highlights the area of the frequencies which one can assume to be related to the second degree. The scatter of the values and the lack of a central point could be interpreted in a variety of ways, among which the fact that the execution of this degree is usually (or always) "tied" to some kind of ornamental figure (*gamaka*). One instance of the execution of a strongly embellished second degree in this particular performance is represented in the lower panel in Fig. 1. Here, the arrow points to a part of the execution where the second degree is reached with quick repeated upward melodic movements[3].

[2] This methodology, as well as the term "tonagram" (or "tonagramme" in French) has been used by various scholars in the past decades in order to analyse scale structures in an empirical way (among these, Tjerlund, Sundberg, and Fransson, 1972; Bel, 1998; Van der Meer, 2000).

[3] In this particular type of transcription of the melody, the rounded rectangles superimposed on the F0 curve correspond to the perceived pitch expressed in terms of scale degrees, and the letters indicate specific types of ornamental figures (M = upper volta; A: short ascending melodic movement to the main note). A complete description of the adopted system of musical representation is in Bravi, 2010. It is worth noting that Robert Morris has recently put forward a new approach for the description of the *rāgas* based on the successions of modulations of *rāga* scale degrees, instead of the succession of the scale degrees with their ornamentations. In his view, in fact, 'this [the latter] description hierarchizes the scale degree over the modulation. Even if it is traditional, and therefore easier to speak of note modulation in this way, we have seen that the modulations will often not distinguish one scale degree (*svara*) from another (unless the note name is sung at the same time). So, thinking of scale degrees embellished by ornaments really doesn't touch the heart of *rāga*, in which the successions of modulations is more definitive than the successions of scale degrees' (Morris, 2011, p. 27).

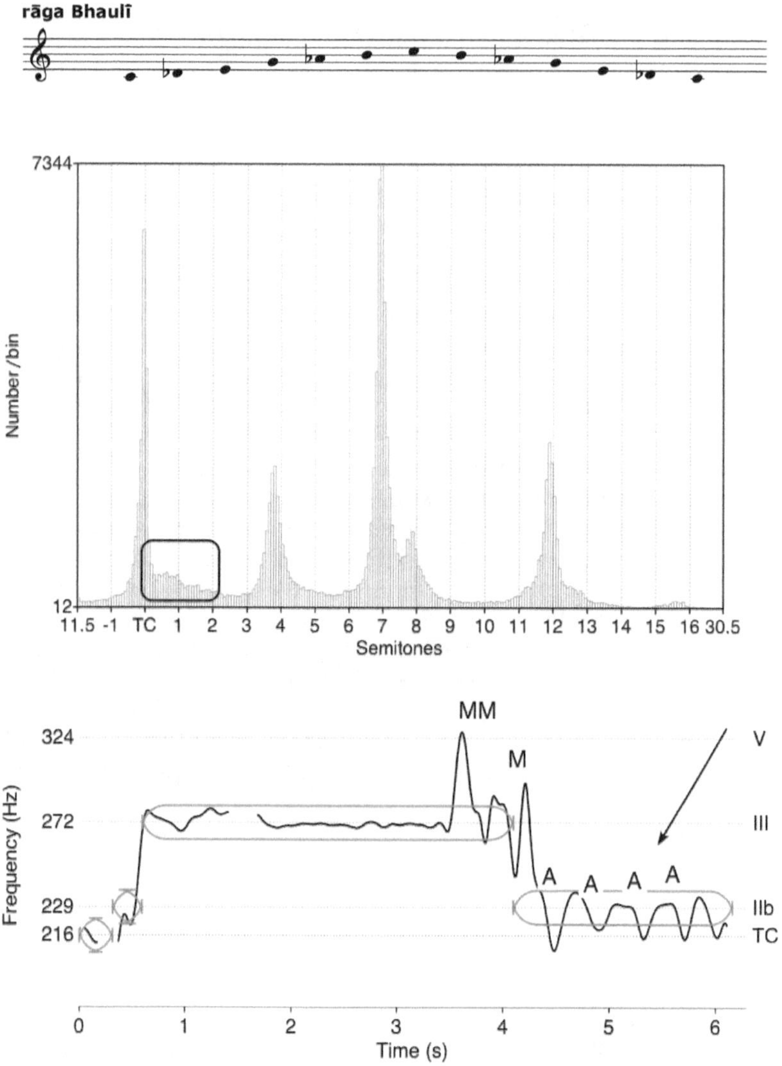

Fig. 1. In the upper panel, the ascending and descending structure of the *rāga* Bhaulī, in Western staff notation (the central C corresponds to the Sa of the *rāga*); in the middle panel, a tonagram with the distribution of the frequencies in the first two Carnatic compositions presented by Prema in her Cagliari concert, based on this *rāga* (the rounded rectangle displays the bins of frequencies, divided in ten-cent classes, in the area of the second degree); in the lower panel, a graphical representation of the melodic profile of a small excerpt of the execution, with the arrow pointing to the strong ornamentation of the second degree.

[I. M.] Of course this kind of representation concerns the physical dimension of sounds. Computers are very useful in this way because they offer very deep descriptions of all the parameters: like a sort of technical metalanguage they allow different grammatical conceptualizations dealing with music from various cultures to be gone over. In Cagliari, we regularly use this kind of device (above all thanks to Paolo Bravi's work) also in the description of Sardinian traditional music because it gives us basic and very detailed information to qualify a musical "oral thought" behind the music making of contemporary people on the island. It's an important step but there are many aspects exceeding the "computer's vision", above all the human interrelationships that are the true essence of every musical culture, starting from postural behaviours.

[Pa. Br.] Indeed, as a preliminary self-introduction to the students who attended her seminar, Prema insisted on asking them to come near her, and not to remain seated in their seats, which were arranged as usual in straight rows on a sloping floor, like a small concert hall, and if they could, they were asked to sit on the floor just like her, forming a circle of people. The "official" reason she maintained was the need for everybody to hear without her having to shout. This was certainly the case, but possibly there was something more to this choice in breaking the strong division set by the strict distinction between the "performer" – alone on one side of the hall – and the "listeners" – grouped in a physically separated space in the hall. I think that Prema's intention was also to cancel or at least to minimize the watershed between the performer and public. I interpreted her desire both as a way to overcome the symbolic valley separating performer and public, and to recreate a warm and intimate setting which could give the performances the right "mood" of soft, delicate, highly refined "chamber" music. Moreover, in this way, teaching in this particular place was really not so different from the traditional fashion in which learners are placed as close to the Maestro as possible.[4] In this case, Prema seemed to me as if she was trying

[4] If the traditional system of musical education based on the figure of the *gurukula* ('preceptor-family') – as witnessed by Prema – is no longer practiced even in India, where institutional courses and academic learning has come into practice for decades, a close and direct relation between the teacher and his/her students is still considered an essential part of the learning process for Indian Carnatic musicians. Private lessons, where the students learn directly with a teacher or in a small group is what is usually practiced today. According to T. Visnawanathan '[w]hatever the extent of verbalization and modern technology as supplementary aids, however, there is no substitute for personal contact with the teacher, either individually or in small groups' (Viswanathan, 1977, p. 16).

to set up a group in a way that could facilitate the experience of living a "shared moment", implying not only a mere "delivery" of "contents" and information towards the students, but even the participation in an event of reciprocal knowledge and, as such, of mutual human and cultural growth.

[Pr. Bh.] As you suggested, the typical classroom atmosphere with some chairs and a table with a blackboard is not suitable for Indian Classical music. In the olden days students stayed with their teacher's family for many years and learnt music, this was called *gurukula* (*guru* means teacher; *kula* means family). While this tradition is not followed anymore, the essence of the tradition is followed where the teacher teaches individually or to a small number of students. Everybody sits on the floor cross-legged without their shoes on. It is very intimate and easy to teach. Since the room I was given was too big (big enough for 100 people) and everybody was scattered around the room, it was not easy for me to teach and so I had to ask everybody to sit closer which the students understood and actually everybody had a better time learning music this way, even though the students were not used to sitting on the floor.

[Pa. Br.] In the presentation of her contents, Prema seemed to have adopted a twofold didactic approach, characterised by two quite opposite departure points. In both cases, however, the focus remained attention, interest, and the concrete possibility for the students to keep pace with the increasing complexity of the songs proposed. The first criterion seemed to me to have been the similarity of the *rāgas* or the *tāla* used in the chosen composition with structures of the Western musical tradition. In this case, the students did not usually find any difficulty in learning the song. The second criterion seemed to me to be the exact opposite of this, i.e. to get the students to live a musically "unusual" experience, since they were asked to sing exercises or short songs with (for an inexperienced Western practitioner) "weird" intervals and scales and "strange" rhythmic structures (see Figure 2). This experience was a chance to really understand how they can broaden the boundaries of their musical language (of course, with the necessary training process, and the necessary emotional and metal investment).

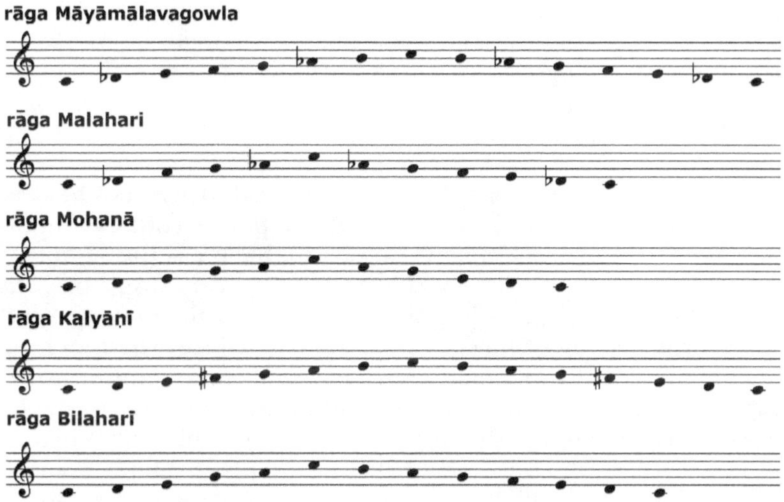

Fig. 2. The *rāgas* used by Prema in the first session of her seminar in Cagliari. After some introductory exercises in *rāga* Māyāmālavagola, the students learnt a few songs (gītā) in the *rāgas* Malahari (a derivative of the *rāga* Māyāmālavagola), Mohanā, Kalyāṇī and Bilaharī. The *rāgas* have been transcribed here in Western staff notation by setting C as the tonal centre (Sa).

[I. M.] The extreme diffusion of musics of the world facilitates the availability to approach "other organized sounds". Today, thanks to the mass media, any person could approach (theorically) every kind of music from all over the planet, the largest availability of music than ever before in the history of man. It's a largely incomplete availability – we could say "*in absentia*" of the performative contexts – because it regards only one sense, hearing (also partially sight, thanks to videos); but music is a "global fact" pertaining to all the human senses. However, the auditive familiarity with "other sounds" is, of course, a basic asset for learning other "musical technical thought": I remember the "enstrangement" of the students of the Italian *Conservatorio* about 20 years ago when I simply proposed that they listen to Indian music sounds.

The new dynamics of the global circulation of music have also radically transformed the idea of ethnomusicological research (see the Ethnomusicology entry in Sadie 2001). Our discipline has progressively dropped the idea of "collecting information" about other music, with interpretative approaches rooted on 'intersubjective and dialogical coproduction of texts, contexts, processes, performances, interpretations, and understandings' (Titon 1995, p. 290). Likewise, even a tiny dialogical experience like the one we had with Prema is very useful from different didactical points of view in order to give an idea of a "complex tradition" so different from one's own.

[Pa. Br.] Presenting the theory, the musical structures, the genres of Indian Carnatic Music, Prema always pointed out the importance of some famous Indian composers, hailed as the "Fathers" of the Carnatic style, who lived in the long period from the 13th CE to the 18th CE. Stressing the importance of the presence and the artistic activity of these composers had effects which permeate the simple information of this remarkable distinction between the Hindustani and the Carnatic traditions. An important "side-effect" was the emphasis on the fact that music is not only a matter of notes, scales, rhythms, *gamakas*, instruments etc., but a creative activity carried out by men/ women, whose names, lives, social activity, artistic works at least in the most relevant cases, are still known. This means considering music as a human fact, not only as a matter of sound structures and sound products. The knowledge of these important figures of Carnatic music appeared not as a peripheral appendix of the training process for Indian singers and musicians, but as an essential part of the Carnatic tradition.

[Pr. Bh.] Your observation on Indian classical tradition is right. Indian music is basically vocal music. In the Southern Indian (Carnatic) musical tradition, the composers and compositions are very important just like Western classical music. Their (the composers') life experience and spiritual approach towards music, when and how a particular song was composed and the context must all be known, in order to present the music effectively since they are not just notes and rhythmic patterns with some lyrics. The songs (also called *Kṛti*) have a variety of themes and they are not not just songs in praise of Gods and Goddesses but they are also philosophical and in many cases, point towards inequality or injustice in society, suggesting solutions.

[Pa. Br.] The possibility of the transmission of emotional contents via music performances outside the internal *milieu* in which the music was originally composed has been widely discussed for a long time. The results of a time-honoured experiment conducted by Angeliki Keil and Charles Keil (Keil and Keil, 1966), in which 87 participants from the USA were asked to express a variety of evaluations on different types of music, showed that not always do the feelings, that the musician (in this case, the sitar player Ravi Shankar) intends to express in his playing, reach the Western listeners: '[i]t would seem [...] that the feeling of religious joy at a Hindu spring flower festival, as expressed by Ravi Shankar, generates confusion, ambivalence or indifference among uninitiated Westerners' (p. 167). In Prema's seminar, the meaning of the lyrics were systematically translated in order to permit students' comprehension, as if musical structures like *rāgas* and *tālas* – albeit being the fundamental ingredients of the musical composition and performance – were not self-sufficient or living in a limbo of "pure" sound structures without any relation with the (let's say in short) "external" world. Obviously, it is virtually (and fortunately!) impossible for a Western student who has only had the chance to listen and to practice Indian music for some hours to "feel" and to "know" this music in the same way as if he had grown up in that cultural context. Nevertheless, Prema's attempts to make Western students aware at least of the meaning of the lyrics and of their intended purposes (often as religious/devotional songs) succeeded in giving the participants at her seminar a first comprehensive introduction to a musical world, and not just notions of musical theory and the practice of particular intervals and rhythmic patterns.

[Pr. Bh.] In my opinion there is a similarity between our Indian and Sardinian culture, especially in daily life. When I demonstrated many songs and taught them some compositions- the depth in the *rāgas* and songs, composers and their life, spirituality and various other topics- the Sardinian students related better than other foreign students I tested in the past. This Indian way of conveying feelings did not seem strange to them. It is interesting to note that in Indian culture, similar to Sardinian culture, there is a social hierarchy in people's roles. Teachers are highly respected in society (especially in the field of fine arts) I could see the same attitude in Cagliari with my students as well. It was a beautiful experience.

[Pa Br.] The idea that music could be something like an (albeit immaterial) "support", capable of transferring "meaning" from a sender to a listener, as posited by the theory of communication of Roman Jacobson (1963) does not usually fit in well with the experience that making music prompts. Musical "objects" are weak and inconsistently real as such, so we can repeat here that the crucial point of the issue (the "ontological fallacy", as Martin Clayton puts it) is that we must overcome the tenet of musical semiology according to which "music is essentially a thing which refers to another thing" (Clayton 2001, p. 4).

Music competence and attitudes are something that everyone develops over the course of time. The acoustic structure of music per se is just a "trace", albeit sometimes very rich and sophisticated, which conveys emotional meaning and social values. This tenet has a good many theoretical and practical consequences, among which the fact that the same acoustic "trace" – melodic pattern, chord sequence, rhythmic schema or any musical element whatsoever – could "mean" different things for different listeners: arouse different feelings, engender different aesthetic effects and evaluations, evoke different memories and associations, express different convictions, ideologies and beliefs, display different social conditions and ways of living.

[I. M.] Musicologists often say "music is more than music", meaning that music is always more than a combination of sounds: 'it's deeply embedded in human culture (just as there isn't a culture that doesn't have language, so there isn't one that doesn't have music). Music somehow seems to be natural, to exist as something apart – and yet it is suffused with human values, with our sense of what it is god or bad, right or wrong. Music doesn't happen, it is what we make it, and what we make of it. People think through music, decide who they are through it, express themselves through it." (Cook 2000, p. 8). Music is an experience that induces people to know and to do, to act and to be.

However, beyond the essential incommunicability of the symbolic meaning, according to the great ethnomusicologist John Blacking, music could set up a communicative tool among cultures at a level of "deep structures" of human musicality, i.e. at the level of general behavioural and brain mechanisms of the psyche (see for instance Blacking 1978). As shared features by human species, the existence of musical "deep structures" could explain the evocative strength of music in the relationship among cultures; it could be the motive for the "ineffable certitude" that music is able to open the way for an immediate understanding regardless of the diversity of surface sound structures. For instance, to sing is a universally shared music behaviour – there is no culture in the world where people do not sing. Everyone recognizes the act of singing by people of other cultures even if he/she is not able to understand the meanings of the formal articulation and sound results. Although they don't go beyond cultural boundaries, this kind of recognitions provides a sensory and emotional communicative experience that might facilitate relationships between peoples.

5 Final Considerations

The idea that music could be something like a multilevel message, capable of transferring complex meaning from performer to listener does not usually fit in well with the immediate "experience of music", especially when it is a "medialised experience": often, the prompt reaction is 'what do words mean?' Maybe, our small virtual discussion has given a faint idea of the multiplicity and deepness of the questions behind musical sounds (and texts).

After all, music is a matter of experience: 'it may be that [...] the impulse to provide analogical or metaphorical interpretations for musical experience is something close to universal. Be that as it may, these interpretations must be terribly transient and unstable – unless and until, that is, we start to fix them through paramusical discourse. This is precisely what happens through the fixing of those imaginary entities, notes, chords, motives and the rest, and the imaginary relationships we call symphonies, *rāgas* and the like. What we conventionally describe as musical meaning is the way in which musical elements and structures are understood to relate to the world – which seems to me a futile endeavour so long as we fail to recognize that these elements and structures are themselves imagined by means of metaphors derived from the relationship between individual and environment' (Clayton 2001, p. 6).

Besides "great divisions" established both by geography and (to say it briefly) culture, various boundaries hamper the sharing of a musical experience, first of all the influences of a socio-political situation. Of course, in our seminars we considered the cultural values of "Carnatic music" (and Prema's knowledge) as exactly equal to our music culture, without any hierarchical relation – which is taken for granted in any ethnomusicological approach. But harsh politic-economic inequalities remarkably condition (maybe unconsciously) the intercultural dialogue, including relationships among musicians that often experience other music through ethnocentric filters and/or naïve/exotic/primitivistic approaches (this is what ethnomusicologists essentially criticize in the attitudes of several Westerner musicians and producers of the so called "world music"- see again Feld 2000 and relative bibliography). After all, music interculturalism is the propensity to relativize one's culture recognizing the equal complexity of other cultures, to go beyond ethnocentrism to aim at the largest possible knowledge of "the others": this is not easy because of the burden of our sense of identity, but within our complex contemporary world, it is an aim that deserves much further consideration and – of course – not only in the musical sphere!

References

Bel, Bernard (1998). "Raga: approaches conceptuelles et expérimentales." In: *Structures Musicales et Assistance Informatique.* Aix-en-Provence – Marseille: CRSM – MIM, pp. 87-108.

Blacking, John (1973). *How Musical is Man?.* Seattle: University of Washington Press.

Bravi, Paolo (2010). *A sa moda campidanesa. Pratiche, poetiche e voci degli improvvisatori nella Sardegna meridionale.* Nuoro: ISRE.

Clayton, Martin (2001). "Introduction: towards a Theory of Musical Meaning (in India and Elsewhere)." In: *British Journal of Ethnomusicology* 10,1, pp. 1-17.

Feld, Steven (2000). "A Sweet Lullaby for World Music." In: *Public Culture* 12,1, pp. 145-71.

Jacobson, Roman (1963). *Essais de linguistique générale.* Paris: Minuit.

Keil, Angeliki and Charles Keil (1966). "Musical Meaning: A Preliminary Report (the Perception of Indian, Western and Afro-American Musical Moods by American Students." In: *Ethnomusicology* 10,2, pp. 153-73.

Levi-Strauss, Claude (1964). *The Raw and the Cooked.* New York: Harper and Row.

Morris, Robert (2011). "Tana Varnams: An Entry into *Rāga* Delineation in Carnatic Music." In: *Analytical Approaches to World Music,* 1,1, pp. 1-27.

Ong, Walter J. (1982). *Orality and Literacy: The Technologizing of the Word.* New York: Methuen.

Patel, Aniruddh D. (2008). *Music, Language and the Brain.* New York: Oxford University Press.

Sadie, Stanley (2001). *The New Grove dictionary of music and musicians.* London: Macmillan.

Seeger, Anthony (2004). *Why Suyà Sing, A Musical Anthropology of an Amazonian People.* Urbana – Chicago: University of Illinois Press

Titon, Todd (1995). "Bi-Musicality as Metaphor." In: *The Journal of American Folklore* 108, No. 429, pp. 287-97.

Tjerlund, Per, Johan Sundberg and Frans Fransson (1972). "Grundfrequenzmessungen an schwedischen Kernplatflöten." In: *Studia Instrumentorum Musicae Popularis* 2, pp. 77-96.

Turino, Thomas (2008). *Music as Social life. The Politics of Participation.* Chicago: The University Chicago Press.

Van der Meer, Wim (2000). "Theory and Practice of Intonation in Hindustani Music." In: *The Ratio Book.* Köln: Feedback Papers, pp. 50-71.

Viswanathan, Tanjore (1977). "The Analysis of Raga Alapana in South Indian Music." In *Asian Music* 9, No. 1, pp. 13-71.

Widdess, Richard (2000). "Coinvolgere gli esecutori nella trascrizione e nell'analisi: un approccio collaborativo al Dhrupad." In: *L'analisi nell'etnomusicologia*. Ed. by I. Macchiarella. Bologna: GATM (http://www.gatm.it/bollettino/2000-1.pdf) (ed. or. 'Involving the Performers in Trascription and Analysis: A Collaborative Approach to Dhrupad'. In: *Ethnomusicolog* 38, No. 1 (1994), pp. 59-79.

Summary of Papers

The editors would like to thank all the authors for having engaged in this project and for the fruitful and suggestive discussions that characterised the workshop. What follows is an attempt to present a brief reasoned résumé of the contributions highlighting the richness of cues and insights that emerged from the presentation and discussion of papers. Special thanks are due to Dr. Sally Davies for revising the English of the whole volume.

Part I. Technical and Speculative Reflections on Signless Signification

Alberto Pelissero (University of Turin, Italy)
Contact: alberto.pelissero@unito.it

Much Ado about Nothing: Unsystematic Notes on śūnya

The paper is an overview of the themes and debates developed in India around the term and concept of *śūnya* 'void'. After a brief survey on the origin of the term, Pelissero focuses on the concept of *śūnya* in Buddhist (mainly Mādhyamika) thought and underlines its being a kind of paradigm of discursive thought: the inherent relational nature of void is a mirror of the mutual dependent nature of any natural phenomenon. As the author timely reminds us "Candrakīrti will declare that vacuity, *śūnyatā*, acts for intellectual activity as a purge acts for the body". Unsurprisingly, in a parallel way, Buddhists extend the usage of apophaticism, from it's original mystic function of expressing the ineffable, to everyday language through the theory of *(anya) apoha* i.e. of framing the meaning of a word through the 'exclusion of the other'. Other well-known devices to express the ineffable show a similar problematic relationship with the otherwise well established couple sign/signified, be it for the absence of the specific sign, such as it happens in metaphorical usage of words or for its inconsistency, as it happens in paradoxes.

ELISA FRESCHI ("Sapienza" University, Rome, Italy)
Contact: elisa.freschi@gmail.com
TIZIANA PONTILLO (University of Cagliari, Italy)
Contact: pontillo@unica.it

When One Thing Applies More than Once: tantra *and* prasaṅga *in Śrautasūtra, Mīmāṃsā and Grammar*

Freschi and Pontillo focus their attention on the usage and cultural history of two crucial terms in Sanskrit technical literature, namely *tantra* (for which the translation 'centralised application' is proposed) and *prasaṅga* (interpreted as an 'automatic involvement'). Both belong to a class of devices used to 'extend' the validity of a given rule outside its proper domain or the application of a given element even in contexts where it is absent. As the authors point out, these devices of functioning *in absentia* entail an organized spatial dimension (a map following the metaphor used in Kahrs 1998), which transforms an absolute absence in a specific one. An organized space (such as language and also ritual) makes a blank grid significant. In this organised space *tantra* and *prasaṅga* represent two different strategies of filling blanks (or, which is the same thing the other way round, of granting multiple applications of a single item); the first one is grounded on 'a common texture, of which all elements benefit' (something akin to the modern concept of anaphora) while *prasaṅga* "represents an extended application, to be carried out if it makes things easier and if needed" (just as it happens in secondary signification).

MARIA PIERA CANDOTTI (University of Lausanne, Switzerland/ Visiting Professor at the University of Cagliari, Italy)
Contact: mariapiera.candotti@gmail.com
TIZIANA PONTILLO (University of Cagliari, Italy)
Contact: pontillo@unica.it

The Earlier Pāṇinian Tradition on the Imperceptible Sign

The paper targets one of the fields where, for the longest time, there has been a definite awareness of the potentialities of a blank sign both in western traditions (with the different theories of zeroing) and in grammatical tradition beginning with the Pāṇinian device of *lopa* 'zero-replacement'. The aim of the contribution is to prove that the *lopa*-device must be put in the wider framework of substitution in order to understand all its features and account for its potentialities. Substitution is the blocking of an otherwise automatically involved (*prasakta*, a term formed from the same basis as *prasaṅga*) element through another element specifically taught that 'takes its place'. Yet, the functions the new element carries out are exactly those of the absent element, and this is true even when the substitute specifically taught has no phonic realisation. Again, it is the role of the organized space (here the language system in its totality) that arises as a crucial prerequisite to make absence as much significant as presence.

Paolo Corda (University of Cagliari, Italy)
Contact: prgcorda@gmail.com

The Infinite Possibilities of Life: Interpretations of the śūnyatā *in the Thinking of Daisaku Ikeda*

Corda's contribution makes us take a great leap forward both in time and space and shows the long lasting presence of Nāgārjuna's thought on emptiness (*śunyatā*) till to contemporary times. This is the case of Daisaku Ikeda, a contemporary thinker and Nichiren Buddhist leader, who interpreted vacuity as potentiality, "not as a mere physical space characterized by the absence of objects [...], but as a situational context fraught with possibilities, from which the multiple manifestations of life arise". An interpretation in which also the well-known 'silence of the Buddha', the most excellent amongst the speakers, on metaphysical matters is reinterpreted not as the only possible answer to the aporias of phenomenal world, but rather as an intellectual attitude propitiating "the cessation of conceptual constructions, i.e. of the proliferations of discursive thought".

Part II. Reflections on Signless Signification in Literature and Arts

Cinzia Pieruccini (University of Milan, Italy)
Contact: cinzia.pieruccini@unimi.it

Presences and Absences in Indian Visual Arts: Ideologies and Events

The paper offers some preliminary and foundational thoughts on the changing patterns of presence and absence that characterise the transmission of artistic works and monuments in India. In the modern representation of Indian art different types of absences can be identified, primary ones (such as – at least in part – in the "aniconic" Vedic culture), fortuitous (due to the material used/ to historical vicissitudes), deliberate (pillage and destructions) or induced (e.g. by modern excavation trends and programmes). It is interesting to note how some unintentional absences (such as absences due to usage of perishable material) nevertheless become significant a posteriori helping, for example, in drawing a divide between public works of art made with costly and durable material and private articrafts.

Mimma Congedo (University of Milan, Italy)
Contact: satyaloka@gmail.com
Paola M. Rossi (University of Milan, Italy)
Contact: usaskanta@hotmail.com

Rethinking the Question of Images (Aniconism vs. Iconism) in the Indian History of Art

The authors address from an innovative point of view the vexed question of the use of images in Indian arts and of the supposed deep divide between a Vedic aniconic cultural and religious context and Hindu image worship. To these well-known categories – whose limits in accounting for Indian culture and art have been recently highlighted – the authors attempt to substitute Umberto Eco's 1984 re-interpretation of 'symbolic' and 'allegoric' medieval meaning modalities. Modern categories nonetheless echoed in terms and concepts as, for example, in the pair *pramā/pratimā* analyzed in the second part of the paper. In the symbolic modality the (ritual) object is just a means to attract the divine into the ritual arena, a divine "that is revealed as fully present when its presence is not taken for granted, but evoked to fill an absence". The allegory, on the other hand, is a sclerotization of the symbol, where the presence of the divine is taken for granted, substituted by the object. Even though the authors rightly insist in denying a perfect equivalence 'symbolic' = 'aniconic' and 'allegoric' = 'iconic', it is interesting how some specific traits of the symbolic modality, such as its inherently impermanent bond with the divine it evokes, match well with some typical 'zero' linguistic phenomena such as metaphor. The impermanence and relativity itself of signless signs are core factors of their semantic creativity, of their being evocative more than denotative in nature.

Patrizia Mureddu (University of Cagliari, Italy)
Contact: pmureddu@unica.it

Denotation in absentia *in Literary Language: The Case of Aristophanic Comedy*

The paper presents a savoury review of the artistic and comic potentialities of what Mureddu calls 'defective communication', that is a communication that asks for an active participation and integration from the hearer to come to fruition. Among the most striking devices of this defective communication, the author presents a) some cases of extreme metonymy where a single word stands for complex set of information coming from previous parts of the comedy asking for an active involvement of the spectator in the comic mechanism b) some cases of extension of a well-known adverbial construction with zero of the adverbial suffix and c) some lengthy compounds where even the active participation of the hearer is not sufficient to focus on the intended sense out of a chaotic bundling of heterogeneous elements. In all these cases "the lack of explicit determination is part of the game, of the challenge that the comic author proposes to his audience" and "the laughter (or at least the smile) that results, serves as recognition of the author's expertise, but perhaps derives also from the interpreter complimenting himself on his own perspicacity".

Ruben Fais (former Curator of the Museo Civico d'Arte Siamese Stefano Cardu, Cagliari)
Contact: rubenfais@alice.it

The Birth of the Buddha in the Early Buddhist Art Schools

The contribution focuses on the yet unsolved issue of the aniconic representation of the Birth of the Buddha, the first of the so-called Great Miracles. The author concentrates on three different but sometimes co-existing iconic themes – the lotus, the vase and the sprinkling of the woman by the elephants – and look for testimony of such images in coeval and later Buddhist texts to help in their interpretation. Instead of looking for a one-to-one relationship between a single iconic element and the miracle of Birth, the author propounds a dynamic interpretation of the three elements that together are able "to subsume the entire cycle of the birth into a single framework." The lotus in the vase (with the occasional addition of the elephant theme) is thus not a mere sign used to denote so to say the birth of the Buddha but it is a complex symbol that, though in an aniconic way, describes it.

Prema Bhat (Emory University, Atlanta, USA)
Contact: pbhat03@yahoo.com
Paolo Bravi (Conservatorio Pierluigi da Palestrina, Cagliari)
Contact: pa.bravi@tiscali.it
Ignazio Macchiarella (University of Cagliari, Italy)
Contact: macchiarella@unica.it

Untranslatable Denotations: Notes on Music Meaning Through Cultures

The contribution here presented is a sort of the transcription of a continuative "intercultural" dialogue held by the three authors on the themes of the meaning of music and on the translatability of that meaning. Starting from Claude Lévi Strauss powerful insight that music combines the contradictory character of being at the same time comprehensible (universally comprehensible, following a wide spread stereotype) and untranslatable, the authors identify one of the causes of this untranslatability in the vagueness and volatility of musical meaning. In fact music cannot be interpreted in jacobsonian terms as "support", capable of transferring meaning from a sender to a listener, that is it is not comparable with language, since only its "morphological" level is always available, while its "meaning" has to rely on something else, which is not included in the sign itself. Its strong communicative power shall find another frame of description.

www.ingramcontent.com/pod-product-compliance
Lightning Source LLC
Chambersburg PA
CBHW021821300426
44114CB00009BA/265
* 9 7 8 1 7 8 3 0 8 3 3 2 9 *